T0210722

Texts in Computer Science

Series Editors

David Gries, Department of Computer Science, Cornell University, Ithaca, NY, USA

Orit Hazzan ⓘ, Faculty of Education in Technology and Science, Technion—Israel Institute of Technology, Haifa, Israel

Titles in this series now included in the Thomson Reuters Book Citation Index!

'Texts in Computer Science' (TCS) delivers high-quality instructional content for undergraduates and graduates in all areas of computing and information science, with a strong emphasis on core foundational and theoretical material but inclusive of some prominent applications-related content. TCS books should be reasonably self-contained and aim to provide students with modern and clear accounts of topics ranging across the computing curriculum. As a result, the books are ideal for semester courses or for individual self-study in cases where people need to expand their knowledge. All texts are authored by established experts in their fields, reviewed internally and by the series editors, and provide numerous examples, problems, and other pedagogical tools; many contain fully worked solutions.

The TCS series is comprised of high-quality, self-contained books that have broad and comprehensive coverage and are generally in hardback format and sometimes contain color. For undergraduate textbooks that are likely to be more brief and modular in their approach, require only black and white, and are under 275 pages, Springer offers the flexibly designed Undergraduate Topics in Computer Science series, to which we refer potential authors.

Torben Ægidius Mogensen

Programming Language Design and Implementation

 Springer

Torben Ægidius Mogensen
Department of Computer Science
University of Copenhagen
Copenhagen, Denmark

ISSN 1868-0941   ISSN 1868-095X   (electronic)
Texts in Computer Science
ISBN 978-3-031-11808-1   ISBN 978-3-031-11806-7   (eBook)
https://doi.org/10.1007/978-3-031-11806-7

This Springer imprint is published by the registered company Springer Nature Switzerland AG
The registered company address is: Gewerbestrasse 11, 6330 Cham, Switzerland

Preface

Design is a funny word. Some people think design means how it looks. But of course, if you dig deeper, it's really how it works.

Steve Jobs

Successful design is not the achievement of perfection but the minimization and accommodation of imperfection.

Henry Petroski

This book aims to provide the reader with an overview of the design space for programming languages and how design choices affect implementation.

It is not a classical compilers book, as it assumes the reader is familiar with basic compiler implementation techniques, nor is it a traditional comparative programming languages book, because it does not go into depth about any particular language, but instead take examples from a wide variety of programming languages to illustrate design concepts.

The book is organised around concepts. Each concept has a chapter that explains the concept, illustrates the concept through examples from past and present (using both mainstream and obscure languages), discussion about pros and cons of design choices, implementation and, where deemed necessary, a bit of formal theory.

It is the opinion of the author that a designer of programming languages should not only know what other language designers have done, but also have an operational understanding of the consequences design choices have on implementation of these languages. Otherwise, the designer is liable to make design choices that renders implementation excessively difficult, impedes performance or makes it very hard for the users of the language to predict the behaviour of programs, especially when several language features are used in combination. Therefore, the description of the design space of various language features includes discussion and sketches of implementation. These sketches are not very detailed, but a competent programmer with knowledge of basic compiler techniques should be able to use the sketches as a guide for implementation.

If this book can help just one language designer avoid making design choices that she or the users of her language later regrets, it is deemed a success.

Do We Need New Programming Languages?

In the 1930s, Alonzo Church and Alan Turing independently proposed models for mechanical computation. These models are now known as the lambda calculus and Turing machines, respectively. Together with the logicians Stephen Kleene and J. B. Rosser, they later proved that any computation that can be done using the lambda calculus can also be done using Turing machines, and vice versa. Given that the two models are radically different, this led Church and Turing to hypothesise that no model of computation that can be realised by a physical machine can perform computations that cannot also be performed by lambda calculus and Turing machines. These models are in this sense *universal*: They can be used to model any computation, and if something is proven to not be computable using a Turing Machine (or the lambda calculus), then it cannot be computed at all on a mechanical device. This hypothesis is called *Church-Turing Thesis*. It is not possible to prove this thesis, as there is no generally accepted formal definition of a mechanical device, but it is generally accepted to be true, as nobody has come up with a physically realisable model for mechanical (or electronic) computation that exceeds the power of Turing machines or lambda calculus. A programming language that (assuming no upper bound on available memory) can do everything a Turing machine or the lambda calculus can do is called *Turing complete*.

Most programming languages are Turing complete, so you can argue that there is no need for new programming languages, as they will not be able to do something that cannot already be done. Even so, new languages appear all the time, so computational power is not the only interesting criterion for programming languages. But it can be very hard to find objective criteria for when a new language is better than an existing language. Common criteria are:

Program size: Are programs in language A shorter than equivalent programs in language B?

Speed: Do programs in language A run faster than equivalent programs in language B?

Ease of programming: Is it easier to write a program in language A than an equivalent program in language B?

Ease of reasoning about programs: Is it easier to prove correctness of programs in language A than in language B.

But these criteria all have problems:

Program size: If both A and B are Turing complete languages, and B can represent the text of programs in A as constants (such as strings) without significant expansion, it is possible to rewrite any sufficiently large program written in A to an equivalent program written in B that is only insignificantly larger. Basically, the rewritten program contains an interpreter for A and the representation of the original program. So any difference in program size will only affect relatively small programs.

Speed: Speed of execution is more a matter of how a language is implemented than how it is designed. You can, at best, compare the speed of a particular program written in language A using a particular implementation of this language to a specific equivalent program in a specific implementation of language B. But it is hard to argue that the two programs represent the fastest way of doing this computation in their respective language implementations, so this says little about the speed of the programs themselves, and even less about the languages.

Ease of programming: This is a highly subjective matter: One programmer can think that it is much easier to program in language A, while another prefers language B. Even if you teach non-programmers to program in two different languages, spending equal effort on both, their preferences may depend on their cultural background, education, or personality, so it is, again, hard so say something objective about the languages themselves.

Ease of reasoning about programs: For Turing complete programming languages, proving that programs are correct with respect to some specification or that they have some desirable property (such as termination) is in general undecidable, so you can argue that all such languages are equally difficult to reason about. On the other hand, in every language, you can prove correctness and termination for *some programs*, so you can discuss the relative ease of doing so for similar programs in different languages. But reaching definitive conclusions from such discussions is difficult, because the requirement that the programs be similar may require one or both programs to be coded in a way that is not typical for the languages in question, so you can easily end up arguing about program style rather than languages.

This does not mean that it is impossible to compare programming languages—one should just avoid very general statements like the above, and one should make reservations clear. But it is perfectly possible to argue that for a specific type of user (programmer), for a specific type of problem, for specific implementations, one language is better suited than another.

This also means that a new programming language typically is designed for a specific type of user (programmer), for a specific type of problem, or for a specific implementation method or machine.

Weak Languages

Many of the observations above rely on languages being Turing complete. If a language is not Turing complete, you can perfectly well and precisely argue about computational power, program size and execution speed (on a non-Turing complete machine). But why would you want to use a language that provably cannot be used for any sort of computation?

Turing completeness may give the highest possible power of computation, but this power itself has a prize: It can be very hard or impossible to decide properties about programs written in Turing complete languages:

- It may be impossible to prove that a program is correct with respect to a formal specification. Some programs can be proven correct, but there are programs that can neither be proven correct nor incorrect.
- It may be impossible to give bounds on computation time or resource use—even if you just want to know if the bounds are finite or not. Again, it is possible to prove bounds on some programs, but some programs will escape proof.

It is possible to design programming languages where such proof or bounds can always be found, but this will be at the cost of Turing completeness. Many domain-specific languages will be deliberately designed this way to ensure specific properties. While these languages can be useless outside the problem domain for which they are designed, they can be very useful for solving problems inside this domain.

General Design Principles

The remainder of the book will investigate design choices for different aspects of programming languages, but there are some cross-cutting guidelines that apply to the design process as a whole. The following guidelines are not hard laws, but something a designer should at least think about.

1. There is no single perfect language design for any given purpose. This does not mean that all designs are equally good—there are plenty of examples of bad language design.
2. Few design choices are good or bad in isolation, but one design choice may fit a given purpose better than others. And some sets of design choices can benefit each other while other sets can interact badly.
3. Make everything as simple as possible, but no simpler.[1] Simplicity is a good design principle, but one should not over-simplify, as that can impact practicality.
4. If a language is difficult to describe precisely, it is likely difficult to understand and use. So make sure syntax and semantics have clear (possibly formal) descriptions.
5. When you design a language or language feature, you should have at least a rough idea of how this can be implemented. This understanding need not be present when a language or feature is investigated (indeed, the investigation may include research for implementation techniques), but it should be before a final design decision is made.
6. Excepting very specialised (domain-specific) languages, a programming language is not very useful unless it is supported by a comprehensive library—if you have to write everything from scratch, all but the most trivial programs will

---

[1] This saying is usually attributed to Albert Einsten.

be major efforts. So, unless you have resources to write a substantial library from scratch, you should enable the use of libraries written in or for other programming languages.

To the Reader

The book has been designed to be used as a textbook in an advanced undergraduate or introductory graduate course in computer science and related fields, but it can also be used by professionals who want to design and implement their own programming languages, regardless of whether these are intended for personal use only or they are hoped to become used by a large number of people.

The book assumes that the reader is familiar with basic compiler techniques such as parsing and code generation at a level corresponding to an undergraduate introductory compilers course. It also assumes the reader has experience with programming in at least a couple of significantly different programming languages. In particular, the reader should have at least a bit experience with polymorphically typed functional languages with pattern matching (such as Standard ML, OCaml, F# or Haskell) imperative languages (primarily C), and object-oriented languages (such as Java or C#). If you haven't already, you can try these languages (and others) out when they are mentioned in the book. There are plenty of online tutorials you can use for this.

Like in most textbooks, each chapter concludes with a number of exercises. These are primarily intended to help the reader get a better understanding of the concepts in the chapter. For this reason, many sections in a chapter will conclude with a few suggestions of exercises that the reader is encouraged to try solving before continuing to the next section.

Every chapter also includes a list of suggested further reading that goes deeper into the subjects covered in the chapter.

Copenhagen, Denmark   Torben Ægidius Mogensen

Contents

List of Figures

A Brief History of Programming Languages

1

> *Those who don't know history are doomed to repeat it. Yet those who* do *study history are doomed to stand by helplessly while everyone else repeats it.*
>
> Tom Toro (New Yorker Cartoons)
>
> *History isn't just the story of bad people doing bad things. It's quite as much a story of people trying to do good things. But somehow, something goes wrong.*
>
> C. S. Lewis

This chapter will give a very brief and incomplete history of programming languages, focusing mainly on the early history up to the end of the 1960s. The early history of programming languages is closely linked to the early history of computers, so this will also be covered, though in lesser detail.

Programming has its origin in mathematical procedures for solving equations, proving theorems and so forth, and the word "algorithm" (effective computational procedure) is, in fact, derived from the name of the mediaeval Persian mathematician Muhammad ibn Mūsā al-Khwārizmī, who devised methods for performing calculations and solving equations. The main difference between mathematics and programming is that mathematical procedures and proofs are formulated in a mixture of formal notation and natural language, where a program is entirely formulated in a formal notation called a programming language. Mathematical logic, however, uses a completely formal notation for mathematical statements and proofs for the purpose of analysing these as mathematical objects and proving properties that are true of *all* statements and proofs expressible in the formal notation. An example of this is Gödel's *incompleteness theorem*, which was proved by representing statements and proofs as numbers. Conversely, mathematical models of computation designed for proving properties of computers and programming, such as Turing machines and the lambda calculus, have influenced the design of programming languages.

© The Author(s), under exclusive license to Springer Nature Switzerland AG 2022
T. Ægidius Mogensen, *Programming Language Design and Implementation*,
Texts in Computer Science, https://doi.org/10.1007/978-3-031-11806-7_1

Programming in the modern sense originated with the advent of programmable computers. The first such computer, the analytical engine, was designed and partially built by Charles Babbage in the nineteenth century, but was never completed. Nevertheless, descriptions of how it would be programmed were written, and Lady Ada Lovelace, who worked with Babbage, is often credited as being the world's first programmer, because she described and published a procedure for calculating sequences of Bernoulli numbers on Babbage's analytical engine.

1.1   Before Computers: Turing Machines and Lambda Calculus

Before electronic computers were built, their future existence was predicted, and logicians made models of how such hypothetical computers could work in order to prove properties about the process of computation.

One such model was made by Alan Turing in 1936, and attempted to simplify and formalise the kind of work done by human computers (people who by hand or using simple mechanical adding machines made calculations): These would have an essentially unbounded supply of paper on which they can write and erase symbols, but they can only look at a small area of paper at any one time. Turing simplified the paper supply to a single unbounded paper tape on which you can write and rewrite symbols. The machine would only be able to look at a single symbol at any one time, there would be a finite number of different symbols to read and write (in the simplest form, only 0 and 1), and the machine can move the tape one symbol left or right. To control this, the machine has a finite number of different internal states, and each state can read the symbol in the current tape position and depending on the symbol write a new symbol, move the tape left or right, and change to a new state. A selected state is the Start state, and the input to the computation would be written to the tape, pointed to by the read/write head. Another selected state is a Stop state, and when this is reached, the machine stops, and the contents of the tape pointed to by the read/write head is the output of the computation. Only a finite portion of the tape is initially non-blank, and after a finite number of steps, this is still true. Figure 1.1 shows a graphical diagram of a Turing machine. A transition labelled 1/0R means that if the current tape symbol is a 1, then write a 0 and move the tape right. Similarly, 0/0L means that if the current tape symbol is a 0, then write a 0 and move the tape left. This Turing machine doesn't do anything particularly interesting.

Starting in the Start state and with the read/write head as shown in Fig. 1.1, the machine makes the transitions shown in Fig. 1.2.

Turing showed, amongst other things, that a universal machine exists: A Turing machine can be encoded as tape symbols, and a machine exists that can read a tape containing a program representation and a representation of its input and simulate the behaviour of this machine. This is essentially a self-interpreter for Turing machines. Given that you can encode machines (programs) as data, Turing wanted to see if machines could decide properties about other machines and found that some

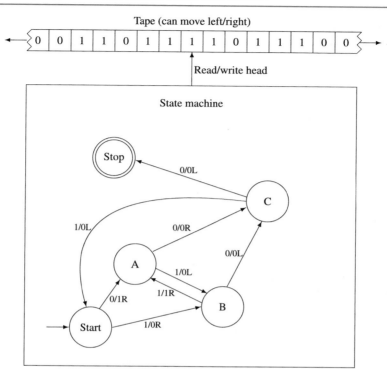

Tape (can move left/right)

| ← | 0 | 0 | 1 | 1 | 0 | 1 | 1 | 1 | 1 | 0 | 1 | 1 | 1 | 0 | 0 | → |

Read/write head

State machine

Fig. 1.1 A Turing machine

Fig. 1.2 Transitions in a Turing machine

State	Tape
Start	...0011011 1̆ 1011100...
B	...001101 1̆ 01011100...
A	...00110 1̆ 101011100...
B	...001100 1̆ 01011100...
A	...001100̆101011100...
C	...001 1̆ 00101011100...
Stop	...0011 0̆ 0101011100...

The position of the read/write head is shown by a ˘ .

properties were not decidable by machines. The proof if this resembles Gödel's proof that not all logical statements can be proven true or false using the rules of logic.

At the same time, and independently of Turing's work, the American logician Alonzo Church formulated a completely different model of computation that is now called the lambda calculus. In lambda calculus, a program is a syntactic term using a very simple grammar:

Fig. 1.3 A reduction
sequence in lambda calculus

$$(\lambda x.(\lambda y.(x\,(x\,y))))\,(\lambda x.(x\,x))$$
$$\rightarrow (\lambda z.((\lambda x.(x\,x))\,((\lambda x.(x\,x))\,z)))$$
$$\rightarrow (\lambda z.((\lambda x.(x\,x))\,(z\,z)))$$
$$\rightarrow (\lambda z.((z\,z)\,(z\,z)))$$

$$T \rightarrow \mathbf{var}$$
$$T \rightarrow (T\ T)$$
$$T \rightarrow (\lambda\mathbf{var}\,.\,T)$$

where **var** is a variable name, $(\lambda x\,.\,t)$ represents a function mapping x to t (similar to (fun x -> e) in F# or (\ x -> e) in Haskell), and $(t_1\ t_2)$ applies t_1 as a function to t_2. A term is reduced using a single reduction rule:

$$((\lambda x\,.\,t_1)\ t_2) \rightarrow t_1[x \mapsto t_2]$$

where $t_1[x \mapsto t_2]$ means "t_1 where every occurrence of x is replaced by t_2". To make this consistent, variables in t_1 may have to be renamed during the substitution. Specifically, substitution is defined by the rules

$$
\begin{aligned}
x[x \mapsto t_2] \quad &= t_2 \\
y[x \mapsto t_2] \quad &= y \ \text{ if } x \neq y \\
(t_3\ t_4)[x \mapsto t_2] \quad &= (t_3[x \mapsto t_2]\ t_4[x \mapsto t_2]) \\
(\lambda y\,.\,t_3)[x \mapsto t_2] &= (\lambda z\,.\,t_3[y \mapsto z][x \mapsto t_2]) \quad \text{where } z \text{ does not occur in } t_2 \text{ or } t_3
\end{aligned}
$$

Note that the renaming of y to z uses the above substitution rules and is done prior to replacing x by t_2.

Computation is done by applying a "program" t_1 to "input" t_2 and using the reduction rule until no further reductions can be made, after which the reduced term is the output. See Fig. 1.3 for an example of this. An important property of the lambda calculus is that the result is independent of the order in which reductions are made (though the number of required steps and termination may depend on the order). By fixing a rule for selecting the next reduction, computation is well defined.

Shortly after Turing machines and lambda calculus were introduced, Turing showed that any computation that can be done by a Turing machine can also be done by the lambda calculus, and vice versa. This is now known as the Church-Turing thesis.

Suggested Exercises: 1.1, 1.2

1.2 Programmable Electronic Computers

Working programmable electronic computers were constructed in the 1940s. Programming these were done on the terms of the computer, sometimes by physically connecting wires between parts of the computer and sometimes by stringing together sequences of very simple operations, such as adding numbers and moving numbers between different parts of the computer memory, using a primitive form of what is today known as "machine code". This programming was often done by the same people who were also employed to make calculations by hand or using mechanical calculators. These people were called "computers", a name that is now mostly used for what was then called *electronic computers*, a term that compared the capabilities of these machines to the capabilities of their human counterparts. Human computers were in the 1940s and 1950s often women, so in the early days of electronic computers, most programmers were women.

When computers were small and computer hours expensive compared to hours of labour, it made sense to spend a large effort on writing programs and less on making it easy to do so. But it was quickly discovered that making nontrivial programs at the very low level required by electronic computers was not only time-consuming, but also an error-prone process. So in the 1950s, high-level programming languages were invented: Formalised notations (using symbols found on a typical teletype terminal) that could be used to express programs in a form that was more readily understandable (for humans) than machine language, and employing higher-level concepts such as floating-point numbers, arrays, records, loops, subroutines, and so on. These high-level concepts were translated into machine code, so they did not, strictly speaking, allow *more* ideas to be expressed than possible in machine language, they just, by employing high-level idioms, allowed these ideas to be expressed more easily, succinctly, and readably. High-level formalised notation also allows a degree of automatic detection of errors, as certain types of incorrect uses of high-level idioms can be detected by a computer program (such as a compiler or interpreter) and reported as errors, whereas machine code has no structure that can be exploited to this effect. Essentially, the high-level concepts introduce a structured syntax that can be verified against a formal grammar and type system, whereas programs in machine code can be seen as strings of words with no structure.

The first step towards actual programming languages was "autocodes" or "assemblers", programs that translate a textual representation (called "assembly language") of machine language instructions into the binary-number format required by the computers, offering only few abstractions such as named addresses and registers and automatically calculated addresses and offsets.

Probably the first high-level programming language was Plankalkül, devised by the German Konrad Zuse in 1942–1945. Plankalkül was, however, not implemented on a computer until much later, so it was mainly used as a tool for designing programs that were later, by hand, translated into low-level code for running on Zuse's Z3 and Z4 computers. Plankalkül included many concepts that did not enter other programming languages until much later, but since Zuse was isolated from the international computer research scene because of World War II and its aftermath, Plankalkül had no direct influence on the development of later programming languages.

The first widespread and actually implemented high-level programming language was FORTRAN (FORmula TRANslating system) from 1957, closely followed by LISP (LISt Processor, a functional language designed for symbolic processing) in 1958, COBOL (COmmon Business Oriented Language, a language intended for business programming) in 1959/1960, and in 1960 ALGOL (ALGOrithmic

Language, a language for expressing algorithms), a language that has been called "an improvement on most of its successors". All of these languages are (in much extended versions) still in use today, and most modern programming languages can trace their origins to one or more of these four languages through a process that is more evolutionary than revolutionary. For example, Java can be seen as a modern form of ALGOL with elements taken from COBOL, LISP, and Simula (see below).

Since 1960, the major new concepts in programming languages are object-oriented languages (Simula, 1967), logic languages (Prolog, 1972), languages with automatic type inference (ML, 1973) and languages for concurrency (Concurrent Pascal, 1975). Object-oriented programming is a way of structuring programs into entities called "classes" that combine declarations of data and operations on this data, and expressing data as "objects" that are instances of such classes. Logic languages express a program as a set of logical statements, so running a program will essentially construct a proof that an instance of a given input-goal is a consequence of these statements. Type inference allows a compiler to verify certain consistency properties (type correctness) without requiring the programmer to explicitly annotate the program with type information. Concurrency is a structured way of expressing interactions between a program and its environment and between several programs that run concurrently on a computer. We will look more closely at these concepts in later chapters.

1.3   Early and Influential Programming Languages

We will briefly describe some design elements of a selection of early programming languages and languages that brought significant new elements to programming.

1.3.1   Plankalkül

Since Plankalkül was not intended for automatic translation to machine language, its notation was made for human understanding rather than machine readability, though in such a way that it could mostly be typed on a typewriter with addition of a few hand-drawn symbols.

Values in Plankalkül are multi-dimensional arrays of bits, which can be indexed to individual bits or to a row of bits, which can represent a binary number.

Plankalkül uses a systematic naming convention: Input variables are written as V, intermediate variables as Z (for "Zwischenwerte"), constant names as C and result variables as R. To allow multiple variables of the same kind, the letters can be supplied with numeric indices. Additionally, a variable or constant can be a multi-dimensional array. Each variable or constant is explicitly typed using "structure types" such as 0 to indicate a single bit and $1.n$ to indicate an array of n bits. Unlike in modern programming languages, a variable, its index, component selection, and type are written on multiple lines, aligned to the same column. For example, the lines

```
  V
V | 3
K | 7
S | 1.n
```

describes component number 7 of the input variable V3 and that this component is
a bit array. The letters V, K and S at the left of the vertical bar indicate "Variablen-
Index" (variable index), "Komponent" (component) and "Struktur" (structure) or,
alternatively, A for "Angabenart" (data type). We can access bit 4 of this component
by the lines

```
  V
V | 3
K | 7.4
S | 0
```

Note that the structure type of the selected value is now a single bit.

Plankalkül has equivalents of assignments, if-then-else statements, while-loops,
and recursive function calls (with multiple result variables). It also has an operation
that can select the first component or all components of an array that fulfil a specified predicate, corresponding to filter operations known from modern functional
languages. We will not go further into the notation for this, referring the interested
reader to the "Further reading" section at the end of the chapter.

1.3.2 FORTRAN

FORTRAN was developed at IBM by a team led by John Backus as an alternative to
hand-coded assembly language. The manual was published in 1956 and a compiler
was completed in 1957. Because computer time was expensive it was required that the
compiler could generate code that ran at a speed comparable to hand-coded assembly.
This meant that the language design was conservative and that the compiler used a
series of optimisations to improve the speed of the code. The language was intended
mainly for scientific computation, so it included support for multi-dimensional arrays
and complex numbers. Control structures were, however, fairly limited, consisting
of (possibly conditional) jumps to labels and a DO loop, which corresponds to for
loops in modern languages.

The syntax of FORTRAN was designed around punched cards, so the 80 characters
found on a standard punched card were divided into fields for different purposes, as
shown in Fig. 1.4. A C in column 1 indicates that the line is a comment, otherwise
columns 1–5 can contain a numeric label. Column 6 indicates whether a statement is
continued from the previous card/line, columns 7–72 contains the statement text and
column 73–80 are ignored and can be used for comments, card numbering (useful if
a stack of cards is dropped on the floor) or other information.

C ◄ FOR COMMENT STATEMENT NUMBER	CONTINUATION	FORTRAN STATEMENT	IDENTI- FICATION
C		PROGRAM FOR FINDING THE LARGEST VALUE	
C	X	ATTAINED BY A SET OF NUMBERS	
		BIGA = A(1)	
		DO 20 I = 2,N	
		IF (BIGA − A(I)) 10, 20, 20	
10		BIGA = A(I)	
20		CONTINUE	

Fig. 1.4 FORTRAN layout as shown in the 1956 manual

In the example, the DO statement indicates that the body of the loop ends at the statement labelled 20 and that the variable I loops through the values 2 to N. The CONTINUE statement is a no-operation that, for readability, is used to mark the end of the DO-loop. The IF statement has three destination labels: The first is used when the value of the expression is negative, the second is used when the value is 0, and the third when it is positive. Blank spaces are ignored except in column 6, so the DO-statement in the example could equivalently be written as DO20I=2,N. A widespread anecdote says that a NASA programmer by mistake typed a period instead of a comma in a DO-loop, making the compiler read it as an assignment (i.e., DO20I = 1.5 instead of the loop DO 20 I = 1, 5), and as a consequence made a rocket launch fail. While there are accounts that such an error was indeed made, it was corrected before it could do harm.

Because memory was scarce in 1956, FORTRAN allowed several variables or arrays to explicitly share the same memory. It was up to the programmer to ensure the correct use of this feature. In addition to saving memory, it allows a two-dimensional array to be viewed also as a one-dimensional array (using a different name), which makes looping over all elements simpler.

Later versions of FORTRAN, most notably FORTRAN 66, FORTRAN 77, and Fortran 90 (note the change to lower-case) are extended with more data and control structures and a freer textual layout. When we later in the book refer to FORTRAN without any specific version indication, it is the early (pre 1977) versions of FOR-TRAN we talk about.

1.3.3 LISP

LISP was designed in 1958 at MIT by John McCarthy. LISP was inspired by the lambda calculus, a mathematical formalism for computing. LISP was intended for symbolic processing and had a single data type: The S-expression (symbolic expression). An S-expression is either an atom (a symbol composed of alphanumeric characters) or a pair of two S-expressions, so examples include AB (an atom) and

((AB.C).D) (a nested pair). A list (A,B,C) is an abbreviation of the S-expression (A.(B.(C.NIL))).

LISP was originally meant to use a syntax called M-expressions (meta expressions) for writing programs, but with each M-expression having an equivalent S-expression, so programs could be used as data. A definition of a function that finds the leftmost symbol in an S-expression is written as the M-expression

$$ff[x] = [atom[x] \;\rightarrow\; x; T \;\rightarrow\; ff[car[x]]]$$

where the arrows indicate conditionals: If x is an atom, x is returned, otherwise (indicated by the truth value T), the function is called recursively on the first component of the list, which is selected using the car function. This function definition would be represented by the S-expression

```
DEFINE ((FF,(LAMBDA,(X),(COND,((ATOM,X),X),(T,(FF,(CAR,X))))))))
```

The first implementation of LISP did not accept M-expressions, so programmers needed to write their programs as S-expressions. Furthermore, the commas could be (and usually were) omitted from lists, so the definition above would be written as

```
DEFINE ((FF (LAMBDA (X) (COND ((ATOM X) X) (T (FF (CAR X))))))))
```

Programmers came to like this notation, so it became the standard for LISP to use S-expressions to write programs, and this notation has survived even in modern LISP-like languages like Scheme and Clojure. In Scheme, the above definition can be written as

```
(define ff (lambda (x) (cond ((atom? x) x) (#t (ff (car x))))))
```

although atom? has to be defined from other functions.

We have already mentioned the CAR function for selecting the first component of a pair. The corresponding function to select the second component is called CDR. This non-obvious nomenclature comes from two assembly language macros on the IBM 704 computer first used to implement LISP: CAR found the Contents of the Address part of a Register and CDR found the Contents of the Decrement part of a Register, which happened to be what was needed to select the components of pairs. Abbreviations such as (CADR X) for (CAR (CDR X)) were introduced, and these became so popular that the nomenclature has survived in Scheme and Clojure in spite of the accidental origin of the names.

LISP was the first programming language to allow functions as values that can be passed as arguments to other functions and returned from these. Though assignments to variables were possible from the start, their usage was (and still is) discouraged. LISP was also the first language to feature automatic garbage collection, see Chap. 4.

1.3.4 COBOL

COBOL was designed by a committee that the US Department of Defence set down in May 1959 with the purpose of defining a portable programming language for business applications, so costly and error-prone recoding of such applications could be avoided. The committee finished its work in late 1959 and the work was approved by the Executive Committee in January 1960. Rear admiral Grace Hopper, a prominent member of the design committee, is widely regarded as the main inventor of the language.

Programs written in COBOL are meant to be readable by business people with no background in programming, so a notation resembling the English language is used. For example, an assignment that in C and similar languages is written as C = A+B can in COBOL be written as ADD A TO B GIVING C, a C-like statement M *= N can be written as MULTIPLY M BY N, and you can write conditions like IF X IS GREATER THAN Y. A more standard math-like notation for formulas is, however, allowed.

Also inspired by English, the MONTH field of the DATE field in a record called MASTER can be written as MONTH IN DATE OF MASTER, using either IN or OF as synonyms for accessing a field.

The basic data structures in COBOL are nested records of numeric or textual fields and files containing sequences of such records. To allow portability between computers with different integer sizes and representations, all numbers in COBOL are specified by a number of decimal digits before and after a decimal point. Similarly, textual variables specify the number of characters they can hold. The underlying idea is that all values can be stored in database records using a fixed number of characters per field. To ensure portability, a standard character set is specified. This was in the first COBOL definition from 1960 limited to 51 different characters, but is in later versions of COBOL extended to include more characters, including lower-case letters. An example record definition in COBOL is shown below:

```
01 STUDENT
   02 NAME PIC A(20)
   02 DATE-OF-ENTRY
      03 YEAR PIC 9(4)
      03 MONTH PIC 99
      03 DAY PIC 99
   02 ECTS-POINTS PIC 9(3)V9
```

The number on the left indicates nesting level, so the fields labelled 02 are fields of the record labelled 01 and the fields labelled 03 are sub-fields of the DATE-OF-ENTRY field. PIC A(20) is a type indicator that specified that NAME is a string (PICture) of 20 alphabetic characters. PIC 9(4) indicates a four-digit number, PIC 99 indicates a two-digit number and PIC 9(3)V9 indicates a fixed-point number with 3 digits before the decimal point and one digit after. The level indicators must be two digits each (in the range 00 to 49), but they do not need to be incremented in steps of 1. In fact, it is common to increase the numbers by 4 to allow easier restructuring of records at a later date. Using this convention, the record description above would use 01, 05 and 09 instead of 01, 02, and 03 for the three levels.

COBOL (in a more modern form) is still one of the most widely used programming languages for business applications. Its use of fixed-point decimal numbers have caused hardware-support for decimal arithmetic (binary coded decimal) to be added to many computer architectures, in particular those aimed at business applications.

1.3.5   ALGOL 60

ALGOL 60 was a further development of a language called both IAL (International Algebraic Language) and ALGOL 58 (ALGOrithmic Language), proposed at a conference in Zürich in 1958. IAL/ALGOL 58 was intended primarily as a language for describing algorithms in reports and articles and secondarily for being implemented on computers. It introduced a number of new concepts including block structure, where the scope of conditional statements and loops are delimited by keywords begin and end rather than by labels, and where blocks can freely be nested within one another. ALGOL 58 did not see much use except as inspiration for other languages, notably ALGOL 60.

ALGOL 60 grew out of discussions at meetings about ALGOL 58, most notably the Copenhagen meeting in February 1959, which led to the publication of an ALGOL Bulletin edited by Peter Naur, then working at Regnecentralen, which at the time were building the first Danish computer DASK. At a meeting in January 1960, the report on ALGOL 60 was finalised. The report was based on a preliminary report written by Peter Naur based on discussions in the ALGOL Bulletin, but had a number of additional authors, including John W. Backus (of FORTRAN fame) and John McCarthy (of LISP fame). It has been suggested that Naur, being a junior member of the committee, got a disproportional influence on the final language design by preempting the discussion in the January 1960 meeting by providing the first coherent draft description of a full language proposal. In any case, the ALGOL 60 report has since been praised as exemplary in its clarity and systematic description of the language, and the language design itself was also praised. In 1973, C.A.R. Hoare said about ALGOL 60 that "Here is a language so far ahead of its time that it was not only an improvement on its predecessors but also on nearly all its successors".

The report had a number of innovations, including using a formal notation for the syntactic description based on a proposal by John Backus for describing the syntax of ALGOL 58. The resulting notation is now called the Backus-Naur form and is equivalent to context-free grammars. The report also described three levels of the ALGOL 60 Language: The reference language, the publication language, and hardware representations. The reference language was primarily what was defined in the report, but it was suggested that an extended notation allowing Greek letters, subscripts , and exponents could be used in articles and reports to increase readability. Even the reference language, however, used many symbols not (at the time) commonly found on teletype terminals and other media used by computers,

Fig. 1.5 Transpose
procedure in ALGOL 60

```
procedure Transpose (a)Order:(n) ; value n;
array a ; integer n ;
begin real w ; integer i, k ;
for i := 1 step 1 until n do
      for k := i+1 step 1 until n do
      begin w := a[i,k] ;
            a[i,k] := a[k,i] ;
            a[k,i] := w
      end
end Transpose
```

including $\neq$, $\leq$, $\geq$, $\neg$, $\supset$, $\uparrow$, $\vee$, $\wedge$, and $\equiv$. As a consequence, the report allowed specific hardware implementations to substitute these characters with sequences of other characters. No suggestions for these substitutions were made, except that they must be specified in the documentation for the specific implementation. The reference language also emphasised keywords by underlining or boldface text, but allowed the emphasis to be omitted in implementations for hardware that did not support boldface or underlined text.

While FORTRAN, COBOL, and LISP were designed almost entirely in the US, ALGOL 60 had a significant European influence and was as a result much more popular in Europe than in the US. Nevertheless, ALGOL has had more influence on modern programming language design than FORTRAN, LISP and COBOL, most notably through strong influences on Pascal, C and Simula, and through these on Java, C#, Python, and most modern mainstream languages. Programs written in ALGOL 60 are, as a consequence, readily understandable to modern programmers, as the example in Fig. 1.5 shows.

A peculiarity of ALGOL 60 is the mechanism for parameter passing. While LISP evaluates parameter expressions before calling a procedure (a mechanism known as *call by value*), and FORTRAN allowed only call-by-reference parameters, ALGOL by default instead substitute unevaluated parameter expressions into the called procedure, so they are evaluated anew every time the corresponding parameter is used, a mechanism known as *call by name*. The main reason for using call by name is *referential transparency*: that a name bound to an expression has the same meaning as the expression itself in the context in which the expression is written (so variables used in the expression retain the scope of the expression, even if the expression is referenced in another scope). This mechanism complicated the implementation of ALGOL, but was solved using a mechanism called "thunks", which we will return to in Chap. 5. This mechanism allows very powerful programming tricks (such as Jensen's Device[1]), but the implementation overhead and the difficulty of analysing program behaviour meant that later variants of ALGOL almost invariably abandoned this mechanism. A variant called *lazy evaluation* has, however, later become popular in pure functional programming languages such as Haskell.

---

[1] https://en.wikipedia.org/wiki/Jensen%27s_Device.

Fig. 1.6 Layout of an APL keyboard. Image source and license: https://commons.wikimedia.org/wiki/File:APL-keybd2.svg

1.3.6   APL

APL, named after Kenneth Iverson's 1962 book "A Programming Language" is based on a mathematical notation for vector and matrix operations that Iverson developed at Harvard University and later at IBM. The notation was used at IBM to give a formal description of the instruction sets of computers. The notation followed the mathematical tradition of using specialised symbols, subscripts, and so on. When work on implementing the notation as an executable programming language began in 1963, the notation was simplified, but still used many symbols not usually available on computers of the day. As a consequence, IBM developed specialised keyboards, screens, and printers to support the notation. The layout of the APL keyboard is shown in Fig. 1.6. Even though the keyboard includes many special symbols, APL needed many more, so some APL-symbols had to be typed by over-striking two symbols on the keyboard. The first commercially available version of APL was released by IBM in 1967.

In addition to using a special character set, the distinguishing feature of APL is that it allows operations on whole vectors and matrices without explicit looping over indices. In fact, early versions of APL did not have explicit looping constructs and relied almost exclusively on vector and matrix operations for repetition (though `goto` was supported). For example, the APL expression $+ / \iota\ 10$ adds the numbers from 1 to 10. Evaluation of APL expressions is from right to left, and all operators have the same precedence, so, first, $\iota\ 10$ creates a vector of the numbers from 1 to 10. The / symbol is called "compress" and applies the operator to its left (in this case $+$) between the elements of the vector to its right, resulting in $1 + 2 + \cdots + 10 = 55$. Complex computations can be written very compactly using the built-in APL operators, and the use of vector and matrix operations make APL programs easy to parallelise. But the compact notation is also hard to read, especially for non-experts, which has made some people jokingly call APL a "write-only" language. As an example, the following program computes the list of primes less than or equal to an integer R:

$$PRIMES : (\sim R \in R \circ . \times R) / R \leftarrow 1 \downarrow \iota R$$

Starting from the right, ιR creates a vector of the numbers from 1 to R. 1 $\downarrow$ drops the first element (leaving 2 up to R), and $R \leftarrow$ assigns the result to R (note that R now has a different type). Inside the parenthesis (still starting from the right), $R \circ . \times R$ creates a cross product of R with itself, using point-wise multiplication, so you get a multiplication table. $R \in$ checks for all numbers in R whether they occur in this table, creating a vector the length of R, where the value is 1 (true) if the corresponding number in R is a product of two numbers and 0 (false) if it is not a product. Finally, $\sim$ negates this, so the vector contains 1 for primes and 0 for non-primes. Moving outside the parentheses, / filters the contents of R using the truth values, leaving only the primes. This program is not very efficient but serves to illustrate typical APL programming style.

APL is still in use, mainly in the financial sector, and many of its vector and matrix operations have been included in modern programming languages, both to facilitate parallelism and for its compactness of notation, even if the single-character symbols of APL are usually replaced by keywords or multi-character symbols. As an example, the *map-reduce* paradigm for parallel computation uses operators similar to those found in APL.

1.3.7   PL/I

PL/I (short for "Programming Language One") was developed from 1964 to 1966 by IBM as a language that could replace FORTRAN, COBOL, and ALGOL 60 for use on the IBM System/360, which was developed during the same period. The idea was to make a single language that could be used for all purposes: Scientific computing (which mandated support for complex numbers), financial computing (mandating flexible treatment of strings, dates, and fixed-precision numbers) as well as concurrent programming ("multiprogramming"), since System/360 supported this.

PL/I borrowed block structure from ALGOL 60, but (like FORTRAN) used call-by-reference as the main parameter-passing mechanism and added extensible arrays, fixed-point arithmetic, complex numbers, exception handling (for handling overflow and other error situations), a module system and much, much more.

One of the design goals of PL/I was extensibility: The language should allow future extensions without breaking existing programs. This meant that variable and procedure names could be identical to keywords, so future keywords would not invalidate old choices of variable names.

The language was first defined in 1964 and compilers were shipped in 1966. A process of standardisation was begun the same year but was not completed until 1976. An unusual feature of the standard definition of PL/I was that the semantics were defined by a semi-formal translation into BASIS/1, a low-level abstract machine that was precisely (though informally) defined.

PL/I was difficult to implement in part because of the overlap between keywords and variables, which made parsing difficult and error messages imprecise, and partly because some of the advanced features made optimisation difficult. A goal of PL/I was to make code that could compete with optimising FORTRAN compilers, but that was never achieved.

PL/I has mostly been used on mainframes (particularly IBM systems), though compilers exist for Windows and Unix. It did not, as intended, replace FORTRAN and COBOL, but it has been used to program large systems such as SAS (though this moved away from PL/I later), and is still in use, primarily in financial institutions.

PL/I can be seen as the first (and probably the last) major attempt to design a language for absolutely everything from system programming through scientific programming to financial programming.

1.3.8 BASIC

BASIC, which is short for "Beginners All-purpose Symbolic Instruction Code" was designed in 1964 at Dartmouth College by John G. Kemeny and Thomas E. Kurtz as a deliberately simple language that would allow students from non-technical fields to use computers.

Like FORTRAN, BASIC programs consist of lines that were typically written on punched cards. For simplicity, each line is a single statement starting with a line number and a keyword. For example, an assignment to a variable A might be done using the line

```
120 LET A = 17
```

Line numbers identify lines as targets for jumps, using statements like

```
170 GOTO 120
```

Control structures were initially limited to GOTO, GOSUB (jump to a subroutine), RETURN (return from subroutine), IF-THEN and a FOR-loop that iterated a variable through a range of values. Later variants of BASIC have added support for structured programming inspired by ALGOL, including WHILE and REPEAT loops and named procedures with parameters.

BASIC became immensely popular in the late 1970s when it became the language of choice for home computers. BASIC was both simple enough to implement in the limited memory available on home computers and simple enough that children could quickly learn to make small programs. Most home computers used their own, mutually incompatible variants of BASIC, so programs running on one home computer could rarely run unchanged on other computers. But the common core allowed many programs to be easily rewritten for other computers, as long as they did not use sound or graphics, which were very machine-specific on home computers.

Due to its popularity, BASIC also became ubiquitous on the more business-oriented "Personal computers" such as the IBM PC, and as computers grew in capacity, more features were added to the language, making BASIC a full-fledged, professional programming language. At the other end of the hardware spectrum, programmable hand-held calculators eventually became programmable in simple BASIC dialects. Microsoft's Visual Basic dialect is, at the time of writing, one of the most used languages for programming on the MS Windows and .NET platforms, but it bears little resemblance to the original Dartmouth BASIC.

1.3.9 Simula

Simula was first defined and implemented in 1965 by Kristen Nygaard and Ole-Johan Dahl from the University of Oslo as an extension of Algol 60 for simulating discrete event networks.

But it is mainly the later extension, Simula 67, that has been influential on later programming language design. Simula 67 added objects, classes, inheritance, subclasses, virtual procedure calls, and dynamic object creation, making it the first object-oriented language, and a major inspiration for later object-oriented languages such as Smalltalk, C++, and Java.

Simula 67 also added garbage collection, which was unusual for Algol derivatives. The reasoning was that dynamic object creation combined with subclassing makes it difficult to track the lifetimes of objects manually, so automatic reclamation of dynamically created objects is needed. Most object-oriented languages (C++ being a notable exception) have inherited the use of garbage collection from Simula 67.

1.3.10 Pascal

Pascal is an ALGOL variant that was designed by Niklaus Wirth in the late 1960s as a language for teaching structured programming to students. Its design goals were consistency and simplicity (of both design and implementation) while still allowing advanced structuring mechanisms such as nested procedure declarations, functional values, and structured data such as subranges, records, and variants. Additionally, the language was designed to prevent certain types of errors, by disallowing certain constructs, checking for potential errors at compile time, and catching a large class of the remaining errors at runtime. For example, Pascal does not allow the construction of null pointers, and all array accesses are checked at runtime to be within the declared bounds.

Pascal became extremely popular in the 1970s and 1980s, being one of the most common languages for teaching programming in higher education, and variants of Pascal were widely used for programming personal computers. The popularity of Pascal has declined somewhat, but variants of Pascal (such as Delphi) are still widely used, and Pascal has been influential in the design of later programming languages such as Java and C#.

1.3.11 C

The C programming language is another variant of ALGOL. It was designed by Dennis Ritchie in the early 1970s for the purpose of implementing large parts of the UNIX operating system. Up to that time, operating systems were almost exclusively implemented in assembly language.

As a language for systems programming, C was designed to allow the programmer to easily predict what the compiled code would look like, and some of the features of the language (such as byte addressability and the ++ and -- pre/post-increment/decrement operators) were directly inspired by features in the PDP-11 assembly language. The language also included features for manipulating machine words at the bit level and for viewing (by almost unrestricted type casting) the same machine word as different types, such as integers or pointers, at different times. Additionally, C does not check anything at runtime, unless this is explicitly coded in the program. So errors such as addressing outside an array, following a null pointer, or following a pointer to something that is no longer allocated, are not caught. The philosophy is that if it is not trivial for the compilers to eliminate unnecessary checks, checks of that kind are not done, and it is up to the programmer to insert these where needed.

C favours brevity, so many of the verbose keywords and operators of ALGOL are replaced by single characters. For example, the ALGOL keywords BEGIN and END are replaced by curly braces, and C omits the THEN keyword in conditional statements (replacing it with a requirement to enclose the condition in parentheses). A macro system allows further abbreviations.

In spite of being designed for systems programming, the relative efficiency of C made it widely popular for programming almost anything (including financial applications), and several later languages have borrowed heavily from C, in particular the use of curly-brace syntax and the flexible for-loop syntax. But most C-inspired languages have moved away from the systems programming focus, have added restrictions on type casting, and have added compiler-inserted runtime checks for things such as addressing outside the bounds of an array and following null pointers, so their similarities with C are often mostly syntactical.

1.3.12 Prolog

Prolog, which is short for "PROgramming with LOGic" was developed in 1972, so it is not quite as early as the languages mentioned above. We have included it in this list because it introduced a radically different way of programming.

Prolog was developed by the French computer scientist Alain Colmerauer for doing natural language processing such as automatic translation. For this reason, it works mainly on symbolic data consisting of words that can be combined into lists or trees (representing grammatical structure). For example, a sentence can be represented as the list of words [the, cat, sleeps], which a Prolog program might parse into the tree structure

```
sentence(nounPhrase(article(the),noun(cat)),verb(sleeps))
```

Such tree structures can contain unspecified parts using *logical variables*. Prolog uses *unification*, a generalisation of pattern matching, to build, take apart and distinguish tree-structured data.

In Prolog, a program is a list of logical statements. To run the program, you provide a logical query containing variables. The Prolog system will then try to find instantiations of the variables that make the query provably a consequence of the logical system defined by the program. If there are no such instantiations, the answer is "false" (or "no", depending on the Prolog variant), but otherwise a set of instantiations is presented and the user is given the option to ask for further solutions.

If the search for solutions in Prolog was perfect, these would be the only two possible answers, but (mainly for efficiency reasons) Prolog uses an incomplete search strategy that can run forever without providing any answers. To alleviate this, Prolog also provides non-logical control features that can be used to guide the search. Used correctly, these can avoid non-terminating searches, but they can also prevent searching parts of the solution space that contain valid solutions, so they must be used with care.

Prolog has inspired many later *logic programming languages* that have added features such as complete search strategies, numeric predicates (such as sets of inequalities), and more. We will look further into Prolog and logic programming in Sect. 9.4.

1.3.13   ISWIM and ML

ISWIM (short for "If you See What I Mean") is a hypothetical language described by Peter Landin in his article "The Next 700 Programming Languages". Landin's thesis was that the then current programming languages did not sufficiently well make it clear to readers what the *intention* of a program was. You could see *what* happened, but not really what the underlying purpose is. ISWIM intended to alleviate this by using a syntax derived from mathematical notation, in particular using **let-in** and **where** clauses to make local definitions and using recursive function definitions instead of loops that modify state.

ISWIM was not implemented, but it was a major inspiration for ML (short for Meta Language), which was developed by Robin Milner in 1973 as a meta language for developing proof tactics in the LCF theorem prover. In spite of this, ML is a general-purpose functional language that has seen use for many other purposes, including financial modelling and computer games.

ML added to ISWIM a type system with the property that "well-typed programs can't go wrong", in the sense that certain kinds of runtime errors provably cannot occur in well-typed programs. The types of variables and functions need not be explicitly written in the program, but can be *inferred* from the definitions and use of these. This was done by the *Hindley-Milner* type inference algorithm that allows polymorphic (generic) types to be inferred automatically, uniquely, and efficiently from program text without explicit type annotations.

ML also added recursive, algebraic datatypes allowing statically typed versions of tree structures similar to those found (dynamically typed) in LISP and Prolog, and pattern-matching to manipulate these in a manner resembling the way Prolog uses unification, but without the logical variables of Prolog.

ML is not a *pure* functional language, as it allows imperative features such as assignment and exceptions, but the preferred programming style is almost purely functional.

An extension of ML called *Standard ML* was defined in 1990. The main additions were a powerful module system and a complete formal specification. A 1997 revision was mainly a simplification of the 1990 definition.

ML has influenced many other functional languages, including OCaml, Scala, Haskell, and F#. In particular, type inference, algebraic data types, pattern matching, and the module system have been strong influences on later languages. Features of ML such as polymorphic types, anonymous tuples, and pattern matching have also made it into object-oriented languages such as Java and C#. Bob Harper (who has worked extensively with ML) is attributed with saying "Over time, any language will evolve to look more and more like Standard ML".

1.4 Further Reading

You can read more about the difference engine in [15]. Plankalkül is described in [3]. Turing machines are described in most books about computability, e.g., [14]. The lambda calculus and its theory is described in great detail in [2].

Backus has described the early history of FORTRAN in [1]. A story of LISP can be found in [6]. The early history of COBOL is described in [13]. Peter Naur describes his experiences with the development of ALGOL 60 in [12]. The main developer of APL gives his personal view of the language in [4]. Pascal is described in [5], and C is described in [7].

Prolog and other early logic programming languages are described in [8]. ISWIM is introduced in [9] and Standard ML is defined in [11], along with a commentary [10].

Several of the references above are from the "History of Programming Languages" conference series, which have many interesting historical overviews of early programming languages. The Software Preservation Group (http://www.softwarepreservation.org) has archived a large selection of both articles about and implementations of early programming languages.

1.5 Exercises

Exercise 1.1 Using the notation from Fig. 1.2, show the transitions starting with the configuration

State	Tape
Start	… 001100̌101011100…

Exercise 1.2 Using the notation from Fig. 1.3, show the steps when reducing the lambda expression

$$((\lambda x \, . \, (\lambda y \, . \, (y \, x))) \, (\lambda y \, . \, y))$$

Exercise 1.3 Rewrite the FORTRAN code shown in Fig. 1.4 to C, Java, or C# and add code to read in the values of the number N and the array A and write the resulting value of BIGA.

Exercise 1.4 Using any of the LISP syntaxes shown in Sect. 1.3.3, write the definition of a function that finds the right-most symbol in an S-expression.

Exercise 1.5 Given the record definition shown in Sect. 1.3.4, write a COBOL statement that adds 7.5 ECTS points to the student record (which is named STUDENT).

Exercise 1.6 Rewrite the procedure in Fig. 1.5 to C, Java, or C#. Add code to build the matrix

$$\begin{pmatrix} 1 & 2 & 3 \\ 4 & 5 & 6 \\ 7 & 8 & 9 \end{pmatrix}$$

and print the transposed matrix (obtained by calling the procedure).

Exercise 1.7 Find a programming language designed after the year 1990 which includes a *significant* language feature, design element or property that is *original* to this language and not found in any earlier non-academic programming language.

By non-academic, we mean a language that has been used outside research communities.

Exercise 1.8 Draw the ancestry tree of one of the programming languages F#, Scala, Rust, or Swift, where an ancestor to a language is an earlier language from which the language draws significant elements. For each edge, write at least one element that the later language draws from the older. Make the ancestry tree go back at least to one or more of the languages FORTRAN, LISP, COBOL, and ALGOL 60.

Exercise 1.9 Write a short essay (1–2 pages) about one of the following programming languages, focusing on why the language was designed, from where the language drew inspiration, what distinguishing features the language had, what impact it had in its time, and what later languages (if any) took inspiration from the language. Choose between the languages COMAL, SNOBOL, LOGO, BCPL, POP, Forth, MUMPS, or REFAL. Use original sources and not just Wikipedia. In your own opinion, what is good about the language, and what is not so good?

References

1. Backus J (1981) The history of FORTRAN I, II, and III. In: History of programming languages. Association for Computing Machinery, Inc
2. Barendregt HP (1984) The lambda calculus – its syntax and semantics. North Holland
3. Giloi WK (1997) Konrad Zuse's Plankalkül: the first high-level, "non von Neumann" programming language. IEEE Ann Hist Comput 19(2):17–24. http://doi.ieeecomputersociety.org/10.1109/85.586068
4. Iverson KE (1991) A personal view of APL. IBM Syst J 30:582–593
5. Jensen K, Wirth N (1975) Pascal user manual and report, 2nd edn. Springer
6. Steele GL Jr, Gabriel RP (1993) The evolution of LISP. In: History of programming languages, pp 231–270. Association for Computing Machinery, Inc
7. Kerninghan BW, Ritchie DM (1978) The C programming language. Prentice-Hall
8. Kowalski RA (1988) The early years of logic programming. Commun ACM 31(1):38–43. https://doi.org/10.1145/35043.35046, http://doi.acm.org/10.1145/35043.35046
9. Landin PJ (1966) The next 700 programming languages. Commun ACM 9(3):157–166. https://doi.org/10.1145/365230.365257, http://doi.acm.org/10.1145/365230.365257
10. Milner R, Tofte M (1991) Commentary on standard ML. MIT Press, Cambridge, MA, USA
11. Milner R, Tofte M, Harper R, MacQueen D (1997) The definition of standard ML. MIT Press, Cambridge, MA, USA
12. Naur P (1978) The European side of the last phase of the development of ALGOL 60. ACM Sigplan Not 13(8):15–44
13. Sammet JE (1981) The early history of COBOL. In: Wexelblat RL (ed) History of programming languages I, pp 199–243. ACM, New York, NY, USA. https://doi.org/10.1145/800025.1198367, http://doi.acm.org/10.1145/800025.1198367
14. Sipser M (1996) Introduction to the theory of computation, 1st edn. International Thomson Publishing
15. Swade D (2002) The difference engine: Charles Babbage and the quest to build the first computer. Penguin

Implementation Strategies

2

It's important to have a sound idea, but the really important thing is the implementation.

Wilbur Ross

I believe that people make their own luck by great preparation and good strategy.

Jack Canfield

The very first automatic computing machines, such as Babbage's difference engine and early electronic computers, were specialised to one particular task such as calculating polynomials or multiplying matrices. Early programmable computers were programmed by connecting wires, so there was no real concept of a program. It was only with the advent of *stored program computers* that programs in the modern sense came to be. These were coded first in binary code, then in symbolic machine language (assembly language), and only after the advent of FORTRAN in 1957 in what can be called "high-level languages".

In the 1950s and early 1960s, computers were few, slow, and expensive, so optimising runtime performance was an issue. There were even some resistance against using assembly language because it made it more difficult to make self-modifying code and to reuse the same machine word as both an instruction and a constant value. The first FORTRAN compilers employed quite a complex optimisation techniques to make FORTRAN programs run at a speed comparable to hand-coded assembly language programs, and even so, it was not uncommon for programmers to hand-optimise central routines by modifying the code produced by the compiler—also because the compiler was quite slow, so it was often faster to fix bugs in the compiled code than to recompile a bug-fixed source program. While runtime performance is still an issue for some applications, implementation techniques that are not solely

T. Ægidius Mogensen, *Programming Language Design and Implementation*,
Texts in Computer Science, https://doi.org/10.1007/978-3-031-11806-7_2

focused on maximising performance have gained a foothold. In this chapter, we will look at some of the techniques and trade-offs.

We assume the reader has basic knowledge of compilation and interpretation techniques.

2.1 Compilation and Interpretation

A compiler works by translating a program from one language (typically a high-level programming language) to another (typically assembly language or machine code). This allows compiled programs to, at least in theory, run at the same speed as programs hand-coded in the target language, and it is even in some cases possible to exceed the performance of programs hand-coded by all but the cleverest programmers, simply because a compiler can keep track of more information than a typical programmer can. This makes compilation suitable for implementing languages intended for high-performance computing. The cost is that time is required for translating the high-level code to low-level code, and this time increases with the optimisation level of the generated code. If frequent modifications are made to a program, the delay between making a modification to the program and being able to execute it can be significant.

An alternative way to implement a programming language is *interpretation*. Here, a representation of the source program as text or as a data structure is stored on the computer, and a program (called the interpreter) walks through this text or data structure to decide which operations it needs to perform on the program state (the values of variables and other data used by the program). There is little or no delay between making a modification to a program and executing this (though reading the program text from a file and parsing it can take some time), but the actual execution is slower because the interpreter has to decode what a program statement or expression means every time this statement or expression is executed. Since most programs employ significant repetition in the form of loops or recursion, this overhead can be significant.

LISP was the first major programming language to use interpretation as the main implementation mechanism. This was done mainly for simplicity and because it allowed easy execution of source-level code that is generated at runtime: In LISP, a program is a value using the same data structure as any other value (S-expressions, see Sect. 1.3.3), so it is fairly easy to make programs that build other programs. By using interpretation, these programs can readily be executed, a technique commonly used in LISP programming. Some implementations of LISP use compilation, but still support runtime generation and execution of programs. In this case, such program bits are first compiled and then immediately executed.

Another early language that uses interpretation as the main implementation technique is APL. In APL, an operation typically affects all values in an array instead of affecting only a single number or symbol, so the overhead of decoding the operation is smaller: Looping over the values of the array is done in a loop in the interpreter (running at native speed) and not in a loop in the interpreted program. This reduces the relative overhead of decoding the program. Many APL programs use no explicit loops but only the repetition that is implicit in array operations, so each operation is decoded only once. Nevertheless, later implementations of APL have used the compilation, mainly because compilation allows optimisations that are not easily done in an interpreter, such as merging loops.

This does not imply that optimisation is not possible in interpreters: It is possible for the interpreter to rewrite programs at the source-code level before executing them, and an interpreter can inspect a program for special cases where operations can be simplified. Such optimisations require runtime inspection and rewriting of programs, so they can slow down execution of programs that are not amenable to these optimisations.

2.2   REPLs and IDEs

An interpreter that holds a representation of the source code of the program that is being executed can allow the program to be edited in memory, so the programmer does not have to edit a text file and load this into the interpreter. The interpreter is, hence, equipped with a specialised editor that allows loading programs from files, editing programs, and saving programs to files. Such combined editors and interpreters are often called *integrated development environments* (IDEs).

Often, such interpreters also allow the programmer to write expressions and statements that are immediately evaluated or executed in the context of the current program. Such *read-eval-print loops* (REPLs) were introduced with LISP and are found in many languages such as BASIC, ML, Haskell, and Python.

It is possible to have IDEs and REPLs also for compiled languages. In these cases, the compiler is invoked from the IDE or REPL to compile and execute the code that is being developed. Often, the compiler is made so it does not need to recompile the whole program, but only the parts that have been modified since the last compilation. This is called *incremental compilation*.

2.3   Intermediate Code and Virtual Machines

Early compilers generated machine-specific code directly from a high-level program. This eases machine-specific optimisations, but it makes it more difficult to port the compiler to a different machine.

By employing a (mostly) machine-independent intermediate language, it is possible to split the compilation into two phases: Generation of intermediate code from the high-level language, and generation of machine code from the intermediate code. When porting the compiler to a different machine, only the latter part needs to be rewritten. Furthermore, compilers for different high-level languages can use the same intermediate language, so the phase that translates from the intermediate language to machine language needs to be written only once. It is also possible to implement the intermediate language with an interpreter instead of a compiler. If the intermediate language is simple to decode, the interpretation overhead can be quite small.

If you want to translate M different high-level languages to N different machines, direct translation requires $M \times N$ compilers. If there is a common intermediate language, you need only M compilers from high-level languages to the intermediate language and N compilers from the intermediate language to the different machines. You can also do many optimisations in the intermediate language, and these can be shared between all the compilers. Theoretically, the compilers from high-level languages to the intermediate language can be very simple, and the compilers from the intermediate language to machine language ditto, since almost all of the complexity can be done as simplification and optimisation of the intermediate code. In practice, it is not quite that simple: If the intermediate language is relatively high-level, it can be easy to compile high-level languages to this, but it becomes more difficult to compile the intermediate language to machine language. Conversely, a low-level intermediate language can be easy to compile to machine language, but more difficult to generate from a high-level language. Additionally, it is no help that the intermediate language is high-level if the abstractions used in the intermediate language are a poor fit for the high-level language. For example, if the intermediate language is object-oriented, it may be easy to compile, say, Java or C# to this language, but not obviously simple to compile functional or logic languages to the intermediate language. Similarly, a low-level intermediate language may be a better fit to some machines than others. For example, a stack-based intermediate language may be an ill fit to a register-based machine and vice-versa, and if the intermediate language assumes a specific word size or endianness, it may be difficult to translate to a machine that employs different word sizes or endianness.

Some of the mismatch problems can be alleviated by employing multiple interme-diate languages: One that is used as the target when translating high-level languages, and one that is used for machine-code generation. A single compiler from the first of these to the other can then be used as a compilation phase by several compilers. It is also possible to have more than one high-level intermediate language and more than one low-level intermediate language. This reduces the sharing potential, but allows better fit between languages and machines. It is even possible that all the intermediate languages are subsets of the same, large intermediate language, such that the translation between different intermediate languages is just rewriting from one subset to another (simpler) subset.

In addition to use inside a compiler, an intermediate language can also be used for transmitting or distributing programs: A program is compiled to the intermediate lan-guage, then sent to the machine where it should be executed, where it is compiled or interpreted. In this case, the intermediate language is often called a *virtual machine*. One example of this is the Java Virtual Machine (JVM), which is used to distribute programs written in Java, Scala, Clojure and several other programming languages. When executing programs on the receiving computer, the programs in JVM are ei-ther interpreted or compiled and executed on this computer. Using a virtual machine allows shipping the same program to a multitude of computers using different machine languages without having to ship the entire source code to the receiving computers or shipping multiple compiled images. Furthermore, compilation from the virtual machine to the machine language (or interpretation of the virtual machine) may be simpler than compilation from or interpretation of the source language, as discussed above.

2.4   Hybrid Methods

If an intermediate language is employed, it is (as mentioned above) possible to combine compilation and interpretation: The compiler translates from the high-level language to the intermediate language, which is in turn interpreted on the machine that executes the program. An interpreter can be written in a high-level language and be compiled on different platforms, so this makes it relatively easy to port the language to different platforms: It only requires that the language in which the interpreter is written is already implemented on the new platform. It is, for example, common to write such intermediate-language interpreters in C, as this is readily available on most platforms and sufficiently low-level that interpreters written in C can be fast.

It is also possible to combine interpretation and compilation when executing the intermediate language: Interpretation gives better over-all performance than compilation if there is little or no repetition, and compiling gives better over-all performance if there is significant repetition, where repetition can be loops or repeated calls to the same function. So some virtual machines are implemented using a strategy where the code is initially interpreted and then, after a piece of code has been executed a certain number of times, it is compiled, and future executions of the code piece are done using the compiled code. This is done with the expectation that a piece of code that has already been executed repeatedly is likely to be executed repeatedly in the future also.

This strategy (employed in several implementations of JVM) is more complicated than either pure compilation or pure interpretation, but it can yield better over-all performance, especially for large programs where some parts are executed many times and other parts few times or not at all. The strategy can be generalised to more levels: First interpretation, then simple compilation, and then (if the compiled code is executed sufficiently often) optimised compilation. The interpreter or the simple compiled code can collect profiling information that can be used to improve optimisation in later stages.

2.5   Cross Compilers, Reverse Compilers, and Obfuscation

When writing a compiler, it is not actually necessary to compile to a low-level language. It is, for example, possible to compile from one high-level language to another high-level language. This can be a simple strategy to implement a new language and can exploit the optimisations that the compiler for the target language performs. Compiling from one high-level language to another is called *cross compilation*. Common target languages for cross compilation are C (because C implementations exist on most platforms) and JavaScript (because nearly all browsers support JavaScript, so you can run the compiled programs in browsers).

In addition to being a relatively easy way to implement a new language, cross compilation can also be used to port software from one language to another language, for example, if the language in which the software is written is not supported any more, or if integration to a system written in another language is required. In this case, the compiler should not only generate correct code, but also code that is readable by humans and, preferably, employs the idioms and coding styles of the target language, so it is easier to maintain the translated software in the new language. This is a much harder task than just getting executable code in the new language, as idioms and coding styles can differ greatly.

If the program is simply required to run on a different platform, simple cross-compilation from the old machine language to the new or, alternatively, emulation by interpretation of the old machine language on the new machine can be employed. Emulation can carry a large performance overhead, and maintenance is not made any simpler, but it can be an easy way of getting old code to run on new machines. Emulation is, for example, used to run programs written for old home computers such as Commodore 64, Sinclair Spectrum, and the BBC Micro on modern machines. Modern computers are easily powerful enough that the performance overhead is not a problem. In fact, slowdown is usually required to prevent games written for 8-bit machines from running much too fast to be playable.

A similar purpose is served by *reverse compilation*: Compiling from a low-level language (such as a machine language or a virtual machine) to a high-level language: Legacy software may be available only as compiled code, so maintaining the code can be tedious and error-prone. And if the machine language is no longer supported by modern hardware, it may not even be possible to execute the code any more. Compiling the code to a high-level language makes it possible to recompile (or interpret) the code for a new platform, and (if the code is sufficiently readable) to maintain it in the high-level language. Reverse compilation is also used to help understand what actually happens in code that you only have in machine language. Reading and understanding code in machine language is tedious and error-prone, so if the code can be automatically translated to more readily readable high-level code, the significant effort can be saved.

Reverse compilation has also been used to "steal" code from other vendors: The code shipped from a vendor is reverse-compiled and then by hand modified and recompiled, making it difficult to prove that the resulting code is copied from the original. A similar problem occurs for programs distributed as source code: These can be cross-compiled to another language, modified and recompiled. To prevent such theft, some companies use *automatic code obfuscation*, a form of compilation from a language to itself, but where the resulting code is made harder to understand and analyse. Simple forms of obfuscation simply remove comments, renames variables and functions randomly, undoes indentation, and translates structured control to unstructured jumps and (when the language defines such) using trigraphs or digraphs to replace common characters. This may make it harder to understand the code by basically breaking all the rules programmers are taught for writing readable code, but it is usually not very difficult to analyse what goes on, and tools for automatic indentation and structuring can help.

More complex obfuscation can change data representation, for example re-ordering elements in arrays or records or coding everything as bit strings. An advanced form of code obfuscation is *software water marking*, where the purpose is not only to make it hard to read and understand the code, but also to prove ownership of the code even after this has been compiled or rewritten by someone else. This can be done by inserting extra code that doesn't affect the working of the program, but computes a value encoding the ownership (so the owner can prove ownership by demonstrating how the value decodes to an ownership claim) or by changing the program structure such that the structure itself encodes such a claim.
Suggested Exercises: 2.1, 2.2.

2.6 Bootstrapping

When writing a compiler, one will usually prefer to write it in a high-level language. A possible choice is to use a language that is already available on the machine where the compiler should eventually run. It is, however, possible to have the following situation:

You have a completely new processor for which no compilers exist yet. Nevertheless, you want to have a compiler that not only targets this processor, but also runs on it. In other words, you want to write a compiler for a language A, targeting language B (the machine language) and written in language B.

The most obvious approach is to write the compiler in language B. But if B is machine language, it is a horrible job to write any nontrivial compiler in this language. Instead, it is customary to use a process called "bootstrapping", referring to the seemingly impossible task of pulling oneself up by the bootstraps.

The idea of bootstrapping is simple: You write your compiler in language A (but still let it target B) and then let it compile itself. The result is a compiler from A to B written in B.

It may sound a bit paradoxical to let the compiler compile itself: In order to use the compiler to compile a program, we must already have compiled it, and to do this we must use the compiler. In a way, it is a bit like the chicken-and-egg paradox. We shall shortly see how this apparent paradox is resolved, but first we will introduce some useful notation.

2.6.1 Notation

We will use a notation designed by H. Bratman [1]. The notation is called "Bratman diagrams" or, because of their shape, "T-diagrams" or "tombstone diagrams".

In this notation, a compiler written in language C, compiling from the language A and targeting the language B is represented by the diagram

In order to use this compiler, it must "stand" on a solid foundation, i.e., something capable of executing programs written in the language C. This "something" can be a machine that executes C as machine code. A machine that directly executes language C is in Bratman diagrams shown as

The pointed bottom indicates that a machine need not stand on anything; it is itself the foundation on which other things can stand.

Alternatively, we can have an interpreter for C running on some other machine or interpreter. Any number of interpreters can be put on top of each other, but at the bottom of it all, we need a "real" machine. An interpreter written in the language D and interpreting the language C is represented by the diagram

When we want to represent an unspecified program (which can be a compiler, an interpreter or something else entirely) written in language D, we write it as

These figures can be combined to represent executions of programs. For example, running an unspecified program on a machine D is written as

Note that the languages must match: The program must be written in the language that the machine executes.

We can insert an interpreter into this picture:

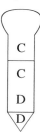

Note that, also here, the languages must match: The interpreter can only interpret programs written in the language that it interprets.

We can run a compiler and use this to compile a program:

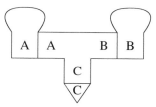

The input to the compiler (i.e., the source program) is shown at the left of the compiler, and the resulting output (i.e., the target program) is shown on the right. Note that the languages match at every connection and that the source and target program are not "standing" on anything, as they are not executed in this diagram.

We can insert an interpreter in the above diagram:

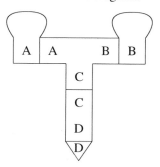

Doing so only makes the compiler run more slowly, but it does not change the code that the compiler generates.

2.6.2   Compiling Compilers

The basic idea in bootstrapping is to use compilers to compile themselves or other compilers. We do, however, need a solid foundation in the form of a machine on which to run the compilers.

It often happens that a compiler *does* exist for the desired source language, it just does not run on the desired machine. Let us, for example, assume we want a compiler for ML to x86 machine code and want this to run on an x86. We have access to an ML compiler that generates ARM machine code and runs on an ARM machine, which we also have access to. One way of obtaining the desired compiler would be to do *binary translation*, i.e., to write a compiler from ARM machine code to x86 machine code. This will allow the translated compiler to run on an x86, but it will still generate ARM code. We can use the ARM-to-x86 compiler to translate this into x86 code afterwards, but this introduces several problems:

- Adding an extra pass makes the compilation process take longer.
- Some efficiency will be lost in the translation.
- We still need to make the ARM-to-x86 compiler run on the x86 machine.

A better solution is to write an ML-to-x86 compiler in ML. We can compile this using the ML compiler on the ARM machine:

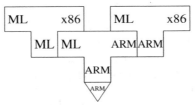

Now, we can run the ML-to-x86 compiler on the ARM and let it compile itself[1] :

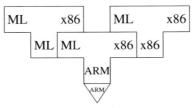

We have now obtained the desired compiler. Note that the compiler can now be used to compile itself directly on the x86 platform. This can be useful if the compiler is later extended or, simply, as a partial test of correctness: If the compiler, when compiling itself, yields a different object code than the one obtained with the above process, it must contain an error. The converse is not true: Even if the same target is obtained, there may still be errors in the compiler.

It is possible to combine the two above diagrams to a single diagram that covers both executions:

---

[1] In this context, we regard a compiled version of a program as the same program as its source-code version.

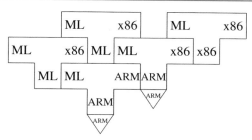

In this diagram, the ML-to-x86 compiler written in ARM has two roles: It is the output of the first compilation, and it is the compiler that runs the second compilation. Such combinations can be a bit confusing: The compiler that is the input to the second compilation step might look like it is also the output of the leftmost compiler. In this case, the confusion is avoided because the leftmost compiler is not running (it does not "stand" on a machine or interpreter), and because the languages do not match. When reading a combined diagram, look for the leftmost machine and see what it runs. If the program that it runs outputs another program, this can then be executed, but only if it stands on a machine or an interpreter (which, itself, must stand on a machine or other interpreter). Still, diagrams that combine several executions should be used with care.

2.6.3 Full Bootstrap

The above bootstrapping process relies on an existing compiler for the desired language, albeit running on a different machine. It is, hence, often called "half bootstrapping". When no existing compiler is available, e.g., when a new language has been designed, we need to use a more complicated process called "full bootstrapping".

A common method is to write a QAD ("quick and dirty") compiler using an existing language. This compiler needs not to generate code for the desired target machine (as long as the generated code can be made to run on *some* existing platform), nor does it have to generate good code, as long as the generated code is correct. The important thing is that it allows programs in the new language to be executed. Additionally, the "real" compiler is written in the new language and will be bootstrapped using the QAD compiler.

As an example, let us assume we design a new language "M+". We, initially, write a compiler from M+ to ML in ML. The first step is to compile this, so it can run on some machine:

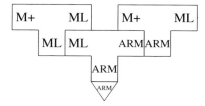

The QAD compiler can now be used to compile the "real" compiler:

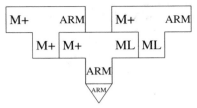

The result is an ML program, which we need to compile:

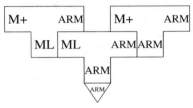

The result of this is a compiler with the desired functionality, but it will probably run slowly. The reason is that it has been compiled by using the QAD compiler (in combination with the ML compiler). A better result can be obtained by letting the generated compiler compile itself:

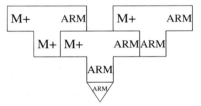

This yields a compiler with the same functionality as the above, i.e., it will generate the same code, but, since the "real" compiler has been used to compile it, it will probably run faster.

The need for this extra step might be a bit clearer if we had let the "real" compiler generate x86 code instead, as it would then be obvious that the last step is required to get the compiler to run on the same machine that it targets. But the simple case underscores a point: Bootstrapping might not be complete even if a compiler with the right functionality has been obtained.

2.6.3.1 Using an Interpreter

Instead of writing a QAD compiler, we can write a QAD interpreter. In our example, we could write an M+ interpreter in ML. We would first need to compile this:

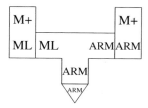

We can then use this to run the M+ compiler directly:

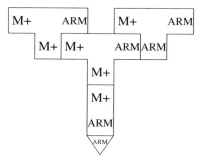

Since the "real" compiler has been used to do the compilation, nothing new will be gained by using the generated compiler to compile itself, though this step can still be used as a test and for extensions.

Though bootstrapping with an interpreter requires fewer steps than bootstrapping with a compiler, this should not really be a consideration, as the computer(s) will do all the work in these steps. What is important is the amount of code that needs to be written by hand. For some languages, a QAD compiler will be easier to write than a QAD interpreter, and for other languages, writing an interpreter is easier. The relative ease/difficulty may also depend on the language used to implement the QAD interpreter/compiler.

2.6.3.2 Incremental Bootstrapping

It is also possible to build the new language and its compiler incrementally. The first step is to write a compiler for a small subset of the language, using that same subset to write it. This first compiler must be bootstrapped in one of the ways described earlier, but thereafter the following process is done repeatedly:

(1) Extend the language subset slightly.
(2) Extend the compiler so it compiles the extended subset, but without using the new features in the compiler.
(3) Use the previous compiler to compile the new.

In each step, the features introduced in the previous step can be used in the compiler. Even when the full language is implemented, the process can be continued to improve the quality of the compiler.

2.6.4   Choosing the Language in Which to Write a Compiler

The purpose of bootstrapping is to obtain a compiler written in the language that it compiles. While this has some advantages: After bootstrapping is complete, there is no need for other compilers or other languages, and bootstrapping is a good (but incomplete) test of the compiler. But there are also disadvantages: The language that we need to compile might not be very suitable for writing a compiler, so writing the compiler in this language adds a burden to the programmer. And if compilers (or interpreters) for other languages are readily available, it is no great problem to rely on these, and a potential source of error is avoided: If a compiler made by bootstrapping fails to produce correct code for a particular feature, this can be caused both by an error in the part of the compiler that handles this feature or by the parts of the compiler that is used to compile the code that handles the feature. This makes it harder to track an error than if you can rely on the correctness of an existing compiler.

Writing a compiler for a nontrivial language is a major programming task, so (as with all large programming tasks), the main concern when picking a language should be its suitability for that type of programming task. In the personal opinion of this author, the following language features are essential for programming a nontrivial compiler:

• Existence of lexer and parser generators or good libraries for writing lexers and parsers (such as parser combinators and regular-expression libraries).
• A module system that allows specification of interfaces between the different components of the compiler (lexer, parser, type checker, intermediate-code generator, register allocator, machine-code generator, etc.).
• Good support for manipulating tree-structured data. This implies automatic memory management (garbage collection), pattern-matching on compound values, and a not too verbose syntax for building compound data.

Most mainstream languages have either lexer and parser generators or libraries that make writing lexers and parsers relatively easy. Both functional and object-oriented languages usually have both garbage collection and module systems where you can separate the specification of a module interface from its implementation. But pattern matching on compound data structures are rarely found outside functional or logic languages, and the syntax for building compound data can also be verbose in some languages.

Suggested Exercises: 2.3.

2.7   How Implementation Techniques can Influence Language Design

Languages are often designed with specific implementation methods in mind, and this can in itself influence the features available in the languages. For example, in a purely interpreted language implementation, it is fairly easy to allow a program to modify itself, by adding or removing function definitions, creating expressions that are evaluated in the current context, and so on. Examples of this include the EVAL function in LISP, which takes an S-expression and evaluates it to a value while using the current bindings of variables and functions as context. LISP also allows changing the global bindings of function names to functions, so functions can be redefined while a program runs. Similar features are found in PROLOG, where clauses can be added or retracted at runtime. Many BASIC implementations allow a string to be evaluated as an expression. While it is possible to do the same things in a compiled implementation, it is much more complicated, so languages designed for compilation (such as C, FORTRAN and Pascal) rarely have such features.

Some languages (NESL, Futhark, . . .) have been designed for execution on graphics processors, and have selected data and control structures that fit this execution model. For example, such languages usually do not support tree-structured data and they support only limited recursion.

Language design can also be limited by available/desirable implementation methods. For example, FORTRAN was originally implemented with static memory allocation only, so procedures were not recursive, and the sizes of arrays must be known at compile time. Pascal was designed mainly for stack allocation, so functions can be passed as arguments, but not returned as results. See Chap. 5 for more details.

Lack of knowledge of implementation methods can also influence language design. Allegedly, the original LISP used dynamic scoping because the implementors did not know how to implement static scoping or did not know the difference. Later LISP variants (such as Scheme and Clojure) support static scoping. Some scripting languages (PHP, Ruby, Perl, . . .) have strange scoping rules, where global and local variables behave differently, and where strange hybrids of static and dynamic scoping are used. It is plausible that these strange rules were originally caused by lack of knowledge of implementation methods, and have stuck for reasons of backwards compatibility.

2.8 Further Reading

Bratman's original article, [1], only describes the T-shaped diagrams. The notation for interpreters, machines, and unspecified programs was added later in [2].

An early bootstrapped compiler was LISP 1.5 [4].

The first Pascal compiler [5] was made using incremental bootstrapping.

Though we in Sect. 2.6.2 dismissed binary translation as only marginally suitable for porting a compiler to a new machine, it is occasionally used. The advantage of this approach is that a single binary translator can port any number of programs, not just compilers. It was used by Digital Equipment Corporation in their FX!32 software [3] to enable programs compiled for Windows on an x86 platform to run on their Alpha RISC processor.

2.9 Exercises

Exercise 2.1 In Sect. 2.5, C and JavaScript are mentioned as popular target languages for cross-compilers. Suggest a third programming language (not a virtual machine) that may be suitable for this purpose, and discuss why it, in your opinion, may in some cases be preferable over both C and JavaScript, and in which cases it may be preferable to use C or JavaScript instead.

Exercise 2.2 In Sect. 2.5, obfuscation is briefly discussed. Discuss the merits of the following idea for code obfuscation:

Every integer variable x is replaced by two variables y and z such that $x = a \cdot y + z$, where a is a constant. Whenever x is modified in the original program, either y or z (and sometimes both) are modified in the obfuscated program in such a way that the invariant is kept. Consider how the following operations on x can be implemented as operations on y and/or z:

- $x := x + k$, where k is a constant.
- $x := x + w$, where w is a variable that in the obfuscated program is represented by two variables p and q, such that $w = a \cdot p + q$.
- The comparison $x < w$, where w is a variable that in the obfuscated program is represented by two variables p and q, such that $w = a \cdot p + q$.
- $i := x * w$, where w is a variable that in the obfuscated program is represented by two variables p and q, such that $w = a \cdot p + q$.

Consider also how this obfuscation impacts performance, and how easy or difficult it would be to recover the original program from the obfuscated program.

Exercise 2.3 Assume that you have a machine that can execute ARM machine code and the following programs:

1: A compiler from C to ARM machine code written in ARM machine code.
2: An interpreter for Haskell written in C.
3: A compiler from Haskell to C written in Haskell.

Now do the following:

(a) Describe the above programs and machine as diagrams.
(b) Show how a compiler from Haskell to C written in ARM machine code can be generated from the above components. The generated program must be standalone, i.e., it may not consist of an interpreter and an interpreted program.
(c) Show how the compiler generated in question b can be used in a process that compiles Haskell programs to ARM machine code.

Exercise 2.4 A source-code optimiser is a program that can optimise programs at source-code level, i.e., a program O that reads a program P and outputs another program P', which is equivalent to P, but may be faster.

A source-code optimiser is like a compiler, except the source and target languages are the same. Hence, we can describe a source-code optimiser for C written in C with the diagram

Assume that you additionally have the following components:

- A compiler, written in x86 code, from C to x86 code.
- A machine that can execute x86 code.
- Some unspecified program P written in C.

Now do the following:

(a) Describe the above components as diagrams.
(b) Show, using Bratman diagrams, the steps required to optimise P to P' and then execute P'.

References

1. Bratman H (1961) An alternative form of the 'UNCOL' diagram. Commun ACM 4(3):142
2. Earley J, Sturgis H (1970) A formalism for translator interactions. Commun ACM 13:607–617
3. Hookway RJ, Herdeg MA (1997) Digital fx!32: combining emulation and binary translation. http://www.cs.tufts.edu/comp/150PAT/optimization/DTJP01PF.pdf
4. McCarthy J, Abrahams PW, Edwards DJ, Hart TP, Levin MI (1962) LISP 1.5 programmer's manual. The M.I.T. Press
5. Wirth N (1971) The design of a Pascal compiler. Softw Pract Exp 1(4):309–333

Syntax

3

Syntax, my lad. It has been restored to the highest place in the republic.

John Steinbeck

Like everything metaphysical, the harmony between thought and reality is to be found in the grammar of the language.

Ludwig Wittgenstein

Syntax, in a broad sense, concerns what programs *look like* without considering their *meaning*. This is closely related to grammars of natural languages: These mandate or describe how to correctly construct texts in a language, but do not describe what these texts mean. The latter is called *semantics*, which we will look at in Chap. 11.

Just like descriptions of natural languages consider vocabulary and spelling separately from grammatical rules (how words are combined to form sentences and how sentences are combined to form texts), syntactic descriptions of programming languages are often divided into *lexical* issues: Which characters or symbols are available, how these are combined to form names, numbers, keywords, and so on, and *grammatical* issues which describe how names, numbers, keywords, and so on are combined to form expressions, statements, declarations, and so on, and how these are combined to form complete programs, following a form of grammar. While, conceptually, lexical and grammatical issues are separate, they are often not entirely isolated: The same lexical token can be classified differently according to contexts: In some syntactic contexts, a token (such as <) can be an operator name and in other contexts, it can be a bracketing symbol, or something else entirely.

We will, in this chapter, consider lexical and grammatical aspects separately, but mention cases where they overlap.

T. Ægidius Mogensen, *Programming Language Design and Implementation*,
Texts in Computer Science, https://doi.org/10.1007/978-3-031-11806-7_3

3.1 Lexical Elements

3.1.1 Character Sets

In most programming languages, a program is a text using characters from a specified character set, just like texts in natural languages are composed of letters, punctuation symbols, and diacritical marks from a language-specific set.

We saw in Chap. 1 that early programming languages had different approaches to character sets: FORTRAN and COBOL use very restricted character sets that are a common subset of several different character sets used in the late 1950s, while ALGOL 60 and APL defined their own character sets that include characters not found in any commonly used character set (until the much later advent of Unicode). Additionally, the ALGOL 60 reference language mandates that keywords are emphasised using either underlining or bold text, such that a sequence of characters is a keyword if emphasised and an identifier if not, where most other languages use emphasis only for presentation purposes (such as syntax highlighting). In the 1960s, inputting emphasised text such as underlining or boldface could be done by overstriking: Moving back on the same line and printing another character on top of an already-written character. But not all input devices supported this, so the ALGOL 60 report allows implementations to omit the emphasis, which requires identifiers to be different from keywords.

The character set that FORTRAN uses does not include the characters < and >, so comparison operators are written as `.LT.` (less than), `.GT.` (greater than) and so on. Even though = is in the character set, the equality operator is written as `.EQ.` for consistency. = is used for assignment and for specifying the initial counter value for do-loops.

Some languages allow variation in the character set, such as allowing regional characters (such as accented letters) to be used in strings, identifiers or comments. A few languages (such as Racket) even allow extension of the character set by allowing arbitrary user-defined bitmaps to be used in program texts.

Additionally, some languages (such as Scratch) compose programs from two-dimensional graphical elements. Such graphical elements can embody both lexical and grammatical aspects by bracketing or linking other elements.

A few languages use different fonts to make lexical distinctions. We already mentioned that ALGOL 60 uses emphasised text (i.e., boldface or underlined fonts) to distinguish keywords from identifiers. Some integrated development environments use different fonts or colours for syntax highlighting, such as **bold** for keywords, *italics* for types and a `typewriter font` for the contents of strings. But almost invariably, the choice of font or colour is redundant and derived from the context. Having the font makes an actual lexical or syntactic distinction is unusual, but not impossible in languages that come with a standardised rich-text editor. A variant of the Forth programming language called colorForth uses colour significantly: Text in a different colour is treated differently by the compiler. For example, white text is a comment, yellow text is executed at compile time, and green text is compiled for execution at run time.

ALGOL 60 defines three different lexical representations: The reference language, as mentioned, emphasises keywords and includes characters such as $\supset$ and $\uparrow$. The publication language extends the reference language with subscripts, superscripts, and Greek letters, and hardware representations can omit highlighting of keywords and substitute characters from the reference language by sequences of symbols from a more restricted set of characters. Syntax highlighting in modern programming environments can be seen as a form of presentation language, but other languages (like ALGOL) exploit more typographical features than just colour and font for presentation languages. A modern example is the language Fortress, which allows math-like notation such as

$$\sum_{k \leftarrow 1:n} a_k x^n$$

in its publication language by providing a mapping from Fortress syntax to LaTeX, which can then be rendered in PDF.

Given that code is more likely to be read more often than written (since debugging and other maintenance involve more reading than writing), it makes sense to have a presentation format that is optimised for readability, even if typing the program (in a rich-text editor or IDE) is made somewhat more complicated. A compromise is to do as ALGOL 60 or Fortress and define separate input and presentation forms, so programs can be input using a simple alphabet and a single font, but presented in a richer typographical form, similar to how some Internet message forums use mark-up symbols in text input, but renders the text with different fonts when showing the result.

Another lexical issue is to what extent symbols are built from multiple characters. In math, variables are usually single letters, possibly with added subscripts, superscripts, or diacritical marks, and often employing Greek letters. Mathematical operator symbols are, likewise, single symbols, again with added superscripts, subscripts, and diacritical marks. The motivation for this is that it avoids ambiguity as to whether two adjacent characters represent a single symbol or two separate symbols, something that can be an issue in many programming languages where, for example, <= or <> are treated as single symbols. Historically, the use of sequences of characters to represent single symbols in programming languages is a consequence of a limited character set. Some languages, like APL and ALGOL 60, avoided this at the cost of requiring special hardware (such as APL terminals) or allowing substitutions (such as hardware representations for ALGOL 60). Unicode defines a very large set of mathematical symbols, so if a language uses the full Unicode character set (or a significant subset thereof), the need for composing operators from multiple characters is much reduced. The disadvantage of this approach is that inputting Unicode characters is tedious using a standard keyboard. Integrated development environments can alleviate this by providing keyboard shortcuts or menus for inputting mathematical symbols. Again, this makes editing programs more cumbersome, but increases their readability.

3.1.2 Case Sensitivity

Letters are found both as UPPER CASE and lower case. In natural language, there are rules that mandate when to use one or the other, for example that words that start a sentence should start with an upper-case letter, and that major words in a title should be capitalised. Usually, this does not change the meaning of a word: "The" is the same word as "the" regardless of differences in capitalisation. Additionally, it is common on signs to use fully capitalised words such as "SALE", again without changing the meaning. There are, however, cases where capitalisation is significant: the first-person pronoun "I" and proper names should always be capitalised, and sometimes this is used to distinguish a proper name from another word, for example, the proper name "Smith" from the profession "smith", and, in Danish, capitalised "I" means "you" (plural) while lower-case "i" means "in".

Most modern programming languages require keywords to be written in lower case, but allow any mix in names of variables, functions etc. in such a way that the variable `list` is distinct from the variable `List` and so on. Some languages are entirely case-insensitive: FORTRAN, COBOL, LISP, and a few other languages designed the days of upper-case-only terminals ignore case, mainly because it would be too tedious to write keywords in all capitals on keyboards that default to lower case. A few modern languages, such as HTML, also ignore case.

There are also examples of languages where capitalisation is used to distinguish classes of names: In Prolog, a variable must start with an upper-case letter, while a symbol starts with a lower-case letter. This allows these to be distinguished syntactically, even when they can occur in the same context. Conversely, Haskell (for the same reason) requires variable names to start with lower-case letters and symbols (nullary constructors) to start with upper-case letters.

Case insensitivity can be somewhat confusing if you are not used to it: It may be a surprise that the variables `list` and `LIST` are the same. Usually, programmers use case consistently, so it is not a big issue. Having capitalisation distinguish different kinds of names (such as variables and symbols) can make programs less verbose as you don't need extra context (keywords etc.) to distinguish these, and it helps reading if you from the capitalisation of an isolated name can determine its kind. In ML (which does not have this distinction), a pattern `node` can be either a variable pattern (matching anything) or a constant pattern (matching only the symbol `node`), and the only way to distinguish these is to check whether a symbol called `node` has been defined previously in the program. For this reason, ML programmers almost universally agree on the *convention* that symbols are capitalised while variables are not, but this is not enforced by the language, as it is in Haskell.

3.1.3 Identifiers

Most programming languages allow identifiers (variable names, function names and other user-definable names), to be built from letters and digits, as long as the name starts with a letter. But there are variations to this theme, for example:

- Many languages allow additional symbols in names. FORTRAN allows spaces in variable names (because spaces are generally ignored in FORTRAN), but these spaces are not significant. Algol 68 allows significant spaces in identifiers, but equates all whitespace, so the names x position and x   position are the same. Many languages allow the underscore character (_) in variable names. LISP allow hyphens (-) in identifiers, ML allows single quotes to be part of names, and Scheme allows a wide range of non-alphanumeric characters. Sometimes it has special significance if an identifier starts with one of these special symbols: In C, a name starting with an underscore is reserved for use by the compiler and should generally not be used by the programmer, and in ML, a name that starts with a single quote is a type variable.
- Some languages put a limit on the length of identifiers. FORTRAN identifiers can be up to six characters long (until Fortran 90, where they can be up to 32 characters long), and COBOL specifies a limit of 30 characters for identifiers (called "words" in the COBOL 60 report). ALGOL 60 does not specify a maximum length, but implementations of ALGOL sometimes limits the number of *significant* characters, so characters in excess of this numbers are ignored when reading identifiers. Pascal requires compilers to use at least eight significant characters.
- Some languages (e.g., TEX) allow only letters in identifiers.
- As mentioned above, upper and lower case characters can be identified, distinguished or have special significance.
- In FORTRAN, the first letter of a variable name determines its type: If the name starts with one of the letters I, J, K, L, M, or N, it is an integer variable, and otherwise it is a floating-point variable. Later versions of FORTRAN allows this convention to be overridden by explicit type declarations.
- In many BASIC variants, an identifier can be suffixed with % to indicate an integer variable and with $ to indicate a string variable. Variables without such suffixes are floating point.
- Many languages allow sequences of certain non-alphanumeric characters as identifiers. These identifiers are typically used for infix operators, but this is not always enforced by the language.

Additionally, recommended coding styles can impose extra restrictions, such as mandating the initial-letter case of certain types of identifiers, even if this is not imposed by the language definition. Scheme, for example, recommends that predicate functions use names that end with a question mark (such as null?, which tests if a value is an empty list).

3.1.4 Whitespace

Whitespace is a term used for spaces, tabs, line feeds, newlines, page feeds, and all other characters that do not show on paper or screen, but affects the positions of the following characters.

In line-based languages like FORTRAN or BASIC (see Sect. 3.2.1), the end of
a line is significant: It signals the end of a statement. FORTRAN ignores all inline
space, so, for example, `DO 20 I = 2 , 5` is read the same as `DO20I=2,5`, and
the compiler recognises the statement as a do-loop. On the other hand, `DO 20 I =
2 . 5` is not recognised as a do-loop, so it is read as an assignment `DO20I = 2.5`.
This can be confusing and cause errors, so in nearly all later languages, space will
separate symbols, so `DO 20 I` will always be read as three separate symbols, no
matter the context.

In ALGOL, LISP, and many modern languages (such as C, Java, or Standard ML),
newlines are (except in string constants and certain forms of comments) not treated
differently from inline spaces, tabs, or page feeds: Any whitespace will separate
symbols, but different forms or amounts of whitespace are equivalent, so layout
across multiple lines and indentation is solely a matter of style.

Some languages, including Haskell, Python, and F#, use indentation to delimit
block structure: Where, for example, a conditional in C is written as

```
if (expression) {
    statement1;
    statement2;
} else {
    statement3;
    statement4;
}
```

where we note that the line breaks and indentation do not affect the parsing, F# would
write the same conditional as

```
if expression then
    statement1
    statement2
else
    statement3
    statement4
```

Note that the else-part is not explicitly terminated, but because both `statement3`
and `statement4` are indented further than the `else` keyword, they are both part of
the else-branch. Similarly, indentation is used to determine the scope of declarations
and other control structures. Note, also, that the statements are not separated or
terminated by semicolons: If the following line has the same or lower indentation
as the previous line, this indicates termination of the statement (or expression) on
the previous line, while a higher indentation indicates a continuation of the previous
line or the beginning of a new block (if a new block is allowed at this point).

Using indentation as an alternative to explicit bracketing reduces the number
of (non-whitespace) characters in the program, and it enforces a consistent layout.

However, it can be confusing for beginning programmers, and it can make error messages less helpful, because an error in indentation may be reported as another kind of error.

Generally, redundancy in syntax helps locate and identify syntax errors, but also increase verbosity, so a balance between redundancy and verbosity must be found.

The *horizontal tab* (or tabulator) character (ASCII code 09) is allowed as whitespace in many languages. The original meaning of the tab is to move the carriage/print head/cursor to the next tabulator stop, which are preprogrammed positions on a line. So a tab character does not represent a specific number of spaces, but just advancement to the next of several position that are usually equally spaced. However, there is no modern standard for how a tab character should be displayed: Sometimes it is displayed as a single space, sometimes as four spaces, sometimes as eight spaces and sometimes as the number of spaces up to the next tabulator stop. So a program that contains tabulator characters might be displayed differently on different printers, terminal windows, or text editors. This is not a great issue if all white space is equivalent, but in indentation-specific syntax, it can be a problem if the compiler interprets tab characters differently than the editor used to write the program or the printer that displays it. For this reason, indentation-specific languages either standardise the interpretation of tabulator characters, making it up to the programmer to ensure that her editors and print programs follow that interpretation, or outright forbid the use of tabulator characters in programs. F# is an example of the latter.

Note that the Tab key (sometimes shown as ⇤ or →) on a keyboard does not necessarily generate a tab character: On some terminals and in some editors, it inserts a number of normal space characters, either a fixed amount, up to the next multiple of four or eight spaces, or to align with the next word (non-whitespace that is immediately preceded by whitespace) on the line above. Some editors (like Emacs) allow this behaviour to be programmed.

Mostly meant as a joke, the language Whitespace ignores all characters *except* whitespace characters (space, tab, and linefeed), which are used to encode syntax. It has been suggested that Whitespace can be used for steganography: Hiding code in something that looks like ordinary text.

3.1.5 Comments

Comments (or *remarks*) are parts of the program that have no effect on their meaning, but which may provide information about the program to a reader of this. FORTRAN defines a comment as a line that has the C character in the leftmost position. This makes the compiler ignore the entire line, so whatever information is given on that line is for human readers only. COBOL uses a similar rule: Any line that has an asterisk (*) in the 7th column is a comment, and BASIC, also being line based, have a REM statement where the rest of the line is considered a comment.

ALGOL 60 chose not to make line breaks meaningful, so comments can be on any part of a line and can extend over multiple lines. A comment begins by the keyword comment and is terminated by a semicolon. Additionally, all characters following the end keyword up to (but not including) the following end, else or semicolon are ignored, so they are also treated as comments. Later ALGOL-style languages such as Pascal and C use a more symmetric notation for comments: A Pascal comment starts with a { or by the sequence (* and ends with a } or the sequence *). C uses a similar notation: A comment starts with /* and ends with */.

When comments use bracketing symbols, it is possible to nest these, writing for example a comment like

```
/*
    outer comment
    /* inner comment */
    outer comment, continued
*/
```

The question is whether the outer comment is terminated at the first or second occurrence of */. The simplest from an implementation viewpoint is to terminate at the first of these, as you don't have to count nesting levels, but it makes it cumbersome to comment out large sections of code: You need to modify the comments in this code so they do not terminate the outer comment. Additionally, if comment-start and comment-end symbols are required to be properly nested, the compiler can warn about potential errors like the above. For this reason, many modern languages allow nested comments such that all of the above is a comment and not a comment that terminates in the third line followed by what is most likely a syntax error. Languages that do *not* allow nested multi-line comments including Pascal, C, and Java, while language that allows nested comments include Standard ML, Rust, Haskell, and Scala.

Some languages that otherwise ignore line breaks have comments that start with a specific sequence of symbols and end at the following line break. For example, LISP comments start with a semicolon and end at the end of the line. C++ also extends the C comment notation with line comments that start with the sequence // and ends at the following line break. If both bracketed comments and line comments are allowed in a language, it is usually possible to nest line comments inside bracketed comments, as long as the line comments do not contain the close-bracket sequence.

While the contents of comments supposedly do not affect the meaning of a program, some languages allow comments to contain information that is interpreted in some way by the compiler, linker, or other tools. This includes *pragmas*, which are directives to the compiler about the selection between several possible implementation-specific behaviours, optimisation flags, linking options, debugging information, and so on. Pragmas sometimes have a syntax identical to other comments and sometimes use a different (but comment-like) syntax. Another use of comments is for generating documentation. In Java, for example, comments starting with /** are extracted by the tool Javadoc to construct a document describing the code in the program. Javadoc comments can use special tags, such as @param and @return, to specify structured information such as argument and result types of methods.

Suggested Exercise: 3.2

3.1.5.1 Literate Programming

A programming style called *literate programming* turns the idea of comments in code on its head: Text in the program is by default comments, so you need to mark the parts of the program that are actual code, using conventions similar to how comments are marked in "normal" languages. The concept was invented by Donald Knuth for his TEX type-setting program: The TEX program is written in WEB, a TEX document where Pascal code is enclosed in comment-like brackets. A tool called TANGLE extracts the Pascal code for compilation and another tool called WEAVE produces a TEX document ready for type-setting.

The language Haskell supports literate programming directly: A compiler flag makes the compiler ignore all text that is not marked in a certain way. You can mark the code in two ways: Either by starting code lines by ">" (similar to line comments) or by enclosing the code in "\begin{code}" and "\end{code}" (similar to bracketed comments), the latter being targeted at the LATEX type-setting system.

3.1.6 Reserved Symbols

Keywords such as `if` and `while` and symbols such as `;` and `.` are in most programming languages *reserved symbols*, which means that a programmer can not redefine their meaning nor use these symbols as names of variables and operators. An exception is PL/I, where nearly all keywords can also be used as variable names.

Allowing redefinition of keywords and predefined symbols has both advantages and disadvantages:

+ If there is a large set of predefined symbols, a programmer may by accident use one of these as a variable or operator name. If this is not allowed, the resulting error messages can be difficult to understand, if the programmer does not know that the symbol is reserved.
+ If a language is later extended with additional reserved symbols (for example by adding keywords), this can break existing programs that use these symbols as variable or operator names.
− Redefining a keyword or predefined symbol can make the program harder to read by people who are not aware that the symbols have changed meaning.
− A coding mistake can make the compiler think that a keyword is a variable and accept erroneous code without complaint. The FORTRAN example where replacing a comma by a decimal point made the compiler read a DO-loop as an assignment is in this category.

If reserved symbols are built from characters that are not available for user-defined names and operators, this will allow extension of the set of reserved symbols without breaking existing programs. As an example, ALGOL 68 (in one of the multiple textual representations) requires keywords to be upper case but variables to be lower case, and allows aliases for keywords to be defined for other languages than English, so `IF` can in German be written as `WENN`. In another textual representation for ALGOL

68, keywords are quoted while variables are not, and in the strict publication format, keywords are shown in boldface (following the tradition of ALGOL 60).

Using different characters for reserved words also gives a visual cue as to whether a symbol is reserved or user defined, which can help a reader.

3.1.7 Separation of Tokens

A *token* is a sequence of characters that is considered as a single symbol, for example a sequence of digits forming a number symbol or a sequence of letters forming a keyword or variable name. Different languages use different rules to determine how a sequence of characters is split into tokens. For example:

- FORTRAN ignores whitespace (except line breaks) and splits a line of text into tokens depending on the kind of statement it can recognise in the line. As mentioned before, the sequence `DO20I` in the beginning of a line is read as three separate tokens if the compiler can recognise a do-loop, but as one token (a variable name) if the compiler recognises an assignment statement.
- Some variants of BASIC extract all sequences that are identical to keywords as such, so the sequence `FORMATION` is split into two tokens: `FOR` and `MATION`, because the subsequence `FOR` is recognised as a keyword.
- PL/I does not a priori distinguish keywords and variable names, except by context. This means that it is legal to have variable names that are identical to keywords, but if a sequence of tokens *can* be read as a legal statement by treating a name as a keyword, it *will be*, but otherwise the name is just a name.
- Most modern programming languages define tokens by regular expressions and splits a sequence according to the *longest prefix* rule: The longest prefix of the input text that matches a regular expression is extracted as a token, and then the remaining text is matched using the same rules. The regular expressions are given priorities, and if the longest prefix matches several regular expressions, the one with the highest priority is chosen. This means that the regular expression defining variable names can overlap the regular expressions defining keywords, but if keywords are given higher priority, a sequence that can be either a keyword or a variable name is read to be a keyword. But note that length takes precedence over priority: Even if a shorter prefix is recognised by a higher-priority regular expression, a longer prefix is preferred, even if this matches a lower-priority regular expression. For example, most modern language will read `iffy` as a variable name and not the keyword `if` followed by the variable name `fy`.

Even though regular expressions can specify very complex tokens, most programming languages generally use simple tokens, the exceptions being numbers (which can have complex rules for specifying, for example, the number base for integers or exponents for floating point numbers) and strings (which may have complex rules for escape sequences, line breaks, or different string delimiters). As with all other design decisions, readability by humans should be considered, and if it is difficult for a human to see where one token ends and the next starts, the language designer should consider simplifying the rules. For example, if a language (like C) defines tokens + and ++ but not +++, it is not obvious how the sequence +++ is split into tokens. The longest-prefix rule will make the split after the second character, but a programmer might be unsure if the sequence "x+++y" is read as "x++ + y" or "x + ++y", both of which make syntactic sense in C. The sequence "x+=++*++y", which is also legal C, may be even harder to read. A programmer can (and should) insert spaces or other delimiters to make it clear where tokens are separated (where this is not obvious), but a language designer should avoid design decisions that make it nontrivial (and non-obvious) for a human reader to separate a character sequence into tokens. This can be done in several ways:

- If keywords and/or operators are built from specific classes of characters, make all combinations of characters from the same class valid tokens. For example, all sequences of letters are either keywords or valid variable names, and all sequences of operator characters (+, -, *, /, <, =, …) are valid operator names (for predefined or user-defined operators).
- Require tokens to be separated by whitespace when they use the same class of characters. For example, if ++ and + are defined symbols (and +++ is not), they must be separated by whitespace, even though the longest-prefix rule would be able to split +++ into two tokens without these being explicitly separated. Unlike in C and unlike the previous suggestion (where +++ would be a legal token), +++ is in this example an illegal sequence of characters.
  Tokens that use different classes of characters (e.g. alphanumeric versus operator versus brackets) can be adjacent without intervening whitespace. For example, (x+y) is easily seen to be five tokens because adjacent characters are from different classes. Some classes of symbols (such as bracketing symbols) need no separation and are always read as single-character tokens. For example, ((is read as two opening parentheses and not a single token, even though the characters are from the same class.
- Make all operators consist of a single symbol. This is the solution used by the language APL, which has a large selection of non-ASCII symbols for that purpose. Mathematical notation uses the same principle: A single symbol $\leq$ is used for less-than-or-equal-to instead of horizontally combining the symbols $<$ and $=$, as is done in most programming languages. In mathematical notation, it is, however, common to add primes, tildes, hats and overlines to operator symbols. Unicode contains a large number of mathematical symbols, and some of these are even available as key-press combinations on standard keyboards, so using some of these in a programming language is certainly possible.

3.1.8 Summary

There are many design choices regarding character sets, handling of whitespace, case sensitivity, token formation (and separation), comment formation, and many more. There is no single best choice, but a language designer should avoid confusing rules while keeping a balance between readability and ease of text entry. It can help using conventions that are familiar to programmers from other languages.

3.2 Grammatical Elements

Where *lexical elements* concern how the individual tokens in a program are written and separated, and which parts of the program text are ignored by the compiler (or interpreter), *grammatical elements* concern how tokens are combined to form complete programs in a way similar to how words and punctuation symbols are combined to form natural-language texts.

Just like natural languages have rules for constructing sentences from words and punctuation, programming languages have rules for constructing expressions, statements, declarations, and so on from tokens. These rules can be described in natural language or by using formalisms such as context-free grammars. In addition to specifying which combinations of tokens form *correct* expressions (or statements, etc.), the rules also specify *structure*, in much the same way that a natural language grammar specifies sentence structure. A program (or procedure) that transforms a flat sequence of tokens or characters to a data structure that reflects the program structure is called a *parser*, and the action of doing so is called *parsing*.

We will, below, look at some examples of syntax design from historical languages and make some general observations.

3.2.1 Line-Based Syntax

The first "real" programming language FORTRAN used *line-based* syntax, or more precisely *card-based* syntax, as the syntax was designed for 80-column punched cards. The layout is as follows:

Columns 1–5: A C in column 1 indicates that the line is a comment. Otherwise, columns 2–5 can be used for an optional statement number (also called a *label*). These need not be in order, but no two lines can have the same number.

Column 6: Any character other than a space or 0 (zero) indicates that the line continues the statement from the line above. If so, columns 1–5 must be blank. It is traditional to use the C character to indicate continuation.

Columns 7–72: These contain one FORTRAN statement.

Columns 73–80: These are ignored by the compiler, so they can be used for short comments or line numbering (which can be useful if a deck of punched cards are dropped on the floor or otherwise get out of order).

In the original FORTRAN, the only statement that spans multiple lines (without explicit continuation) is the DO-loop. This has the following form:

> DO *label variable* = *expression* , *expression*
> One or more statement lines
> *label* Last statement in loop

The label indicated after the DO keyword indicates the label of the last line of the loop. This line traditionally contains the CONTINUE statement, which is a no-operation, but any legal FORTRAN statement is allowed. The variable is initially set to the value of the first expression, incremented by 1 in every iteration until it exceeds the value of the second expression, after which execution continues after the last loop line. An optional step value can be specified.

Apart from the DO loop, statements are not structured, so all other control uses (conditional or unconditional) jumps to labelled statements or calls to functions. More structured control was added in later versions of FORTRAN.

BASIC is another example of a language that uses line-based syntax. Every line starts with a line number, and these must be in increasing order. The rest of the line is a single statement (though some variants of BASIC allow multiple statements on a line, separated by colons). Like FORTRAN, the only structured statement is a loop, in BASIC called a FOR-loop. This has the form

> FOR *variable* = *expression* TO *expression*
> One or more statement lines
> NEXT *variable*

The variable used in the NEXT statement must be the same as in the FOR statement, Some variants of BASIC allow this to be omitted, as it is implicitly known which variable is incremented. Like in FORTRAN, all other control is done by jumps to line numbers. Some later versions of BASIC have added more structured control.

Unlike FORTRAN (where an assignment starts with the variable or array element that is assigned to), each BASIC statement starts with a keyword, so assignments start with the LET keyword, though this has also been made optional in some variants of BASIC.

Since line numbers in BASIC must be increasing, adding lines to an existing program can be a problem: If two adjacent lines are numbered 17 and 18, it is not possible to add a line between these unless you renumber the line numbered 18 (and possibly additional lines after that). Since jumps target line numbers, these must be modified as well, which is a tedious and error-prone process. It is traditional in BASIC to increment line numbers by 10, so you can add up to nine new lines between two lines, and if you need more, you may need to renumber only a few lines. For example, if adjacent lines are numbered 170, 180, and 190, you can add 18 lines between line 170 and line 180 by renumbering line 180 to 189. Even so, tools are common that automatically renumber BASIC programs to use increments of 10 while modifying jumps accordingly.

3.2.2 Multi-line Syntax

Konrad Zuse's Plankalkül language (see Sect. 1.3.1) used a notation where a line of program text is followed by two or three more lines, labelled V, K (optional), and S. These following lines contain information that must be aligned vertically below the symbols in the first line, so the lines are read as a sequence of vertical columns, where each column denotes, for example, a typed component of a variable. Additionally, Plankalkül used brackets that span multiple lines and multi-line connectors that allow a variable in the first line to specify a component that would normally be specified in the third (K) line, essentially using a variable to index a vector.

This syntax was not designed for machine readability, but for writing programs for human readers on paper using a type writer and added hand-written multi-line brackets and lines. The multi-line symbols can be composed of several single-line characters such as |, ⌈, ⌊, ⌉, and ⌋, if these are available in the character set, but the result is difficult for a computer to parse and not really very suitable for human reading. A compiler for Plankalkül was never implemented by Zuse, but several interpreters and compilers have later been implemented, both with the original syntax and a modified syntax that looks more like modern programming languages.

3.2.3 Syntax that Looks Like a Natural Language

COBOL was designed to be used (or at least understandable) by business-people who might not have a mathematical background nor programming experience. For this reason, the designers chose to make the syntax close to English, allowing statements like

```
ADD A TO B GIVING C
```

which will add the contents of A and B and place the result in C, being equivalent to the C statement C = A+B;. Similarly, a conditional can be written as

```
IF A IS GREATER THAN B THEN SUBTRACT B FROM A
```

which is equivalent to the C statement if (a>b) a -= b;.

In spite of attempting to look like English, COBOL originally used a line-based format similar to FORTRAN, where certain columns on a punched card were reserved for different purposes, such as line numbers, comment indicator, and so on. Also, it originally used GO TO as the main control structure, which made programs difficult to understand. Additionally, all variables were global, so procedures could not be given parameters and not use local variables.

The ambition to get business people to write their own code was only partially successful: Most COBOL programs are written and maintained by professional programmers.

Other languages that attempt to look like English include AppleScript, HyperTalk (both used for programming Apple computers), and Inform 7, a language for writing text adventures. While making programs resemble natural language can make programs more understandable by non-programmers, it is only a superficial advantage for the people who write programs:

- Natural languages are very verbose, especially if there is little or no implied context to refer to.
- It is unrealistic for a programming language to accept a complete natural language, and programmers will be frustrated by missing syntactic and conceptual constructs.
- The main challenge when programming is not *expressing* concepts and procedures in whatever syntax is available, but *developing* these concepts and procedures in the first place.

3.2.4 Bracketed Syntax

Originally intended as a temporary measure, LISP introduced a syntax where all statements or expressions are explicitly bracketed by parentheses, and where line breaks are treated like other whitespaces.

In LISP, a conditional expression can look like

```
(COND
    ((EQ N 0) 0)
    ((EQ N 1) 1)
    (T (+ (FIB (- N 1)) (FIB (- N 2)))))
```

The COND indicates a conditional, whose body consists of any number of two-element lists, where the first element of each is a condition. The conditions are evaluated in order until one evaluates to a non-NIL value, whereupon the second element of the list is evaluated to be the value of the conditional. NIL is used as the false logical value, and T evaluates to itself, which is a non-NIL value. Note that even arithmetic and comparison use prefix notation where the first word after the opening parenthesis is the operator name and the operands follow this, separated by spaces. For example (EQ N 0) corresponds to the comparison $N = 0$.

HTML is another example of a language that uses the bracketed syntax: Elements in HTML start with a keyword enclosed in angular brackets, for example <b> (which indicates boldface text) and end with the same keyword preceded by a slash and enclosed in angular brackets, e.g., </b>. Some keywords, such as <br>, which indicates a line break, are not bracketing. XHTML, a variant of HTML that conform to the XML format, require non-bracketing keywords to be suffixed with a slash, e.g., <br/> instead of <br>.

Apart from being easy to parse, the bracketed syntax is also easy to learn and understand because of the simplicity and consistency of the syntax rules. It is, however, somewhat verbose (especially if keywords are repeated both at the beginning and at the end of a bracket), and the lack of infix operators makes arithmetic expressions look very different from mathematical notation, which hinders readability.

In both LISP and XHTML, the concrete syntax is an easily parsed textual encoding of a syntax tree, in LISP using the S-expression structure and in XHTML using the XML format. This makes it relatively easy to make programs that manipulate the syntax of LISP and XHTML.

3.2.5 Prefix, Post Fix and Operator-Precedence Syntax

If every operator or keyword has a fixed number of operands, parentheses are not necessary as long as operators and keywords have fixed arities (number of operands) and either consistently precede or consistently follow their operands. For example, the arithmetic expression $2 * (3 + 4!) - 5$ (where ! is the factorial operator, which binds more tightly than multiplication) can be written in prefix notation (also known as Polish notation) as $- * 2 + 3 !4\ 5$ and in postfix notation (also known as reverse Polish notation) as $2\ 3\ 4! + * 5-$. In prefix notation, an operator is applied as soon as it is followed by the required number of values. For example, an operator (like $+$) which needs two arguments is applied when followed by two evaluated values and the operator and its arguments are replaced by the result. In the prefix expression $- * 2 + 3 !4\ 5$, only ! (which requires one argument) is followed by the required number of values, so the expression reduces to $- * 2 + 3\ 24\ 5$. Now $+$ is followed by two values, so the next expression is $- * 2\ 27\ 5$. The next step is applying $*$ to get $-54\ 5$ and finally apply $-$ to get 49. In postfix notation, an operator is applied if it is preceded by the required number of values, so $2\ 3\ 4! + * 5-$ is reduced to $2\ 3\ 24 + * 5-$, then to $2\ 27 * 5-$, $54\ 5-$, and finally 49.

Both prefix and postfix notation are simple for machines to parse and execute using stacks, and they are compact because no parentheses are needed. However, they are difficult for humans to read and write.

Nevertheless, some programming languages have used systematic prefix or postfix notation. Forth, a language designed for writing control software for telescopes, and PostScript, a document format language, both use postfix notation, and Logo, a language for teaching children to program, uses prefix notation.

For example, in PostScript, the code `0 0 moveto 0 40 mm lineto stroke` moves to coordinates (0, 0), enters the numbers 0 and 40, converts the latter from millimetres to points (40mm equalling 113.385827 points), constructs a line from the current point (0, 0) to the point specified by the two numbers (0, 113.385827), and draws the line.

In Logo, the code `setxy sum :x quotient :y 2 :z` adds the contents of the variable `x` to the quotient of the contents of variable `y` and 2, and sets the current point to the coordinates made from this value and the contents of `z`. Note that `:` is a prefix operator that fetches the contents of a variable. Some versions of Logo allow infix arithmetic in addition to pure prefix notation, so the example can be written as `setxy (:x + :y /, 2) :z`.

Apart from consistency and ease of implementation, there is little that favours pure prefix or pure postfix notation.

A third alternative is to allow both prefix, postfix, and infix operators as well as brackets (one or more kinds) and define the syntax solely by precedence and associativity (left, right, or none) of the operators (and whether they are infix, prefix, or postfix operators), and by making brackets override precedences. Normal mathematical notation for arithmetic expressions can be expressed in this way, and it is possible to express other programming languages constructs such as assignments and statement sequences. Even conditionals can be expressed as operators using the C-style $e_1 ? e_2 : e_3$ notation, but the requirement that ? and : are coupled is not purely a matter of operator precedence, so extra mechanisms are needed to handle such ternary constructs. Parsing using operator precedences of unary and binary operators as well as bracketing symbols is relatively simple (though not quite as simple as pure prefix or pure postfix notation) by using a stack and a table of precedences and associativities of the operators involved.

The syntax of SNOBOL, a programming language for string manipulation, is entirely specified by operator precedence and associativity.

Suggested Exercise: 3.6

3.2.6 Context-Free Syntax

Context-free grammars are a formalism for defining sets of strings and organising the parts of each string in a tree structure. Context-free grammars were used first in the ALGOL 60 report to specify the syntax of the language using a notation that has later been called "Backus-Naur form", though Naur himself preferred the term "Backus normal form". Nearly all modern programming languages use syntax that is at least partially specified by context-free grammars.

Context-free grammars can define and describe unlimited bracketing, operator precedences for infix, prefix, and suffix operators, repetition (lists), and much, much more, so they are well suited for specifying programming language syntax. Furthermore, there are systematic and automatic methods for constructing parsers from context-free grammar specifications, so specifying syntax with context-free grammars can ease the burden of writing a compiler.

The notation for context-free grammars is simple and compact, and (once you understand recursion) also easy to understand. The structure that a grammar imposes on a string reflects the rules of the grammar, so this is also fairly easy to grasp. The main complication is that some grammars may not impose a *unique* structure on a string. Such grammars are said to be *ambiguous*. While ambiguity is generally accepted in natural languages, it is expected that a program written in a programming language has a single, well-defined meaning, so ambiguity is a bad thing in a language specification. Though it is undecidable whether a context-free grammar is ambiguous, most tools that construct parsers from grammars will warn about potential ambiguity. These warnings can be false positives (since the question is undecidable), but if the tool gives no warning, the grammar is definitely unambiguous.

Some ambiguity can be dealt with outside the grammar specification. Operator precedence and associativity are, for example, tedious to specify in the grammar notation itself, so it is common to specify these outside the grammar. Tools that generate parsers will be able to determine if the rules are sufficient to resolve all ambiguity and give warnings if not. In other cases, ambiguity can be resolved by knowing the declaration of a name, such as the number of parameters a function needs, or whether a name refers to a type or a variable. In these cases, a symbol table can be maintained during parsing to allow the parser to resolve such ambiguities. For example, in C++ the text a<b,c>(d) is a template instantiation and application if a is declared to be a template with two parameters, and it is an expression that denotes two comma-separated comparisons if a is declared to be a variable or constant.

A context-free grammar can, however, usually not fully specify the set of legal programs in a programming language, so after parsing, additional checking is usually required. A context-free grammar can, for example, not specify that a name must be declared before it can be used, nor that no two lines may have the same label. Type-checking must also (except in simple cases) be done after parsing.

We will not, here, go into detail about the notation for context-free grammars and parsing of languages specified by context-free grammars. Most compiler textbooks do that, so we refer the reader to these.

3.2.6.1 Lookahead

Parsers for languages defined by context-free grammars generally look only one token ahead to decide on a parse action. For example, most parser generators are limited to LL(1) (which must select a production by looking one symbol ahead) or LALR(1) (which must decide on whether to *shift* or *reduce* by looking on the next symbol).

Limiting lookahead allows compact and efficient parsers to be made, but it makes parsing of some natural and unambiguous grammars impossible (without relying on additional attributes). For example, in Haskell the syntax for patterns and expressions overlap, and in some cases you cannot decide if a string in the common subset of patterns and expressions is one or the other before reading a symbol that follows the pattern or expression. This disambiguating symbol may be arbitrarily far ahead, so a parser with bounded lookahead will not be able to determine whether it is parsing a pattern or an expression. A possible solution is to parse the common superset of patterns and expressions and fix possible mistakes later. Another is to use backtracking or similar mechanisms (such as generalised LR-parsing) that effectively give unlimited lookahead, but can make parsing slower.

Generally, humans are fairly good at looking ahead to determine whether they are looking at, say, a pattern or an expression, as long as they don't have to look more than a couple of lines ahead, so from a human readability viewpoint, unlimited lookahead is generally not a problem, as long as the *typical* lookahead is not more than a line or two of code. Since patterns in Haskell are rarely large, this applies here.

3.2.7 Stronger Grammar Formalisms

Because context-free grammars are unable to precisely specify all restriction on the shape of programs (even if we don't consider such things as type safety and declaration-before-use), several suggestions have been made for stronger grammar formalisms that more precisely can specify language syntax.

For example, the language ALGOL 68, intended as a successor to ALGOL 60, specified the syntax using a two-level grammar formalism called *Van Wijngaarden grammars* after its inventor. This formalism is very powerful and allows some complex restrictions to be expressed compactly, but readers found the notation hard to understand, and there was no obvious implementation method for parsers of languages specified by Van Wijngaarden grammars. In fact, it was later determined that parsing of languages defined by Van Wijngaarden grammars is in general undecidable unless restrictions are added to the formalism.

In most modern languages, non-context-free syntax restrictions are handled by attributes: Values passed between terminals and nonterminals in a context-free grammar rule. An attribute can, for example, be a list of names that are already declared and what kind of names they are (variable, type, template, ...). This list is constructed by the rules for declarations and passed to the rules for statements and expressions. Usually, attributes are built and handled using a normal (Turing-complete) programming language instead of a grammar formalism. This allows all decidable restrictions to be specified, but it limits reasoning about the language syntax.

3.2.8 Other Syntactic Considerations

We will look at some considerations regarding syntax that are not directly concerned with the syntax styles described above, but which a language designer (or implementer) should keep in mind.

3.2.8.1 Operator Precedence

In mathematical notation, giving infix operators different precedence is standard, and the precedences are well known from school math, so it is natural to use these also in programming languages. In math, multiplication binds tighter than addition and subtraction, and exponentiation binds even tighter. Relational operators bind less strongly than arithmetic, and logical connectives $\wedge$ and $\vee$ bind even less strongly, in that order. But that is about where mathematical notation stops having standardised operator precedences.

In mathematical notation, there is even some debate about how strongly division binds. Using fractional notation, such as $\frac{x+1}{x+2}$ makes the binding explicit by the extent of the line, but if you write $1/2x$ (using an implicit multiplication operator), this can be interpreted as either $\frac{1}{2}x$ or $\frac{1}{2x}$. Mathematical calculators and most programming languages give division (whether shown as $/$, $\div$ or $:$) the same precedence as multiplication and associate from left-to-right, so $1/2x$ will be parsed as $\frac{1}{2}x$.

Some (non-mathematical) calculators don't use precedence at all, but evaluate all operators left-to-right, so $2 + 3 \times 4$ is evaluated as $(2 + 3) \times 4 = 24$. Some programming languages (such as APL and Smalltalk) give all operators the same precedence. APL calculates from right to left, where Smalltalk calculates from left to right.

While using identical precedence for all operators simplifies implementation (though not by much) and is simple to read for a human, it can come as a surprise for programmers who are used to the usual math/calculator precedence rules. Hence, it may be a good idea to use the standard precedence rules. But programming languages typically have many more operators than those for which mathematics have standardised precedence rules. For example, C++ has more than 50 operators with 16 different precedence levels. That can be a challenge for humans to remember, so it may be worthwhile to limit the hierarchy to fewer levels, provide some mnemonic to help remember what precedences the different operators have, or both. Pascal defines fewer precedence levels than most languages, giving and (corresponding to the mathematical $\wedge$) the same precedence as multiplication and or (corresponding to $\vee$) the same precedence as addition. This means that the expression x>0 and x<10 is read as x>(0 and x)<10, since relational operators bind less tightly than multiplication. Furthermore, Pascal defines relational operators as non-associative, so the above is a syntax error because the sequence x>e<10 is interpreted neither as (x>e)<10 nor as x>(e<10) but as a syntax error. The Pascal behaviour is not obvious, so it may be best to include at least the six levels that are standard in mathematical notation, so x>0 and x<10 (or equivalent syntax) is read as (x>0) and (x<10). Adding a few more levels is no problem, but more than ten levels may be too difficult to remember. If there at each level is a large number of unrelated operators, this can also make it hard to remember what precedence a specific operator has, so some visual or semantic clue to help placing an operator in the hierarchy may be helpful. For example, even though there are many different relation operators ($=$, $<$, $>$, $\leq$, $\geq$, and $\neq$ just for numbers, and more if you include set relations like $\subset$ and $\in$), the fact that they are all relation operators makes it easy to remember that they all have the same precedence. Which, by the way, is *not* the case in C and many languages derived from C, as == and != (corresponding to $=$ and $\neq$) bind less tightly than <, >, <=, and >= (corresponding to $<$, $>$, $\leq$, and $\geq$).

Some programming languages allow a programmer to define her own infix operators for use later in the program. A consideration is what precedence rules should be applied to these operators. There are several possible answers to this:

- In Smalltalk, all operators have the same precedence, so adding more operators does not complicate parsing or readability.
- C++, for example, only allows a programmer to redefine an existing operator on new types (overloading). The precedence is unchanged by this. This means that the parsing process is not affected by user-defined operators.
- Some languages (such as Standard ML and Haskell) allow specification of precedence and associativity of user-defined operators. This means that parsing now depends on previous declarations. One possible way to handle this in a parser is to allow only a limited number of different precedences and define one abstract token for each of these, so, for example, a token L4 denotes a left-associative infix operator with precedence 4. When encountering an infix operator, the lexer will look its declaration up in a symbol table and emit an abstract token that has the same precedence. The name of the actual operator is given as an attribute to the token in the same way that the name of a variable is given as an attribute to a variable token. Another possibility is to initially parse as if all operators have the same precedence, and then later rewrite the tree structure to reflect the actual precedences. A third way is to use an ambiguous grammar and whenever there is more than one possible parse action consult the declarations of the involved symbols to determine which action (such as shift or reduce) is taken.
  In addition to adding complexity to parsing, user-defined operators with arbitrary precedences hinder readability: A reader will have to search the program text for the operator declaration to correctly read an expression that involves a user-defined operator.
- The languages OCaml and F# also allow an unlimited number of user-defined operators, but the precedence of these are implicitly given by the first symbol in the operator name. For example, all operators beginning with + (e.g., +>) have the same precedence as +. This allows the reader to easily determine the precedence of the operator (assuming that the set of characters allowed in operator names are not too large), and it allows the lexer to emit the same abstract token for all operators that have the same initial symbol.

Hybrids methods are possible, for example giving all user-defined operators the same precedence, but still having different precedences for predefined operators. Precedences in F# are also somewhat hybrid, as *predefined* operators with the same initial character can have different precedences, while all user-defined operators with the same initial character have the same precedence.

If mathematical Unicode characters are allowed as operators, a possibility is to classify these by similarity to standard operators. For example, all operators that are modifications of +, such as $\oplus$ (Unicode 2295) and $\uplus$ (Unicode 228E) can have the same precedence as +, and all relation symbols can be given the same precedence as <. This does not give obvious precedences to all mathematical Unicode symbols, either because there is no similar-looking standard operator (for example ≀, Unicode 2240) or because there can be two similar-looking standard operators with different precedences (such as ∓, Unicode 2A72, which could share precedence with either = or +). So a compromise might be to allow only the subset where precedence is obvious, or to give all other symbols the same precedence.

3.2.9 Bracketing Symbols

Block-structured languages allow statements to span multiple lines that are explicitly delimited. Historically, several different styles have been used:

Uniform bracketing.   This is the style used in ALGOL 60 (where blocks are delimited by **begin** and **end**) and C (where curly braces are used).
Statement-specific terminators.   In ALGOL 68, compound statements (such as conditionals and loops) extend until explicitly terminated by a keyword that is the initiating keyword spelled in reverse. So an **if**-statement is terminated by **fi**, a **while**-**do** loop by **od**, and so on. A variant of this style used in PHP and some dialects of BASIC is to make the terminating keyword the same as the initiating keyword but prefixed with `end`, so an `if` statement is terminated by `endif` (or `end if`), a `while` loop by `endwhile` (or `end while`), and so on.
Indentation-sensitive syntax.   As mentioned earlier, an alternative is to let the extent of a statement be determined by indentation: Subsequent lines that are indented further than the start of the statement are considered part of the statement, but lines that are indented the same or less start new statements.

Using uniform bracketing makes the grammar simpler, but can be more verbose, because you need an extra symbol to start a block, where, if statement-specific terminators are used, a block is implicitly started by any statement. On the other hand, in the latter case you must always explicitly terminate a statement with a statement-specific terminator, even if the body is a single statement. Compare

```
if a<b then
  b = a + b
endif
```

and

```
if a<b then
  b = a + b;
```

An option (used in some BASIC dialects) is that if a statement occurs after the `then` keyword on the same line as this, the extent of the if-then statement is a single line and needs no closing keyword, as it is terminated at the end of the line, but if the `then` keyword ends the current line, then the statement spans several lines and must be explicitly terminated with the `endif` keyword.

Statement-specific terminators add redundancy that can make it easier to see at a glance where a statement ends. Indentation-sensitive syntax is less verbose than either of the above, and also gives visual cues to the extent of a statement, but wrong indentation can give errors that are difficult to locate.

3.3 Concerns that Span Both Lexing and Grammar

Not all syntax can be neatly divided into lexical and grammatical aspects. We have already touched on indentation-sensitive syntax, which is both lexical and grammatical, as whitespace is mostly a lexical issue, but when syntax is indentation sensitive, it affects parsing as well. This makes it more difficult to use lexer/parser generators that make a strong division between the two, but it can be handled by letting the lexer emit one token at a line break where the indentation increases, another when it decreases, and a third when it stays the same. The parser must then be able to handle these tokens even in contexts where line breaks are not significant.

Other elements that span both lexing and parsing are discussed below.

3.3.1 Macros

A *macro* is a definition where uses are expanded by substitution during the translation process. In C, for example, a macro definition

```
#define square(X) X*X
```

defines a macro that makes later occurrences of `square(e)` be replaced by $e*e$.

Macros in C are handled by a preprocessor that runs before the lexical analysis, so the macro invocation `square(/)` will expand to `/*/`, which will be read as the start of a comment. Furthermore, the invocation `square(y+3)` will expand to `y+3*y+3`, which may not be what the user expected.

While expanding macros before lexing and parsing makes it possible to define macros that are not just inlined function calls, it can also lead to code that is hard to read for humans. In addition to the above examples, a definition

```
#define plusY(X) X+y
```

will use a variable y that is not necessarily in scope where the macro is *defined*, but whatever variable y (if any) is in scope where the macro is *used*. Furthermore, a macro can define a variable that can be used after the macro invocation:

```
#define zeroInitialize(X) int X=0;
```

will make a invocation zeroInitialize(i) define and initialise the variable i, which can be used after the macro invocation.

These are instances of *dynamic binding* (see Chap. 5) in a language that otherwise uses static binding.

To overcome these issues, some languages (including Scheme and Rust) define what is called *hygienic macros*, where static scoping is preserved, and where macro expansion is done during parsing rather then in a preprocessor.

It can be discussed whether macros are needed (or desirable) at all: If there are sufficiently powerful abstraction mechanisms in a language, and parameters are not evaluated before a call (e.g., if call-by-name or lazy evaluation is used), the need for macros is much reduced. For example, in ALGOL 60 (which uses call-by-name), a for-loop can be defined as a function. It can also be argued that macros hinder readability: If you can not see whether code such as something(*e*) is a function call or a macro invocation, and what happens to *e* depends on this distinction, then readability suffers.

Many modern languages (like Haskell, C# and Swift) do perfectly well without macro systems.

3.3.2 Visual Languages

Up to now, we have considered a program as being written as text, though we have discussed using different fonts or text colours. But in some languages, programs are more akin to pictures or diagrams. These are often called "visual languages", but since text is visual too, "graphical languages" may be a better term.

For example, the language Scratch (designed by MIT for teaching children to program) combines nested graphical elements to build programs, essentially making the syntax tree visible as nesting of coloured building blocks (see Fig. 10.3). While the building blocks have textual names, these are parts of the graphical elements and are not read by the compiler. In fact, it is possible to change the names of these elements to, say, a different language (such as German or Danish) instead of English for use in different countries. It is only the graphical images for the building blocks that change by this renaming—since the compiler does not look at the names at all, it is unaffected by this.

Another example is Kyma, a domain-specific language for mixing and composing sounds. Here, boxes representing sound sources or filters are connected by arrows to form a sound pipeline. Kyma has been used to produce sound for both games and films.

More mainstream graphical languages are spreadsheets such as Microsoft Excel or Google Sheets. A program in a spreadsheet is a rectangular grid of cells, each containing an element such as a formula, number, date, or string. Cells can refer to other cells or groups of cells by their coordinates, so the grid is an integral part of the language. Spreadsheets are somewhat hybrid between textual languages and (almost) pure graphical languages like Scratch and Kyma, since formulas are written as text and lexed and parsed to form syntax trees that are used during evaluation.

Common for all visual or graphical languages is that they need special editors: It is not possible to edit programs using a text editor (such as Emacs or Vim) or process them using text-processing tools (such as grep), and you need special programs just to look at a program. This may limit the availability of the language, as these special tools need to be ported to new platforms. If these tools are browser-based (such as Google Sheets and the browser version of Scratch), this need not be a significant limitation.

Using special tools to edit programs can ensure that programs are always syntactically correct, but this does not ensure that programs are without error. There can still be type errors and logical errors in the program, and there may be runtime errors (such as division by 0) too. And hybrid languages like spreadsheets can still have syntax errors in formulas, since these are parsed from raw text. Many of the advantages of using a graphical editor can also be provided by integrated development environments (IDEs) for textual languages: Using IDEs, you can compose programs almost entirely by selecting syntactical constructs from menus and filling in details, so syntax errors are (mostly) avoided. IDEs can also provide syntax highlighting and similar semi-graphical cues, and they can collapse and expand parts of the code for viewing. Hence, the borderline between textual languages with IDEs and graphical languages with graphical editors is getting increasingly narrow. Graphical languages will, however, need special tools for things that for textual languages can be done with standard text-processing tools. If a graphical language supports import from and export to a textual format, this difference vanishes too.

Text is fairly compact, so you might be able to see more code logic at any one time in a textual language compared to a graphical language. But since textual syntax is usually at least a bit redundant (to help parsing, error messaging, and readability), the difference may be small.

3.4   Considerations When Designing Syntax

As with all design, you should consider the type of user of your product. While some users prefer a programming language to looks like mathematical notation, others might prefer a language that (superficially) looks like a natural language such as English, or even graphical languages.

Syntactic details are some of the first things programmers forget when they leave a programming language for a while. So, for casual or beginning programmers, a simple and consistent syntax is preferable, even if this may be a bit verbose. Graphical languages are also well suited to casual and beginning programmers. Programmers that work for an extended period in the same language can become familiar with complex syntax, but for most of them, brevity is important.

Syntactic style can also affect error reporting. Line-based syntax has the advantage that it is easy to pinpoint the line where a syntax error occurs, but with a syntax with little redundancy, a mistake might not be discovered by the compiler until many lines after the error, and the compiler may only be able to give a vague indication of the location and nature of the error. Redundancy, on the other hand, increases verbosity, so a balance must be struck between brevity and redundancy. In this context, redundancy does not mean that you can write the same thing in several different ways, but that the syntax includes symbols or keywords that, strictly speaking, are not required to make the syntax unambiguous, but which aid readability, in particular by helping a reader to see the extent of a syntactic construct, such as a loop or declaration.

Being able to write the same thing in different ways can allow personal styles, but it can also be confusing, especially if there are subtle differences between the different notations. For example, you can write an anonymous squaring function in F# either as `fun x -> x*x` or `function x -> x*x`, but while `fun` allows multiple arguments (such as in `fun x y -> x*y`), `function` does not. On the other hand, `function` allows pattern matching with multiple rules (such as in `function 0 -> 0 | n -> n-1`), which `fun` does not. Because F# combines elements from both ML and C#, there are also two equivalent ways of writing polymorphic types: `'a list` (ML style) means exactly the same as `list<a>` (C# style). When inferring types, the F# compiler will sometimes write types using one notation and sometimes using the other.

Some programming languages have ambiguous grammars where declarations of symbols may affect parsing. In C++, for example, the right-hand side of the assignment

```
x = a<b,c>(d);
```

can either be two comma-separated comparisons (`a<b` and `c>(d)`), or a template instantiation, instantiating the template function `a` with template parameters `b` and `c`, and applying the function to the argument `d`. How this is parsed depends on whether `a` is previously declared to be a template function or a variable.

A similar problem occurs in Standard ML: In the definition

```
fun f a = 7
```

`a` can be either a constructor pattern or a variable pattern, depending on whether a constructor named `a` has previously been declared.

In both cases, the declaration of `a` can be far away and even in an imported module, so it may not in any given program be easy to see how these examples are parsed. Resolving ambiguities concerning precedence of user-defined operators can similarly require knowing a far-away declaration. Generally, syntactic ambiguity should be avoided, even if it can be resolved by inspecting the declaration of names.

In C++, the ambiguity could have been avoided by choosing a different notation for templates, such as using different bracket symbols. In ML, the problem could be avoided by making the language enforce the convention that constructors are capitalised and variables not (as Haskell does).

3.5   Further Reading

Most compiler textbooks have a section about grammar, usually using context-free grammars. Noam Chomsky describes various forms of grammars for language description in [2].

Various textbooks, such as [1,4] discuss *formal languages*, i.e., languages that can be described using a system of formal grammars or automata.

A grammar formalism for visual languages is discussed in [3].

3.6   Exercises

Exercise 3.1 Select a language that you are familiar with and determine the complete set of characters that in that language can be used:

1. Inside strings.
2. Inside comments.
3. Outside strings and comments.

Exercise 3.2 In C, a multi-line comment starts and ends with different symbols (/ * and * /, respectively), but in Python the same symbol (' ' ') is used both to start and end a multi-line comment.

a. What are the advantages and disadvantages of using two different symbols versus using the same symbol to start and end multi-line comments?
b. Assume you want to extend C and Python, respectively, with nested multi-line comments. What notation would you suggest for these in the two languages?

Exercise 3.3 Select a language that you are familiar with and give examples of ambiguities in the syntax that can only be resolved if the declaration of a name or symbol is known. Do not use the examples given already in this chapter. If there are no such cases in the language that you select, try selecting a different language.

Exercise 3.4 Find a language outside the ALGOL family of languages that defines both a standard pure textual form (for program entry) and a standard publication language that uses typographical elements not available in the textual form.

Exercise 3.5 Below is shown the syntax in three different languages for declaring two variables: An array a with indices from 0 to 100 and elements that are pointers to floating-point numbers, and a pointer b to an array with indices from 0 to 9 whose elements are floating-point numbers. Discuss advantages and disadvantages of these notations.

C:

```
double *a[101];
double (*b)[10];
```

Pascal:

```
type realArray = array[0..9] of real;
var a : array[0..100] of ^real;
    b : ^realArray;
```

Standard ML:

```
val a = Array.array(101, ref 0.0)
val b = ref (Array.array(10, 0.0))
```

Note that:

- A separate type declaration is needed in Pascal because you can only declare pointers to named types.
- In Standard ML, the array elements must be given an initial value (here, `ref 0.0` and `0.0`, respectively) and the type of the elements are implicitly given by the initial value.
- In C and Pascal, array values are not initialised when declared, though C allows optional initialisation.

Exercise 3.6 a. Assuming the usual operator precedences, convert the following infix expression to prefix (Polish) and postfix (reverse Polish) notation. Keep the constants in the same order as below.

$$(2 + 3 * (4 - 5)) * 6/7$$

b. Write a program/function (in any language of your choosing) that inputs an infix expression and outputs the equivalent prefix and postfix expressions, while keeping the constants in the same order. The syntax of infix expressions is given by the grammar

$$E \rightarrow \textbf{digit}$$
$$E \rightarrow (E)$$
$$E \rightarrow E \textbf{ binop } E$$

where **binop** is one of the infix operators $+$, $-$, $*$, and $/$ with the usual precedence and associativity. Note that numbers are one digit only. You can decide whether or not spaces are allowed. Your tests should include the expression from part a of this exercise.

Exercise 3.7 Addition ($+$) and multiplication ($\times$) are associative in the mathematical sense, meaning that $x + (y + z) = (x + y) + z$ and $x \times (y \times z) = (x \times y) \times z$, which is the reason mathematics allows expressions like $x + y + z$ and $x \times y \times z$ without explicit parentheses. Most programming languages also allow expressions like x+y+x and x*y*x without parentheses, but they usually specify that the meaning of these are equivalent to (x+y)+x and (x*y)*x, respectively, and not to x+(y+x) or x*(y*x). An alternative would be to let the grouping be unspecified (as in mathematics).

What are the benefits and hazards of letting the grouping of + and * be unspecified in a programming language? You can assume that there are no side effects when evaluating the arguments.

References

1. Aho AV, Hopcroft JE, Ullman JD (1974) The design and analysis of computer algorithms. Addison-Wesley
2. Chomsky N (1956) Three models for the description of language. IRE Trans Inf Theory IT-2(3):113–124
3. Marriott K (1995) Parsing visual languages with constraint multiset grammars. In: Programming languages: implementations, logics and programs, 7th international symposium, PLILP'95, Utrecht, The Netherlands, Sept 20–22, 1995, Proceedings, pp 24–25. https://doi.org/10.1007/BFb0026810, http://dx.doi.org/10.1007/BFb0026810
4. Sipser M (1996) Introduction to the theory of computation, 1st edn. International Thomson Publishing

Memory Management

4

Without memory, there is no culture. Without memory, there
would be no civilization, no society, no future.

Elie Wiesel

'It is a poor sort of memory that only works backwards', the
Queen remarked.

Lewis Carrol

4.1 Introduction

Most programs work on more data than a typical processor can hold in its registers,
so data needs to be stored in memory or long-term store (such as disk storage).
Most programming languages use memory as their primary data storage, relying
on input/output or virtual memory to access long-term store. Virtual memory is
usually not handled at the programming language level, but as a service provided
by the operating system to transparently give the appearance of more memory than
physically available. Input/output is usually explicit in programs, but memory access
is often abstracted into access to data structures such as arrays, records, lists, and so
on.

Since memory is a finite resource, it is not enough for a program to claim memory
for data storage, it must also be able to release it again. This can be done crudely—
such as implicitly releasing memory only when the program ends, or more finely
during program execution. Regardless of whether memory management is explicit
in a program or abstracted as scoping rules or such, a programming language must
supply mechanisms for managing memory. And since memory management is a
central part of program execution, the choice of mechanism can affect programming
language design. We will look into the three most common memory management
techniques: Static allocation, stack allocation, and heap allocation, and how these

T. Ægidius Mogensen, *Programming Language Design and Implementation*,
Texts in Computer Science, https://doi.org/10.1007/978-3-031-11806-7_4

are implemented and used in various programming languages. We will focus mostly on arrays, as most other data structures can be implemented using arrays, so when we say "an array is allocated", this applies equally well to records, strings, and other data structures. We will also use the word "object" as a general term covering arrays, records, strings, and other data units that reside in memory, even when these are not objects in the object-oriented sense, let alone the physical sense.

4.2 Static Allocation

Static allocation means that data is allocated at a place in memory that has both known size and known location (address) at compile time. Furthermore, the allocated memory stays allocated throughout the entire execution of the program. This mechanism is simple to implement and understand, and for many applications it is sufficient.

Static allocation was the only way to allocate memory for data in early programming languages like FORTRAN and COBOL. In C, all global variables, regardless of size, are statically allocated.

Static allocation may apply also to return addresses for function calls. In the original FORTRAN and COBOL languages, each procedure has statically allocated space for a single return address, so a call to a function must return before another call to the same function happens. This means that general recursion is not possible.

4.2.1 Limitations

If it is statically allocated, the size of data (including arrays) must be known at compile time, and the size can not change during execution. So if a program is to work on data of different sizes, space enough for the maximum expected size must be allocated. This can be wasteful, and it often turns out that the estimates are wrong, so the program needs to be rewritten to allocate more memory when it turns out that it needs to work on inputs that are larger than was expected when the program was written.

On systems that use virtual memory, it is a common strategy to allocate a lot more memory than needed. Most of the space is only ever allocated on disk; so in essence, the virtual memory mechanism provides memory that can expand by demand. But even virtual memory has its limitations: There is a finite number of logical pages that can be allocated, and if a programming language mandates that arrays are initialised, time might be needed to initialise a large amount of data on disk, even if only a small fraction of that is ever going to be used.

Furthermore, the space is allocated throughout the entire execution of the program, even if the data is only in use for a small fraction of this time. In essence, there is little reuse of statically allocated space within one program execution. Again, virtual memory can allow reuse of physical memory, but not of logical pages.

FORTRAN and COBOL allow a programmer to specify that several statically allocated arrays can share the same space, but this feature is rarely seen in modern languages. This sharing mechanism does not guarantee that two arrays that share the same space are not in use at the same time. In fact, it is often used to provide different views to the same data, e.g., both as a one-dimensional array and as a two-dimensional array.

It is, in theory, possible to analyse the liveness of arrays and other compound data in the same way that the liveness of local variables are analysed for register allocation, and use the result of the analysis to automatically make multiple arrays or other data objects share the same space. This is, however, rarely done, as it requires an expensive analysis of the entire program. It is more common to rely on virtual memory for sharing of physical memory across multiple data objects.

4.3 Stack Allocation

A simple way of allowing data to have the input-dependent size and be only temporarily allocated during execution is to use a stack.

A stack is typically a contiguous block of memory that initially holds no data. A *stack pointer* points to one end of this block. Space for data can be allocated and freed by moving this pointer. An invariant is that all space on one side of the pointer is in use, but space on the other side of the pointer is unallocated.

If data of size N needs to be allocated, it is first checked if there are at least N units of unused space, i.e., that the space between the stack pointer and the end of the block is at least of size N. If so, the pointer is moved N units into the free space of the block. Depending on whether the pointer moves to higher or lower addresses inside the block (i.e., if the free space is above or below the used space), the address of the allocated data is either the old or new value of the stack pointer. If there is insufficient memory available, either an error is reported and the program stops or the block used for the stack is extended. Whether it is possible to extend the block depends on the operating system.

Data is freed by a symmetric process: The stack pointer is moved back N units. Note that this implies that it is only possible to free the most recently allocated data. This is called *the stack discipline*: Allocation and freeing are nested like balanced parentheses.

If a programming language allows unbounded recursion, it needs unbounded space, so static allocation does not suffice. The language can, instead, store return addresses and local variables on a stack: Space for the return address and all local variables are allocated on the stack when a function is called, and all this is freed when the function returns. Algol 60 and many later languages use this mechanism for function calls.

Stack allocation has both advantages and disadvantages:

- The space for the array is freed up when the function that allocated the array returns. This allows easy reuse of the memory for later stack allocations in the same program execution.
- Allocation is quite fast: You just move the stack pointer. If released memory does not have to be cleared, releasing the memory again is also fast—again, you only move a pointer. If clearing is required, you additionally need to overwrite the released memory with a default value (usually 0, but 0xDEADBEEF has also been used).
- The size of an array does not need to be known at compile time: At runtime, you can move the stack pointer to make room for an array of any size, limited only by the amount of free memory on the stack. An array that is currently at the top of the stack can even be extended after its initial allocation.
- Excepting the array that is currently topmost on the stack, it is not possible to extend arrays after they are allocated. It is possible to allocate a new and larger array to replace an array that is too small, but unless this happens in the same function invocation as the original array allocation, the new array may be freed too soon.
- An unbounded number of arrays can be allocated at runtime, since a recursive function can allocate an array in each invocation of the function.
- The array will not survive return from the function in which it is allocated, so it can be used only locally inside this function and functions called from there, but not after return from the function, as the space may later be reused for other data.
- Data allocation and freeing obeys stack discipline: The most recently allocated data is the first to be freed. This means that data that is no longer needed can stay allocated for a long time afterwards, as all data allocated on top of this on the stack must be freed first.

In C, arrays that are declared locally in a function are stack-allocated (unless declared static, in which case they are statically allocated). C allows you to return pointers to stack-allocated arrays, and it is up to the programmer to make sure her program never follows a pointer to an array that is no longer allocated. This often goes wrong. Other languages (like Pascal) avoid the problem by not allowing pointers or references to stack-allocated data to be returned from a function—but it is still possible (and safe) to pass references to stack-allocated data as arguments to calls.

ALGOL 60 uses stack allocation as the only memory management mechanism—global variables are simply stack allocated at the beginning of execution and freed at the end. Languages that rely solely on stack allocation are sometimes called ALGOL-like languages, though later variants of ALGOL (such as ALGOL 68) use additional memory management mechanisms such as heap allocation, which we will look at below.

4.4   Heap Allocation

The limitations of static allocation and stack allocation are often too restrictive: You might want arrays that can be resized or which survive the function invocation in which they are allocated, for example, so you can return an array from a function call. Hence, most modern languages allow *heap allocation*, which is also called *dynamic memory management*.

Data that is heap-allocated stays allocated either until the program execution ends (when all data is freed), until the data is explicitly deallocated by a program statement, or until the data is deemed dead (no longer used) by a runtime memory management system, which then deallocates the dead data. The size of an array (or other data) need not be known until it is allocated, and if the size needs to be increased later, a new array can be allocated and references to the old array can be redirected to point to the new array. The latter requires that all references to the old array can be tracked down and updated, but that can be arranged, for example, by letting all references to an array go through an indirection node that is never moved, or, if using concurrent copying garbage collection (see Sect. 4.8.3), by immediately forwarding the array into a block of larger size.

Languages that use heap allocation nearly all make allocation explicit in the program, so they are mainly classified by how heap-allocated data is deallocated: Either explicitly by commands in the program or automatically by a runtime memory management system. The first is called "manual memory management" and the latter "managed memory management", "automatic memory management", or "automatic garbage collection".

Even though manual memory management is simpler than automatic memory management, automatic memory management came first: LISP in 1958 used automatic garbage collection.

4.5   Manual Memory Management

Most operating systems allow a program to allocate and free (deallocate) blocks of memory while the program runs. These blocks are, typically, fairly large and operating system calls to allocate and free memory blocks can be slow. Furthermore, some operating systems restrict allocation and deallocation to a stack discipline, so you must free the most recently allocated block first. This "stack" is separate from the function-call stack.

A program (or a runtime system that supports a programming language) can allocate one or more blocks of memory from the operating system and then manage allocation and deallocation of smaller pieces of these blocks. Many programming languages provide a memory manager that hides most of the details of this, so a programmer (or compiler) only sees an interface to a runtime system that provides library functions for allocating and freeing arbitrarily sized blocks of memory.

In C, these library functions are called `malloc()` and `free()`. A call `malloc(n)` allocates a block of at least n bytes on the heap and returns a pointer to this block. If there is not enough memory available to allocate a block of size n, `malloc(n)` returns a null pointer.[1] `free(p)` takes a pointer to a block that was previously allocated by `malloc()` and deallocates this. If p is a pointer to a block that was previously allocated by `malloc()` and not already deallocated, `free(p)` will always succeed, otherwise, the result is undefined. The behaviour of following a pointer to a deallocated block is also undefined and is the source of many errors in C programs.

In Pascal, similar operators are called `new` and `dispose`.

Some object-oriented languages (such as C++) allocate and free heap-allocated objects with object constructors and destructors, but these typically work the same way as `malloc()` and `free()`, except that object constructors and destructors may do more than just allocation and deallocation, e.g., initialising and clearing fields or opening and closing files. Some object-oriented language (like Java and C#) free memory used by objects using automatic memory management (which we will return to in Sect. 4.6), so destructors do not actually free memory (this is done later), but they can clear fields and close files.

Below, we will look at how manual memory management for heap allocation can be implemented.

4.5.1 A Simple Implementation of `malloc()` and `free()`

Initially, the heap management library will allocate a large block of memory from the operating system. If this later turns out to be too small to satisfy a `malloc()` call, the library will allocate another block from the operating system and so on, until the operating system refuses to allocate more memory to the library, in which case the call to `malloc()` will fail (and return a null pointer).

All the blocks that are allocated from the operating system and all blocks that have been freed by the program (by calling `free()`) are linked in a list called *the free list*: The first word of each block contains the size s (in bytes) of the block and the second word contains a pointer to the next block. In the last block in the free list, the next-pointer is a null pointer. Note that a block must be at least two words in size, so it can hold the size field and the next-pointer field. Figure 4.1a shows an example of a free list containing three small blocks. The number of bytes in a word (*wordsize*) is assumed to be 4. A null pointer is shown as a slash. We assume n is a multiple of the word size and at least $2 \cdot wordsize$. Otherwise, `malloc()` will round n up to the nearest acceptable value.

---

[1] According to the C99 standard.

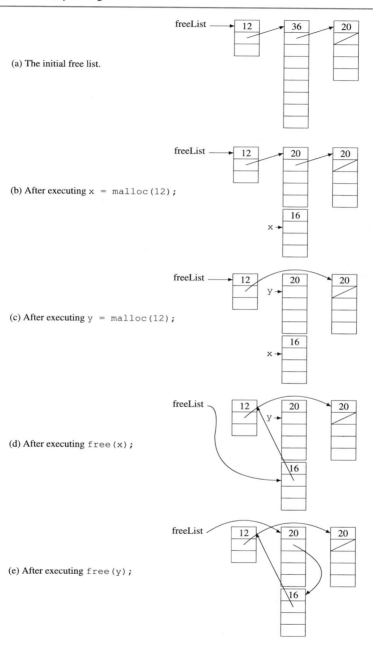

(a) The initial free list.

(b) After executing x = malloc(12);

(c) After executing y = malloc(12);

(d) After executing free(x);

(e) After executing free(y);

Fig. 4.1 Operations on a simple free list

A call to malloc(n) with $n \geq 2 \cdot wordsize$ will do the following:

1. Search through the free list for a block of size at least $n + wordsize$. If none is found, ask the operating system for a new block of memory (that is at least large enough to accommodate the request) and put this at the end of the free list. If the operating system refuses to allocate more memory, return a null pointer (indicating failure to allocate).
2a. If the found block is just large enough (between $n + wordsize$ and $n + 2 \cdot wordsize$ bytes), remove it from the free list (adjusting the next-block pointer of the previous block or the free list pointer if it is the first block) and return a pointer to the second word. The first word still contains the size of the block. Note that the allocated block may be a bit larger than needed, but the excess is too small to be used as another block.
2b. If the found block is more than $n + 2 \cdot wordsize$ bytes, it is split into two blocks: The last $n + wordsize$ bytes are made into a new block, the first word of which holds its size (i.e., $n + wordsize$). A pointer to the word after the size field is returned. $n + wordsize$ is subtracted from the size field of the original block, which stays in the free list.

Figure 4.1b shows the free list from Figure 4.1a after a call x = malloc(12);. The second block in the free list is large enough (case 2b) and is split in two blocks, and a pointer to the second word of the second block has been returned. Note that the split-off block has size 16, since it needs to hold the requested 12 bytes plus 4 bytes for the size field.

A subsequent call y = malloc(12); finds the second block in the free list to be large enough, but not large enough to split (case 2a), so y points to the second word of this block. The last word in the allocated block is unused, since y only needs three words. Such excess space in allocated blocks is called *internal fragmentation*. Figure 4.1c shows the free list from Fig. 4.1b after this allocation. Note that, to update the next-block pointer in the previous block (the first in the free list) to point to the block after the allocated block (the last in the free list), we need two pointers when searching the free list: One to the current block and one to the previous block. An alternative is to use a doubly linked list, which we will look at in Sect. 4.5.2.

A call subsequent call free(x) adds the block pointed to by x to the front of the free list: The second word of the block is updated to point to the first block in the free list, and the free list pointer is updated to point to $x - wordsize$, i.e, to the size field of the released block. freeing the previously allocated 12-byte block. Figure 4.1d shows the free list from Fig. 4.1c after freeing the block allocated to x, and Fig. 4.1e after also freeing the block allocated to y.

As allocating memory involves a search for a block that is large enough, the time is, in the worst case, linear in the number of blocks in the free list, which is proportional to the number of calls to free() that the program has made previously. Freeing a block is, however, done in constant time, as the freed block is just added to the front of the free list.

Another problem with this implementation is *external fragmentation*: We split blocks into smaller blocks, but never join released blocks, so we will, over time, accumulate a large number of small blocks in the free list. This will increase the search time when calling `malloc()` and, more seriously, a call to `malloc(n)` may fail even though there is sufficient free memory—the memory is divided into a lot of blocks that are all smaller than n bytes even though the total size of the free blocks may be larger than n bytes. For example, if we, with the free list in Fig. 4.1d, try to allocate 20 bytes, there is no block in the free list that is large enough, even though two of the available blocks are adjacent in memory and have a combined size of 28 bytes. So if the operating system will not give more memory to the memory allocator, the call to `malloc()` will fail.

If all blocks are of the same size

If all heap-allocated objects have the same size, we don't need the size field, the first block in the free list is always large enough, and fragmentation is not an issue. Some languages restrict all heap allocated objects to fit within a predefined block size to ensure efficient allocation without fragmentation.

Resizing heap-allocated arrays

It is possible to resize heap-allocated arrays if all accesses to the array happen through an indirection node: A one-word node that contains a pointer to the array. When the array is resized, a new block is allocated, the elements of the old array are copied to the new array and the old array is freed. Until the copying is complete, values may have to be fetched from the old array and updates happen in both copies. Finally, the indirection node is made to point to the new array. Using an indirection node makes array accesses slower, but the actual address can be loaded into a register if repeated accesses to the array are made (and no resizing happens between these accesses).

Suggested Exercises: 4.1.

4.5.2   Joining Freed Blocks

We can try to remedy the external fragmentation problem by joining a freed block to a block already in the free list: When we free a block, we don't just add it to the front of the free list but search through the free list to see if it contains a block that is adjacent to the freed block. If this is the case, we join these blocks into one large block. Otherwise, we add the freed block as a new block to the free list. Since we may need to replace a block in the free list by a larger block with a different start address, we need the free list to be doubly linked, so we can update the next-block pointer of the previous block to point to the new block. Figure 4.2 shows operations on a doubly linked free list, using the same operations as in Fig. 4.1. Note that the minimum size of blocks in the free list is now three words. In this example, we don't actually need the backwards pointer, as the joined block has the same start address as the block that was already in the free list, but if the freed block had a lower address than the free list block to which it is joined, the backwards pointer would be needed.

Executing `free(x);` at the situation in Fig. 4.2c can not join the freed block, since the adjacent block is allocated to y. So, we get the situation shown in Fig. 4.2d.

However, subsequently executing `free(y);` joins the freed block to the first block in the free list, creating a 36-byte block (see Fig. 4.1e). Since we replace a block already in the free list by one that has a different start address, we must adjust the next-pointer of the previous block or, in this case (since there is no previous block), the free list pointer.

With this joining, `malloc()` and `free()` both use time that is linear in the length of the free list, but the free list is likely to contain fewer blocks. In the worst case, no blocks are ever joined, so we could just be wasting time in trying to join blocks. But if, for example, n same-sized objects are allocated with no other calls to `malloc()` or `free()` in between, and they are later freed, also with no calls to `malloc()` or `free()` in between, all blocks that were split by the allocation will be joined again by the deallocation. Overall, joining blocks can reduce external fragmentation, but not completely eliminate it, as free blocks that are separated in memory by allocated blocks can not be joined.

If we add an "in-use" mark to the size field of allocated blocks, we can quickly see if a freed block can be joined with the next block in memory: We can use the address and size of the freed block to find the address of the next block in memory, and if the in-use field of this block is clear, we can join the two blocks. This does not require searching through the free list (but does require a doubly linked free list). A freed block can with this method only be joined with the next block in memory (if free), but not with the previous block in memory, even if this is free: We have no way of knowing where the previous block in memory starts. So, the method works for the sequence shown in Fig. 4.2, but not if y was freed before x. With this modification, `free()` is again constant time, but we merge fewer blocks than otherwise.

We can use the least significant bit in the size field for the in-use mark. Sizes are always a full number of machine words, so the size will always be an even number. Adding 1 to the size (making it an odd number) when a block is allocated can indicate that it is in use. When freeing a block, we subtract one from the size (removing the bit that indicates that it is in use), then look ahead to that many bytes to find the size field of the next block. If that size field is even, the blocks can be joined, so we add the sizes and store the sum in the size field of the released block. We then remove its (now joined) neighbour from the free list and add the newly joined block to the free list.

Suggested Exercises: 4.2, 4.3.

4.5.3 Sorting by Block Size

To reduce the time used searching for a sufficiently large block when calling `malloc()`, we can keep free blocks sorted by size. A common strategy for this is limiting the size of a block (including its size field) to powers of two and keeping

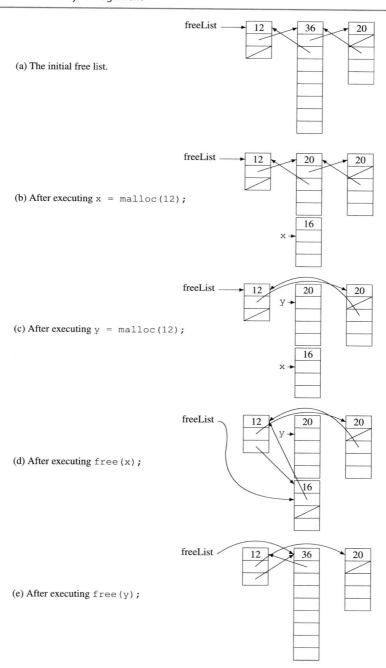

(a) The initial free list.

(b) After executing x = malloc(12);

(c) After executing y = malloc(12);

(d) After executing free(x);

(e) After executing free(y);

Fig. 4.2 Operations on a doubly linked free list with joining

a free list for each size. Given the exponential growth in sizes, the number of free lists is modest, even on a system with large memory. The cost is increased internal fragmentation: When allocating a block, the size (including size field) is rounded up to the next power of two, which can make almost half the block unused.

When `malloc(n)` is called, we find the nearest power of two that is at least $n + wordsize$, remove the first block in the free list for that size and return this. If the relevant free list is empty, we take the first block in the next free list (which holds blocks twice the size) and split this into two equal-size blocks, put one of these into the previous free list, and return the other. If the next free list is also empty, we go to the next again, and so on. If all free lists are empty, we allocate a new block from the operating system. The worst-case time for a single call to `malloc()` is, hence, logarithmic in the size of the total heap memory.

If neighbouring free blocks are joined, these must be of the same size to preserve that sizes are powers of two. This can create a cascade of joinings. For example, if free blocks of sizes 4, 8, 16, and 32 are neighbours in the listed order, they can not be joined, as joining any two neighbouring blocks would create a block that is not a power of two. But if we free new size-4 block that located just before the size-4 block, these two can be joined to a size-8 block, which can then be joined with the size-8 block to form a size 16-block, which can be joined with the other size-16 block to form a size-32 block, which can be joined with the other size-32 block to a size-64 block.

Some memory managers restrict block addresses to be aligned to their block size. So, a 16-word block would have an address that is 16-word aligned, a 32-word block would be 32-word aligned, and so on. When joining blocks, we can only do so if the resulting joined block is aligned to its size. So, some blocks can only be joined with the next (higher address) block of the same size, and some can be joined only with the previous (lower address) block of the same size. Two blocks that can be joined if they are both free are called "buddies", and each block has a unique buddy. While this restricts the joining of blocks, it reduces the risk of having a large number of neighbouring blocks that can not be joined. For example, a sequence of blocks sized 4, 16, 4, and 16, …can not be joined, as joining a block with one or both neighbours will create a block that is not a power of two in size. But such sequences can not occur with the buddy system.

Even when joining blocks as described above, we can still get external fragmentation. For example, we might get a heap that alternates between four-word blocks that are in use and four-word blocks that are free. The free blocks can have an arbitrarily large combined size, but, since no two of these are adjacent, we can not join them and, hence, not allocate a block larger than four words.

Suggested Exercises: 4.4, 4.5.

4.5.4   Large Objects

Large objects, which typically mean objects larger than half a page of virtual memory, are often treated differently than small objects. Instead of rounding their size up to the nearest power of two, their size is just rounded up to the nearest number of virtual-memory pages. Information about which pages are free or in use is kept in a data structure outside the heap, so you don't have to traverse a large number of virtual pages to find a sufficiently large number of adjacent free pages. Basically, a vector is used that for each page holds two bits that tell whether the page is free, is in use for smaller objects (typically using a buddy system as described above), is in use as the beginning of a large object, or is in use as a later part of a large object. When allocating an object that requires N pages, you step through this array skipping N pages per step until you find a free page. You then go back and forward from this to see if there are N adjacent free pages. If not, you step N pages ahead again and so on, until you either find N adjacent pages or reach the end of the table, in which case you ask the operating system for more pages. When deallocating a large object stored in N pages, the object pointer should point to the start of a page marked as holding the beginning of a large object. This and the subsequent $N-1$ pages can now be marked as free in the bit vector. If these are at the end of the bit vector, the pages can be released back to the operating system. To avoid continually releasing and requesting pages to and from the operating system, it is normal to only release pages if a significant number can be released in one go, and when asking the operating system for more, the total number of requested pages is rounded up to a significant number, so there is less risk of having to ask for more shortly afterwards.

The advantage of handling large objects this way is twofold: There is less internal fragmentation, as you only round up to multiplies of the page size (and not to a larger power of two) and you don't need to swap as many virtual-memory pages to and from disk, as the structure that describes the status of the pages does not reside in the pages themselves, but in a separate vector that is rarely swapped out to disk. The disadvantage is that the time to allocate or free a large object is linear in the size of both the object and the total heap memory (as scanning the array of pages is done linearly), but since the number of pages of memory is usually modest, and large blocks are allocated and freed only rarely, this is not a great overhead.

4.5.5   Summary of Manual Memory Management

Manual memory management means that both allocation and deallocation of heap-allocated objects (arrays, etc.) are explicit in the code. In C, this is done using the library functions `malloc()` and `free()`.

The heap-manager library uses one or more free lists. By using free lists sorted by size and joining adjacent freed blocks, the worst case of allocation and deallocation can both be made logarithmic in the size of the total heap memory (but is usually close to constant time). Deallocation can be made guaranteed constant time, but that makes allocation slower and increases fragmentation.

Large pages can be handled separately to get better behaviour from virtual memory.

Manual memory management has two serious problems:

- Manually inserting calls to `free()` in the program is error-prone and a common source of errors. If memory is used after it is erroneously freed, the results can be unpredictable and can compromise the security of a software system. If memory is not freed or if it is freed too late, the amount of in-use memory can increase unboundedly, which is called a *memory leak*.
- The available memory can over time be split into a large number of small blocks. This is called external fragmentation.

Memory leaks and fragmentation can be quite serious in systems that must run uninterrupted for a long time, such as telephone exchange systems or web servers.

Fragmentation can *only* be fully avoided if either all heap-allocated blocks have the same size (so no joining of blocks is required) or if the heap manager can move heap-allocated objects around in memory, thereby making freed blocks adjacent. When a heap-allocated object is moved, this requires modification of all references to this, so the heap manager must have access to all pointers that point into the heap. Furthermore, if it is visible to the program that a pointer is moved (e.g, if the pointer can be converted to an integer), moving a pointer can change the behaviour of the program.

So in languages like C or C++, where pointers can be cast to integers, the heap manager can not prevent fragmentation. Good programmers can avoid fragmentation by careful coding, but this is a time-consuming and fragile task.

4.6   Automatic Memory Management

Because manual memory management is error-prone, many modern languages support automatic memory management, also called *garbage collection*. Garbage collection was introduced with LISP in 1958.

With automatic memory management, heap allocation is still done in the same way as with manual memory management: By calling `malloc()` or invoking an object constructor. But the programmer does not need to explicitly call `free()` or object destructors: It is up to the compiler to generate code that frees memory without programmer intervention. This is usually *not* done by making the compiler insert calls to `free()` in the generated code, as finding the right places to do so requires very complicated analysis of the whole program.

Instead, a block is freed when the program can no longer access it. If no pointer to a block exists (and new pointers to the object can not be created by, say, converting integers to pointers), the program can no longer access that block, so the lack of an incoming pointer is typically the property that is used to determine if freeing a block is safe. Note that this can cause blocks to stay allocated even if the program will never access them: Just because the program *can* access a block does not mean that it *will* ever do so. To reduce memory leaks caused by keeping pointers to blocks that will never be accessed, it is often advised that programmers overwrite (with null) pointers that will definitely never be followed again. The benefit of automatic memory management is, however, reduced if programmers spend much time considering when they can safely overwrite pointers with null, and such modifications can be error-prone and make programs harder to maintain. So, overwriting pointers for the purpose of freeing space should be considered only if memory leaks can't be prevented by other means.

If a pointer can point anywhere within a block, it can be difficult to identify the block that the pointer points into, so automatic memory management usually requires pointers to point only to the start of blocks. With manual memory management, calling `free(p)` requires p to point to the start of a block, but otherwise, pointers are free to point anywhere within a block. Some languages support *weak pointers* that are not used to identify accessible blocks. These can point to the middle of blocks.

We will look at two types of automatic memory management: Reference counting and tracing garbage collection.

4.7   Reference Counting

Reference counting uses the property that if no pointer to a block of memory exists, then the block can not be accessed by the program, and can, hence, safely be freed.

To detect when there are no more pointers to a block, the block maintains a count of incoming pointers. The counter is an extra field in the block, typically located next to the size field. When a block is allocated, its counter field is set to 1 (representing the pointer that is returned by `malloc()`). When the program adds or removes pointers to the block, the counter is incremented and decremented. If, after decrementing a counter, the counter becomes 0, the block is freed by calling `free()`. Apart from this, `malloc()` and `free()` are implemented as described earlier, with a few modifications which we will touch upon in a bit.

The cost of maintaining the counter is significant: If p and q are both pointers residing in registers, an assignment p := q requires the following operations:

1. The counter field of the block B_1 to which p points is loaded into a register variable c.
2. If $c = 1$, the assignment will remove the last pointer to B_1, so B_1 can be freed. Otherwise, $c-1$ is written back to the counter field of B_1.
3. The counter field of the block B_2 to which q points is incremented. This requires loading the counter into c, incrementing it, and writing the modified counter back to memory.

Even if no memory is freed, a total of four memory accesses and one hard-to-predict conditional jump are required for an operation that could otherwise just be a register-to-register move.

A further complication happens if a block can contain pointers to other blocks. When a block is freed, pointers inside the block are no longer accessible by the program, so the blocks that these pointers point to can have their counters decreased. Hence, we must go through all pointer fields in the freed block and decrement the counters of their targets, recursively freeing those targets that get their counters decremented to zero.

This requires that we can determine which fields of a block are heap pointers and which are other values (such as integers) that might just look like heap pointers.

In a strongly typed language, the type of an object will typically have information about which fields of the object are pointers. In a statically typed language, the type information is available at compile time when code to free an object is generated, so code for decrementing the targets of pointers in the freed object can be inserted into the code that frees the object. In a dynamically typed language, type information is available at runtime in the object itself, so when freeing a block, this type information can be inspected and used to determine which pointers need to be followed. In both cases, freeing a block is done by calling `free()` with the type information as argument in addition to the pointer. In a statically typed language, the compiler can generate a specialised `free()` procedure for each type and insert a call to the relevant specialised procedure when freeing an object. A dynamically typed language implementation can store a pointer to a specialised `free()` procedure in the object. In a class-based object-oriented language, this can be part of the class descriptor of the object.

If full type information is not available (which can happen in weakly typed languages and polymorphically typed languages), the compiler must ensure that sufficient information is available to distinguish pointers from non-pointers. This is often done by observing that heap pointers point to word boundaries, so these will be even machine numbers. By forcing all other values to be represented as odd machine numbers, pointers are easily identifiable at runtime. An integer value n will, in this representation, be represented as the machine number $2n + 1$. This means that integers have one bit less than a machine number and that care must be taken when doing arithmetic on integers, so the result is represented in the correct way. For example, when adding integers m and n (represented as $2m + 1$ and $2n + 1$), we must represent the result as $2(m + n) + 1$, which can be done by subtracting 1 from one of the arguments before adding them.

The requirement to distinguish pointers from other values also means that the fields of an allocated block must be initialised, so they don't hold any spurious values that look like pointers. Initialisation is not normally done by `malloc()` itself, but can be done by object constructors that call `malloc()`.

If a list or tree structure loses the last pointer to its root, the entire data structure must be freed recursively. This takes time proportional to the size of the data structure, so if the freed data structure is very large, there can be a noticeable pause in program execution—unless the recursive freeing is made concurrent, see Sect. 4.8.3.

Another complication is circular data structures such as doubly linked lists or more general graphs. Even if the last pointer to a doubly linked list disappears, the elements point to each other, so their reference counts will not become zero, so the list is not freed. This can be handled by not counting back-references (i.e, pointers that create cycles) in the reference counts. Pointers that are not counted are called *weak pointers*. For example, in a doubly linked list, the backward pointers are weak pointers, while the forward pointers are normal pointers.

It is not always easy for the compiler to determine which pointer fields should be weak pointers, so it is usually up to the programmer to declare pointers as weak.

In general, reference counting is primarily used for objects that are non-circular, and rarely allocated, moved, and freed, such as large arrays of numbers, shared libraries, and memory-mapped files. There are, however, programming languages that use reference counting even for managing small and short-lived objects. Swift is an example of this.

Since freeing an object is an explicit action by the heap manager, a finaliser can be invoked immediately when an object loses its last pointer.

Suggested Exercises: 4.6, 4.7.

4.8 Tracing Garbage Collectors

Tracing garbage collection was first introduced with LISP in 1958 and is the most common class of garbage collection used in modern language implementations. In LISP, all objects have the same size, so allocation is fast and blocks do not need to be joined.

A tracing garbage collector first determines which blocks are directly or indirectly reachable from variables in the program, and then frees all unreachable blocks, as these can never be accessed by the program. Reachability determination can handle cycles, so tracing collectors (unlike reference counting) have no problem with freeing circular data structures.

The variables from which pointers are traced include register-allocated variables, stack-allocated variables, global variables, and variables that have been spilled on the stack or saved on the stack during function calls. The set of all these variables is called *the root set* of the heap, as all reachable heap-allocated tree or graph structures will be rooted in one of these variables.

As with reference counting, we need to distinguish heap pointers from non-pointers. This can be done in the ways described above, but as an additional complication, we need such distinctions for the root set as well as for objects allocated in the heap. So all stack frames and global variables must have value descriptors, which (like for heap-allocated objects) can be separate from the values themselves or by using distinct (even/odd) representations for pointers and non-pointers.

A tracing collector maintains an invariant during the reachability analysis by classifying all nodes (roots and heap-allocated blocks) into three categories represented by colours:

White: The node is not (yet) found to be reachable from the root set.
Grey: The node itself has been classified as reachable, but some of its children might not have been classified yet.
Black: Both the node itself and all its immediate children have been classified as reachable.

By this invariant, called the *tricolour invariant*, a black node can not point to a white node, as this would contradict the definition of black and white nodes. A grey node represents an unfinished reachability analysis: The node itself and its children are reachable, but some children may not yet have been visited by the reachability analysis.

Initially, all nodes in the root set are classified as grey, and all heap-allocated blocks are classified as white. Each step in the reachability analysis consists of picking a grey node, making its white children grey, and then reclassifying the node itself as black. When no grey nodes remain, the reachability analysis is complete. At this point, all reachable nodes are black and all white nodes are definitely unreachable, so white nodes can safely be freed. We can summarize this in pseudo-code, where G is the set of grey nodes:

```
G := the set of pointers to root nodes
while G is non-empty do
    remove a pointer p from G
    if the node pointed to by p is not already marked as black
        for all fields q in the block pointed to by p do
            if q is a pointer, add q to G
        mark the node pointed to by p as black
free all white nodes
```

The difference between different types of tracing collectors is how the set G is represented, how nodes are marked as black, white, or grey, and how nodes are freed.

While manual memory management and reference counting free memory blocks one at a time using a relatively short time for each (unless a large data structure is freed), tracing collectors are not called every time a pointer is moved or a block is freed—the overhead would be far too high. Instead, a tracing collector will typically be called when there is no unallocated block that can accommodate an allocation request. The tracing collector will then free all unreachable blocks before returning to `malloc()`, which can then return one of these freed blocks (or, if it is still the case that no block is large enough, ask the operating system for more space). Reachability analysis is proportional to the total size of the reachable nodes, including the root set, so noticeable pauses in execution can happen when using tracing collection. We will look at ways to reduce these pauses in Sect. 4.8.3.

4.8.1   Mark-Sweep Collection

Mark-sweep collection marks all reachable blocks using depth-first traversal starting from each root in the root set. When marking is complete, the collector goes through (sweeps) the entire heap and frees all unmarked nodes. Freeing (as well as allocation) is done using free lists as described in Sect. 4.5. The set G of grey nodes is represented as a stack. We can sketch the two phases with the pseudocode in Fig. 4.3.

Initially, G is set to hold the root set. When `mark()` returns, b is set to point to the first heap node, and `sweep()` is called.

```
mark()
   push all elements of the root set onto stack G
   while the stack G is non-empty
      pop a node pointer p off the top of G
      if the mark at the node b pointed to by p is clear
         for all fields q in b do
            if q is a heap pointer then push q to G
         set the mark on p (* which is now black *)
   return

sweep()
   set b to start of heap
   while b ≤ end-of-heap do
      if the block at b is unmarked (* classified as white *)
      then add it to the free list
      else clear the mark bit
      b := b + the size of the block at b
   return
```

Fig. 4.3 Pseudocode for mark-sweep collection

The stack G used in the mark phase can, in the worst case, hold a pointer to every heap-allocated object. If blocks are at least four machine words, this overhead is at most 25% extra memory on top of the actual heap space.

The sweep phase needs no stack, as it runs through the heap memory from one end to the other. When the sweep phase frees an object, it can call a finaliser for the object.

If all blocks have the same size, you can integrate the sweep phase into the allocation procedure: Instead of finding a node in the free list, it will sweep the heap until an unmarked node is found and then return this. When the end of the heap is reached, a new garbage collection is initiated.

It is possible to implement mark without using recursion or stacks by replacing the mark bit of a block with a counter that can count up to the size of the block plus one. In white nodes, the counter is 0, and in grey nodes, it is between 1 and the size of the block, and in black nodes, it is equal to 1 + the size of the block. Part of the invariant is that, if the counter is a number n between 1 and the size of the block, word number n of the block points to the parent node instead of to the nth child node. When the counter is incremented, this pointer is restored to its original value and the next word (if any) is made to point to the parent. When the last word is restored, mark follows the parent-pointer and continues traversing from there.

This technique, called *pointer reversal*, requires more memory accesses than a traversal that uses an explicit stack, so what you save in space is paid for in time. Also, it is impossible to make pointer reversal concurrent (see Sect. 4.8.3), as data structures are temporarily changed during the mark phase.

Suggested Exercises: 4.10.

4.8.2 Two-Space Collection

The methods we have described above for reference counting and mark-sweep collection use free lists and do not move objects after they are allocated, so they suffer from the same fragmentation issues as the manual memory management methods we have described.

Two-space collection avoids both internal and external fragmentation completely at the cost that garbage collection needs more space and nodes are moved to new locations during garbage collection. Also, while mark-sweep collection uses time both for live (reachable) and dead (unreachable) nodes, two-space collection uses time only for live nodes, unless finalisers need to be called for freed objects. Functional and object-oriented languages often allocate a lot of small, short-lived objects, so the number of live objects will often be a lot smaller than the number of dead objects. So having to use time only for live objects can be a substantial saving, even if the cost of handling each dead object is small (as it is in the sweep phase of mark-sweep).

In two-space collection, allocation is done from a single, large contiguous block of memory called the *allocation area*. The memory manager maintains a global pointer called *next* to the first unused address in this block and a global pointer called *last* to the end of this block. Allocation is simple:

```
malloc(n)
    n := n + wordsize;    (* add space for size field *)
    if last - next < n then do garbage collection
    store n at next    (* set size field *)
    next := next + n
    return next - n    (* pointer to start of object *)
```

When garbage collection and initialisation are not required, allocation is done in constant time regardless of the size of the allocated object and the size of the heap. After returning from a garbage collection, it is assumed that there is sufficient memory for the allocation, so allocation goes ahead regardless. We will later, briefly, return to the case where garbage collection fails to free sufficient memory.

In addition to the allocation area, The garbage collector needs an extra block of memory (called the *to-space*) at least as large as the allocation area, which we during collection will call the *from-space*. Collection copies all reachable nodes from the from-space to one end of the to-space, and then frees the entire from-space. The to-space becomes the new allocation area, and in the next collection, the rôles of the two spaces are reversed, so the previous from-space becomes the new to-space, and the allocation space becomes the new from-space. When collection starts, a global pointer called *scan* is made to point to the first address in to-space and the *last* pointer is made to point to the end of to-space. As a first step, all nodes pointed to by the root set are copied to the beginning of the to-space and *next* is made to point to the first free word after these nodes.

When a node is copied from from-space to to-space, all nodes that point to this node have to have their pointers updated to point to the new copy instead of the old.

At the end of garbage collection, there should be no pointers into from-space, and all pointers are updated to point to the new copies of objects.

The colours of the garbage collection invariant indicate the status of copying of nodes and updates of pointers:

White: The node has not been copied to to-space.
Grey: The node has been copied to to-space, but some of the pointer fields in the new copy may still point to nodes in from-space. Grey nodes are located between the pointers *scan* and *next* in to-space.
Black: The node has been copied to to-space and all pointer fields in the new copy have been updated to point to nodes in to-space. Black nodes are located between the start of to-space and the *scan* pointer.

When $scan = next$, all nodes are black, and garbage collection is complete.

We illustrate this in Fig. 4.4, in which the top left shows a very small heap before garbage collection. For simplicity, there is only one root pointer. The to-space is empty, so both *next* and *scan* point to the start of to-space. Top right shows the state after the node pointed to by the root pointer is copied to to-space. The new copy is a grey node, so only *next* has been updated. The original copy of the node is made into a *forwarding node* by replacing the size field by a pointer to the new location, and the root pointer now points to the new copy.

To turn the grey node black, we move the *scan* pointer downwards and *forward* all pointer fields we see. Forwarding a pointer p consists of the following steps:

1. If p points to to-space, leave it alone. The test can be made by comparing p to the start and end of to-space.
2. If p points to from-space, there are two possibilities:

   i. It points to a forwarding node. This can be seen by checking if the machine word pointed to is a size or a pointer (see above). If so, replace p by the forwarding pointer.
   ii. If it is not a forwarding node, copy the entire object that p points to to-space, updating *next* in the process. Then, replace the size field of the original node pointed to by p by a forwarding pointer. p is then replaced by this forwarding pointer.

The first pointer field encountered by *scan* is a pointer to a forwarding node, so we replace it by the forwarded address and get the situation shown mid-left in Fig. 4.4. The second pointer field encountered by *scan* points to a size field in from-space. So, we copy the node to to-space, replace the size field in the original by a forwarding pointer, and replace the pointer at *scan* by this forwarding pointer. This gives the situation shown mid-right in Fig. 4.4. After forwarding another two pointers (bottom left and bottom right in Fig. 4.4), *scan* has caught up with *next*, so all nodes in to-space are black, and garbage collection is complete. Note that the two nodes have changed relative order after garbage collection.

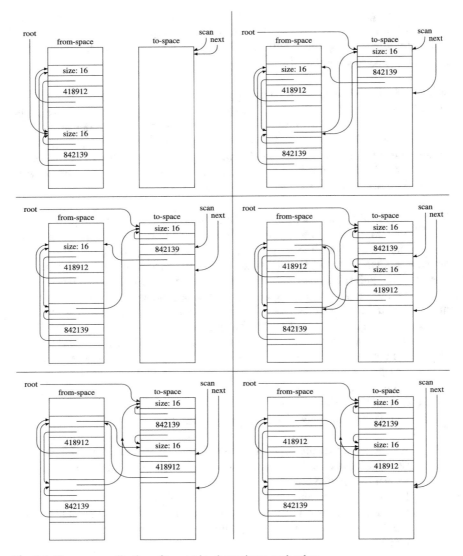

Fig. 4.4 Two-space collection of two nodes that point to each other

Once all nodes in to-space are black, all live blocks have been copied to to-space and no pointers exist from to-space to from-space. So, the entire from-space can be safely freed. Freeing requires no explicit action—the from-space is just re-used as to-space in the next collection. An exception is if finalisers need to be called for freed objects: In this case, a sweep phase is required.

The basic operation of two-space collection is *forwarding* a pointer: The block pointed to by the pointer is copied to to-space (unless it is a forwarding node, indicating that this has already happened) and the address of the new copy is returned. To show that the node has already been copied, the first word of the old copy (i.e, its size field) is overwritten with a pointer to the new copy, making the old copy a forwarding node. To distinguish sizes from pointers, sizes can have their least significant bit set (as we in Sect. 4.5.2 used this bit to mark a block in use). In pseudo-code, the forwarding function can be written as

```
forward(p)
    if p is not a pointer to from-space
    then return p
    else
        q := the content of the word to which p points
        if q is even   (* a forwarding pointer *)
        then return q
        else
            p' := next
            s := q - 1   (* clear mark bit to find size *)
            copy s bytes from p to next
            overwrite the word at p with the value of next
            next := next + s
            return p'
```

Forwarding a pointer copies the node to to-space if necessary, but it does not yet update the pointer fields of the copy to point to to-space, so the node is grey. The necessary updating of pointers is done by the function update, that takes a field in a grey node (located in to-space between scan and next) and forwards it.

```
update(p)
    p := forward(p)
```

The entire garbage collection process can be written in pseudo-code as

```
next := first word of to-space
scan := next
last := last word of to-space
for all variables p in the root set do
    update(p)
while scan<next do
    update(the word at scan)
    scan := scan + wordsize
```

By the invariant, nodes between the start of to-space and scan are black, and nodes between scan and next are grey. So, when scan=next, all nodes in to-space are black, and all reachable nodes have been copied to to-space. White nodes are the nodes in from-space that have not been forwarded.

If this garbage collection does not free up sufficient space to allocate the requested block, the memory manager will ask the operating system for memory for a new larger to-space, and immediately make a new garbage collection to the new to-space. The two old spaces can (if adjacent) be joined to become the next to-space. If the total size of allocated objects is much smaller than the to-space after a collection, the from-space can be freed, and the to-space is split into two equally sized spaces.

Two-space collection changes the value of pointers while preserving only the property that a given pointer field or variable after collection points to a copy of the node that it pointed to before collection. So, a programming language that uses copying collection must allow pointer values to change in this way without this being observable to the program. This means that it is not possible to cast a pointer to an integer and cast the integer back to a pointer, since the new pointer might not be valid. Also, since the order of blocks in memory is changed by garbage collection, pointers to different heap blocks can not be compared to see which has a lower address, as the relative order of nodes can change after a collection. The only operations on pointers that do not visibly change behaviour after a collection are following pointers and comparing pointers for equality (since pointer equality is preserved by the copying collection described above).

Since collection time is proportional only to the live (reachable) nodes, it is opportune to do collection when there is little live data. Often, a programmer can identify places in the program where this is true and force a collection to happen there. In a computer game, this might be after completing a frame, and in a web server, this might be after completing a request. Not all memory managers offer facilities to force collections, though, and when they do, it is rarely portable between different implementations of a language.

Suggested Exercises: 4.11.

4.8.3 Generational and Concurrent Collectors

Tracing collectors can be refined in various ways. We will look at generational collectors and concurrent collectors.

A problem with copying collectors is that long-lived blocks are repeatedly copied back and forth between the two spaces, which takes time. To reduce this problem, we can use two observations: Larger blocks tend to live longer than smaller blocks, and blocks that have already lived long are likely to continue living for a long time. So we aim to not copy such blocks as often as small, young blocks. We do this by having not only two spaces but also n spaces, where each space is larger than the previous (typically 4–16 times larger). These spaces are called *generations*, and the small spaces are called the young generations, with the smallest often called *the nursery*. Small blocks are allocated in the smaller (younger) generations (typically the nursery) and large blocks in the larger (older) generations. We keep as an invariant that generation $g + 1$ should have at least as much *free* space as the total size of generation g, so when collecting generation g, the free space of generation $g + 1$ can be used as to-space. All collections start with collecting generation 0 (the nursery) using the free space of generation 1 as to-space. If generation 1 after the collection does not have enough free space for another collection, we collect this, using the free space of generation 2 as to-space and so on. After a collection, there will be a g such that all generations between 0 and g are empty, and generation $g + 1$ has free space at least the size of g (as, otherwise, we would have collected this too).

If a new block is to be allocated in generation g, and there is not sufficient space, we collect all generations up to and including g before allocating the block.

The last generation does not have a next generation to use as to-space, so we collect this using a non-generational collection method such as mark-sweep or two-space copying collection with equal-sized spaces.

Generally, there will be 10–100 collections of generation g between collections in generation $g + 1$, so blocks in the older (higher numbered) generations are not copied very often. Also, collection of a small (young) generation is very fast, so pauses, though occurring more often, are typically much shorter than in non-generational two-space collectors. When the oldest generation needs to be collected, the pause is pretty much the same as with a normal non-generational collector. The smallest generations will typically be made to fit in the cache of the system, so allocation of small objects and collection of the nursery can be done quite quickly.

Because objects in generations older than the one currently being collected are not moved, we need to update only pointers into the generation that is being collected (the from-space).

Remembered Sets

Generational collectors, as described above, do not work if a pointer from an old generation can point to a younger generation: When an object in the younger generation is collected, only pointers to that object from the same or younger generations to that object are updated to point to the new copy, so a pointer from an older generation will still point to the old copy, which after the next collection can be overwritten with something unrelated.

So, we need a mechanism for updating pointers from older generations to younger generations. Calling update() on all objects in older generations will do the trick, but this defeats the purpose of generational collection.

The traditional solution is to let each generation g (except the oldest) have a list of pointers to fields in generations older than g that point into g. This list, called *the remembered set*, can be allocated in the generation itself (starting from the opposite end of normal allocations). When a generation is collected, we need only call update() on the forwarded blocks and the fields pointed to by the remembered set. The fields pointed to by the remembered set are also used as extra roots when collecting the generation into which they point. This way, we don't have to trace reachability through the older generations: Only root nodes that point directly into the collected generation and fields pointed to by the remembered set of the generation are treated as roots when collecting this generation.

Remembered sets add an extra burden on the program, though: Whenever the program updates a pointer field in an object, it has to check if the pointer points to a generation younger than the generation in which the object itself is allocated. This test is called a *write barrier*. If a pointer is made to point to a younger generation, the program must add a pointer to the updated pointer to the remembered set of the younger generation. Adding an element to the remembered set of a generation might cause the free space in the generation to fall below the collection threshold, so this must be checked at any pointer-field update, and a collection started if this is the case.

Studies have shown that adding pointers from old generations to younger generations happens relatively rarely (especially in functional languages), so remembered sets are typically small and the overhead of maintaining these relatively modest. When writing a program in a language where memory management might be implemented using generational collection, it is generally a good idea to avoid updating pointer fields except immediately after they are created. For example, if you build a list over time, it is better to add new elements to the front of the list rather than to the back of the list, as the latter requires overwriting a (null) pointer in an old object to point to a new object.

Concurrent and Incremental Collection

While generational collectors can reduce the average length of pauses caused by garbage collection, there can still be noticeable pauses when older (larger) generations are collected. For highly interactive programs (such as computer games) or programs that need to react quickly to outside changes, such pauses can be unacceptable. Hence, we want to be able to execute the program concurrently with the garbage collector in such a way that the long pauses caused by garbage collection are replaced by a larger number of much shorter pauses. So, at regular intervals, the program gives time to the garbage collector to do some work. This can be done by letting the garbage collector be a separate thread which synchronises with the program in the usual way, or the program can simply call the collector regularly and expect the garbage collector to return after a short time, so the program and the garbage collector work like co-routines. This is often called *incremental garbage collection*. The garbage collector can rarely complete a collection before returning control to the program, so it is important to keep both the program state and the garbage collection state consistent when control passes between the program and the collector.

Reference counting is easily made incremental: It is only when freeing large data structures that pause can be long, but the collector can return to the program before freeing is completed and resume the freeing process when next called. Making tracing collectors concurrent is more difficult, though.

A tracing collector uses the invariant that a black node can never point to a white node. If the program updates a pointer field in a root or heap-allocated block, it might violate this invariant. To avoid this, the program must, when it stores a pointer p into a node n, ensure that it is not the case that p is stored in a black node and n is a white node. It can do that by forcing either of these nodes to become grey, as a grey node can point to any colour, and any colour can point to a grey node.

If using a mark-sweep collector, we can make an object grey by setting its mark bit and pushing a pointer to it on the stack of grey objects. When updating a pointer field, we can push either the object that contains the field or the object that this is made to point to. Since we do this when overwriting a field, we call this *write barrier*. This is similar to the write barrier used for generational collection, and the purpose is similar: To ensure that the object pointed to by an updated pointer is correctly preserved by the garbage collector.

The sweep phase is easily made concurrent: The program can only access black nodes, and the sweep phase modifies only white nodes, so the invariant will not be violated by adding a white node to the free list (as long as this is done atomically). Blocks that are allocated by the program during an unfinished mark phase are immediately made grey by marking them and adding them to the stack. Objects that are allocated during the sweep phase can never point to white objects, so no action is required.

In a copying collector, things are more complicated, as blocks are moved by the collector, making it necessary to update pointers. If a pointer is followed before it is updated, it will access a possibly invalid old copy. We can avoid this by forwarding the object a pointer points to before following that pointer. This is called *a read barrier*. In a generational collector, we only need to forward pointers that point to the generation that is currently being collected. If the program allocates memory during a collection, this should be allocated in the to-space of the current collection or in an older generation.

Concurrent collectors risk running out of space even when there is free memory, since the free memory might just not have been collected yet. If this happens, the collector can continue collection until enough free space is available, even if this takes time, or it can ask the operating system for more space. A two-space copying collector can not easily increase the size of the to-space in the middle of a collection, but a concurrent collection can either allocate the new object in an older generation that has space enough for this or extend the oldest generation and allocate the object there.

4.9   Summary of Automatic Memory Management

Automatic memory management needs to distinguish heap pointers from other values. This can be done by using explicit type information or by having non-overlapping representations of pointers and non-pointers (such as even/odd). Newly allocated blocks must be initialised so they contain no words that look like pointers.

Reference counting keeps in every block a count of incoming pointers, so adding or removing pointers to a block requires an update of a counter for the block. Reference counting can not (without assistance) collect circular data structures, but it mostly avoids the long pauses that (non-concurrent) tracing collectors can cause.

Mark-sweep is a simple tracing collector that uses a free list.

Copying collectors don't use free lists, so fragmentation is avoided and allocation is constant time (except when garbage collection is needed). Furthermore, the time to do a collection is independent of the amount of unreachable (dead) nodes, so it can be faster than mark-sweep collection. There is, however, an extra cost in copying live blocks during garbage collection. Also, the language must allow pointers to change value. If finalisers need to be called on freed objects, a sweep phase using time proportional to the size of the from-space is needed.

Generational collection can speed up copying collectors by reducing copying of old and large blocks at the cost of increasing the cost of updating pointer fields. We have only shown generational copying collection, but it is possible also to make mark-sweep generational.

Concurrent (incremental) collection can reduce the pauses of tracing collectors, but adds overhead to ensure that the program does not invalidate the invariant of the collector and *vice versa*.

4.10 Memory Management and Language Design

The mechanisms used for memory management can influence language design and vice versa. For example, by having static allocation only, FORTRAN and COBOL did not allow true recursion. Because C was designed for writing operating systems and real-time systems, pauses caused by garbage collection are unacceptable, so manual memory management was chosen. On the other hand, LISP was designed to be purely abstract rather than a thin abstraction of a concrete machine, and requiring manual memory management or restricting allocation and deallocation to follow a stack discipline would be counter to this goal. So automatic garbage collection was chosen (and invented) for LISP, and used in nearly all functional and object-oriented programming languages since.

ALGOL 60 was designed to allow recursion, and block structure (even without recursion) follows a stack discipline, so using stack allocation was natural.

Generally, manual memory management restricts abstraction: If you can not even abstract away whether an object is shared or not, the abstraction is rather limited. For this reason, most object-oriented languages use automatic memory management.

Stack allocation does not limit abstraction to the same extent, but it does limit the kinds of values that you can return from a function or assign to variables and fields. Pascal makes these restrictions explicit in the syntax, so it is, for example, not possible for a function to return a pointer to a stack-allocated value. There is no restriction on the use of pointers to heap-allocated values, and since Pascal uses manual management of heap memory, it is possible to follow a pointer to an object that has been deallocated and later overwritten by another value.

Many languages combine static, stack, and heap allocation, and use them for different aspects of the implementation. C, for example, uses static allocation for global variables and stack allocation for local variables and return addresses. Heap allocation is in C only used in libraries and user programs and not for implementing language features. C does not restrict how pointers to stack-allocated or heap-allocated objects are used, so it is entirely possible to follow a pointer to an object that has been un-stacked or freed and where the memory used for that object has later been overwritten by another value—regardless of whether that object was allocated on the stack or the heap. Some languages (or implementations thereof) use a single mechanism for all memory management. We have already mentioned (the first versions of) FOR-TRAN and COBOL as entirely based on static allocation, and ALGOL 60 as based entirely on stack allocation. Some implementations of LISP and other functional languages have been based entirely on automatically managed heap allocation, but many implementations of these also use a stack, for example, for return addresses for function calls. But where C and Pascal syntactically distinguish if values are al-located statically, on the stack, or on the heap, most functional languages don't make this distinction but leave it up to the compiler to decide where values are allocated. A language designer should decide to what degree it is visible to the programmer where values are allocated and by what mechanism they are freed. Making more details about memory management and pointers visible to the program not only can give a programmer more control but can also reduce abstraction.

This chapter has only concerned programs that run a single process. Memory management in the presence of multiple concurrent processes that share memory is discussed briefly in Sect. 6.5.

4.11 Further Reading

Techniques for manual memory management including the buddy system mentioned in Sect. 4.5.3 is described in detail in Knuth's The Art of Computer Programming [5]. Allocation of large objects, as described in Sect. 4.5.4, is described in more detail by P.H. Kamp [4].

Automatic memory management, including generational and concurrent collec-tion, is described in detail in various places [1,3,7].

In a weakly typed low-level language like C, there is no way to distinguish point-ers and integers. Also, pointers can point into the middle of blocks. So, automatic memory management with the restrictions we have described above can not be used for C. Even so, garbage collectors for C have been made [2]. The idea is that any value that *looks like* a pointer into the heap is treated as if it *is* a pointer into the heap. If unlimited type casting is allowed (as it is in C), any value can later be cast into a pointer, so this is not an unreasonable strategy. Any heap-allocated block that is pointed (in)to by something that looks like a pointer is preserved during garbage col-lection. This idea is called *conservative garbage collection*. A conservative collector is not allowed to change the values of pointers (as it might accidentally change the value of a non-pointer that just happens to look like a pointer), so copying collectors are not suitable. Typically, variants of the mark-sweep collection are used.

Automatic memory management based on compile-time analysis of lifetimes of objects is discussed in [6]: A stack of *regions* is made, and a new region is pushed on top every time a new scope is entered and popped when the scope is exited. A type-based analysis finds a region in which to allocate a new object such that the object is guaranteed to be dead when the region is popped from the stack. The main difference to stack discipline is that values are not only allocated on top of the stack but also in regions deeper down the stack. But values are (like in the stack discipline) freed from the top of the stack only. This may keep some values around longer than necessary, so space leaks can occur.

4.12 Exercises

Exercise 4.1 Show the free list from Fig. 4.1c after a call `free(y);`.

Exercise 4.2 In Sect. 4.5.2, a fast method for joining blocks is described, where a newly freed block can be joined with the adjacent block at higher address (if this is unallocated), but not with the adjacent block at lower address. If a memory manager uses this method (and the allocation method described in Sect. 4.5.1), what is the best strategy: Freeing blocks in the same order that they are allocated, or freeing blocks in the opposite order of the allocation order? Explain why.

Exercise 4.3 In Sect. 4.5.2, a fast method for joining blocks is described, where a newly freed block can be joined with the adjacent block at higher address (if this is unallocated), but not with the adjacent block at lower address. This is because the size field can be used to locate the start of the next block, but not the start of the previous block.

To remedy this, we can modify the block layout, so the size is stored both in the first word of the block and the last word of the block. Sketch modified versions of `malloc` and `free` that can use this to join any two adjacent, free blocks. Estimate the extra cost of allocation and freeing when this strategy is used.

Exercise 4.4 In the buddy system described in Sect. 4.5.3, block sizes are always powers of two, so instead of storing the actual size of the block in its size field, we can store the base-2 logarithm of the size, i.e, if the size is 2^n, we store n in the size field.

Consider the advantages and disadvantages of storing the logarithm of the size instead of the size itself.

Exercise 4.5 Given the buddy system described in Sect. 4.5.3, the worst-case execution time for `malloc()` and `free()` is logarithmic in the size of the total heap memory. Describe a sequence of allocations and deallocations that cause this worst case to happen every time. You can assume that the initial heap memory is a single block of size 2^n for some n.

Exercise 4.6 In Sect. 4.7, it is suggested that heap pointers can be distinguished from other values by representing heap pointers by even machine numbers and all other values by odd machine numbers.

An integer n would, hence, be represented by a machine number with the value $2n + 1$, which is guaranteed to be odd.

a. Consider how you would effectively (using the shortest possible sequence of machine-code instructions) add two integers m and n that are both represented this way (i.e., as machine numbers $2m + 1$ and $2n + 1$) in such a way that the result is also represented in the same way (i.e., as a machine number $2(m + n) + 1$). Assume registers A and B hold $2m + 1$ and $2n + 1$, respectively, and that the result $2(m + m) + 1$ should be written to register A while preserving register B. Write the sequence of instructions using any assembly language (x86, ARM, MIPS, …). You can use additional registers, but keep the number to a minimum.

b. Do the same for multiplication of m and n. The result in register A should be $2(m \times m) + 1$.

Exercise 4.7 Instead of using one bit in each machine word to distinguish heap pointers from numbers (and other non-pointers), you can keep a separate bitmap with one bit per word of memory that can potentially hold heap pointers, i.e., stack and heap memory. If a bit in this bitmap is set, the corresponding word is a heap pointer, otherwise it is not.

Discuss the advantages and disadvantages of this approach compared to using the least significant bit of every word to distinguish pointers and non-pointers.

Exercise 4.8 Pointers are typically word-aligned, so the last 2 or 3 bits (depending on whether words are 32 bits or 64 bits) are all 0. When we use the least significant bit to distinguish pointers from non-pointers, there are bit patterns that are not used. For 32-bit words, these are binary numbers that end in 10, and for 64-bit words, they are binary numbers that end in 010, 100, and 110.

a. Discuss (in the context of memory management) possible uses of the unused bit patterns in 32-bit words.

b. Discuss (in the context of memory management) further possible uses of the unused bit patterns in 64-bit words.

Exercise 4.9 Instead of keeping the size of a block and its reference count in separate words, you can pack both in one word. Suggest methods to handle the limitations that this gives on block sizes and reference counts.

Exercise 4.10 At the end of Sect. 4.8.1, it is suggested that the sweep phase can be integrated into the allocation procedure, so a free list is not required. It states that this only works if objects are all of the same size.

If objects can have different sizes, what can go wrong with this approach of not having a free list (that can not also go wrong when a free list is used), and how would you suggest fixing the problem?

Exercise 4.11 In Sect. 4.8.2, the space between `scan` and `next` works like a queue, so copying live nodes to to-space is done as a breadth-first traversal of the live nodes. This means that adjacent elements of a linked list can be copied to far-apart locations in to-space, which is bad for the locality of reference. Suggest a modification of the `forward` function that will make adjacent nodes of a singly linked list be copied to adjacent blocks in to-space. You should only use a constant amount of extra space, so a full depth-first traversal is not possible, nor should you use (non-tail) recursion. Be careful to return the correct value from `forward`.

While your changes should not assume that blocks are list nodes, you can focus on solving the problem for the linked-list case. You can assume that a node in a linked list has two fields: A value field (which may or may not be a pointer) and a tail field (which is always a pointer, though it can be a null pointer).

Exercise 4.12 The tricolour invariant requires that no black node ever points to a white node. This is sufficient to ensure the correctness of incremental collectors, but it is not necessary: If a black node points to a white node, this is harmless, as long as there is a path from a grey node to the white node, so it will eventually be reached (and coloured grey) by the garbage collector. So, an alternative write barrier for ensuring correctness of incremental garbage collection is:

Whenever a write to a pointer field *removes* a reference to an object, colour that object grey.

The difference from the write barrier we presented in section "Concurrent and Incremental Collection" is that when we make the assignment $p = q$, we, instead of colouring the object that q points to grey (since p may be a field in a black node), colour the object that p points to before the assignment grey.

Note that, if q points to a white node and p is a field of a black node, this does not preserve the tricolour invariant, but it ensures that everything that was reachable at the start of garbage collection is eventually coloured grey (and later black). To ensure that objects allocated after the start of garbage collection are preserved, these are immediately coloured black.

Discuss the advantages and disadvantages of this approach.

Exercise 4.13 The root set of the heap is the set of all pointers from outside the heap that can point into the heap, so this includes the contents of registers and stack frames. To reduce the size of the root set, frames can be allocated in the heap (forming a linked list of frames) instead of on the stack, using garbage collection to reclaim the frames instead of unstacking them immediately at function returns. This reduces the root set to the set of registers and a single frame pointer, which may also reside in a register.

Discuss the advantages and disadvantages of this approach with emphasis on how this affects generational collection.

Exercise 4.14 We have in this chapter discussed using a stack for memory allocation, a strategy that fits well with block structure and recursion, as these follow a stack discipline.

An alternative structure is a *queue*: A data structure where the oldest allocated object is the first to be freed, so you allocate objects at one end of the queue and free them from the other end.

Is there any programming language feature (existing or hypothetical) that would lend itself naturally to using a queue for memory management?

References

1. Appel AW (1998) Modern compiler implementation in ML. Cambridge University Press
2. Boehm H, Weiser M (1988) Garbage collection in an uncooperative environment. Softw Pract Exp 18(9):807–820
3. Jones RE, Lins RD (1996) Garbage collection: algorithms for automatic dynamic memory management. Wiley
4. Kamp PH (1998) Malloc(3) revisited. In: Proceedings of the annual conference on USENIX annual technical conference, ATEC '98, pp 36–36. USENIX Association, Berkeley, CA, USA. http://dl.acm.org/citation.cfm?id=1268256.1268292
5. Knuth D (1997) The art of computer programming, volume 1: fundamental algorithms. Addison-Wesley
6. Tofte M, Talpin JP (1997) Region-based memory management
7. Wilson PR (1992) Uniprocessor garbage collection techniques. In: IWMM '92: proceedings of the international workshop on memory management, pp 1–42. Springer, London, UK

Scopes, Functions, and Parameter Passing

5

If you have a procedure with 10 parameters, you probably missed some.

Alan Perlis

I saw in details while she saw in scope. Not seeing the scope is why I am here and she is not. I took each element separately and never looked to see that they never did fit together properly.

from "The Night Circus" by Erin Morgenstern

JavaScript's global scope is like a public toilet. You can't avoid going in there, but try to limit your contact with surfaces when you do.

Dmitry Baranovskiy

In most programming languages, you can declare named entities such as variables, functions, classes, and types. Each declaration has a *scope*, which defines from where the declared name is visible. The rules that determine visibility of declarations are called *scope rules*.

Functions and procedures use various means to pass information to and from their callers using *parameter-passing mechanisms*. We use this phrase to cover both passing arguments to a procedure or function and passing results back from a procedure or function to its caller.

5.1   Scope Rules

Overall, scope rules can be divided into two classes:

Static scoping   (also called *lexical scoping*) means that visibility of a declaration is
    determined solely by syntax: You can, by inspecting the program text, determine
    where a declaration is visible.
Dynamic scoping   in contrast means that the visibility is determined (at least in
    part) by the execution history. Roughly speaking, a declaration is visible if it has
    already been visited during the execution, unless the scope of the declaration is
    explicitly ended or a declaration encountered later hides the declaration.

Static scoping is typically used in programming languages originally designed for
implementation by a compiler, while dynamic scoping is typically used in languages
designed for implementation by an interpreter. But since a language can be implemented by both compilation and interpretation, you cannot simply assume that
interpreters use dynamic scoping and compilers use static scoping.

5.1.1   Global Scoping

In early programming languages, it is common that a declaration is visible throughout
the program, though sometimes only after the place of declaration (whether in the
text, as in static scoping, or after visiting the declaration, as in dynamic scoping).

    In COBOL, for example, all variable declarations are placed in the beginning
of the program in a DATA DIVISION followed by procedure declarations in a
PROCEDURE DIVISION. Procedures in COBOL have no parameters nor local
variables, so all communication between a procedure and its caller is done through
the global variables declared in the DATA DIVISION. Since all declarations are
syntactically placed in the beginning of the program, there is no observable difference
between static and dynamic scoping.

    The original 1957 version of FORTRAN did not have procedures or functions,
so all variables were global. Scalar variables need not be declared, but hold an
unspecified value until first assigned. The type of a variable is implicitly given by
the first letter of the name. Arrays must be explicitly declared by a DIMENSION
statement and are only available in the parts of the program that syntactically follow
the DIMENSION statement, so this is an instance of static scoping.

    In (most variants of) BASIC, variables can be declared anywhere in a program
but are accessible only after the declaration has been visited during execution, thus
making this an example of dynamic scoping.

    As mentioned in Chap. 4, global scoping can be implemented using static memory
allocation: Every variable has a unique address and stays allocated until the end
of execution. If static scoping is used, the compiler can compute the addresses of
variables at compile time. If dynamic scoping is used, a mapping between variables

and addresses must be maintained during execution, but once a variable has been declared, its location is fixed through the remainder of execution.

5.1.2   Local Variables Only

In FORTRAN II from 1958, procedures (called *subroutines*) and functions were added to the original FORTRAN language. In FORTRAN II, a procedure or function can only see variables that are declared locally in the procedure or function, and these variables are not visible outside the procedure or function. Procedures can have parameters, and functions additionally have results.

Procedures and functions use different mechanisms for parameter passing: A function takes values as arguments and may not modify the variables that locally hold these arguments, and returns its result by writing it to a local variable with the same name as the function before returning. A procedure call takes variables as arguments and transfers the locations (addresses) of these to the called procedure (the *callee*). The procedure uses these locations to read from or write to the variables passed as parameters. This mechanism is called *call by reference*. It allows, for example, a procedure to swap the contents of two variables passed as parameters:

```
SUBROUTINE SWAP(A,B)
TEMP = A
A = B
B = TEMP
RETURN
END
```

calling this procedure with `CALL SWAP(X,Y)` will swap the contents of variables X and Y.

FORTRAN II does not allow recursion, so all variables (local or global) can be statically allocated. Procedures and functions can not be declared inside other procedures or functions, so this is sometimes called a *flat procedure scope*.

5.1.3   Block Structure

Introduced in ALGOL 60, block structure means that the scope of a declaration is explicitly delimited by a block, which in ALGOL 60 starts with the keyword BEGIN and ends with END. In later ALGOL-like languages like C, curly braces are used to delimit blocks. Variables declared inside a block will be removed at the end of the block. If a variable named x is in scope before a block is entered, and the block declares a variable with the same name, the version of x that is declared in the block will shadow the version of x declared outside the block, so any reference (by name) to x inside the block will be to the version that is declared locally in the block. When the block is exited, local x is removed and the original x becomes visible again, with its original value. LISP also use a form of block structure: A variable declared in a LAMBDA expression is in scope inside the body of this expression, and since the body can hold other LAMBDA expressions, scopes of variables are nested like in ALGOL 60.

5.1.3.1 Static Versus Dynamic Scoping

Most block-structured languages use static scoping, but a few (such as the original LISP) use dynamic scoping. The difference between static and dynamic scoping happen when a function that is declared outside a block is called from inside this block.

- With static scoping, the variables declared inside the block are not visible from the called function, but variables that are visible where the function is *declared* are visible from the called function (unless shadowed by local declarations inside the function).
- With dynamic scoping, the variables declared inside the block are visible from the called function. Basically, all variables that are visible where the function is *called* are visible from the called function (unless shadowed by local declarations inside the function). Variables that are visible where the function is declared *may* be visible, but only if they have not been shadowed by similarly named variables in a block that has been entered and not exited since the function was declared. Essentially, encountering a declaration pushes the declaration on a global stack, and when the block that contains this declaration is exited, the declaration is popped off the stack.

The difference can be observed by code similar to the below:

```
int x = 2;

void f()
{
  x = 1;
}

int main(int argc, char *argv[])
{
  {
    int x = 0;
    f();
    printf("%d", x);
  }
  printf("%d", x);
  return 0;
}
```

The above uses C-style syntax, but similar code can be written in most block-structured languages. If static scoping is used, the first `printf` command will print 0, since the assignment inside `f` affects the global variable declared in the first line. The second `printf` command will print 2, since only the globally declared `x` is visible. If dynamic scoping is used, the first `printf` command will print 1 because the declaration of `x` inside the block just prior to the call overrides the global declaration until this block is exited, at which point the global variable is restored, so the second `printf` command will print 2. C, like most ALGOL-derived languages, uses static scoping, so the result would be 0. Some scripting languages (like Perl and Bash) as well as some extended forms of BASIC that include procedure declarations use dynamic scoping.

The original LISP from 1958 used dynamic scoping, but while this was probably a mistake in the implementation (because the lambda-calculus that LISP was inspired by uses static scoping), it stayed as the main scoping rule for LISP and LISP variants until Scheme in the 1970s chose static scoping. Later LISP variants like Clojure have also adopted static scoping.

Some scripting languages use a mixture of static and dynamic scoping. JavaScript, for example, use dynamic scoping for global variables and static scoping for local variables. A function can declare a variable to be global, after which it is available in all other functions.

5.1.3.2   Implementing Static Scoping

With static scoping, several different mappings of names to variables can exist at the same time. For example, in the example above, `x` is bound to the global variable inside `f` but to a local variable inside `main`, even though the two functions are both active at the same time. This means that each function has its own mapping of variables to locations. When a function is declared, the function name is bound to a pair of the address of the code for the function and the environment (a mapping of names to locations, which may be addresses or offsets from a frame pointer) that is active at the time and place of the declaration. When the function is called, this mapping is activated and possibly extended with mappings of parameters and local variables of the function. This extension is local to this particular invocation of the function, so if the function is called again before it returns, a new extension of the environment is made.

If, as in standard C, functions are all globally declared, the mappings that are active at the time and place a function is declared are mappings of global variables to their addresses. Since this never changes, there is no need to store a copy for each function, so a new environment is made from scratch every time a function is called. This new environment is called a *frame* or *activation record* and is usually put in the call stack, and local variable names are at compile time translated into offsets into this frame. Global variables are at compile time translated into static addresses.

It is a bit more complicated when functions can be declared locally inside other functions. We will return to this in Sects. 5.1.4 and 5.1.5.

5.1.3.3   Implementing Dynamic Scoping

Dynamic scoping can be implemented in two ways: Deep binding and shallow binding. In both cases, a global mapping of names to values is maintained, but what happens when a variable is used and when a block is entered and exited is different:

- With deep binding, the global mapping is a stack of name/value pairs. When using a variable x, the stack is searched from the top downwards until a pair with x as the name is found. The value in this pair is read or overwritten depending on whether the variable is read or overwritten.
  When a new, local variable is declared in a block, a pair of its name and value is added to the top of the stack. When the block is exited, the pairs for locally declared variables are removed from the top of the stack. Note that there can be several variables with the same name on the stack.
- With shallow binding, a fixed-size array of values is used with one element for every different variable *name* in the program. The index for a given variable name can be calculated at compile time, or a hash table can be used at runtime to find the index for each variable. When using a variable, the index is found and the value at that index is read or overwritten.
  When a new, local variable is declared in a block, its index is found, and the value stored there is pushed onto a stack (called *the dump*) and the initial value of the local variable is written into the indexed place. When the block is exited, the values are popped from the dump (in the opposite order of which they were pushed) and put into the respective indexed places, thereby restoring the values of variables to what they were before the block was entered.

In most cases, there is no observable difference between these two implementation strategies, so shallow binding can be seen as an optimisation (especially if indexes are calculated at compile time). But there are cases where a difference can be observed:

- If the address of a variable can be taken (such as by using the & operator in C), then the addresses of all variables with the same name will be the same when shallow binding is used. If, between the time an address is taken and the time the address is used, a new scope declares a variable with the same name, the address will point to the value of the new variable. With deep binding, the old variable is in the same location it always was, so the address will point to the value of the old variable.
- With *call by reference* parameter passing (see Sect. 5.1.7), a parameter is essentially the address of a variable, so the same thing applies.

5.1.4   Nested Function Declarations

ALGOL 60 and LISP both allow functions to be declared inside other function definitions, making the inner function declarations visible only in the function in

Fig. 5.1 Local function
declaration in Gnu C

```
double twice(double (*f)(double), double x)
{
    return f(f(x));
}

double addTwice(double a, double b)
{
    double add(double c)
    {
        return c+b;
    }

    return twice(add,a);
}
```

which it is declared, but allowing the inner function to access variables declared in the outer function. In contrast, standard C, though block structured, only allows globally declared functions (so it has flat procedure scope). The Gnu C compiler (GCC) allows nested function declarations, and since C is likely to be more familiar to the reader than ALGOL, Pascal, and other languages that allow nested function declaration as standard, we will use the Gnu C notation in the examples below.

Having only globally declared functions simplifies implementation (which we will return to later), but nested declarations allow more flexible use of functional values. For example, the Gnu C program in Fig. 5.1 declares a local function that is passed as parameter to another function. addTwice declares a local function add that adds the value of b to its argument. It then calls twice with that function as argument. The end result is that the value of b is added twice to a.

If static scoping is used (which C does), b is not in scope in twice, so when passing add as a parameter to twice, we must pass not only the address of the code of the function add, we must also pass the value (or location) of b, so when twice calls add (through the functional parameter f), it can be given access to b. Such a combination of a code address and values or addresses of variables used in this code is called a *closure*, which we will return to later.

If dynamic scoping is used, a global mapping of variables to values is maintained, and b is added to that mapping when the function addTwice is entered and only removed when that function exits. So b is implicitly available (in scope) inside twice (as long as it is called from addTwice), so it is sufficient to pass the address of add as a parameter to twice. When add is called from inside twice, it can access b through the global mapping. Hence, no closure is needed. Dynamic scoping, hence, simplifies implementation of functional values when function declarations can be nested, but the dynamic scoping can lead to surprises. If, for example, twice declares its own local variable called b, it is the value of this that will be used when add is called.

5.1.5 Recursion

As mentioned above, FORTRAN II and COBOL do not allow functions to call themselves, neither directly or indirectly. The ability to do so was introduced with LISP in 1958 and ALGOL 60 in 1960.

If no recursion is allowed, there can only ever be one active copy of a local variable at any one time, and a function can use a fixed location to store the address to which it must return, so all variables and return addresses can be statically allocated. This static allocation must, however, distinguish variables with the same name in different scopes (e.g., in different procedures), giving these different locations.

If recursion is allowed, there can be several different active versions of local variables and return addresses. This can be implemented using a stack.

With static scoping, local variables and return addresses are stored in a *call frame* or *activation record* on a stack and addressed relatively to a stack or frame pointer. This allows several copies of the same local variable and several different return addresses for the same function to coexist in different locations on the stack, and a closure for a local function can be built by combining a pointer to the function code with a pointer to the frame of the function in which the local function is declared. We will go into more detail about closures in Sect. 5.3.

With dynamic scoping, a global mapping of variables to addresses is used, so no closures are built. But a stack is nevertheless needed to implement either shallow or deep binding.

Mutual recursion is when several declarations can refer to each other. If function definitions can be nested, this usually allows a limited form of mutual recursion: A function f can call the functions that are defined locally within f, and these can call f. But this does not in itself allow declaration of three functions that can all call each other. Full mutual recursion requires that definitions in the same scope can all refer to each other.

In some languages, a declaration can only see declarations that syntactically occur before this declaration (or inside it), but most of these allow a *forward declaration* or *function prototype* that specifies the name and type of a function that is not defined until later. This is the case in, for example, Pascal and C. Other languages (like Standard ML and F#) allow a number of declarations to be explicitly mutually recursive. In Standard ML, this is done by combining the declarations with the keyword and. Some languages, such as Haskell, implicitly allow all declarations at the same level to refer to each other.

5.1.6 Macros

Macro definitions usually employ textual substitution, making variables in macros dynamically scoped. If a macro can declare a variable, this can be used after the macro invocation, so macros can affect scoping in complex ways. As a consequence, some macro systems called *hygienic macros* use renaming to ensure that the scopes of variables declared or used in macros mimic static scoping. See also Sect. 3.3.1.

5.1.7 Parameter-Passing Methods

Different languages use different methods for passing parameters to functions and procedures. We have already briefly mentioned a few, but here is a more comprehensive list with more explanation.

Call by value. Call by value means that a value is passed from the caller to the called function (the callee). Generally, any expression can be used as argument in the call. This expression is evaluated prior to the call, and the resulting value is passed to the callee. This is the most common parameter-passing method.

Call by reference. Call by reference was introduced in FORTRAN II, as described above. If a variable is passed, the *location* (address) of this variable is passed to the callee. When the callee accesses a parameter, it fetches the value from the passed location, and when the callee updates a parameter variable, it does so at this location. If a non-variable expression is passed as argument to a call, a new location is created for the result of this expression, and this location is passed. If the callee updates the corresponding parameter, the value of the parameter location is modified, but this can not be observed at the caller since the location for the expression variable is not given a name.

Call by reference is used in many languages. Pascal, for example, allows both call by value and call by reference, specifying the latter by prefixing a parameter in a procedure declaration by the `var` keyword. In Pascal, only variables (including array elements and record fields) may be passed by reference, so an error will be reported if a non-variable is passed to a by-reference parameter. But if a variable is passed as parameter in a call, you will need to inspect the declaration of the called function to see if it is passed by value or reference. C does not use call by reference as such, but it allows taking the address of a variable and passing that as a parameter. The callee has to explicitly follow this pointer to access the variable, unlike in FORTRAN II and Pascal, where this is implicit.

Call by reference can introduce *aliasing*. If a call, such as f (x, x), using Pascal notation, or f (&x, &x), using C notation, passes the same variable to two different reference parameters, two different variable names (in the callee) can refer to the same location, so updating one of these implicitly also updates the other. In addition to giving unexpected behaviour, aliasing also hinders optimisation: If a compiler temporarily fetches the content of a reference parameter into a register and it afterwards writes to another reference parameter, it should re-fetch the first parameter because the write might affect this (if the two parameters are aliases of the same location). Aliasing can also occur if a variable that is in scope in the callee (such as a global variable) is passed by reference to this. This gives similar issues with fetching values into registers.

Call by value result. Call by value result (also called "call by copy restore" or "call by value return") was introduced in FORTRAN IV, where it replaced call by reference. The values of arguments are passed to the callee, which copies these values into local variables. When returning, the values of the local variables are passed back to the caller, and if an argument is a variable, the new value is copied back into this variable. If a variable is passed, it will, hence, be overwritten with a new value when the procedure returns. If an expression is passed, it is an unnamed temporary variable that is overwritten, so this is not observable.

Call by value result leads to an ambiguity: If the same variable is passed twice in the same function (such as in CALL F(X,X), using FORTRAN notation), the value of that variable is copied into two different local variables in the callee. If these have different values when the call returns, which value is copied back to the variable? This ambiguity can be resolved by specifying an order in which the parameters are copied back, or by not allowing repeated variables in a call, which removes the source of the ambiguity.

Call by reference and call by value result give the same visible behaviour if there is no aliasing, i.e., if no global variables are passed as parameters and no variable is passed twice in the same call. If there is no aliasing, call by value result can be seen as an optimisation of call by reference, as values can be passed in registers, but call by reference forces a variable to be in memory.

Call by name.   Call by name was introduced in ALGOL 60 as the default parameter-passing mechanism. In call by name, a parameter expression is not evaluated before the call, but it is evaluated *every time* the callee accesses the parameter. If a variable is passed, it can be updated by the caller like for call by reference. The motivation for call by name is to make function inlining transparent: Inlining can be done by replacing a call by the body of the callee where all occurrences of parameters have been replaced by copies of the corresponding argument expressions (possibly with some renaming to avoid name clashes). It is also a very powerful mechanism: It allows a procedure to implement a loop, where an argument expression is re-evaluated until a condition is true. ALGOL 60 also allows call-by-value passing if this is declared explicitly.

If static scoping is used (as it is in ALGOL 60), care must be taken to evaluate the parameter expression in the scope of the caller and not the scope of the callee. Hence, a parameter is passed as a closure (in ALGOL called a "thunk") that combines the code for the argument expression with a pointer to the frame in which the expression must be evaluated.

Call by name is an instance of *lazy evaluation*, because it postpones evaluation of arguments until absolutely necessary. Call by name is rarely used in modern programming languages, but the related call by need mechanism (see below) is used in what is called "lazy functional languages", such as Haskell.

Call by need.   Like in call by name, a parameter expression is not evaluated prior to the call, but only when the callee accesses its parameter, so a parameter expression is passed as a thunk like in call by name. But unlike call by name, evaluation happens once only, after which the value is stored (by overwriting the thunk) and reused if the callee accesses the parameter again.

In a pure functional language, call by need has the same observable behaviour as call by name, except for execution time, which can be a lot lower with call by need, as expressions are not reevaluated. But by avoiding re-evaluation, call by need can without huge loss of efficiency be used for more things: Not only parameters to functions are unevaluated until used, components of pairs, lists and other data structures are not evaluated until used. This means that you, for example, can recursively define an infinite list (say, of all square numbers) and pass this to a function. The function will force evaluation of only the parts of the list that it actually uses, leaving the remainder unevaluated. This makes it easier to split a task into separate functions that produce data and process it. For example, a program for a chess game can let one function produce an (unevaluated) tree of all possible future moves, and pass this to a function that searches and prunes this tree, only forcing evaluation of the parts that it inspects.

Call by need is what is usually meant by *lazy evaluation*, and is used in Haskell and other pure functional languages. Because call by need carries an overhead for building thunks and updating these when they are evaluated, most compilers for languages that use lazy evaluation use call by value for parameters that the compiler can prove *will* eventually be accessed. In a pure functional language, order of evaluation is not observable, so this is a safe optimisation.

Hybrid methods.   Some languages (like Pascal) allow the user to specify different parameter passing methods when declaring functions or procedures. Other languages (like C) pass scalar types (numbers, Booleans and characters) and structs by value but arrays and strings by reference: Instead of copying a complete array, only a reference to the start of the array is passed. In contrast, Pascal makes deep copies of arrays and strings when these are passed by value, so you explicitly need to specify call-by-reference passing if you only want to pass a reference to an array or string.

The difference between deep copying (copying the entire structure) and shallow copying (copying only a pointer to the structure) is observable only if the callee can modify the structure: With deep copying, the modification is not visible to the caller, but with shallow copying (like in call by reference), all modifications are visible to the caller. So while the semantics of imperative languages must specify whether deep or shallow copying is used, this is not always needed for functional languages. It can be up to the compiler to decide which is best suited in each particular case. Standard ML, for example, only specifies that updatable references and pointers to mutable arrays should not be followed when copying arguments, but allows the compiler to decide if, say, pairs are copied or not. Some implementations of Standard ML pass pairs by reference and other implementations make deep copies, but this doesn't change the behaviour of programs—only their performance.

Suggested Exercises: 5.1 and 5.2.

5.2 Implementing Functions and Function Calls

We will in this section mostly focus on static scoping, as dynamic scoping is comparatively simple to implement. We will, for simplicity, assume that local variables are allocated on a stack and that parameters, return values, and return addresses are

passed on the same stack. In reality, most compilers will allocate some local variables in registers and use registers to pass parameters, results and return addresses.
We refer to compiler textbooks (such as [6]) for details about register allocation,
using registers for parameter passing, and other details about generating code for
function calls for C-like languages where function declarations can not be nested.

Interpreters will usually not store program variables in registers, using these for
variables in the interpreter itself, so the description below about using stacks for
everything is fairly accurate when it comes to interpreters.

5.2.1 Summary of Implementing Function Calls

The code for calling a function and returning from it can be divided between the
caller and the called function (called the *callee*) in different ways. The net effect of
the code for a function call should be:

1. Creating a *frame* for the callee on the stack.
2. Storing the parameters and the return address in this frame.
3. Jumping to the callee.

The callee can allocate its own local variables in the frame. The net effect of returning
from a function should be:

1. Removing the *frame* from the stack.
2. Storing the function result on the stack.
3. Jumping to the caller using the return address saved at the call.

Care must be taken to do this in the right order, so, for example, the return address
is not overwritten by the function result. This means that some parts of the frame
for the callee may be created in the caller prior to jumping to the callee, and other
parts of the frame are created in the callee itself after the jump. Similarly, the code
for removing the frame may be split between the callee and the caller.

The details of the above are usually governed by the *procedure call standard* for
the processor that the code is generated for. Interpreters manage their own stack, so
they have more freedom of frame layout and the order in which things are done.

5.2.2 C-Style Functions

Function declarations, calls and values in C are easy to implement because all function
declarations occur at top level (flat procedure scope). For example, a functional value
is just a pointer to the code of that function. We will not go into further detail about the
implementation of C-style functions but refer to compiler textbooks such as [6].

Fig. 5.2 Nested function
declarations in Gnu C

```
int f(int x)
{
  int a;
  int g(int y)
  {
    int b;
    int h(int z)
    {
      if (z != 0) {
        a = a + z;
        return b + x;
      } else {
        x = x - 1;
        return f(b) + a;
      }
    }
    b = x - 1;
    return h(y) + h(b);
  }
  a = x + 1;
  return g(a) + 3;
}
```

5.2.3   Nested Function Declarations

Many languages allow a function to be declared inside another function and have access to the variables declared in the outer function. In Gnu C, you can write a nested function declaration like shown in Fig. 5.2.

The main thing to note is that, since C uses static scoping, h can access variables declared in both f, g and in h itself. Also, while f can call g, it can not call h, since all declarations inside g are local to g, and thus invisible from the outside. On the other hand, h can call both f and g, since all declarations of functions and variables from outer scopes are visible in inner scopes.

During compile-time type checking, we can add variables from inner scopes to the current symbol table when entering these scopes and remove them when exiting the scopes. But things get a bit more complex when generating intermediate code or machine code, as there is no concept of nested scopes in these low-level languages.

We, for now, ignore registers and assume that all variables are stored either statically or on a stack. So when h accesses variables declared in f or g, it must do so through static memory or the stack. Using static memory for this amounts to shallow dynamic scoping, and since C mandates static scoping, we will use the stack. We note that h can both read and modify variables declared in f and g, so it is not enough to give h access to a copy of the *values* of these variables: It must have access to their *locations*, so it can modify the contents of these locations. We can pass these locations as pointer parameters to h. In C, a pointer parameter is indicated by prefixing the parameter name with a * (or suffixing its type name with a *). You get the address of a variable by prefixing it with &. You get the contents of the variable pointed to by pointer p by writing *p.

Now that all in-scope variables are passed as pointers, we can move all functions out to top level as shown in Fig. 5.3

Fig. 5.3 Adding reference
parameters to the functions
from Fig. 5.2

```
int f(int x)
{
  int a;
  a = x + 1;
  return g(&x, &a, a) + 3;
}

int g(int *X, int *A, int y)
{
  int b;
  b = *X - 1;
  return h(X, A, &b, y) + h(X, A, &b, b);
}

int h(int *X, int *A, int *B, int z)
{
  if (z != 0) {
    *A = *A + z;
    return *B + *X;
  } else {
    *X = *X - 1;
    return f(*B) + *A;
  }
}
```

For readability, we use the name A for the variable that points to a and so on. Note that, when we pass X and A from g to h, these are already pointers, so we do not need to take their addresses again. In fact, doing so would be a type error.

Instead of passing A and X as separate parameters, we can pack these into a single struct and pass only one pointer. We will, in the following, pack all local variables in a function into a single struct, emulating (part of) the frame of this function. This changes the code to that shown in Fig. 5.4. Recall that, in C, fields of a struct can be accessed through a pointer to the struct using the -> operator.

We have one less parameter in calls to g and h, but accessing the variable a requires an offset to a field in the struct fFrame. Often, such small constant offsets to addresses cost nothing extra in terms of code size and execution time when accessing memory, and it is often possible to use registers for temporarily storing fields. The disadvantage is that it requires multiple indirections to access a variable that is multiple scopes away.

The pointer to the frame representing the scope in which a function is declared (before flattening the program) is called a *static link* to distinguish it from the link to the return address, which is called the *dynamic link*. Note that the dynamic link is always to the calling function, but the static link is always to the frame of the (originally) syntactically immediately enclosing function, representing the static scope.

Having a single parameter (such as gFrame in Fig. 5.4)) holding all references to variables from outer scopes makes it easier to pass functions as parameters, as we shall see in Sect. 5.3. The disadvantage is that it requires multiple indirections to access a variable that is multiple scopes away. For example, h has to follow two

```
typedef struct FFrame {
    int x, a;
} fFrame, *fFrameP;

int f(int x)
{
  fFrame fFrame;
  fFrame.x = x;
  fFrame.a = fFrame.x + 1;
  return g(&fFrame, fFrame.a) + 3;
}

typedef struct gFrame {
    fFrameP fFrameP;
    int y, b;
} gFrame, *gFrameP;

int g(fFrameP fFrameP, int y)
{
  gFrame gFrame;
  gFrame.fFrameP = fFrameP;
  gFrame.y = y;
  gFrame.b = gFrame.fFrameP->x - 1;
  return h(&gFrame, y) + h(&gFrame, gFrame.b);
}

int h(gFrameP gFrameP, int z)
{
  if (z != 0) {
    gFrameP->fFrameP->a = gFrameP->fFrameP->a + z;
    return gFrameP->b + gFrameP->fFrameP->x;
  } else {
    gFrameP->fFrameP->x = gFrameP->fFrameP->x - 1;
    return f(gFrameP->b) + gFrameP->fFrameP->a;
  }
}
```

Fig. 5.4 Packing local variables into structs

pointers to access x. Such double indirections can often be optimised away: Since h
accesses fFrame multiple times, it can store the address of that in a local variable,
so it only needs one indirection for later accesses.

Suggested Exercise: 5.3.

5.3   Functions as Parameters

Gnu C also allows functions to be passed as parameters to other functions. We saw
one example in Sect. 5.1.4. Another example is shown in Fig. 5.5.

Note that, in Fig. 5.5, the function h that is passed as arguments to f is locally
declared in g and that it accesses the variable a that is declared in g and not in scope
in f. So, unlike in "normal", flat C (see Sect. 5.2.2), it is not sufficient to pass a
pointer to the function code when passing a function as a parameter: We must also
pass references to the non-local variables used by these functions.

Fig. 5.5 Function
parameters in Gnu C

```
int f(int x, int (*p)(int))
{
  return p(x) + p(1);
}

int g(int a)
{
  int h(int c)
  {
    a = a + 1;
    return a + c;
  }
  if (a%2 != 1)
    return f(a, h) + f(17, g);
  else
    return a;
}
```

Like in Sect. 5.2.3, we use a linked list of frames in the style of Fig. 5.4, but we also add a static link for functions declared at top level, so all functions have a static link, even if this is a null pointer or a pointer to an empty struct. All functions can potentially be passed as parameters, and if a callee expects a function parameter to have a static link, it has better have one. For example, f is passed both h and g as parameters, and while it is strictly speaking only h that needs a static link (since g is globally declared), f doesn't know what function it is passed, so it needs to assume that any parameter it gets has a static link.

A functional parameter is now a pair of a function pointer and a static link. This pair is called a *closure*, and the translation of the code to use explicit closures is called *closure conversion*. The translation is shown in Fig. 5.6.

Since the static links can have different types depending on the function to which it is paired in a closure, we cast static links to void pointers and cast them back to their actual types before accessing them. We do the same with the function pointers.

Note that both the frames and the closures are allocated on the call stack (as they are just local variables). This means that a closure only stays allocated until the end of the function in which it is created. For this reason, it is undefined in Gnu C what happens if a closure is used after the function in which it is created returns, for example, if the function stores the closure in a global variable.

Note that the Gnu C compiler does not actually implement nested scopes and closures using source-to-source translation—the transformations shown here just illustrate one of many ways of implementing nested scopes and closures.

In Sect. 5.4, we will look at a mechanism for handling *first-class functions*, i.e., functions that can be used and stored as freely as any other values such as integers or reals.

Suggested Exercise: 5.4.

```
void *nullLink = NULL;

typedef struct GFrame {
  void *link;
  int a;
} gFrame, *gFrameP;

typedef struct Closure {
  void *link;
  void* function;
} closure, *closureP;


int f(void* dummyLink, int x, closureP p)
{
  int (*pf)(void *, int) = (int (*)(void *, int))(p->function);
  return pf(p->link, x) + pf(p->link, 1);
}

int h(gFrameP gFrameP, int c)
{
  gFrameP->a = gFrameP->a + 1;
  return gFrameP->a + c;
}

int g(void* dummyLink, int a)
{
  gFrame gFrame;
  closure hClosure, gClosure;
  gFrame.link = NULL;
  gFrame.a = a;
  gClosure.link = NULL;
  gClosure.function = (void *)g;
  hClosure.link = (void *)&gFrame;
  hClosure.function = (void *)h;
  if (a%2 != 1)
    return f(NULL, a, &hClosure) + f(NULL, 17, &gClosure);
  else
    return a;
}
```

Fig. 5.6 Closure conversion in C

5.4 First-Class Functions

Function values that can be stored and passed around as freely as, say, integers, are called *first-class functions*. This freedom of use means that it is no longer possible to allocate the closures for the functional values on the stack used for function calls, as the closures can be returned from the functions in which they are allocated or stored in global variables. Also, the static links stored in a closure may point to frames of functions that have long returned by the time the closure is used. Hence, we can store neither closures nor frames pointed to by closures on the stack. Instead, closures and frames are stored where they can stay as long as the closure is live. This usually means the heap (see Chap. 4).

Since the lifetimes of first-class functions can be hard to predict, we can not (easily) find natural places to deallocate closures and frames. This implies that C-style manual heap management can not be used, as calls to `free()` can seldom be safely inserted by a compiler. Hence, languages that support first-class functions nearly always use automatic memory management (i.e., garbage collection), see Sect. 4.6.

Apart from allocating closures and frames on the heap and making deallocation automatic, no further changes are required to implement first-class functions. Functional languages often have properties that allow simplification or optimisation of what we have seen, though. See Sect. 5.5.

5.5   Functional Programming Languages

A functional programming language is a language that uses recursive function calls as the primary control feature, often omitting explicit loops. Most functional languages support first-class functional values as described in Sect. 5.4, but they usually also impose restrictions on assignments to variables. Pure functional languages do not allow *any* assignments to variables, array elements, or record fields after they are initialised, while impure functional languages allow assignments, but often in a restricted form.

5.5.1   Impure Functional Languages

When an impure functional language (such as Scheme) allows unrestricted assignments to variables, we can not make any simplification of the implementations of nested scopes and closures compared to what we have described above. But there are impure languages such as Standard ML that disallow assignments to *variables* but allow assignments through explicit references. Basically, an immutable variable (which can not be modified after initialisation) can point to a place in memory the contents of which can be freely modified.

Since variables never change value after their initialisation, it is safe to make local copies of non-local variables instead of accessing them through references or static links. A nested function declaration in Standard ML is shown in Fig. 5.7. Compared to Fig. 5.2, we have used ML-style syntax and we have removed the non-initial assignments to a and x (which are not allowed in Standard ML), but otherwise the program has the same structure.

In Fig. 5.8, we have moved the declarations of g and h to the top level and added extra parameters corresponding to the non-local variables. Compared to Fig. 5.3, we pass the *values* of these variables instead of pointers to them, which greatly simplifies the translation.

Like in Fig. 5.4, we can combine the extra variables to a single frame record (or tuple) as shown in Fig. 5.9. Note that pairs like (x, a) are usually allocated in memory (on the heap), so the cost is not that different from using static links as in Fig. 5.4.

A Standard ML program that uses functions as first-class values is shown in Fig. 5.10. This is similar to the Gnu C program in Fig. 5.5, but we have omitted the non-initial assignment to a and, instead, added h as part of the result of g to

Fig. 5.7 Nested function
declarations in Standard ML

```
fun f x =
    let
        val a = x + 1
        fun g y =
            let
                val b = x - 1
                fun h z =
                    if z = 0 then
                        b + x
                    else
                        f b + a
            in
                h y + h b
            end
    in
        g a + 3
    end
```

Fig. 5.8 Lifted function
declarations in Standard ML

```
fun f x =
    let
        val a = x + 1
    in
        g (x, a, a) + 3
    end

and g (x, a, y) =
    let
        val b = x - 1
    in
        h(x, a, b, y) + h(x, a, b, b)
    end

and h (x, a, b, z) =
    if z = 0 then
        b + x
    else
        f b + a
```

illustrate closures escaping the function in which they are built. Using static links like in Fig. 5.9, we can translate this into the "flat" program shown in Fig. 5.11. The result is now straightforward to translate to intermediate code. Note that since environments may have different numbers of variables and types of these, the closure-converted program is not always well typed using the ML type system, so closure conversion is usually done after type checking.

Suggested Exercise: 5.5.

5.5.2 Defunctionalisation

An alternative to closure conversion using code/function pointers is to convert closures to values in a datatype where the constructor indicates the function part of the closure and the argument of the constructor is the environment part of the closure. When a functional value is called, a dispatch function inspects the data type and calls the intended function. The program in Fig. 5.10 can with this method be

```
fun f x =
  let
    val a = x + 1
    val env_f = (x, a)
  in
    g (env_f, a) + 3
  end

and g (env_f, y) =
  let
    val (x, a) = env_f
    val b = x - 1
    val env_g = (env_f, b)
  in
    h(env_g, y) + h(env_g, b)
  end

and h (env_g, z) =
  let
    val (env_f, b) = env_g
    val (x, a̅) = env_f
  in
    if z = 0 then
      b + x
    else
      f b + a
  end
```

Fig. 5.9 Using static links in Standard ML

```
fun f (x, p) =
  p x + p 1

fun g a =
  let
    fun h c = a + c
  in
    (f (a, h) + f (17, g),
     h)
  end
```

Fig. 5.10 Functional values in Standard ML

closure converted to the program shown in Fig. 5.12. While there is an overhead in the dispatch, the resulting program *is* actually well typed in the ML type system, which the program in Fig. 5.11 is not.

5.5.3 Pure Functional Languages

Pure functional languages do not allow non-initialising assignments of any kind, nor do they allow functions to have effects such as reading from input or writing to output. While this does not further simplify implementation of nested scopes or closures, it allows some optimisations that are not valid in impure languages. We observe that if a function call can cause no effects or assignments, two calls to the same function with the same arguments will always return the same value. So we can replace an

```
fun f (env_0, x, pc) =
  let
    val (p, env_p) = pc
  in
    p (env_p, x) + p (env_p, 1)
  end

fun g (env_0, a) =
  let
    val env_g = (env_0, a)
  in
    (f (env_0, a, (h, env_g)) + f (env_0, 17, (g, env_0)),
     (h, env_g))
  end

and h (env_g, c) =
  let
    val (env_0, a) = env_g
  in
    a + c
  end
```

Fig. 5.11   Closure conversion in Standard ML

```
datatype intIntClosure = G of () | H of ((), int)

fun dispatch (G env, x) = g (env, x)
  | dispatch (H env, x) = h (env, x)

fun f (env_0, x, pc) =
  dispatch (pc, x) + dispatch (pc, 1)

fun g (env_0, a) =
  let
    val env_g = (env_0, a)
  in
    (f (env_0, a, H env_g) + f (env_0, 17, G env_0),
     H env_g)
  end

and h (env_g, c) =
  let
    val (env_0, a) = env_g
  in
    a + c
  end
```

Fig. 5.12   Defunctionalised closure conversion

expression like $f\ x + f\ x$ with $\mathtt{let}\ y = f\ x\ \mathtt{in}\ y + y$, which is guaranteed to have the same result and which evaluates $f\ x$ only once. Without assignments or effects, we can also freely rearrange the order of evaluation without risking changing the result.

The cost is that mechanisms for input and output are more complicated than in impure functional languages. For example, an input stream can be implemented as a function that, when you call it, returns both the read value and a new modified stream. The old stream is no longer valid, so the language must ensure that this is not used afterwards. This can be done by using linear types (that ensure that a value can be accessed only once) or by using monads (which use syntactic restrictions to ensure single use of values).

5.5.4 Lazy Functional Languages

Pure functional languages (such as Haskell) often use *lazy evaluation*. Lazy evaluation means that a variable initialisation, function parameter or structure field is not evaluated at the time the variable is declared, the function is called, or the structure built, but postponed until the value of the variable, parameter, or field is actually used, which may be never.

The simplest form of lazy evaluation is called *call by name* and implies that a parameter is reevaluated *every time* it is used. In a pure language, this will give the same result every time, but it can be quite costly to reevaluate an expression many times. The ALGOL 60 language use call-by-name by default for function parameters (but not variable initialisations). Since ALGOL 60 is not a pure language, evaluating an expression several times can give several different results, which is sometimes used purposefully in ALGOL 60 programs, but normally re-evaluation is avoided by the programmer by using call-by-value (if the parameter is certain to be used) or by copying the parameter to a local variable (thereby forcing evaluation) when it is known to be used, and afterwards use the local variable instead.

Call-by-name is implemented by passing a closure (in this context called a "thunk") instead of a normal value. When the value of a parameter is needed, the thunk is called to evaluate the parameter expression. Basically, every parameter expression is made into a locally-declared parameterless function, and every use of an incoming parameter is replaced by a function call with no parameters. Applying this transformation to the program in Fig. 5.7 produces the program in Fig. 5.13. The notation fn () => e defines an anonymous function that takes no argument (indicated by the empty brackets) and returns the value of e as a result.

Note that, when a variable (which is already a parameterless function) is used as a parameter in a call, there is no need to build a new closure. Essentially, this exploits the equivalence of fn () => x () and x when x is a parameterless function. This corresponds to *eta reduction* in the lambda calculus.

To avoid re-evaluation of parameters, a more advanced form of lazy evaluation called *call by need* is used by most lazy functional language implementations, including Haskell. Call by need, like call by name, postpones evaluation of a parameter or variable initialiser until its value is used, but it is evaluated *at most* once regardless of how many times it is used. This can be achieved by overwriting the thunk of the parameter or variable by a new thunk that immediately returns the already-computed value, once this is computed the first time. The initial thunk can be made to do this once it is applied. Call-by-need transformation of the program in Fig. 5.7 is shown in Fig. 5.14. In order to overwrite the original thunks, we store them in updatable references. ref x creates an updatable reference containing x as the initial content. ! x gets the content of the updatable reference x and $x := y$ updates the content of the updatable reference x to be the value of y. Since ML does not

Fig. 5.13 Call-by-name
transformation applied to
Fig. 5.7

```
fun f x =
  let
    val a = (fn () => x () + 1)
    fun g y =
      let
        val b = (fn () => x () - 1)
        fun h z =
          if z () = 0 then
            b () + x ()
          else
            f b + a ()
      in
        h y + h b
      end
  in
    g a + 3
  end
```

```
exception Dummy

fun f x =
  let
    val a = ref (fn () => raise Dummy)
    val _ = a := (fn () => let val v = (!x) () + 1
                           in a := fn () => v; v end)
    fun g y =
      let
        val b = ref (fn () => raise Dummy)
        val _ = b := (fn () => let val v = (!x) () - 1
                               in b := fn () => v; v end)
        fun h z =
          if (!z) () = 0 then
            (!b) () + (!x) ()
          else
            f b + (!a) ()
      in
        h y + h b
      end
  in
    g a + 3
  end
```

Fig. 5.14 Call-by-need transformation applied to Fig. 5.7

allow recursive reference variables, we first bind the closure to a dummy function
(that raises an exception because this imposes no restrictions on the return type) and
then overwrite this with a function that can update the closure.

5.5.5 Strictness Analysis

It should be evident that, if a parameter is actually used, there is considerable overhead
in using call-by-need rather than evaluating the parameter immediately using call by
value, so if a parameter or variable is guaranteed to be needed, it is better to evaluate
the argument expression immediately and pass its value rather than build and pass
a thunk. An analysis that can determine if a parameter is guaranteed to be needed

is called *strictness analysis*. Most compilers for lazy languages use some form of strictness analysis.

A simple strictness analysis takes an expression and returns the set of variables whose values are definitely needed to evaluate the value of the expression. If the expression is the body of a function, this will tell us which parameters of the function can safely be evaluated before the call: If a parameter x to f is definitely needed, the value of x can be evaluated in advance. We say that f is strict in argument x.

Suggested Exercises: 5.7 and 5.6.

5.6 Exceptions

An exception allows a function to return across multiple calls to an exception handler, so it has a non-trivial interaction with function calls. So we describe the implementation of exceptions in this chapter, but we will return to exceptions as a control structure in Chap. 6.

In most languages, exceptions involve two program constructs: An exception *raiser* and an exception *handler*. In Standard ML, these are called `raise` and `handle`, while the equivalent constructs in Java and C# are called `throw` and `try-catch`.

The semantics of these constructs is that an exception raiser causes control to pass to the most recently encountered active handler, where a handler is active if it has been entered during execution but not yet exited (so handlers are, in effect, dynamically scoped). If there is no active exception handler when an exception is raised, an error message (such as "uncaught exception") is typically given. The exception raiser can usually pass some information to the exception handler.

If there is an active exception handler in the function that raises an exception, passing control to the handler can be done by a local jump and does not involve the function-call mechanism. But if not, control passes down the call stack to the closest function that has an active exception handler. The saved registers of that function must be restored from the call stack to ensure a correct state for the handler.

There are various ways to handle this. We look at three of these: *Tagged return*, *stack unwinding*, and using a *handler stack*.

5.6.1 Tagged Return

Tagged return is the simplest way to implement exceptions. When a function returns, it not only returns a value in the usual way but also an indication of whether the value is a result of a normal function return or the result of an exception being raised. This indication can be stored in a dedicated normal register, in a flag (condition) register, or in a dedicated memory location. Immediately after a call, the caller must check this indication to see if it can continue normally or must pass the exception to the next active handler. If there is an active handler in the same function, this can be done with a local jump, otherwise control is passed to the previous caller by immediately returning with the exception indicator still set. This way, control is eventually passed to the most recent active handler.

While tagged return is a simple mechanism, it is quite costly: Every call must on return check the exception indicator, so the cost is paid even by functions that do not raise or handle exceptions—even if no exception is ever raised. As a general principle, the implementation of a specific language feature should not adversely affect programs that do not use this feature. Given that exceptions in Java or C# normally indicate exceptional (unusual) behaviour, adding a cost to every call to methods/functions that *might* raise exceptions is not ideal.

An alternative to returning an explicit exception indicator is to have every call use two return addresses, both of which are passed when a function is called: One used for normal return and one used for exception return. The exception return address points to the local exception handler (if any), which restores the correct state (by restoring saved registers and adjusting the stack pointer) before executing the handler code. If the function has no local handler, one is added which just restores registers and returns using the previous exception-return address.

This still has a significant cost: When saving registers across a function call, both variables live after the call and variables live at the entry to the exception handler must be stored. And to ensure that the exception handler can find the variables it needs to restore, these must be at the same offsets in all function calls. Additionally, an extra parameter (the exception return address) must be passed in every call.

5.6.2 Stack Unwinding

Stack unwinding is an attempt to move the cost of exceptions to the cases where an exception is actually raised, so there is virtually no cost for programs that do not raise exceptions.

It is easy to see from the program text whether a call is inside an active exception handler in the same procedure. So we can compile time make a global table that maps each return address (call point) to the address of the active exception handler that encloses the call point (if any exist in the same function) and to 0 if there is no enclosing exception handler in the same function.

When an exception is raised (and not handled locally), the stack frames are inspected until a return address that maps to a non-zero handler is found, and control is passed to this handler. As stack frames are popped off the stack, registers that were saved in the stack frames must be restored, so the handler will be executed in the correct state.

So while there is no cost except when an exception is raised, the cost of processing a raised exception is proportional to the number of stack frames that are popped off the call stack until the handler is found.

5.6.3   Using a Handler Stack

It is possible to avoid inspecting call frames altogether by having a stack dedicated to exception handling: Whenever an exception handler is entered, the address of the handling part (i.e., the catch clause of a `try-catch` statement or the matching part of a `handle` expression) is stored along with the current value of the call-stack pointer and the values of all variables that are lived at the entry to the handling part. When an exception handler is exited (regardless of whether this was due to a normal exit or because the handler was activated), the topmost record (containing a handler address and variable values) is popped.

When an exception is raised, control is immediately passed to the handler address at the top of the handler stack, the variables stored there are restored, and the call-stack pointer is set to the stored value. Hence, the cost of raising an exception is very low and independent of the number of calls between the exception raiser and the handler. On the other hand, entering and exiting handlers is no longer free. Typically, very few variables are live in exception handlers, so the cost is not large, and functions that do not have exception handlers pay no cost at all.

Whether stack unwinding or using a handler stack is more efficient depends on the frequency of raising exceptions compared to the frequency of entering and exiting exception handlers. If exceptions are rarely raised, stack unwinding is more efficient, but if exceptions are raised frequently and the handler may be many calls away, using a handler stack may be more efficient.

5.7   Further Reading

We have made references to a compiler book [6] in this chapter, both for translation of expressions and statements to intermediate code and for translation from intermediate code to machine language. Numerous other compiler textbooks can provide that information as well.

We have used Gnu C as an example language. This is described in [7]. The lambda calculus is described in [2], Standard ML in [5] and Haskell in [3]. For more about translating functional languages, see [1] for translation of Standard ML and [4] for translation of a language similar to Haskell.

5.8   Exercises

Exercise 5.1 Find documentation for one of the languages Ruby, Lua or Perl. Specify which version of the language you discuss.

a. Describe the scope rules for the chosen language, focusing on static versus dynamic scoping, whether function definitions can be nested, rules for global and local variables, and rules for mutual or simple recursion.
   If there are any of the scope rules you find strange, discuss why you find them strange and consider if there are good reasons for these.
b. Describe the available parameter-passing methods in the chosen language, including how (and if) functions can be passed as parameters or results, and how scopes work for these.

Exercise 5.2 A common trick for swapping the values of two variables is to use exclusive OR three times. In C, a procedure for doing this can be declared as

```
void swap(int *x, int *y)
{
    *x ^= *y;
    *y ^= *x;
    *x ^= *y;
}
```

This procedure can be called by passing the addresses of two variables, e.g., swap(&a, &b);, which will swap the contents of a and b.

a. What is the value of c after executing the statement sequence c = 42; swap(&c, &c);?
b. Describe requirements for the locations of variables a and b that ensure that a and b will have swapped their values after a call swap(&a, &b);.
c. Write a C macro SWAP such that SWAP(a, b); will swap the contents of two integer variables a and b, regardless of their locations.

Exercise 5.3 Section 5.2.3 shows a method for converting nested function definitions to global function definitions. Consider the C program fragment with nested function definitions (as allowed by Gnu C) in Fig. 5.15.

a. Change the local function definition of binS to a global definition by adding parameters for non-local variables, as shown in Fig. 5.3 for the program in Fig. 5.2.
b. Pack the parameters for non-local variables into frame structs as shown in Fig. 5.4.

Exercise 5.4 Section 5.3 shows how local functions can be passed as arguments in the Gnu extension of C. Consider the code fragment in Fig. 5.16.

a. Convert this into standard C by closure conversion, as shown in Fig. 5.6 for the program in Fig. 5.5.

```
int binSearch(double k, double a[], int size)
{
  int binS(int low, int high)
  {
    int mid;
    if (a[low] == k) return low;
    else if (low >= high) return -1;
    else {
      mid = (low + high)/2;
      if (a[mid] > k) return binS(low, mid-1);
      else return binS(mid, high);
    }
  }
  return binS(0, high-1);
}
```

Fig. 5.15 Nested functions for Exercise 5.3

```
double differentiate(double (*f)(double), double x)
{
  double epsilon = 0.0000001;
  return (f(x+epsilon) - f(x))/epsilon;
}

double g(double a, double b)
{
  double parabola(double x)
  {
    return x*x+a*x+b;
  }

  return(differentiate(parabola, 0.0));
}
```

Fig. 5.16 Functions for Exercise 5.4

Exercise 5.5 In Sect. 5.5.1, we use nested frames, so a frame consists of a tuple of the frame of the surrounding function (if any) and the values of the variables of the current function. Instead of using nested frames, we can make frames flat by copying the values of the variables from outer scopes into the current frame—since variables are never updated, we can copy them freely. In Fig. 5.9, this would mean that env_g contains copies of the local variables of f instead of f's frame env_f.

a. Rewrite the program in Fig. 5.9 so it does this.
b. In Fig. 5.11, a closure is a pair of a function and a frame that consists of a static "link" (the frame for the outer scope) and copies of local variables. Like above, we want to flatten frames so the frame of a function is a flat tuple of all variables that the function can access. A closure is still a pair of a function and a frame, but the frame is flat as described above.

Rewrite the program in Fig. 5.11 to use flat frames.

Exercise 5.6 An alternative definition of strictness is defined in terms of termination: We say that f is strict if *whenever* evaluation of an expression e does not terminate, it is also the case that evaluation of the application $f(e)$ does not terminate.

If f definitely uses its argument, evaluation of the argument is eventually forced, so if evaluation of e doesn't terminate, nor does evaluation of the call to $f(e)$. So all functions that are strict by the definition in Sect. 5.5.5 are also strict by the alternative definition.

Is the converse also true? i.e., are all functions that are strict by the definition involving termination also strict by the definition used in Sect. 5.5.5? Argue your answer.

Exercise 5.7 Section 5.5.5 suggests a strictness analysis based on the set of variables definitely needed to evaluate an expression.

a. Given the expression grammar below, where expressions have the usual meaning, sketch an algorithm that given an expression returns the set of variables the values of which are *definitely* used when the expression is evaluated.

$$E \rightarrow \textbf{num}$$
$$E \rightarrow \textbf{id}$$
$$E \rightarrow E + E$$
$$E \rightarrow E == E$$
$$E \rightarrow E \;\&\&\; E$$
$$E \rightarrow \texttt{if } E \texttt{ then } E \texttt{ else } E$$

Notes: $==$ is comparison for equality. $\&\&$ is logical conjunction using *short-circuit semantics*, so the second argument is not evaluated if the first argument evaluates to false. **num** represents any number, and **id** represents any variable identifier.

Write your algorithm by completing the following function definition. You can (and should) use recursion.

$$
\begin{aligned}
needs(n) &= \emptyset, \quad \text{when } n \text{ is a number constant} \\
needs(x) &= \{x\}, \text{ when } x \text{ is a variable} \\
needs(e_1 + e_2) &= \cdots \\
needs(e_1 == e_2) &= \cdots \\
needs(e_1 \;\&\&\; e_2) &= \cdots \\
needs(\texttt{if } e_1 \texttt{ then } e_2 \texttt{ else } e_3) &= \cdots
\end{aligned}
$$

b. Discuss how calls to recursively defined functions can be handled in the above algorithm. Hint: Use and update a mapping from function names to lists of Booleans that indicate which parameters are needed.

Exercise 5.8 The ability to create and call functional values with static scopes (i.e., closures) is very powerful and can simulate many features found in programming languages. For example, we can (using F# syntax) define truth values by

```
let True = fun x y -> x
let False = fun x y -> y
```

which allows us to define a conditional by

```
let If = fun c t e -> c t e
```

which makes If True *t e* reduce to *t* using the following steps:

```
  If True  t e
↝ If (fun x y -> x) t e
↝ (fun c t e -> c t e) (fun x y -> x)  t e
↝ (fun x y -> x) t e
↝ t
```

Similarly, If False *t e* reduces to *e*.

When solving the exercises below, you can use notation from F#, Haskell, ML, or any statically-typed language that supports closures.

a. What are the types of `True`, `False` and `If`?
b. Define a function `Not` such that `If (Not True) 3 4` reduces to 4 and `If (Not False) 3 4` reduces to 3.
c. Show, in the style used above, the sequence of function calls that reduce `If (Not True) 3 4` to 4.
d. Define in a similar way (using functional values only; no tuples, records, datatypes, arrays, etc.) functions `Pair`, `Fst`, and `Snd`, such that `Fst (Pair 3 4)` reduces to 3 and `Snd (Pair 3 4)` reduces to 4.
e. Show, in the style used above, the sequence of function calls that reduce `Snd (Pair 3 4)` to 4.
f. When implemented in F# or ML, a problem with the definition of `If` above is that it (unlike an if-then-else expression) evaluates *both* branches (*t* and *e* above), even though it returns only one of these. Why does it do that? Discuss what could be done to prevent evaluation of both branches.

References

1. Appel AW (1992) Compiling with continuations. Cambridge University Press
2. Barendregt HP (1984) The Lambda calculus – its syntax and semantics. North Holland
3. Jones SLP (2003) Haskell 98 language and libraries: the revised report. Cambridge University Press. http://haskell.org/onlinereport/
4. Jones SLP, Lester D (1992) Implementing functional languages – a tutorial. Prentice Hall
5. Milner R, Tofte M, Harper R, MacQueen D (1997) The definition of standard ML. MIT Press, Cambridge, MA, USA
6. Mogensen TÆ (2017) Introduction to compiler design, 2nd edn. Springer
7. Stallman RM (2019) The GCC developer community: GCC online documentation. https://gcc.gnu.org/onlinedocs/. Accessed on September 2019

Control Structures

6

Trust is good, control is better.

Attributed to Vladimir Lenin

'Who controls the past', ran the Party slogan, 'controls the future: who controls the present controls the past'.

George Orwell, 1984

Execution of a program is generally done by computing (executing or evaluating) different parts of the program (possibly repeatedly) in some order that may be dependent on data. *Control structures* are features in a programming language that allows the programmer some control over this order.

Some programming languages (such as Pascal or ML) specify very precisely the order in which computations are executed/evaluated, and allow implementations only to deviate from this to the extent that the differences are not observable. Other languages (such as C) allow implementations limited freedom in ordering computations, even when the differences *are* observable. No matter how strictly ordering is otherwise defined, the change in ordering affected by a control structure is usually defined precisely.

Function/procedure calls is one form of control structure, which we have already looked at in Chap. 5. In this chapter, we will look at other control structures, both structures that are used to determine the sequence of computation within one procedure or function and structures that determine sequence across function/procedure boundaries. Some languages support control structures that are similar to function/procedure calls, and we will also look at these.

© The Author(s), under exclusive license to Springer Nature Switzerland AG 2022
T. Ægidius Mogensen, *Programming Language Design and Implementation*,
Texts in Computer Science, https://doi.org/10.1007/978-3-031-11806-7_6

6.1 Jumps

The control structures in early programming languages like FORTRAN and COBOL
were heavily inspired by the control features available in computer hardware, which
is to say conditional and unconditional jumps.

The first version of FORTRAN from 1956 has a multitude of different jump
statements:

GO TO n jumps to the line numbered n. Recall that lines in FORTRAN can option-
ally be numbered with a five-digit line number (which originally was limited to
0 to $2^{15}-1$).

GO TO $(n_1, \ldots, n_m), i$, where i is an integer-typed variable containing the value
j, jumps to the line numbered n_j. If j is outside the range $1, \ldots, m$, no jump is
made.

GO TO $i, (n_1, \ldots, n_k)$, where i is an integer-typed variable, jumps to the line number stored in i, which must be one of $n_1, \ldots, n_m$. Line numbers are not internally
represented as the integers they resemble, so i must be given a line-number value
by a command ASSIGN n TO i, where n is a line number.

IF $(e)\, n_1, n_2, n_3$ evaluates the expression e. If the value is less than zero, the statement jumps to n_1, if the value is equal to zero, the statement jumps to n_2 and if
the value is greater than zero, the statement jumps to n_3.

Additionally, a number of machine-specific conditional jumps that depend on sensors or error statuses.

In early FORTRAN, only jumps can be conditional, and only in the forms above.

COBOL separates conditionals and jumps. We will return to conditionals shortly
and look only at jumps now. The PROCEDURE section of a program consists of a number of named paragraphs and sections (collectively called *procedures*). The GO TO
p statement jumps to the procedure named p. GO TO $p_1, \ldots, p_m$ DEPENDING
ON i, where i is a variable containing the value j, jumps to procedure p_j. These
are equivalent to the two first forms of the FORTRAN GO TO statement mentioned
above, but COBOL additionally has a rather strange (from a modern viewpoint) feature to control jumps: The statement ALTER p_1 TO PROCEED TO p_2 changes a
statement of the form GO TO p_3 located at paragraph p_1 to thereafter jump to p_2
instead of to p_3, until another ALTER statement changes the destination again. This
feature, which essentially allows a program to modify itself, was removed from the
official COBOL standard in 2002 because it can make programs very hard to read
and analyse.

COBOL procedures can be used both as targets of jumps and as subroutines. A
subroutine is called with the PERFORM statement, which jumps to the procedure,
but when the end of the procedure is reached, it returns to the statement located
right after the PERFORM statement. The end of the procedure is implicitly just
before the next procedure declaration or the end of the PROCEDURE section of
the program. COBOL (in its original form) conceptually stores the return address
as a jump statement placed after the last statement in a procedure, so recursion is

not supported (because a recursive PERFORM would overwrite the return address). Furthermore, if a jump jumps out of a procedure, control is not passed back to the caller, as it never encounters the return jump statement. Later versions of COBOL have added recursion by using a stack for return addresses and adding a command GO BACK that explicitly returns from a procedure. COBOL allows chaining several calls after each other in a single PERFORM statement, and allows adding a condition such that the PERFORM statement repeats until this condition is true (making this a structured loop).

ALGOL 60 allows statements to be prefixed by alphanumeric labels. Labels implicitly have scope in the enclosing block, so you cannot jump into a block from outside the block, but you can jump out of a block. The go to statement allows (almost) arbitrary expressions to specify the target of a jump, which gives capabilities similar to ASSIGNed or indexed jumps in FORTRAN.

Pascal, in spite of being designed for structured programming also includes a goto statement. Labels are declared using block structure, so like in ALGOL 60, you cannot jump into blocks. Unlike ALGOL 60, Pascal only supports jumps that name the target labels as constants, but it is possible to jump out of procedures to labels in enclosing scopes.

C also allows labels and goto statements, but unlike Pascal, the scope of a label is the entire function in which it is declared, so it is possible to jump into branches of conditionals or bodies of loops, but it is not possible to jump out of a function. Gnu C extends the standard C jumps by allowing a label to be stored in a variable and a goto to jump to a label stored in a variable, corresponding to the ASSIGNed jumps in FORTRAN.

To summarise, a jump transfers control to a specified other part of the program. Different languages can specify different restrictions on the range of such jumps. Jumps can depend on data, either by being conditional or by letting a value select between several specified jump targets. A variant of the "normal" jump is a jump that records a return address so control can be resumed just after the jump by an implicit or explicit return command. This is often called a subroutine jump. Subroutine jumps may or may not support recursion.

Using jumps as control can make programs hard to read, so it is usually recommended that they be used as little as possible, even in languages that support them. Jumps can be quite useful in program-generated code, such as lexers and parsers, so if a language is intended to be used as a target for code generators (in addition to being coded by humans), support for jumps can be a good thing, even if few human programmers will ever use this feature.

It is, in theory, always possible to avoid unstructured jumps in a language that has structured conditionals and loops or recursive function calls. We will look at this in the next section.

6.2 Structured Control

Structured control usually refers to control structures that are explicitly bracketed, so two control structures can only overlap if one is properly nested within another, similar to how parentheses are nested. We will look at different kinds of structured control structures below.

6.2.1 Conditionals

A conditional is a control structure that chooses between one or more computations/execution paths (called branches) depending on the value of an expression or variable. A structured conditional will syntactically contain the possible branches that it can select from, unlike conditional, assigned or indexed jumps where the branches can be located far from the conditional selection of these. If no explicit jumps are made inside the branches, control will resume immediately after the conditional regardless of which branch is chosen.

The simplest form of conditional is binary selection: One of two possible branches is chosen depending on a value. One subset of possible values will select the first of these branches, and the complement of this subset will select the other. Often, the value is required to be Boolean, so it only has two possible values, but in other cases, more values are allowed, but only some of these will select the first of the two branches, while the remaining values select the other. For example, in C, conditions are integers and all non-zero values are considered to be true (selecting the first branch), while only 0 is considered false (selecting the second branch).

A structured binary conditional was found already in COBOL in 1959, where it has the form

IF *condition* THEN *statement* OTHERWISE *statement*

If the condition evaluates to the true Boolean value, the statement after the THEN clause is executed, otherwise the statement after the OTHERWISE clause is executed. These statements may be compound statements, i.e., consist of multiple statements including other conditionals. The OTHERWISE part is optional. If it is not present, it is equivalent to an OTHERWISE part with an empty statement. ALGOL 60 has a similar binary conditional using the keywords if and else.

Conditions can be used to select between the evaluation of two or more expressions instead of execution of two or more statements. LISP, for example, has a condition of the form

(COND (*condition*$_1$ *expression*$_1$) ... (*condition*$_n$ *expression*$_n$))

The conditions are evaluated in sequence and the expression associated with the *first* condition that evaluates to true is evaluated. The remaining expressions are ignored. If no condition evaluates to true, a default value (nil) is returned. The LISP COND statement is equivalent to a sequence of nested binary conditions. Using ALGOL-like syntax, the above is equivalent to

```
if condition₁ then expression₁
...
else if conditionₙ then expressionₙ
else nil
```

Not all languages have a suitable default value for when no condition is true. These languages will either syntactically require a default/otherwise/else branch or give a runtime error if no conditions evaluate to true. For example, ALGOL 60 has conditional expressions as well as conditional statements using essentially the same syntax for both, but demands that conditional expressions have $\underline{else}$ parts.

The LISP conditional is not a true multi-way selection, as it is equivalent to a sequence of binary selections, but it is not unusual for programming languages to have multi-way conditionals that select from an arbitrary number of branches based on the value of an expression. The general form of these is some syntactic variant of

```
case expression of
    pattern₁ : branch₁
    ...
    patternₙ : branchₙ
end
```

The expression is evaluated to a value, and if a pattern *matches* the value, the corresponding branch is selected. We will call the combination of a pattern and its corresponding branch a *rule*.

Different languages have different forms for patterns and different rules for how to select branches. Some examples (ignoring syntax differences):

- Pascal requires the expression to be a scalar type (excluding reals). A pattern is a list of constants of that type, and a value matches a pattern if it is listed in the pattern. All constants occurring in patterns of the same case statement must be different. This ensures that the order of the rules is immaterial. If there is no matching rule, the behaviour is undefined.
- C has a similar construction (called switch) with similar restrictions, but there are a couple of differences:

  - C allows constant expressions in patterns. These are evaluated at compile time and are equivalent to the constants they represent.
  - C allows a default pattern that matches any value not covered by the other patterns. The default rule must be the last rule in the switch statement.
  - When a rule is selected, both the corresponding branch *and* all subsequent branches are executed. It is possible to explicitly exit the conditional using a break statement, and it is normal practice that all branches are terminated with a break statement.

- ML, Haskell and other functional languages allow almost any type for the expression in a case expression, and patterns can be more than just constants:

  - A pattern can be a variable. This matches any value and binds the variable to be equal to this value in the corresponding branch.
  - A pattern can be a tuple of patterns. A tuple pattern matches a value if the value is a tuple of the same size (usually ensured by the type system) and if the components of the value are matched by the corresponding pattern components. For example, the pattern $(7, x)$ will match any pair where the first component is equal to 7, and it will bind x to be equal to the second component of the pair.
  - A pattern can be a constructor applied to a pattern. The pattern matches if the value is built by applying the same constructor to an argument value and the argument pattern matches the argument value.

Patterns can be nested arbitrarily, so it is, for example, possible to make a pattern that matches all lists that are at least five elements long and where the third element is the string `"abc"`.

If patterns can overlap, the language must specify a rule for which of several matching rules are selected. The most common rule is that the *first* matching rule is selected. Some languages forbid overlapping patterns, and some say that if two patterns overlap, the *most specific* rule is applied. This implies that if two patterns overlap, one of these must be more specific than the other. Most compilers for functional languages give warnings if there are values not covered by any pattern (non-exhaustive pattern matching) or if a rule cannot be reached because all values matched by the rule are matched by higher-priority rules.

Some functional languages allow a variable to occur several times in a pattern. The pattern will only match a value if all the occurrences of the variable match identical sub-values. For example, a pattern (x, x) will match any pair consisting of two identical values.

As an alternative, some languages (like Haskell or F#) allow a pattern to be supplemented by a *guard*, which is a condition that must be true for the pattern to match. A pair consisting of two identical values can, for example, be matched by the pattern/guard combination (x, y) | x==y (using Haskell notation, where the vertical bar is read as "where"). In F#, the keyword when is used.

6.2.1.1 Short-Circuit Condition Evaluation

In logic, a conjunction $p \wedge q$ is false if p is false, regardless of the value of q. So if p is found to be false, there is no need to evaluate q. Similarly, $p \vee q$ is true when p is true, no matter the value of q, so evaluation of q can be skipped. This is called *short-circuit evaluation*.

In a programming language, it is not always possible to safely skip evaluation of q in such cases: There might be side effects when evaluating q, or the evaluation of q might not terminate, so it is observable whether q is evaluated or not. So applying the shortcut as an optimisation can change the observable behaviour of a program, which optimisations generally should not do.

However, some languages define logical operators corresponding to ∧ and ∨ as having short-circuit behaviour, meaning that the second operand is not evaluated if the first is sufficient to determine the truth value—even if the second expression could cause side effects, errors or nontermination. C, C#, Java, and ML are examples of such languages. Conversely, Pascal is an example of a language that specifies that both operands of a logical operator must be evaluated always.

In addition to saving time, short-cut evaluation of logical operators allow expressions like `x!=0 && y/x >3` (using C notation) which, if both operands of `&&` are evaluated, will lead to a division-by-zero error, but will evaluate to false without error if sequential short-circuit evaluation is used.

Short-circuit evaluation is normally implemented using jumps: The code for evaluation of $p \vee q$ will jump past the code for evaluating q if p evaluates to true. Conditional jumps can be expensive to execute on processors with long pipelines, especially if the condition is hard to predict, so short-circuit evaluation is not always faster than full evaluation, but this depends a lot on hardware specifics (such as whether conditions are only available in jumps or also in assignments), so it is hard to give a definite answer about which strategy is most efficient. So a language designer should not choose between short-cut or full evaluation based on efficiency, but on which observable behaviour is desired—or include both options in the language.

6.2.2 Loops

Loops are a means of repeating a computation (with different values) a number of times (iterations). We can classify loops by when the number of iterations is known:

Type 1: The number of iterations is known at compile time. This can, for example, be looping over the elements of an array the size of which is known at compile time.

Type 2: The number of iterations is known before the first iteration begins. This usually means that the number of iterations is computed at the beginning of the loop and not changed after that.

Type 3: The number of iterations is not known in advance. Instead, the loop repeats until a certain condition is fulfilled, which may be never.

We will look at some loop structures from various languages and relate them to these categories.

FORTRAN   defines a loop: DO n $i = m_1, m_2, m_3$. The label n specifies the end of the repeated code: All code starting with the line following the DO statement up to and including the line labelled n is repeated. The i is an integer-typed index variable that starts with the value of m_1 and increases by m_3 after each iteration. The loop exits to the line following the line labelled n when i reaches a value that equals or exceeds m_2. m_1, m_2, and m_3 are either integer-typed variables or integer constants. m_3 can be left unspecified, in which case it is taken to be 1. The body of a DO loop is always executed at least once. This allows the compiler to place the exit test at the bottom of the loop, which saves a small amount of code.

FORTRAN does not allow the index variable to be modified inside the body of the loop. This ensures that the number of iterations is known before the first iteration begins, so this is a type-2 loop using the above classification. If m_1, m_2, and m_3 are all constants, it is also a type-1 loop.

COBOL uses PERFORM for looping. PERFORM executes a list of procedures in sequence, but has an optional clause that causes this sequence to repeat. This clause can have several forms:

- EXACTLY n TIMES, where n is either a non-negative integer constant or a variable that holds a non-negative integer value. As the name indicates, this repeats the sequence n times, making this a type-1 or type-2 loop depending on whether n is a constant or a variable.
- VARYING i FROM m_1 TO m_2 BY m_3. This has the same meaning as the FORTRAN DO loop, but m_1, m_2 and m_3 must all be (variables holding) positive numbers. This is also either a type-1 or a type-2 loop depending on whether m_1, m_2, and m_3 are all constants. COBOL allows the FROM, TO and BY clauses to be in any order, so VARYING X BY 1 FROM Y TO Z is a legal statement.
- UNTIL c, where c is a condition. This recomputes c before every iteration, and if c is true, the loop stops. This may mean that the body of the loop is never entered, in spite of the syntax where the UNTIL clause is specified *after* the loop body. This is a type-3 loop.

ALGOL 60 uses a loop of the form

for i := *list* do s

where i is an index variable, *list* is a list of value specifiers separated by commas, and s is a statement. This loops assigns i to be the sequence of values specified by *list* and executes s for each of these in the order specified. The elements of *list* can each be one of the forms:

- An expression e. This is evaluated and used as the value of i.
- e_1 step e_2 until e_3. This makes i start with the value of e_1, stepping it by the value of e_2 and stopping when i is either greater than or equal to or smaller than or equal to e_3, depending on the sign of e_2. This works like the similar constructions in FORTRAN or COBOL, except that the step value can be negative, in which case the iteration continues until i is smaller than or equal to the value specified in the until clause. The ALGOL 60 report does not forbid the loop body to modify i.

- e_1 <u>while</u> e_2. This initially sets i to the value of e_1 and repeats the body (which may modify i) while e_2 is true, similarly to the UNTIL form of the COBOL loop, except that the condition is negated.

If all list elements are of the first form, the loop is a type-1 loop. Otherwise, it is a type-3 loop. Even the step-until form does not guarantee that the number of iterations is known before entering the loop, since the index variable can be modified inside the body of the loop, thereby changing the number of iterations required to reach the value specified in the <u>until</u> clause.

Pascal   has several different loop structures:

- while e do s evaluates e and if this is true, executes s and repeats from the top, re-evaluating e, executing s if e is still true, and so on, until e evaluates to false (if ever), in which case the loop exits. This is a type-3 loop.
- repeat s until e executes s and then evaluates e. If this is true, the loop exits, otherwise it repeats from the top, executing s and evaluating e, repeating until e becomes false, if ever. This is a type-3 loop.
- for $i := e_1$ to e_2 do s executes s with i having the values from e_1 up to e_2 inclusive. If $e_2 < e_1$, the loop exits without executing s. An alternative form uses downto instead of to, in which case i is decremented until it reaches the value of e_2, and the loop exits if $e_2 > e_1$. In neither case can the i be modified inside s, so this is a type-2 loop and also a type-1 loop if e_1 and e_2 are constants.

C   has equivalents of the while and repeat loops from Pascal, excepting syntactic differences and that C has negated forms of both loops, so a loop with the test before the body can repeat until the condition is true and a loop with the test after the body can repeat while the test is true. C additionally has a for loop of the form for $(e_1; e_2; e_3)$ s.
First, e_1 is executed, then e_2. If e_2 is false, the loop exits, otherwise the body s and the expression e_3 are executed. Then, the loop repeats from evaluating e_2, continuing until e_2 becomes false, if ever. This is obviously a type-3 loop.
Usually, e_1 initialises a variable and e_3 increments or decrements that variable, but they can be arbitrary expressions.d Note that, in C, assignments are expressions. A typical for-loop in C is of the form

```
for (i = 0; i<n; i ++) s
```

which makes i run through the values from 0 to $n-1$ in steps of 1, assuming i is not modified in s (which is allowed).
Java, C# and other descendants of C have the same loop structures as C and possibly more.
APL   Operators in APL can operate on all elements in a vector, so you can add all the elements of a vector or multiply two vectors without using an explicit

loop. Since the sizes of the vectors are known, this is a type-2 loop. APL also has unstructured jumps that can be used to implement type-3 loops.

Haskell,   being a pure functional language, doesn't have loops in the sense of FOR-TRAN, COBOL, ALGOL, Pascal or C, since these work by repeating execution of a state-modifying statement. Haskell, like most functional languages, uses recursion where imperative languages use loops, but Haskell has a looping structure called *list comprehensions*. A list comprehension builds a list by taking elements from other lists, filtering them by conditions, and operating on the resulting elements. As an example, the following list comprehension builds a list of all the pairwise sums of elements from the lists a and b that consist of two different values:

```
[i+j | i <- a, j <- b, i /= j]
```

i ranges over all the values in a, and for each value of i, j ranges over all the values in b. The condition i /= j ensures that i and j are different. Finally, the values of i+j are used to build a new list. If, for example, a = [1,3] and b = [3,4], the resulting list will be [1+3, 1+4, 3+4] = [4,5,7].

This comprehension in the example above is conceptually similar to (and designed to look like) the set comprehension $\{i + j \mid i \in a, j \in b, i \neq j\}$, except that it works on lists instead of sets, so the order of elements is important, as is the number of occurrences of each element.

Lists in Haskell are lazily evaluated, so their sizes may not be known in advance, and they may indeed not be finite. So this is actually a type-3 loop.

Loops of type 1 can be unrolled completely at compile time, which can make them run faster but also increases code size. Very long loops are typically not unrolled, but short loops often are.

Loops of type 1 and 2 are relatively easy to parallelise: If it can be verified that iterations are independent (i.e., that the computation that happens in one iteration is independent of the computations done in other iterations), some iterations can be computed on some processors at the same time that other iterations are computed on other processors. Vector processors are parallel processors where a large number of processing elements do the same thing, except on different data. These are ideally suited to run such loops in parallel. Early supercomputers were nearly all vector processors and were made to run FORTRAN programs very fast. Since the FORTRAN DO-loop is a type-2 loop, this is a good match. Modern graphics processors are also vector processors, and programming these is usually done by writing parallelisable type-1 or type-2 loops. The full-vector operations in APL (being implicit type-2 loops) are also amenable to running on vector processors.

Another property of type-1 and type-2 loops is that they are guaranteed to terminate. In addition to making reasoning about running times easier, it also allows running the code after the loop in parallel with the loop itself, to the extent that this code does not depend on the computations in the loop. It is not unusual for two loops where one is placed immediately after the other to be independent, so they can be executed in parallel.

Compilers can also optimise loops where an index variable increases by a constant amount in every iteration. For example, if the index variable is multiplied by a value inside the body of the loop, and that value does not change between iterations, the multiplication can be replaced by an addition. For example, the loop (using Pascal notation)

```
for i:=1 to n do
  a[i] := a[i] + K*i
```

can be optimised to

```
ki := 0;
for i:=1 to n do begin
  ki := ki + K;
  a[i] := a[i] + ki
end
```

Since multiplications are used to calculate offsets into arrays, this is a relatively common occurrence. This kind of optimisation is called "strength reduction" or "incrementalisation".

While type-1 and type-2 loops are easier to parallelise, optimise and reason about, type-3 loops are more powerful: There are computations where you cannot in advance predict the number of iterations required before a condition becomes true. We will return to this in Chaps. 10 and 12.

6.2.3 Whole-Collection Operations

APL was the first programming language to offer built-in operations that operate on whole collections instead of requiring element-by-element iteration. Modern languages often offer such whole-collection operations as library functions, list comprehensions, or other mechanisms.

There are several reasons to supply whole-collection operations:

- It can make programs shorter and more readable than programs using loops. For example, the APL code +/v adds all elements in the vector v, which is shorter than using an explicit loop, and (once you know the notation) also more readable.
- In an interpreted language implementation, whole-collections operations are faster because the looping structure does not need to be interpreted.
- The implementation has freedom to access elements in the collection in different orders and can even parallelise the computation.

There are in particular two kinds of function that are interesting for whole-collection operations:

1. Linear functions (also called *map homomorphisms*).
2. Homomorphic functions.

We illustrate these on lists, but the principles carry over to other collections. Lists are appended using the ++ operation (borrowing syntax from Haskell). In other types of collections, ++ may be an operation that concatenates to arrays or (multi)set union, as long as it is associative: a++$(b$++$c)$ = $(a$++$b)$++c. The empty list (usually denoted by [ ]) is the neutral element of ++, so [ ] ++ x=x=x ++ [ ]. In other collections, the neutral element of ++ can be the empty array or the empty (multi)set.

A function f is *linear* if $f(x$++$y) = f(x)$++$f(y)$. Since [ ] is a neutral element of ++, this implies $f([ ]) = [ ]$. A linear function is one that operates on all elements individually and combines the results using ++ to form a new list (or other collection). In functional languages, map and filter functions for lists and other collections are linear. It is trivial to parallelise a linear function: Different processes can work on different parts of the collection without interfering—as long as f does not have side effects.

A function f is *homomorphic* if there exists a value ι and an operation $\oplus$, such that $f([ ]) = \iota$ and $f(x$++$y) = f(x) \oplus f(y)$. This implies that $\oplus$ is associative and that $z \oplus \iota = z = \iota \oplus z$ for all values z in the range of f. Examples of homomorphic functions are

- Adding all elements in a collection: $\iota = 0$, f [x] $= x$, and $\oplus$ is +.
- Finding the maximal number in a collection: $\iota = minint$ (where $minint$ is the smallest representable integer), f [x] $= x$, and $\oplus = $ max.
- Finding the first value in a collection that fulfils a specified property (if any such value exists). We need an option type to represent the result, so if no value in the collection fulfils the property, we return NONE, and if there is a first value v that fulfils the property, we return SOME v (using ML-style notation for option types). We get $\iota = $ NONE, f [x] $= $ SOME x, and $\oplus$ is a function that given a pair where the first element is NONE, returns the second element, but otherwise returns the first element, i.e., fn (NONE, y) => y | (SOME x, y) => SOME x.
- Sorting: $\iota = $ [ ], f [x] $= $ [x] and $\oplus$ merges two sorted lists.

A homomorphic function f can be implemented by applying f to singleton lists for each element and then combining the results using $\oplus$. It is easy to parallelise, as different processes can operate on different parts of the collection and later communicate to combine their results. The *map-reduce* framework (used in, e.g, Hadoop) is based on homomorphic functions.

Note that, since ++ is associative, $\oplus$ must also be associative. This means that not all functions that are defined using foldl or foldr in Standard ML, fold or foldBack in F#, or / in APL are homomorphisms. For example, a function that reduces with the − operator is not a homomorphism, since − is not associative. It is, however, the case that if a function f can be defined *both* in terms of `foldl` and `foldr` (or `fold` and `foldBack`), then it is a homomorphism. It is, however, not always easy to find ⊕ from definitions of f using `foldl` and `foldr`. For example, you can define sorting as folding (left or right) a function `insert` that inserts a value into a sorted list. But ⊕ is a merge function, which is not obvious from the definitions using `insert`.

Suggested Exercise: 6.6.

6.2.4   Break and Continue

Many of the languages described above that support both jumps and structured control allow jumps to labels or line numbers outside the loop or other control structure from where the jump originates, but there is a somewhat more structured way to do this: Break statements.

As implemented in C and most other languages that support break statements, `break` jumps to right after the closest enclosing loop or multi-way branch (`switch`). It is easier to write and read than using explicit jumps because you don't need to write a label at the end of the loop/`switch` and because it is clear from the `break` statement that it is relatively local. In C, `break` cannot exit nested loops, but Java allows naming a loop and using this name in a `break` statement. This is a mix between explicit jumps and breaks with implicit destinations. An alternative is to allow a break to specify the number of nested control structures it exits, so `break 2` exits two nested loops. The scripting language Bash allows this.

C implements another semi-structured jump: If you inside a loop execute the `continue` statement, the program will immediately terminate the current iteration of the loop and continue at the next iteration, after updating loop variables and testing exit conditions. The effect is equivalent to an explicit jump to a label positioned at the end of the loop body (but still inside the loop). Bash allows `continue` to specify a number, so `continue 2` corresponds to a jump to the end of the body of the closest loop that is outside the current loop. This will skip all remaining iterations of the inner loop and start a new iteration of the outer loop.

It is somewhat inconsistent that, in C, `break` affects both `switch` and loops, while `continue` affects loops only. There is no meaningful way to apply `continue` to a `switch` statement, so the consistent thing to do would be to let `break` affect loops only (like in Bash) and use a different keyword to exit branches of a `switch` statement, or simply (as in most languages not derived from C), make this the default behaviour.

6.2.5   Structured Versus Unstructured Control

Since processors don't have structured control, compilers need to translate structured control into a combination of conditional and unconditional jumps. This is not very difficult and is covered in all compiler textbooks, so we will not go into details here. The converse is not so simple: Can any program using unstructured control be rewritten to use structured control only?

To investigate this, we look at a simple language that has labels (which are positive integers) and four kinds of jump:

- A simple unconditional jump goto l, where l is a label *or* a variable that holds a label.
- A conditional jump if c then l_1 else l_2, where c is a condition and l_1, l_2 are labels.
- A subroutine jump gosub l_1 then l_2, where l_1, l_2 are labels. This jumps to the subroutine l_1, which after completion will return to l_2. Usually, the return address of a subroutine call is implicit, but it makes it easier to express the translation if it is explicit.
- A return jump return that returns to the return label specified by the most recent active subroutine jump. Subroutines are recursive.

This covers (using different syntax) all the kinds of jumps we have looked at except indexed jumps, which can easily be simulated by a sequence of conditional jumps. We assume that the program starts at label 1 and that any jump to the label 0 (which is not used in the program) ends program execution. We divide the program into *basic blocks*, where each basic block starts with a label and ends with a jump and contains no labels or jumps between these.

We will translate this into a program that uses a repeat loop and a case statement. We use an array stack to hold return addresses. We assume this is large enough.

The overall form of the translated program (using Pascal notation) is

```
stackPointer := 0;
currentLabel := 1;
repeat
   case currentLabel of
     translated basic blocks
   end
until currentLabel = 0;
```

Each basic block l: s; j, where l is a label, s is a statement, and j is a jump, is translated into l: s; j', where l is now a case label, s is unchanged, and j' is the translation of j. We translate jumps as follows:

- goto l is translated to currentLabel   := l;. Note that l can be either a constant or a variable.

- `if` c `then` l_1 `else` l_2 is translated to
  `if` c `then` `currentLabel` `:=` l_1 `else` `currentLabel` `:=` l_2 `;`
- `gosub` l_1 `then` l_2 is translated to the block

```
begin
   stack[stackPointer] := l₂;
   stackPointer := stackPointer + 1;
   currentLabel := l₁;
end;
```

- `return` is translated to the block

```
begin
   stackPointer := stackPointer - 1;
   currentLabel := stack[stackPointer];
end;
```

Assigning labels to variables is done using normal assignment statements. All non-control statements are left unchanged.

The translation is not particularly efficient, since an extra variable is needed to hold the current label, and a case statement is needed to select the basic blocks. A case statement can be implemented using a lookup table that translates case labels into code addresses, so the overhead does not need to be very high.

But, apart from readability and ease of writing code, are there any advantages to using structured control? We mentioned earlier that certain optimisations can be applied to type-1 and type-2 loops, which seems to favour using these over unstructured control. But it is possible for compilers to recognise a type-1 or type-2 loop implemented using unstructured jumps, so it mainly just makes it easier for the compiler if such loops are explicitly structured. In fact, compilers can recognise structures in seemingly unstructured code, so it is mainly if unstructured code has a form that does not correspond to a combination of loops and branches that the compiler cannot apply structure-specific optimisations. So it is mainly programmers and readers of programs that benefit from structured control. An exception is dynamic control, i.e., jumps through variables. This can be all but impossible to analyse at compile time (and even harder for a human to follow), so this can seriously impede optimisation. This is one of the reasons assigned jumps in FORTRAN must specify the set of possible destinations: A static analysis will tend to over-approximate the set of possible destinations, but a programmer will have a pretty good idea about what these can be, and specifying this knowledge to the compiler can enable optimisations that are otherwise not possible. It can be hard to maintain the set of possible destinations if a program evolves, though: If a programmer adds a label assignment to the program, the programmer also has to add the label to all assigned jumps that might use this label, and that can be nontrivial to figure out. The result is often that labels are added to jumps that cannot, in fact, use these labels, resulting in over-approximation.

But even if only static control (jumps to constant labels) are used, this does not imply that parallelisation and optimisation is always possible: Data flow that is hard to analyse can seriously impede optimisation.

Suggested Exercise: 6.2.

6.3 Exceptions and Continuations

We have already looked at `break` that can exit control structures, but even when being able to exit multiple nested control structures, `break` cannot exit procedures.

In some languages (such as Pascal), explicit jumps can jump out of procedures. Since Pascal is block structured, the target of the jump must be in a statically enclosing procedure. The compiler can identify this procedure and generate code that follows the static link (see Chap. 5) to find the stack frame of this procedure, unstacks the frames on top of this, and then jumps to the address associated with the label.

Another mechanism that can jump out of procedures is *exceptions*, which we briefly covered in Chap. 5. Unlike out-of-procedure jumps in Pascal, an exception jumps to a dynamic destination, i.e., to a handler in the most recently called but not completed procedure that contains a handler. See Sect. 5.6 for details of how this can be implemented.

This means that the destination of an exception does not need to be in a statically enclosing procedure. In fact, it commonly is not, since exceptions are often used to signal error conditions: If a procedure is unable to provide a sensible result because the input (or other data) does not have the form required to do so, the procedure can raise an exception that can be handled by the caller. Exceptions can also be implicitly raised by in-built operations, for example when the program tries to follow a null pointer, address out of the range of an array, divide by zero or when an arithmetic operation would overflow.

An alternative to using exceptions for this purpose is to make procedures return an error indication instead of a normal result. In languages where almost any type includes null pointers by default, it is common to return null pointers as error indicators. But since null pointers are also used for other purposes (such as indicating empty lists or leaf nodes in a tree), this is not always possible. In C, it is common to let the result value of a function indicate success/error status and let the actual result be passed by reference through a parameter. In ML, Haskell and other functional languages, it is common to use an option/maybe type to indicate something that can either be a normal value or no value at all. In ML, both exceptions and option types are commonly used for signalling inability to produce normal results. Haskell does not support exceptions, as these make evaluation order observable, and many of the optimisations (such as strictness analysis) that Haskell use depend on the inability to observe the order of evaluation.

In addition to signalling errors, exceptions can also be used for backtracking: A recursive procedure that searches for a solution can first try one possibility, and if (possi-

```
exception Backtrack

// check if placement of a queen in row m
// is compatible with previously placed queens in qs
// d is distance between columns
let rec incompatible m qs d =
  match qs with
  | [] -> false
  | q :: qs -> m=q || abs(m-q)=d || incompatible m qs (d+1)

// n is board size, m is try for current column
// qs holds already placed queens in previous colums
let rec queens1 n m qs =
  if n = List.length qs then qs  // solution found
  else if m > n then raise Backtrack // m too high, backtrack
  else if incompatible m qs 1 // if current row doesn't work
       then queens1 n (m+1) qs  // try next row
  else
     try queens1 n 1 (m :: qs)  // add another queen
     // if that doesn't work, try next row
     with Backtrack -> queens1 n (m+1) qs

let queens n = queens1 n 1 []
```

Fig. 6.1 Using exceptions for backtracking to solve the N-queens problem

bly deep inside further recursions) finds that this possibility does not lead to a solution, raise an exception that is caught by a handler that will try another possibility. To illustrate this, Fig. 6.1 shows a program in F# that finds a solution to the N-queens problem.

6.3.1 Continuations

A *continuation* is an explicit representation of the potential remainder of the computation at a specific point during the execution of a program: At any given point during the computation, the *current continuation* represents all the work that needs to be done to complete execution. The current continuation includes the current program point (the address of the next instruction), the stack of return addresses, and all the data currently used by the program including global variables, stack-allocated variables and heap-allocated data. Given a data structure that represents the current continuation, it is possible to store this data structure somewhere, stop the execution, do something unrelated, read the data structure back in and set up program state to what this represents, and then restart computation from this state.

When an exception handler such as try s h, where s is the body of the try block and h is the handler (consisting of one or more catch clauses) is encountered during execution, a continuation is stored. This is not quite the current continuation but a continuation that holds the same information as the current continuation except that the program point is the start of the handler h instead of the start of the body s.

If no exception is raised the continuation is not used, and execution continues from the end of *s* to whatever code follows the `try` block. But if an exception is raised inside *s*, the current continuation at this point is replaced by the continuation stored by the `try` block, making execution continue in the handler *h*.

Usually, the continuation is represented by a *shallow copy*: the values of the registers and a pointer to the current top frame in the stack (which contains return addresses and values of local variables). This frame (and all frames below it) will still be on the stack when the exception is raised, so the stored continuation can be restored just by setting the current frame pointer to the stored frame pointer and restoring the saved registers. An observant reader will notice that the restored continuation will not be exactly that which was stored, because the values of global variables, local variables and heap-allocated data might have changed. Storing a continuation that will allow resumption in exactly the same state would require a *deep copy*: a copy of the entire state including global variables, stack and heap. This would be prohibitively expensive, so shallow copies with the implied inexact resumption of the continuation is accepted as the normal behaviour of exceptions. In a pure functional language, the stored continuation will not have been modified, so resumption will be exact even if only a shallow copy is stored.

6.3.1.1   First-Class Continuations

First-class continuation is a term used to indicate that a programmer can explicitly store the current continuation and invoke this at any later time.

C defines a library function `setjmp()` that stores the current continuation in a data structure (using shallow copying as described above). Another library function `longjmp()` invokes a continuation stored in a data structure.

Since only a shallow copy is stored, behaviour is undefined if a continuation is stored, the function that stored the continuation returns, and the continuation is later invoked.

While this is not required by the C99 standard, implementations of `setjmp()` usually copy the top frame rather than just a pointer to the top frame, making this a semi-deep copy. This allows a continuation to be invoked after the function is returned, but only if no further returns are made. This allows jumping back and forth between two or more active procedures, something called *coroutines*, which we will look at shortly.

If frames are stored in a garbage-collected heap rather than on a stack, a frame will be retained as longs as a pointer to this frame exists, even if the function that created the frame has returned. This allows a continuation to be invoked at any future point, regardless of subsequent calls and returns. Scheme was the first language to allow this fully flexible form of first-class continuations, using the function `call-with-current-continuation` that passes the current continuation to the argument function.

6.4   Function Calls as Control

If mutual recursion is allowed, a programmer can make code using func-
tion/procedure calls that is just as unstructured as code using jumps to labels. In
fact, it is easy to translate a program using jumps and labels to a program with mutually recursive procedures: Make one procedure for each basic block (see Sect. 6.2.5)
and then translate jumps to calls.

All the calls are at the end of a procedure, so nothing further happens in the
procedure after the call returns. Such calls are called *tail calls*. If all calls are tail
calls, no call returns until the last called function finishes, at which point all calls
return without doing anything further. Tail calls can be optimised to not use stack
space, so a compiler can translate the above back into jumps, making tail calls as
efficient as jumps and tail recursion as efficient as loops.

So if unstructured jumps can be translated into procedure calls, what makes pro-
cedure/function calls more structured than jumps?

The translation above uses procedures with no parameters and no results, so all
interaction between procedures is through global variables. So one possible answer
is that the ability to pass parameters and results allow more structured coding when
using functions than when using labels and jumps: While the control flow may be
equally hard to follow, the data flow is much easier to follow. This is particularly the
case in pure functional languages, where functions do not have side effects, so all
interaction with a function is through its parameters and results.

Another answer is that a function returns to its caller, which makes control easier to
follow. This is not really the case if all calls are tail calls, and a function return can be
bypassed by raising an exception, so a combination of function calls and exceptions
can be as difficult to follow as unstructured jumps. First-class continuation can make
control even more difficult to follow.

For this reason, John Backus (the main designer of FORTRAN) in his 1977 Turing
Award lecture [1] proposed a functional programming style and language (called
FP) without named variables and where explicit recursion is minimised. Control and
data flow is instead done using a set of predefined functions (including arithmetic
operators), a set of operators for function composition, and combining forms that
operate on vectors, similar to the APL vector operations. For example, a function for
computing the inner product of two vectors can be defined by

$$\textbf{Def } \text{IP} \equiv (/+) \circ (\alpha \times) \circ \text{trans}$$

$\circ$ is function composition, so $f \circ g$ will first apply g to a value and then pass its
result to f, so the operators will be applied right to left. Reading from the right,
trans transposes the input from a pair of two vectors into a vector of pairs. $(\alpha \times)$
applies multiplication $(\times)$ to all these pairs, and $(/+)$ reduces the resulting vector of
products into a single number using the $+$ operator.

While this style of completely avoiding named parameters and explicit recursion
has not caught on, most modern functional languages include many of the composition operators and combining forms proposed by Backus, such as mapping a function
over the elements of a list of vector (equivalent to the α operator in FP), reducing a

list or vector using a binary operator (equivalent to /), zipping two vectors or lists (equivalent to trans), and so on. List comprehensions are also a way to reduce explicit recursion in functional programs.

In summary, recursive functions and procedures can lead to code that is as unstructured and unreadable as code using jumps and labels. Structure and readability can be improved by using parameters and results instead of side effects and by using operators that apply functions to whole data structures instead of using explicitly recursive functions that walk these data structures.

6.5 Multithreading

Multithreading is a way to construct a program out of multiple *threads* that take turns executing in such a way that one thread can pass control to another before it is finished and later resume where it left off. There are various mechanisms for this, which we will look at below.

Note that multithreading does not imply parallelism: Parallelism can exist without multithreading, and multithreading can exist without parallelism. For example, parallel execution of a loop is not multithreaded (as only one program point is active), and coroutines (which we cover below) are not parallel.

6.5.1 Coroutines

Coroutines is a mechanism that allows a procedure A to pass control to another procedure B, which at a later time can make procedure A resume. The difference between this and procedure calls is that procedure B does not need to finish before passing control back to A: It can do so at any time, and when A again passes control to B, B resumes at the point it was before passing control to A.

This can make two procedures take turns using resources such as a printer. The following example declares two coroutines and calls the first using the keyword resume. The two coroutines pass control back and forth until one of them returns.[1]

```
coroutine A
{
   print "Twas brillig, and the slithy toves";
   resume B;
   print "All mimsy were the borogoves,";
   resume B;
}
```

---

[1] Text taken from Lewis Carroll's poem "Jabberwocky".

```
coroutine B
{
  print "Did gyre and gimble in the wabe:";
  resume A;
  print "And the mome raths outgrabe.";
  resume A;
}


resume A;
```

Executing the program will print the text

```
Twas brillig, and the slithy toves
Did gyre and gimble in the wabe:
All mimsy were the borogoves,
And the mome raths outgrabe.
```

Any number of procedures can pass control to each other in this way.

Used this way, coroutines can implement what is called *cooperative multitasking*, where multiple threads run concurrently and explicitly pass control to each other in contrast to *preemptive multitasking*, where an outside agent can pause any thread at any time to pass control to another.

If no recursion is allowed, coroutines can be implemented by giving each coroutine a globally allocated frame for its local variables and resume address. If recursion is allowed, each coroutine needs its own stack. Alternatively, if frames are heap allocated and explicitly linked as described in Sect. 6.3.1.1, this will allow recursive coroutines. In fact, first-class continuations can be used to implement coroutines.

A variant of coroutines are called *generators*. A generator is called (usually with keywords resume or next), but instead of passing control to an explicitly named coroutine using another resume, it returns a value using the keyword yield, which passes control back to the caller. The difference between resuming a generator and calling a function is that the generator is resumed at the place from which it yielded instead of starting over. This can be used, for example, to implement a random-number generator:

```
generator random
{
  int seed = 1111;
  while true do {
    seed := (seed * 8121 + 28411) mod 134456;
    yield seed;
  }
}
```

```
print next random;
print next random;
print next random;
print next random;
```

This will give the output

```
42290
64877
95920
91123
```

A generator is a mixture of a normal function and a coroutine, as a generator will return a value to its caller (like a normal function) but resume at the point where it yielded control (like a coroutine).

Another variant of coroutines is called *cooperative multitasking*. Like in normal coroutines or generators, a routine will explicitly give control to another routine, but it does not specify which. So instead of passing control to an explicit other routine using `resume` or return to a caller using `yield`, it will simply say `pause`. This means that the current routine will stop until control is passed back to it, at which point it will resume at the point after the `pause` statement. The run-time system of the program will maintain a queue of waiting routines. When a routine pauses, it will be put at the end of this queue, and the first routine in the queue will get the control, so the routines are executed in a round-robin fashion.

6.5.2 Threads

A *thread* is a computation that runs simultaneously with other computations in the same program. This does not imply that these computations physically happen at the same time, it can just mean that the computations take turns to proceed, just like coroutines do. In fact, coroutines are threads that explicitly pass control to other threads, so at any one time at most one thread is active.

A more interesting case is when control is not passed or given up explicitly but is controlled by an outside agent such as the operating system or the runtime system of a programming language implementation. Threads can be stopped and resumed at any time during their execution (with a few exceptions, which we will see below) and might even be running in parallel on different processors.

We classify multithreaded systems by whether or not they share mutable state. If they share mutable state, two threads can communicate by writing to and reading from this state, but there is also a need of synchronisation so one thread does not read from the shared state while another has only partially updated the state. If, for example, the state is a number of variables that must have a constant sum, and one thread has subtracted a value from one of these but not yet added it to another,

another thread that adds up the variables will get an incorrect sum. Even worse is if two threads write to the same variable: The final value of the variable depends on which thread writes first. This is called a *race condition*. Note that neither are issues with coroutines, as a coroutine can ensure that the shared state is consistent before passing control to another. We will look at various synchronisation methods below. If threads do not share mutable state, they need some other way to communicate, such as by passing messages between them. We will also look at this later.

6.5.2.1 Synchronisation Mechanisms

The shared state can consist both of variables and other resources such as i/o channels. In either case, unsynchronised use of these resources can lead to errors such as inconsistent memory states or two texts being intermingled in random order in a file or on a printer. Hence, we want threads to have *mutually exclusive* access to these resources, meaning that only one thread at a time has access to a resource, so other threads must wait until this thread has finished using the resource. This can lead to situations where two threads both wait for the other thread to release a resource. This is called a *deadlock*. It can be difficult to decide if a multithreaded program can result in deadlock when running, but it is often easy to detect when it *has* happened: If thread A is waiting to access a resource X that thread B has exclusive access to, and at the same time B is waiting to access a resource Y that A has exclusive access to, there is a deadlock. There is, however, no easy fix: If either thread is forced to release its resource, this might be in an inconsistent state, so if a deadlock is detected, the usual response is to stop the program with an error message.

Synchronisation between threads that share resources is usually done through *semaphores*.

In its simplest instance, a semaphore is a Boolean variable that signals whether a resource is in use or not: If the value is true, some thread is using the resource, and if it is false, it is available for any thread to grab.

If a thread wants to access a resource, it tests if the semaphore is false, and if this is the case it sets it to true, uses the resource, and resets the semaphore to false. However, it might happen that two threads test the semaphore at the same time, both finding it to be false, both setting it to true, and both using the resource, which is what we wanted to avoid. Therefore, testing and setting a semaphore must be a single, atomic operation that cannot be interrupted by another thread.

With an atomic test-and-set operation, a thread can check if the resource is available, use it if it is, and do something else if not. If it gains the resource, it operates on it and then *releases* it by setting the semaphore to false.

But it is often the case that the thread cannot do something sensible until it has access to the resource, so it will repeatedly test the semaphore until it is available, which is called *busy waiting*. For this reason, semaphores often offer a *wait* operation instead of test-and-set: If a thread waits on a resource, it is suspended until it can gain exclusive access to the resource. This makes the semaphore a queue instead of a bit: When a thread waits, it is put at the end of the queue. When the resource is free, the thread at the front of the queue (if any) is activated. When this releases the resource, the next thread in the queue is activated, and so forth. Threads can be given priorities so a high-priority thread can push itself in front of low-priority threads in the queue. This is implemented using a *priority queue*.

While a semaphore can be used for *synchronising* access to a resource, it does not enforce *exclusive* access unless a thread cannot access to the resource unless it has checked the semaphore first. Also, if threads fail to release resources, this can prevent other threads from accessing the resource and ultimately lead to deadlocks. So it is common to encapsulate a resource in an abstraction that waits for access, performs a limited set of operations on the resource, and releases it again, thus both enforcing exclusive access and preventing overlong claims on a resource. One such mechanism is a *monitor*: A monitor is similar to a static class: It has fields (representing resources) and methods for accessing and modifying the fields. The monitor allows only one method to be active at any one time (using a semaphore to do so) and requires methods to be designed in a such a way that the resources are left in a consistent state when a method finishes (which releases the monitor). What it means for a state to be consistent depends on the resource, so there is no way for a programming language to ensure this. But it restricts the code that must be verified for consistency to the methods in the monitor.

6.5.3 Message Passing

With message passing, there are no explicitly shared resources: Every resource is by scoping local to a thread. Instead, the threads communicate by sending messages to each other. A message is usually a piece of data, but messages can also be identifiers for threads or mailboxes (see below). Threads that do not share resources are often called *processes*.

Messages are sent and received through *mailboxes*. A mailbox holds a queue of messages, so the oldest messages are by default read first. But it is also possible to assign priorities to messages, so they are read in order of priority (preserving the order of messages that have the same priority). The difference is whether a mailbox is a simple queue or a priority queue. In some cases, each thread has its own mailbox for incoming messages and on other cases mailboxes are independent entities that can be shared by multiple threads.

Message passing is categorised as *synchronous* or *asynchronous*. With synchronous message passing, a thread that sends a message to another is suspended until the message has been read by the receiver. This is similar to waiting on a semaphore and is implemented in a similar way: A thread that sends a message is suspended and entered in the queue, and is activated when it (and its message) is removed from the front of the queue.

With asynchronous message passing, the thread can continue as soon as the message is sent. The mailbox is still a queue and can still use priorities, but only the messages are queued. The sending thread can not see when (or if) the message is read.

Asynchronous message passing can emulate synchronous message passing by making the sender wait for acknowledgement of receipt, which the receiver sends as it reads the message. Synchronous message passing can emulate asynchronous message passing by building a queue out of threads each with their own mailbox: When a thread in the queue reads a message, it will immediately send it to the next thread in the queue, which does the same, until the last thread in the queue sends it to the actual receiver mailbox. The original sender can continue as soon as the first thread in the queue reads the message, which will be almost immediately unless the queue is full. The main difference is performance: If threads are distributed on multiple processors or even over a network, synchronous message passing can require a thread to wait a long time for acknowledgement of receipt even if the receiver has an empty mailbox.

Occam and C# are examples of languages that implement synchronous message passing, in C# by using the *send* function. C# also implements semi-asynchronous message passing: The *asend* function does not wait for the receiver to read the message, but it does wait for the receiver to indicate whether it intends to read it at a later time.

There is similarly a choice whether a receiver that tries to read a message can continue if there are no messages in its mailbox. or it must wait until a message arrives. To avoid busy waiting, it is common to make the receiver wait, even if message passing is otherwise asynchronous, but a receiver is often allowed to wait for messages from several mailboxes at the same time. C# has functions for both cases: `receive` waits for a message to arrive, while `try_receive` returns immediately even if the mailbox is empty.

Erlang and Scala are examples of languages that implement asynchronous message passing. In Scala, threads that communicate by message passing are called *actors*. Scala also supports synchronous message passing, though this is implemented by asynchronous message passing and hand-shaking. Both Erlang and Scala allow threads to be created by other threads and passed as messages to other threads. For example, a thread can build a buffer out of new threads it creates and send identifiers for the end points of this buffer to two other threads that thereafter can use the buffer to communicate between each other.

Regardless of whether message passing is synchronous or asynchronous, deadlocks can occur if two threads are waiting for messages from each other.

Another design choice is whether messages are shallow or deep copies of data: With shallow copying, only a pointer to structured data is transferred, while deep copying will send a complete description of the data to the receiver. Shallow copying will only work if the sender and the receiver share a single memory space, but it is more efficient than deep copying if this is the case. Shared memory scales badly to a large number of parallel processes, though. Deep copying is more expensive than shallow copying (unless messages are small) but can allow sender and receiver to be on different computers and to use different internal representation of the data. Separate memory for different processors scales better than shared memory.

6.6 Exercises

Exercise 6.1 Consider the following restriction to labels: Only one jump (conditional or unconditional) may exist to any single label in the program. In essence, jumps and labels are paired, so every label occurs exactly two times in the program: Once in a jump and once as a label definition (i.e., as a destination).

Discuss advantages and disadvantages of this restriction.

Exercise 6.2 Section 6.2.5 describes a method for translating unstructured control to structured control. Use this to translate the following unstructured statement to a structured statement.

```
1: f := 1; t := 3;
   gosub 2 then 0
2: if n=0 then 6 else 3
3: n := n-1; t := 6-f-t;
   gosub 2 then 4
4: t := 6-f-t;
   writeln("from ", f, " to ", t);
   f := 6-f-t;
   gosub 2 then 5
5: n := n+1; f := 6-f-t;
   goto 6
6: return
```

Exercise 6.3 Convert the unstructured code from Exercise 6.2 to a recursive procedure `hanoi` that has n, f and t as parameters, and an initial call to `hanoi`. Avoid using assignments to variables—use expressions such as `n-1` and `6-f-t` only as argument expressions. You can use structured control statements (such as if-then-else) but you can not add extra variables. You can use C, Pascal, ML, Python, or whatever syntax you want, including pseudocode, as long as the syntax includes recursive procedures with parameters.

Exercise 6.4 Consider the following form of loop for functional languages like ML, Scala and F#: $\text{loop } f \ e$, where (for some type t) f has type $t \rightarrow t$ and e has type t, first evaluates e to a value v_0 and gives v_0 as an argument to f. If the evaluation of $(f \ v_0)$ throws an exception (of any kind), v_0 is returned as the result of the loop. If $(f \ v_0)$ returns a value v_1, this is passed as argument to f, and if $(f \ v_1)$ throws an exception, v_1 is returned from the loop, otherwise the result v_2 of $(f \ v_1)$ is passed to f, and so on.

So f is called repeatedly, passing its result in as a new argument, until the evaluation throws an exception, at which point the latest argument to f is returned.

a. Is this loop a type-1 loop, a type-2 loop, or a type-3 loop? Why?

b. Define a non-recursive function gcdStep such that loop gcdStep (a,b) returns the pair $(g, 0)$, where g is the greatest common divisor of a and b. You can assume that division by zero or getting the remainder of division by zero throws an exception.

Exercise 6.5 Consider a variant of the C language where there is no distinction between expressions and statements. This means that structures that in C are statements that do not return values must now be allowed as expressions and, hence, must be extended to return values. Exceptions to this requirement are statements that change the place of execution to elsewhere (such as return, break, and continue), but the behaviour of these may need to be modified to ensure that other statements do return values.

For example, a C assignment $x = e$ is allowed as an expression and returns the value of e, which must have the same type as x. We want to extend this to all statement types.

Note that while C defines a default value for all type (such as 0 for integers, a null pointer for pointer types, and 0.0 for floats), we want to use default values as results of statements only if no other reasonable option exists. In other words, the value of a statement s is preferably the value of an expression or (sub)statement in s, even if we have to modify the syntax of the statement to ensure this. Only if there are no sensible ways to modify the statement syntax will we use default values.

Since empty statements do not have subexpressions, substatements, or default values, we do not allow these in the language.

Consider the following C statements and discuss how these can be extended or restricted (by modifying syntax and/or imposing restrictions to the types of expressions or statements) to ensure that they always (if they return at all) return a value of a well-defined type, and what that value and type is. You can use informal descriptions like in the description of the assignment statement above. Discuss for each case whether using default values is the most sensible choice and, if so, which default value.

As an example, we consider a block $\{s_1, \ldots, s_n\}$. Empty blocks are equivalent to empty statements, which we do not allow, so we restrict blocks to contain at least one statement, i.e., $n > 0$. The value a block returns could be the value of any statement in the block, but it seems most natural to let it be the value of the last statement in the block, i.e., the value of s_n. The type of the block is thus the type of s_n. Use similar reasoning below, and allow yourself to be inspired by functional languages where conditionals and loops are expressions.

a. if (e) s_1 else s_2
b. if (e) s
c. do s while (e)
   Consider if and how break and continue statements should be modified to ensure a well-defined return value of a well-defined type for loops that contain break or continue statements.
d. while (e) s

Consider if and how `break` and `continue` statements should be modified to ensure a well-defined return value of a well-defined type for loops that contain `break` or `continue` statements.

e. `while (e) s`

Consider if and how `break` and `continue` statements should be modified to ensure a well-defined return value of a well-defined type. Are the modifications (if any) the same as above?

f. `switch (e) {case statements}`, where a case statement is of the form `case c:s`, where c is a constant expression and s is a statement, or of the form `default : s`. A default clause is optional in switch statements in C. If a default clause is included, it must be the last case statement in the `switch` statement.

Note that the statements in *all* case statements after the selected case statement are executed, unless a `break` statement explicitly exits the `switch` statement. We want to preserve this behaviour.

Consider if and how `break` statements should be modified to ensure a well-defined return value of a well-defined type. Is the modification (if any) the same as for the loops above?

Exercise 6.6 Section 6.2.3 considers whole-collection operations such as maps, folds and filters. In particular, it considers *linear* and *homomorphic* functions. In the following, we assume collections are lists.

a. Show that a linear function is also homomorphic.

b. Argue which of the following functions are linear, homomorphic, or neither. When they are homomorphic, describe what ι and $\oplus$ are. These should be sufficiently precise that you can define the function by a rule for f `[x]`, and the rules f `[]` $= \iota$ and $f(xs\text{++}ys) = f\ xs \oplus f\ ys$, where the definition of $\oplus$ does not use f.

For example, if `maximal` is the function that returns all elements in a list that have the maximal value in the list (so `maximal [2,3,0,1,3]` should return `[3,3]`), then you cannot just define $x \oplus y = maximal(x\text{++}y)$, since that could cause infinite recursion. A suitable definition could be

$$
\begin{aligned}
\iota &= [] \\
\texttt{maximal } [x] &= [x] \\
xs \oplus [] &= xs \\
[] \oplus ys &= ys \\
(x\texttt{::}xs) \oplus (y\texttt{::}ys) &= \begin{cases} y\texttt{::}ys, & \text{if } x < y \\ (x\texttt{::}xs)\text{++}(y\texttt{::}ys), & \text{if } x = y \\ x\texttt{::}xs, & \text{if } x > y \end{cases}
\end{aligned}
$$

- The function `length` that returns the length of a list. For example, `length [2,3,0,1,3]` should return 5.
- A function `primes` that return all prime numbers from a list of integers. For example, `primes [2,3,0,1,3]` should return `[2,3,3]`.

- A function `singletons` that returns the list of values that occur exactly once in the argument list. For example, `singletons [2,3,0,1,3]` should return `[2,0,1]`.
- A function `different` that returns the list of different values in the argument list in the order of their first occurrence. For example, `different [2,3,0,1,3]` should return `[2,3,0,1]`.
- The `reverse` function that reverses the order of elements in a list. For example, `reverse [2,3,0,1,3]` should return `[3,1,0,3,2]`.
- The function `oddlength` that returns `true` if the length of its input list is odd and `false` of the length is even.. For example, `oddlength [2,3,0,1,3]` should return `true`.
- A function `last` that returns the last element in a list of integers, and 0 if the list is empty. For example, `last [2,3,0,1,3]` should return 3. and `last []` should return 0.

Exercise 6.7 As in exercise 6.6, argue which of the following functions are linear, homomorphic, or neither.

a. A function `upToLength` that takes a list of integers of length n and returns the list of integers from 1 to n. For example, `upToLength [] = []`, and `upToLength [3, 17, 11, 5]` should return `[1, 2, 3, 4]`.
b. A function `everyOther` that takes a list of values and returns a list of every other element of that list (i.e., the first element, the third element, the fifth element, and so on). For example, `everyOther ['e', 'v', 'e', 'r', 'y']` should return `['e', 'e', 'y']`.
c. A function `returnEmpty` that takes any list and returns the empty list (no matter what the input is).
d. A function `appendAll` that takes a list of lists and returns a single list that is obtained by appending all the lists in the input list. For example, `appendAll [[1], [4, 2], [], [1]]` should return `[1, 4, 2, 1]`.
e. A function `sorted` that takes a list of integers and returns a list using the following rules:

  - If the list is empty, it should return the empty list. I.e., `sorted [] = []`.
  - If the list is sorted, it returns a list containing two elements: The smallest and the largest element in the list. For example, `sorted [1, 3, 3, 7]` should return `[1, 7]`, and `sorted [5]` should return `[5, 5]` (as 5 is both the smallest and largest element).
  - If the list is not empty and not sorted, it should return a list of one element, which is the first element of the list. For example, `sorted [1, 3, 2, 7]` should return `[1]`.

Exercise 6.8 The function that finds the average of a list of numbers is not homomorphic (see Sect. 6.2.3). Show this (by example).

The average function can, however, be implemented by applying a homomorphic function to the list and afterwards applying a constant-time operation on the result of this. Show how to do this.

Exercise 6.9 A program is said to be *deterministic* if several executions of the program with the same input will always yield the same output. Conversely, a program is *nondeterministic* if this is not always true.

(a) Discuss for each of the multithreading mechanisms described in Sect. 6.5 whether or not it can *introduce* nondeterminism (if no other feature is nondeterministic), and why/why not.
(b) Discuss which strategies you can employ for testing nondeterministic programs.

Reference

1. Backus J (1978) Can programming be liberated from the von Neumann style?: A functional style and its algebra of programs. Commun ACM 21(8):613–641. https://doi.org/10.1145/359576.359579

Types

7

The beautiful has but one type, the ugly has a thousand.
Victor Hugo
Well-typed programs don't go wrong.
Robin Milner

In a programming language context, *types* are used to distinguish values that have different properties. The main reason for using types is to avoid errors: If a value is used in a context where it is expected to have a certain property, and it does not have that property, this is an error. Conceptually, it is an error even if it does not lead to an error message: It is an error in the logic of the program, just like adding apples and oranges and expecting bananas is a logical error.

Above, we use "value" in a broad meaning. Types are often used about elements that cannot (in the language in question) be used as values, such as procedures or modules.

A simple view of types is that a type represents a set of values, and a value is said to be of that type if it is an element of the set. For example, the type int can, in some languages, represent the set of all integers that can be represented as 64-bit two's complement binary numbers and in other languages the infinite set of all integers. If int represents the set of all integers, type int $\rightarrow$ int represents the set of all (partial) functions from integers to integers, which is not only an infinite set, but an uncountably infinite set. If we limit the set to the set of computable functions, it becomes countable, but it is difficult to work with concepts such as computability using set theory.

It is even more problematical if types can be recursive: The ML-style data type

```
datatype ff = I of int | F of (ff --> ff)
```

T. Ægidius Mogensen, *Programming Language Design and Implementation*,
Texts in Computer Science, https://doi.org/10.1007/978-3-031-11806-7_7

does not even represent a well-founded set, so we get into paradoxes like the set of all sets that do not contain themselves (Russell's paradox). To remedy this, a branch of mathematics called "domain theory" has been established, so types represent *domains* instead of sets. Domains are similar to sets but have different properties that allow well-defined recursive definitions.

So while thinking of types as representing sets of values is useful for simple types, it can be problematical for complex types, in particular for recursive types or types of mutable arrays. For more complex types, it is more useful to think of a type as representing a finite set of *properties* or *operations* that exist for elements of the type: The type int $\rightarrow$ int, for example, is represented by the property that something of type int $\rightarrow$ int can be applied to something of type int to give a result of type int. Since, for example, addition is not a property of the type int $\rightarrow$ int, we cannot add two functions nor add a function to an integer.

A *type system* is a set of rules for determining if an operation in a program violates the properties associated with types. These rules can be applied either before the program is executed (static type checking), while the program is running (dynamic type checking), or a combination of both. We will look at formalisms for type systems in Chap. 11.

We can classify type systems by how and when they are applied:

Static   type systems apply their rules before the program is executed (i.e., at compile time).

Dynamic   type systems apply their rules while the program is running (i.e., at runtime).

Strong   type systems verify that *none* of the properties associated with a type are violated.

Weak   type systems allow some (or even all) of the properties associated with a type to be violated.

Explicit   type systems assume that names (or values) in a program are explicitly specified to have specific types, and verify that the names (or values) are not used in a way that conflict with the properties of the specified types. Type checking can be done either prior to execution (for static types, where types of names are specified)) or during execution (for dynamic types, where types of values are specified).

Implicit   type systems do not need declarations for names or values in the program but will find types for these that avoid violations of properties at runtime. Doing this prior to execution is called *type inference*.

Many type systems combine several of these concepts. For example, Java uses a mostly static type system (as types are nominally checked at compile time), but downcasts and element types of arrays are type-checked dynamically at runtime (see Sect. 7.4.3). C does all its type checking at compile time, so it is a pure static type system. But some properties are not checked at all: For example, a pointer to a function can be cast into a pointer to an integer, which allows the program to add an integer to a function, which violates the property that addition is not defined for functions. So the type system for C is somewhat weak. C# allows types of local variables to be omitted as long as the variables are initialised, so some types are inferred, but most types in C# must be explicitly declared. Standard ML and Haskell infer the types of all variables and functions, but they both require types of constructors in datatypes to be declared. So while types are mostly inferred, a few are just checked, but all type checking is done at compile time, making Standard ML and Haskell purely statically typed. In fact, many implementations of Standard ML use *type erasure*: After types are inferred/checked, all type information is discarded because it is not needed anymore. Some implementations use the type information for optimisations during compilation, though. Scheme tags values with types and checks the tags before applying an operation to ensure that the operation is defined for the involved types. So it is a strong type system, but entirely dynamic.

If the purpose of type systems is to detect errors, strong type systems are clearly better than weak type systems, but strong type systems can be more costly in terms of compile time or execution time than weak type systems. Given that a static and a dynamic type system detects the same errors, it is better to do so statically, to detect errors early. But static type systems may be more restrictive than dynamic type systems. For example, static type systems usually require all elements of an array to have the same type, but a program using dynamic types can, without errors, use an array where every odd element is a string and every even element a number. You can say that static type systems can have false negatives, but can provide positive guarantees for all future executions, where dynamic type systems can not provide any guarantees for future executions. Type inference relieves the programmer from the burden of specifying types and, especially, to modify these specifications when a program is rewritten to use a different type to represent a value. But type specifications can work as partial documentation, so they (to some extent) help a reader understand a program. Additionally, some properties can be checked but not inferred, as inference can be undecidable. For example, combining polymorphism with subtyping makes inference undecidable while statically checking specified types that combine polymorphism and subtyping is decidable.

Programming languages can be *untyped*. This means that all operations are valid on all values. This differs from weak types, where some operations are (at least logically) invalid on some values, but violations are not caught. The pure lambda calculus is an example of an untyped language, and many machine languages can be viewed as untyped: All values are machine words and all instructions work for all possible machine words. So operations are only logically invalid if we apply an outside interpretation on what specific machine words represent.

7.1 Checking Types

Dynamic type checking is the simplest form of type checking: Every value in the program is paired with a type descriptor. Whenever an operation is performed on a value, the type descriptor is checked to see if the operation is valid on the value, and whenever an operator produces a new value, it pairs it with a type descriptor.

A type descriptor can be anything from a single bit to an explicit list of properties such as a list of the operations allowed for values of this type, and even pointers to code that implements these operations. We will look at this in more detail in Sect. 7.4.1.1.

Static type checking is often done as *pseudo evaluation* (a term coined by Peter Naur): Evaluating expressions and executing statements on non-standard values, such as type descriptors.

For example, an expression is evaluated with variables bound to type descriptors instead of values. An operation calculates a new type descriptor for its result from the type descriptors of its arguments, reporting errors if the operation is not valid on the argument types.

The type descriptors that names are bound to are usually derived from the declarations of these names, but it is also possible to type-check if variables do not need to have declared types: When a variable is assigned to or initialised, it is given the type found by pseudo evaluating the expression that gives the variable its value. This is often called *type inference*. Two complications can occur:

1. A variable is used before it is given a value.
2. A variable is given different types in different parts of the program.

The simplest solution to the first problem is to report an error, but it is also possible to give the variable a default type, such as integer, under the assumption that most values are integers. This can lead to misleading error messages if the variable is, in fact, not used as an integer. Another option is to give the variable an unspecified type (using a *type variable*) which is filled in later, when and if the context in which the variable is used mandates a specific type or specific properties of the type. If no context demands anything of the type of the variable, it can safely be left unspecified or parametric (see Sect. 7.4.4).

If, say, different branches of a conditional give different types to the same variable, what is the type of the variable after these branches join? The simplest possibility is to make this an error, but it can sometimes be possible to find a type that is compatible with the different types of the different branches. For example, if one branch leaves the type unspecified, the type found in the other branch can be used. If the language uses subtyping (see Sect. 7.4.3), a type that is a supertype of the types used in the branches can be used. For example, if a variable in one branch is given an integer type and in the other branch a floating-point type, the variable can after the join be given a floating-point type. This may require a type conversion, see Sect. 7.2.

A similar problem occurs with loops: If different iterations of a loop give different types to the same variable, this is an error unless the types can be reconciled in the way we described for branches. A common case is that a variable has an unspecified type before pseudo evaluating the body of the loop and is given a type during this evaluation. The loop is then re-evaluated with the variable bound to this type. If this does not change the type of the variable, pseudo evaluation of the loop stops. But if the variable has a different type, we can try to reconcile this with the previous type. If this is possible, we reevaluate with the reconciled type, otherwise we report an error message. To avoid infinite loops during type evaluation, there should not be an infinite number of different types that can be reconciled this way. For example, a subtype hierarchy should be of finite height to avoid an infinite chain of ever-larger (in the hierarchy) types.

Some languages use both static and dynamic type checking. Java and other object-oriented languages do static type checking but still have values carry type descriptors (class descriptors) at run-time. These are used both to find implementations of the operators defined for the value, to check downcasts (dynamic type checking), and to perform superclass calls.

Another way of combining static and dynamic type checking is called *soft typing*. Soft typing is type inference for a dynamically typed language, but made in such a way that it does not reject programs as faulty, but instead inserts dynamic type checks only where the type inference cannot determine the type. Additionally, the types inferred by soft typing (and the inserted dynamic checks) can be used to give feedback to the programmer, who can use this information to detect errors. Even when not used to give feedback to the programmer, many compilers for dynamically typed languages use soft typing for optimisation.

Suggested Exercises: 7.5.

7.2 Type Conversion

Values of one type can sometimes be converted to values of another type, which is called type conversion or type casting. This can be explicit (written in the program text) or implicit (not written in the program text), and it can either be an identity conversion (the representation of the value does not change) or by using code to convert the value to a different representation.

Examples of explicit conversions are downcasts or when a floating-point value is converted to an integer through truncation or rounding. Examples of implicit conversions are automatic conversion of an integer to a floating-point value when an integer is added to a floating-point number, or when an object of class A is passed to a method that expects an object of a superclass of A.

Downcasts and superclass conversions are usually identity conversions: The representation of the value does not change. Conversion from integer to floating point requires a change of representation, since an integer is not represented in the same way as the floating-point value that has the same magnitude.

Additionally, type conversions can be *safe* or *unsafe*. A safe conversion means that the converted value is guaranteed to have all the properties associated with the type it is converted to, and that the conversion can always happen. An unsafe conversion can either fail, or it can be incomplete, which can lead to errors later on, which may or may not be detected.

Converting an integer to a floating-point value is normally safe (if the range of floating-point values is larger than the range of integers), but precision can be lost. This is normally not regarded as a type error, though. Using an object at a supertype is also safe, but downcasts can fail, so they are not safe. Converting (in C) a void-pointer to a function pointer is definitely unsafe: Unless the void-pointer happens to point to a function, all sorts of errors can occur. In fact, most explicit type casts in C are unsafe.

Some languages (like Standard ML) require all type conversions to be explicit, while some (like Pascal) only require unsafe conversions to be explicit. Some (such as Java and C#) allow some unsafe conversions to be implicit.

7.3 Atomic and Composite Types

Types are either *atomic* (representing a simple value such as a number, a character, or Boolean value) or *composite*, meaning that they are composed of several other types, which themselves may be simple or composite. At some level, all values stored on a computer can be broken down into bits, but we do not consider this a reason to classify as composite all values that require multiple bits to represent. In a high-level language, values such as integers or floating point values are considered atomic, even though you can observe the bit patterns used to represent them.

We will here look at various forms of atomic and composite types.

7.3.1 Numbers

Mathematics operate with many kinds of numbers: Natural numbers, integers, rational numbers, real numbers, complex numbers, and so on. Normally, natural numbers are seen as a subset of integers, integers as a subset of rational number, rational numbers as a subset of real numbers, and real numbers as a subset of complex numbers.

Mathematical integers are unbounded and mathematical reals have infinite precision, so it is not possible to represent all integers or all real numbers precisely on a computer. Consequently, types called `integer` or `real` in a programming language will rarely correspond to the set of mathematical integers or real numbers.

Integers are typically bounded to what can fit in a machine word, so the range of integers can be machine-dependent and differ across different implementations of the same language. Some languages mandate a minimum range for the integer type, while others just require that a running program can detect the range of integers on the machine on which it is running. For example, Pascal requires that the constant `maxint` is defined and that all integers between `-maxint` and `maxint` are representable in the `integer` type. Some languages implement several different integer types with different ranges. Pascal, for example, allows arbitrary intervals of integers as types as long as the interval is a subrange of the interval represented by the `integer` type. For example, Pascal allows a variable to be declared to have the type `-3..7`, which allows it to have only integers in the range -3 to 7, so if a value outside this range is given to the variable, an error is reported. C defines the types `char`, `short`, `int` and `long` and unsigned variants of these. `char` is at least 8 bits in size, `short` and `int` are at least 16 bits, and `long` is at least 32 bits. Some C implementations define a `long long` type that is at least 64 bits in size. C also defines types that have an exact number of bits, such as `int32_t`, which denotes 32-bit signed numbers using two's complement representation. The `sizeof` operator will, given a type, return the number of bytes used to represent this type.

Some languages (including Haskell, Python and Scheme) implement integers that are bounded only by the available memory. Operations on such (somewhat imprecisely named) *unbounded integers* are more expensive than operations on machine integers, but avoid the problems inherent in machine-dependent and fixed-size numbers.

Some languages allow strings containing only digits (and, possibly, signs and decimal points) to represent numbers, so integers of almost any size can be represented. COBOL, for example, requires number variables to specify the number of digits for both integer and fixed-point numbers. A type `picture 9(27)`, for example, specifies an unsigned number with 27 digits, and `picture S9(7).999` represents a signed number with seven digits before a decimal point and three digits after a decimal point. The similar type `picture S9(7)V999` also represents a signed number with seven digits before a decimal point and three digits after, but the decimal point is implied and not actually represented as a character. COBOL numbers are stored as strings but can be optimised to use *binary coded decimal* (BCD) format, which uses four bits per digit. Many early computers and some modern mainframe computers have hardware support for operations on numbers represented in BCD or as strings of digits.

Rational types can be represented as pairs of integers. It is usually only languages that support unbounded integers (such as Scheme and Haskell) that have built-in support for rational numbers, as addition of fractions quickly leads to very large numerators and denominators.

Non-integral numbers are often represented as fixed-point numbers or floating-point numbers. We have already seen that COBOL allows fixed-point numbers with an arbitrary number of digits before and after a decimal point, but few modern languages directly support fixed-point numbers, though many have libraries that implement these using either integers (with implied decimal point) or strings as representation.

FORTRAN and most modern languages support *floating point numbers*. Floating point numbers emulate scientific notation for real numbers such as 2.345×10^{-42}, but with limited precision of the mantissa (the part before the $\times$ symbol) and limited range of the exponent (the power that 10 is raised to). Also, most floating-point formats use powers of two instead of powers of ten. Historically, there have been many different machine-specific variants of floating point numbers with different precision, binary or decimal exponent, and so on, but most modern computers and programming languages use the IEEE 754 standard for floating point numbers, which in addition to specifying how results are rounded offers single precision, double precision and extended precision numbers, where single-precision numbers pack signs, mantissa and exponent into 32 bits, double precision packs everything into 64 bits, while extended precision does not have a specified format, but is usually represented using 80 bits (following a format used by Intel). C uses the names `float`, `double`, and `long double` for the three IEEE formats. Many languages support only a single floating-point type, which is usually the IEEE double precision format.

7.3.2 Characters

As mentioned in Chap. 3, programming languages have used many different character sets to represent syntax. The character set available for character-typed values does not need to be the same as used for syntax. For example, while APL uses a special character set for its syntax, character values are typically restricted to a more standard character set such as ASCII. Conversely, many languages that use ASCII only for syntax allow characters from the 8-bit IEEE 8859-1 character set or the full Unicode alphabet as values.

In ASCII, all upper-case letters precede all lower-case letters in the order implicit by the numeric encoding of characters, so sorting using this implied order will not yield the same order as in dictionaries. This issue becomes even worse in IEEE 8859-1 and Unicode, as letter symbols are not even contiguous in the numeric encoding, and different countries/languages may use different dictionary ordering for the same set of characters. For this reason, many programming languages provide only the simple encoding-based ordering as a built-in operator and rely on library functions that can be parameterised by location to make dictionary comparison and sorting. Alternatively, characters can only be compared for equality and must be explicitly converted to their encoding for order comparison.

7.3.3 Boolean Values

There are only two Boolean values: truth and falsehood. Some programming languages (Pascal, Standard ML, Haskell, …) support specific Boolean types, but other languages (C and many variants of BASIC) choose to represent Boolean values as integers, typically with 0 representing falsehood and anything else representing truth. Some dynamically-typed languages use null objects or null pointers to represent falsehood and anything else to represent truth.

In terms of implementation, there is not a lot of difference between these representations, but using a specific type for Boolean's prevent some errors such as adding a Boolean to a number. Conversely, representing Boolean values as 0 and 1 allows a programmer to multiply a number by a truth value, which can make code for conditionally adding a value to a number more compact. Not having a unique representation for truth can be a problem when you compare Boolean values: Two different integers (such as 7 and 9) can both represent truth, so comparison of the underlying integer representations is not the same as comparison of the logical values.

7.3.4   Enumerated Types and Symbols

An *enumerated type* is a type that holds a finite number of named values, for example, `Monday`, `Tuesday`, `Wednesday`, `Thursday`, `Friday`, `Saturday`, and `Sunday`. Enumerated types are usually implemented as small integers, and the main reason to use enumerated types instead of numbers is readability: It is easier to understand what the value `Thursday` means than if the number 4 is used instead. Also, a compiler can check if a case statement/expression covers all possible cases and if a variable is given a value that is not in the type.

Pascal was one of the first mainstream languages to include explicit enumerated types. A Pascal declaration of an enumerated type is done by listing the values in parentheses:

```
type weekday =
        (Monday, Tuesday, Wednesday, Thursday,
         Friday, Saturday, Sunday);
```

C allows declaration of an `enum` type using a similar notation, but the values are just synonyms for small integers, and no checking is done. Java has enumerated types using a syntax similar to C, but instead of being represented as numbers, an `enum` type is a class, and values in the type are instances of the class. Java allows enum values to have parameters, making enums a form of sum type (see Sect. 7.3.8).

LISP has symbolic values called *symbols* or *atoms* similar to values in enumerated types, but since LISP is dynamically typed, there is no declaration of symbols: Any sequence of letters and digits (and a few other characters) that start with a letter is a symbol. The differences between symbols and strings are that strings allow more different characters and that symbols are *internalised*: A symbol is represented as a pointer to its name, and it is ensured that all occurrences of the same symbol point to the same name, so comparison of symbols can be done as pointer comparison. In addition to LISP variants, Prolog, Ruby, Smalltalk, and several other (mostly dynamically typed) languages also support symbols.

7.3.5   Product Types

A *product* type (also called a *tuple type*) is similar to a Cartesian product in mathematics: A value in a product type is constructed by choosing an element from each of the component types and putting them next to each other, in the order specified in the product.

Most programming languages allow multiple arguments to functions using a tuple-like notation, but there are often not tuple values as such: You cannot store a tuple in a variable or return it as a result from a function call. We will here focus on tuple types that allow tuples to be used as values.

The simplest form of product type is a pair: We know pairs from mathematics, where we often work with pairs of numbers (such as Cartesian coordinates), but the components of a pair need not be of the same type. You can, for example, use a pair of a name and a number to represent a person and his year of birth. In mathematical notation, such a pair could be written as (Peter, 1982). Note that this is different from the pair (1982, Peter): The order matters, even if the types of the components could be used to identify which is the name and which is the year. In maths, a set that contains pairs of names and years would be written as *name* × *year*. In some programming languages, the notation is similar. In Standard ML and F#, for example, the type would be written as name * year, using the * symbol because × is not available in the ASCII character set. We have used the types name and year to be synonyms to strings and integers. The example pair above can be constructed by ("Peter", 1982). In Haskell, the type is written as (name , year), mimicking the notation for pair values. Values are constructed in the same way as in ML or F#. In Java, the pair type is written as Pair < name, year >, and a value in this type is constructed by new Pair < name, year > ("Peter", 1982). In LISP, a pair of Peter and 1982 is represented as (Peter . 1982) and constructed by the expression (cons Peter 1982). There is no notation for types in LISP, as it is dynamically typed. There are no tuples longer than pairs, but lists serve a similar role.

This generalises to more than two components. A product (tuple) with three elements is called a *triple* or *triplet*, a product with four components is called a *quadruple* or *quartet*, and so on. Some languages (like Standard ML) allow tuples of any size, while other languages put a limit to their size. For example, Java, limits tuples to ten components. Note that while set products in mathematics are often seen as associative, so $A \times (B \times C) \equiv A \times B \times C \equiv (A \times B) \times C$, this is not usually the case in programming languages. Tuple types corresponding to the above three products of three sets would be different in all of the languages mentioned. For example, the ML types int*(int*int), int*int*int and (int*int)*int are three different types.

To access elements of a product, you use a *projection*. A projection is a mapping from a product type to one of its component types. In mathematics, these projections are usually called π_i or $proj_i$, where i is the (1-indexed) number of the desired component, so π_1 (or $proj_1$) is the function that takes the first component of a pair or other tuple. In Standard ML, projection functions are named #1, #2, and so on, so #1 ("Peter", 1982) = "Peter". In F#, projection functions fst and snd take the first or second component of a pair, respectively. There are no standard functions for longer tuples, but these can be defined using pattern matching (see below). In Java, tuples define projection methods getValue0(), getValue1(), and so on, and also a getValue() method that takes the position number as argument (and returns a value of type Object, which is a supertype of all the component types). Note that these projection functions are 0-indexed, where the ML projections are 1-indexed. LISP, Scheme and other LISP-derived languages use the functions `car` and `cdr`, respectively, to access the first and second component of a pair. Many of these define `caar` to take the first component of the first component of a value, and generalise this to other combinations of a and d between c and r. For example, Scheme has the operator `cadddr` to take the fourth component of a list (defined as nested pairs).

In functional languages, it is common to use pattern matching to access components of a tuple. If a variable p in Standard ML has type `name * year`, you can write

```
let val (n, y) = p in e end
```

to, inside *e*, give the variables n and y the values of the first and second component of p. F# and Haskell use a similar notation. In fact, it is recommended to use pattern matching rather than projection functions to access the components of tuples.

A special case of product types is the empty product. This type has only one possible value, so it is mainly used when a function has no parameter or no result. In C, which does not have tuples except for passing arguments to functions, a parameter tuple can be empty, but a special type `void` is used when a function does not return any value. No variable can be declared to have the `void` type, so it is not a proper value type. In Standard ML and F#, the empty tuple type is called `unit` and has the single value `()`. Variables can have the type `unit`, and the value can be freely used like any other. In Haskell, the type is called `()`, following the Haskell design choice that type notation resembles value notation.

7.3.6   Records and Structs

Record types are similar to tuples, but instead of components being identified by their position, they are identified by name.

COBOL was the first mainstream language to support records. Records in COBOL were mainly used to describe entries in files, so they are specific about the number of characters used to store each field and locations of specific symbols such as decimal points, signs and other symbols. Records in COBOL can be nested, which is indicated by giving each field a level number. Any field with a higher number than a preceding field is considered to be a sub-field of the preceding field. An example of a COBOL record declaration is shown below:

```
01 STUDENT
   05 NAME PIC A(20)
   05 DATE-OF-ENTRY
      09 YEAR PIC 9(4)
      09 MONTH PIC 99
      09 DAY PIC 99
   05 ECTS-POINTS PIC 9(3)V9
```

The declaration indicates that a student record has a 20-letter name, a date of entry, and a number of ECTS points, which is given by three digits before an implicit decimal point and one digit after. The date of entry is itself a record with fields for year, month and day. The year is four digits and the month and day are each two digits. The keyword PIC indicates that the field is a picture, which is a fixed-length string of symbols. The following characters specify the kind of symbols used: A represents alphabetic characters, 9 represent digits, V represents an implied decimal point. So the number of ECTS points is represented by four characters all of which are digits, with an implied decimal point before the last digit. A number in parentheses after a symbol specifier indicates that the symbol specifier is repeated, so A(20) is equivalent to 20 As in a row. Other symbol specifiers indicate alphanumeric characters (X), blanks (B), explicit decimal points (.) and more. The level numbers need not be successive integers. It is, in fact, recommended that level numbers increase by 4 (as in the example), so extra levels can easily be added between two existing levels.

In COBOL, a record field is accessed just by its name, so using the name MONTH as a variable implicitly accesses the MONTH field of the DATE-OF-ENTRY record inside the STUDENT record. This also means that two different records cannot use the same field names. The above example defines only a single student record. To make an array of student records, you add, for example, OCCURS 500 TIMES after the STUDENT name. Note that the type information is mixed with the name information, so you can not define a record type and use that as the type of multiple variables.

Pascal was one of the first languages to separate names and types for records: You can declare a record type that can be reused for multiple variables. Declaring a record type similar to the COBOL example is done by

```
type student = record
                name: array[1..20] of char;
                date_of_entry : record
                                  year: 0..9999;
                                  month: 1..12;
                                  day: 1..31
                                end;
                ECTS_points : real
              end
```

after which you can declare an array of students:

```
var students : array[1..500] of student
```

Unlike COBOL, you have to specify full paths to access fields, so getting the month field of student number 7 is done by students[7].date_of_entry.month (though you can use a statement with students[7].date_of_entry do S, where you in S can just write year, month, or day to access the fields).

Allowing a type to be declared separately from a variable of that type allows different record types to use the same field names, as the context will always make it clear which record this is a field of. C has record types similar to those of Pascal, except they are called *structs* instead of records, the syntax follows the C style with curly braces, and types are mentioned before names in declarations.

Records and tuples are equivalent except for the notation used, so many languages provide only one of these. Pascal and C, for example, provide records/structs but not tuples, while Python provides tuples but not records. Providing both (like ML, Haskell and F# do) can give notational convenience. Generally, tuples are preferred if the number of elements is small, and records if the number of elements is high or might change when the program is modified: Using position would make references to elements go wrong if a new element is inserted into or removed from the middle of a tuple.

7.3.7   Collection Types

While product/tuple/record types are used to represent values with a small, fixed number of elements, *collection types* are used to represent a large and possibly variable number of elements.

In statically typed languages, the elements of a collection are usually required to have the same type, but it is common in dynamically typed languages to use *heterogeneous* collections, where elements can be of different types.

7.3.7.1   Arrays

The original collection type is the *array*: An indexed collection of elements that is usually implemented as a contiguous area in memory, which allows uniform access time to any element.

The size of an array is generally fixed after it is created, but some languages allow increasing the size of arrays after creation. This usually involves copying the contents of the array to a new, larger location and freeing the space for the old copy. This can be quite costly, so even when it can be done, it is used sparingly. Also, if an array can be moved during its life time, it must be accessed through an indirection.

The index set is usually an integer interval. In FORTRAN, the index set is an interval from 1 to n, where n is specified as a constant in the program. In C and languages derived from it, the index set is an interval from 0 to $n-1$, where n must be constant for global arrays but can be a variable for local arrays. Pascal allows any finite interval of integers as index set, so you can, for example, define an array with indexes from -10 to 10. Pascal, actually, allows any finite type as index set, so you can, for example, use Booleans, characters, or weekdays (defined as an enumerated type, see Sect. 7.3.4) as indexes.

If the index set can be a set of tuples, the array is called *multi-dimensional*. Many languages (including FORTRAN and Pascal) that do not support general tuple values allow multi-dimensional arrays. A multi-dimensional array can be implemented by laying out the dimensions of the array in a single line. For example, a 10×20 array can be laid out as 20 consecutive rows of 10 elements each or as 10 consecutive columns of 20 elements each. The difference is not normally observable except in running time, but there are a few cases where it makes more of a difference: FORTRAN allows EQUIVALENCE declarations that allows a two-dimensional array to be viewed as a one-dimensional array, so a 10×20 array can be viewed as a one-dimensional array with 200 elements. FORTRAN lays out arrays column by column, so the first 20 elements of the one-dimensional array will be from the first column, the next 20 from the second column and so on. Layout also matters in languages that do not enforce index checks (so you can address outside the declared bounds of an array). What you get as a result from addressing out of bounds can depend on the layout, and it is even possible to emulate the behaviour of FORTRAN EQUIVALENCE declarations by addressing out of bounds. In C, arrays are laid out row by row, so you can access a 10×20 array as a one-dimensional array by fixing the column number to 0 and changing the row number from 0 to 199. A local array in C must have the sizes of all but the first dimension of an array specified as compile-time constants, but the first dimension can be specified at run-time. The reason is that the size of the first dimension does not appear in address calculations for indexing into arrays (when there are no bounds checks), so it is not needed for code generation. For example, indexing element (i, j) of a zero-based array of size $M \times N$ is done by the address calculation $s \times (N \times i + j) + b$, where s is the size of elements and b is the address of the first element. Since M is not used in this calculation, the code can easily be generated at compile time even if M is unknown. If N is unknown, code can still be generated, but it must use a variable access to get N, and $s \times N$ cannot be pre-computed at compile time.

Another possible layout for multi-dimensional arrays is as arrays of arrays: An $M \times N$ array is laid out as M pointers to M one-dimensional arrays of size N. Accessing an element requires two memory accesses compared to one memory access for contiguous layouts, but in a loop, the first of the two memory accesses can often be moved out of the loop. The advantage of this layout is that the M one-dimensional arrays need not have the same size, nor do they need to be adjacent in memory.

So far, we have assumed that the index set of an array is known when the array is created (except that we may allow resizing), and that it is simple to translate an index into an address. *Associative arrays* lift these restrictions by allowing composite values (such as strings, records or arrays) as indices, and allows the index set to be initially unspecified, so indexes can be added to and removed from the set during the life time of the array. Associative arrays are usually implemented as hash tables, but small tables can also be implemented as linked lists or sorted trees of index/value pairs. The first language to have built-in associative arrays was SNOBOL4, but many modern languages (Lua, Python, Swift, F#, Haskell, ...) implement associative arrays using various names such as *tables*, *maps*, or *dictionaries*. Indices to associative arrays are often called *keys*.

7.3.7.2 Lists and Streams

Lists are similar to arrays in the sense that elements are organised in sequence. The main difference is that lists are designed to be of unspecified size and easily extensible by adding new elements to one or both ends of a list. LISP was the first language to offer lists as a built-in data structure. Lists in LISP can have other lists as elements, so they can be used to build arbitrary tree structures. Most statically-typed languages require elements of a list to have the same type, so trees are built from other types, notably recursive sum types (see below).

In the simplest form, a list is implemented as a sequence of pairs each holding an element and a pointer to the rest of the list. If the pointer is a null-pointer, there are no further elements. This makes access to the first element of a list fast and simple, and it is fast and simple to add elements at the front of a list: You just create a new pair that holds a new element and a pointer to the old list. It is also easy and fast to walk through a list from the first element to the last. Randomly accessing the Nth element of a list, however, requires following N pointers. List elements are usually heap allocated, and garbage collection greatly eases writing programs that use lists.

An element can be added to the end of a list by overwriting the null-pointer in the last pair by a pointer to a new pair. This can also be used to append two lists in constant time. Both of these operations destructively change the value of the original list, so if there are multiple pointers into the old list, these will afterwards see a different list. So in functional languages (that generally avoid mutable data structures), this method is normally only used as an optimisation when there is only one incoming pointer to a list (which can be detected with reference counting, see Sect. 4.7, by using linear types, or by static data-flow analysis). In imperative languages, where values are generally accepted to be mutable, it is quite common to overwrite the null-pointer at the tail of a list when adding elements. This can, however, adversely affect generational garbage collection (see Sect. 4.8.3). If adding elements to the tail of a list is commonly done, a list can be a pair of pointers to both the first and the last nodes of the list structure.

It is also possible to add or delete elements from the middle of a list: To add an element after an existing element, you create a new pair with the value of the new element and which points to the next element, and you update the next-element pointer in the pair after which the new element is added. Similarly, you can delete an element by updating the next-element pointer to point to the pair following the next element. All of these, obviously, destructively update the list.

It is easy to iterate over the elements of a list from the start to the end, but it is not so easy to move backwards in the list, since a pair only points to the next element. To make walking a list in both directions easy, you can have pointers both ways. This, however, makes adding elements to the front of the list as destructive as adding them to the end of the list, so doubly-linked lists are rarely used in functional languages.

To make random access faster, a list can be implemented as a tree structure. This can make access time proportional to the logarithm of the index rather than linearly proportional to this, but it adds a small overhead to accessing the first element of a list and taking the tail of a list compared to a simple linked-list implementation.

Streams are usually distinguished from lists by being generated on demand: It is not known if there is a next element until it is accessed, and if there is not already an element, it is generated. This on-demand generation can be done using lazy evaluation (Sect. 5.5.4) or by using coroutines (Sect. 6.5.1). In lazy functional languages like Haskell, there is no difference between lists and streams.

7.3.7.3 Strings

Strings are sequences of characters, and they are often implemented as arrays or lists of characters. In C and Pascal, for example, a string is just an array of characters, and in Haskell, a string is just a list of characters. But many languages have additional support for strings:

- String constants may be supported even if general array constants are not. Similarly, printing strings may be supported even if printing of other array types are not.
- Lexicographic comparison of strings may be predefined even if lexicographical comparison of arrays or lists in general are not.
- Conversion of numbers to strings and vice-versa may be built into a language.
- Allocation of strings may have special support.
- There may be support for substring operations even if similar operations are not defined for general arrays or lists.

In BASIC, for example, strings are values that can be concatenated, extracted, and more, while arrays need explicit loops to implement similar operations. Also, an expression can evaluate to a string, but not to an array. Some BASIC dialects use automatic garbage collection to handle allocation and freeing of strings, while arrays can only be allocated, but never freed. Additionally, strings are often paired with their lengths, so finding the length of a string does not require walking down the string until a null character or the end of a list is found.

Additionally, lexicographical comparison may be nontrivial. While covering character types, we already mentioned that letters are not ordered in dictionary order, because upper- and lower-case characters are separated and non-ASCII letters (such as Æ, Ö, Þ and Ł) are located far from A–Z, and that different countries/languages may order the same characters differently. When we go from single letters to strings, there may be further complications: Normally, upper and lower case letters are considered equal when ordering words, but if two words differ only by one being capitalised and the other not, the capitalised version comes first. There can also be local rules: In the Danish language, it is common to alphabetise AA as Å, and in England, it is normal to consider Æ a ligature of A and E and alphabetise it as this combination. How words with apostrophes and accents (such as "apă", "Glück", and "O'Connor") are alphabetised can also follow local rules. Most programming languages by default use ordering based on the numeric encoding of characters, which can be used for search trees and other purposes where any total ordering will do, but allow location-specific libraries to either override the default ordering or provide additional order relations.

7.3.7.4 Sets and Multisets

Sets are collections of values where the order and number of occurrences of values are unimportant. This mimics the mathematical concept of a set where, for example, $\{3, 2\} = \{2, 2, 3\}$.

Sets should allow fast checks for whether an element is in a set, whether the set is empty, for selecting an arbitrary element in the set, and for finding the union or intersection of two or more sets. Sets should also support either adding elements or converting an element into a singleton set (which can be enjoined with another set to add this element). The efficiency of these operators can depend on properties of the element type: It must at least be possible to compare elements for equality, otherwise a membership test cannot be made, but membership tests can be made faster if the values can be represented as small integers or if there is a total order on the values.

Pascal supports sets where the element type is an enumerated type, Boolean, or integer or character subrange. Sets are implemented as bit vectors: The values in the element type are numbered from 0 to N, and a set of that type will have $N + 1$ bits. If bit i is 1, this means that the element numbered i is in the set. Membership test is, hence, done by indexing into the bit vector. Union is done by bitwise OR, and intersection by bitwise AND. There is no operator for picking an element in a set, but this can be implemented by looping over the possible elements until a member is found. The time required to do a membership test is independent of the size of the set, but union, intersection, emptiness test, and other operations require time proportional to the size of the bit vector, which depends on the number of different values in the element type. So Pascal sets work best if the element type is small.

There are other ways to represent sets: F#, for example, implements sets as sorted binary trees, so elements can be from a large (or even infinite) type, as long as there is a total order defined on that type. Membership test requires $O(\log n)$ comparisons, where n is the size of the set, and union and intersection require $O(m + n)$ time, where m and n are the sizes of the sets. Test for emptiness is, however, constant time, as is picking an arbitrary element from the set. However, to ensure deterministic behaviour, the smallest element in the set is always chosen, which increases the time to $O(\log n)$. Another common set implementation is a hash table: Membership test is done by hashing the element and using the hash value to index a table, where each entry is a list of the elements in the set with that hash value. If the table is sufficiently large, membership test is proportional to the size of the element. Emptiness test, union and intersection take time proportional to the size of the hash tables, as does picking an arbitrary element.

The language SETL (Set language) is a language where the primary data structure is set. SETL has set comprehensions (similar to list comprehensions in Haskell) and APL-style operations for operating on whole sets. For example, the product of all numbers from 1 to n can be written as `*/[1..n]`.

Multisets (also called *bags*) are like sets, except that elements can occur multiple times in a multiset. A multiset can be seen as a mapping from the element type to non-negative integers that represent the *multiplicity* of elements. Often, multisets are more natural representations of real-world data than sets or lists. For example, the coins in a wallet are naturally represented by how many there are of each coin type rather than the number of different coins (a set) or a specific listing of these (a list). Many languages have libraries that implement multisets, but few languages have built-in support for these as predefined types. An exception is SQL, where selecting elements from a database naturally results in a multiset.

7.3.8 Union and Sum Types

Product types (tuples and records) are used for "this and that" values that must contain both an instance of one type *and* an instance of one or more other types, corresponding to a Cartesian product.

Sum or union types are used for "this or that" values, types that can contain either an instance of one type *or* an instance of one or more other types. These types do not have a simple mathematical equivalent: While "union" is often used to describe these, they are not always mathematical unions of the component types. For example, a union of integer and integer may not be equivalent to integer.

In C, a union type is syntactically similar to a struct type: A number of named and typed fields are specified, such as in

```
union Number {
    int x;
    double y;
};
```

that declares a union type called Number with fields x and y. A field in a union is accessed just like a field in a struct by specifying the field name, so to access the integer field of a variable n of type Number, you write n.x, and to access the floating-point field, you write n.y. But while a struct requires *all* fields to be present in a value, a union requires *exactly one* of the fields to be present. It is, however, in C not possible to inspect a value to determine *which* value is present. If you set the integer field of n by, say, n.x = 3; and try to access the other field by n.y, the result is undefined, but no error is reported. This is a case where C has weak types. A union value is implemented as a pointer to a space in memory that has room enough for the largest field.

To ensure stronger typing, Pascal uses a slightly different construction: A *variant record*. A variant record analogous to the C union above can be declared by

```
type Number =
    record
        case integral : Boolean of
            true:  (x : integer);
            false: (y : real)
    end
```

This defines a record with two fields: A Boolean field `integral` and a field that depends on the value of this field: If `integral` is true, the second field is called x and is an integer, and if `integral` is false, the second field is called y and is a floating-point number. It is now possible to determine which field is present, so it can be detected if a non-present field is accessed, and most compilers will generate code that reports this at runtime. The variable defined after the `case` keyword is called the *tag field*. If the tag field is changed, the fields corresponding to its new value are undefined. If an assignment is made to a field that does not correspond to the current value of the tag field, the tag field can automatically changed. For example, if (in the Pascal example above), the tag field is true, and an assignment is made to n.y, the tag can be updated to false. Not all compilers do this, however.

In mathematics, the concept used by variant records in Pascal is called a *tagged union*, *discriminated union* or *coproduct*. A discriminated union of two sets or types *s* and *t* are sometimes written as $s + t$, which gives rise to the name *sum types*.

In Java, enumerated types allow values to have fields, effectively making these equivalent to tagged unions.

Statically-typed functional languages like Standard ML, Haskell, and F# have tagged union types usually called *sum types* or *datatypes*. Like with variant records, a sum type has a finite number of tags (here called *constructors*), each of which may have a value of a specified type. A type equivalent to the `Number` type above can in Standard ML be declared by

```
datatype Number = x of int | y of real
```

The vertical bar is usually read as "or". Note that, while the usual convention in ML is to use upper case for constructors, we have written x and y in lower case to make the example more similar to the equivalent Pascal and C examples.

To construct a value of type `Number`, you can write x 7 or y 3.14. The values are not mutable, so you can not change the tag and the value after creation, and it is easy to statically check that a value is type correct. Accessing values of sum types is done by pattern matching, so a function that converts a `Number` to a string can be written as

```
fun toString (x v) = Int.toString v
  | toString (y v) = Real.toString v
```

It is also possible to use a case expression:

```
fun toString n =
  case n of
    x v => Int.toString v
  | y v => Real.toString v
```

While Pascal must at runtime check that an accessed field corresponds to the current tag, type correctness of the above can be checked at compile time. By using pattern matching to access values of sum types, it can also be ensured that a function accounts for all possible values. For example, if the toString function above did not specify a case for y, the compiler would report a warning. To enable type inference, constructors must be unique: In a given scope, only one type can have a constructor named x.

Standard ML, F#, OCaml and Haskell use similar syntax (with minor differences) for declaring and using sum types.

Dynamically typed languages do not need sum types: Any variable can at sometimes be an integer, at other times be a floating-point value, or anything else, and dynamically typed languages usually have operators for determining the type of a variable, which corresponds to testing tags in variant records or sum types.

Object-oriented languages with dynamic subtyping and type-case statements can also emulate sum types: An abstract superclass can have each variant as subclasses. At runtime, a type-case can determine which variant a value has, so different actions can be taken. If type-case is not possible, the different actions can be different implementations of a method.

If function values are available, these can also emulate sum types: A discriminated union of types s and t can be modelled by the type $\forall \alpha ((s \rightarrow \alpha) \times (t \rightarrow \alpha) \rightarrow \alpha)$, where $\forall \alpha$ indicates uniform parametric polymorphism, see Sect. 7.4. If s is an integer type and t a floating point type, values can, for example, be $\lambda(f, g).(f\ 7)$ or $\lambda(f, g).(g\ 3.14)$. A function corresponding to the toString function above can be written as $\lambda v.v$ (Int.toString, Real.toString). We have here used lambda calculus notation, where $\lambda x.e$ defines an anonymous function similar to fn x => e in Standard ML, fun x - > e in F#, \x - > e in Haskell, and (LAMBDA (x) e) in LISP.

7.3.9 Function Types

Most languages have procedures and functions (even if they are called "methods" or something else), and if the language is statically typed, the parameters of functions and procedures and the results of functions must have specific types, and the type of a function is the combination of its argument and result types. This is also true when functions or procedures are used as parameters or values.

Some languages, however, provide additional type information for functions and procedures, for example:

- Java and Swift specify which exceptions a function or method can raise, using the throws and (for Swift) rethrows keywords.
- GNU C++ allows functions to specify that they do not modify any non-local memory (pure) or that they neither read nor modify non-local memory (const).
- Clean and Mercury can specify that a parameter or result is *unique*, meaning that the value is unshared, i.e., that no other function has access to it. This allows a function

to do side effects on this value without affecting other functions. This is useful in lazy evaluation, concurrency or parallelism, where the order of evaluations is unspecified, so side effects can cause different results with different evaluation orders. In Clean and Mercury, uniqueness types are mainly used for file handling and i/o. Rust has a similar concept called *ownership types*, but these are properties of general pointer types, not just function parameters and results.

All of the above specify *effects* that a function may have that makes it behave unlike a mathematical function that always returns the same result given the same argument and which does not cause or depend on any side effects.

We use $s \rightarrow t$ to specify the type of a function that takes an argument of type s and produces a result of type t. The arrow associates to the right, so $s \rightarrow t \rightarrow u \equiv s \rightarrow (t \rightarrow u)$.

Unrestricted functional values can emulate almost any other data structure: An array is a function from indices to values, $i \rightarrow v$, where i is the index set and v is the value set. A pair of values of type s and t is a function of type $\forall u((s \rightarrow t \rightarrow u) \rightarrow u)$. We covered sum types in Sect. 7.3.8, and a list with elements of type s is a function of type $\forall u((s \rightarrow u \rightarrow u) \rightarrow u \rightarrow u)$, corresponding to a `fold` function over the list. The types can restrict the use of these data structures. For example, the list representation just shown does not permit general recursion over the list structure but only fold-like operations. A sufficiently permissive type system (or dynamic types) can allow functions to represent any data structure that can be operated on by any kind of iteration or recursion. Not always very efficiently, but semantically equivalent to the usual data structures.

7.3.10   Recursive Types

A recursive type is a type that is partially defined in terms of itself, using recursion. If types are viewed as sets, these are not well-founded sets, giving problems similar to Russel's paradox. So there are usually restrictions to how recursive types can be defined.

It is not hard to define recursive types that do not have any finite values, for example by the equation $t = s \times t$, which conceptually defines infinite nested pairs. In a strict language, no infinite values can exist. In a lazy language, infinite values can exist (as long as only a finite part is ever evaluated), but lazy languages usually forbid infinite nested pairs.

If the recursive case is combined with a non-recursive alternative, finite values are possible: $t = u + s \times t$ defines a type t, where values are either of type u or pairs of s and t. Finite values of this type are equivalent to list of elements of type s, ending with a value of type u. In a lazy language, infinitely nested values are also possible, but in a strict language they are not. Lists in many functional languages are defined as recursive sum types:

```
datatype 'a list =   [] | :: of 'a * ('a list)
```

Here (in ML notation), using a binary constructor : : (which is infix in expressions
and patterns) and a nullary constructor [ ] representing the empty list.

If a recursive sum type has no infinite values, it is called an *inductive type*, because
it corresponds to an inductively built set, i.e., a set built from a finite number of base
values and a finite number of rules for how values can be combined to form new
values. Mathematical induction can often be used to reason about functions that are
defined on inductive types. Most functional languages restrict recursive types to be
sum types but often allow recursive types with only recursive summands. In Standard
ML, for example, the declaration

```
datatype 'a infList = ::: of 'a * ('a infList)
```

is legal, but since there are no finite values of this type, none can ever be built.
Haskell allows similar non-inductive type declaration, but because Haskell uses lazy
evaluation, it is possible to define and work with infinite values (that are just not
ever fully evaluated). Even in Standard ML, you can define useful types with only
recursive summands:

```
datatype 'a tree = Node of 'a * ('a tree list)
```

which defines a tree type where a node has a list of children. Since the list can be
empty, it is possible to build finite trees, for example the value Node (7, [ ]),
which is a node with no children. What makes this work is that the recursive instance
is guarded by a type constructor (list) that includes values that do not use the type
given as parameter. Similarly, an alternative to infList can be a stream:

```
datatype 'a strm = ::: of unit -> 'a * ('a strm)
```

which guards the recursion by a function arrow. This means that elements of streams
are not evaluated until forced to do so by applying the function. It is not an inductive
type because it, even in a strict language, has infinite values. The stream type is,
however, *coinductive*, which is a concept dual to inductive.

Other interesting non-inductive recursive types can be defined, for example:

```
datatype lambda = Fun of lambda -> lambda
```

which defines values that functions that can take functions as arguments and results.
This can be used as the value domain for the untyped lambda calculus. The identity
function $\lambda x.x$ can, for example, be defined by Fun (fn x => x), and the reverse-
apply function $\lambda xy.y\,x$ can be defined as

```
Fun (fn x => Fun (fn (Fun y) => y x))
```

If a language allows null pointers, it is possible to define recursive types even without sum types. For example, in C, a list of numbers can be defined by the declaration

```
typedef struct List {
  int head;
  struct List *tail;
} *list;
```

A list is terminated by using a null pointer in the `tail` field. Pascal similarly allows recursive record types using pointers. Since object pointers in most object-oriented languages can be null pointers, recursive classes can similarly be defined.

7.3.11   Named Types and Type Equivalence

Most languages that allow user-defined types also allow the programmer to declare a named type, for example by a declaration like (using Pascal notation)

```
type complex = record re, im : real end;
```

Some languages require structured types to be named, and declarations of variables must use the name rather than the type description. Pascal, for example, allows variables to be declared using either named types or type descriptions but requires array elements and function parameters and results to be declared using only named types. Except parameters that are of functional type, which must be declared by a type description that looks like a full function declaration. C requires struct and union types to be named but allow array and pointer types to be described in variable and parameter declarations. ML requires sum types to be declared by name, while record types, tuples and function types to be described in variable/parameter declarations (and types in variable/parameter declarations are generally optional). In Java, classes must be named and variable declarations must use the names.

If you can name a type, you can in theory give two different names to the same type description (e.g. by writing `type t1 = t2;`). Do these then represent the same type, or do they represent different types, such that using one where another is expected is a type error?

If two different names with identical description represent the same type, the language is said to use *structural equivalence* for types. If they are different, the language is said to use *name equivalence*. Languages (like Java) that use name equivalence normally requires variable declarations to use type names rather than type descriptions, while languages that use structural equivalence allow both type names and type descriptions in variable declarations. Many languages use a mixture of structural and name equivalence. As mentioned, Java uses name equivalence for classes and structural equivalence for array types and pointer types, while Standard ML and

Haskell use name equivalence for sum types (datatypes) but structural equivalence for everything else.

There are advantages and disadvantages to both kinds of type equivalence:

Structural equivalence allows compound types (such as pairs or function types) to be without name, which reduces the number of type declarations needed.

Name equivalence allows details of a type to be hidden from the programmer, providing *abstraction*. Languages with structural equivalence require other mechanisms (such as modules) to provide abstract types.

Name equivalence can prevent, for example, adding meters to seconds by defining both as differently named variants of a floating point type. This requires all arithmetic operations to be redefined for the named types, though.

Type inference generally infers type based on structure, so structural equivalence is natural. Type inference with name equivalence is possible but requires that differently named types have different descriptions. For example, Standard ML does not allow two differently named sum types (datatypes) in the same scope to have constructors with the same name. On the other hand, even if arbitrary types can be named, type inference will (excepting sum types) use the full descriptions in inferred types, which can make type expressions very large if printed.

Structural equivalence of recursive types can be an issue: Comparing two recursive type descriptions for equality requires keeping track of names that are *assumed* to be equal until proven otherwise. In technical terms, comparison of recursive types requires *coinduction* while non-recursive types can be compared using *induction*. Standard ML uses name equivalence for recursive types partly for this reason.

In languages (like Standard ML and Haskell) that use name equivalence for sum types, you can give a compound type a short printed name by using a sum type with one summand. For example, in Standard ML, the datatype declaration

```
datatype person = Person of {name : string, age : int}
```

will make values of type `person` to be shown to have a named type rather than a record type, whereas the declaration

```
type person = {name : string, age : int}
```

will show values of type `person` as record types. Note that both allow variable declarations to use the type name. This does not enforce abstraction, though, as pattern matching on a value of type `person` is possible in both cases, assuming the programmer knows the constructor `Person` used in the datatype declaration in the first case.

7.3.11.1   Units of Measure

We mentioned above that name equivalence can prevent adding numbers that represent different units (such as meters and seconds) at the cost of having to redefine arithmetic operations. This quickly breaks down if units can be combined into, for example, meters per second or meters per second squared, as the number of types that must be declared becomes very large and the number of variants of arithmetic operators even larger.

A better solution is to use *units of measure* types (also called *dimension types*). Note that this is different from *unit types* that are types with only one value, such as unit in ML and () in Haskell.

Units of measure types are found in the languages Fortress and F#. Essentially, a unit of measure is a named variant of a number type (which can be integer or floating point). In F#, you can declare, for example

```
[<Measure>] type m
[<Measure>] type s
[<Measure>] type kg
[<Measure>] type N = kg m / s^2
```

which defines meters (m), seconds (s), kilograms (kg), and Newtons (N), where the latter is defined to be kilograms times meters per second squared. You can define unit constants by suffixing with a unit. For example, the gravitational constant can be defined as

```
let G = 6.67408e-11<m^3/(kg s^2)>
```

You can then calculate the gravitational force between two masses by using Newton's law of gravitation[1] :

```
let m1 = 1000.0<kg>
let m2 = 2000.0<kg>
let r = 3000.0<m>
let f = G*m1*m2/(r*r)
```

you get val f : float $< kgm/s \char94 2 > = 1.483128889e - 11$. Note that the unit is not abbreviated to N. This is because F# uses structural equivalence for units of measure, so units are expanded in full to allow comparison.

With unit-of-measure types, you cannot add or subtract values with different units, but you can freely multiply and divide such values, which makes the resulting unit of measure the product or fraction of the involved units of measure. The example above shows this: G*m1*m2 gets the type float $< kgm \char94 3/s \char94 2 >$, and

---

[1] https://www.britannica.com/science/Newtons-law-of-gravitation.

by dividing with the square of a distance in meters makes the resulting type float < kgm/s ^ 2 >. Note that the unit fractions are shortened by cancelling units if they appear in both numerator and denominator.

Suggested Exercises: 7.11, 7.12.

7.4 Polymorphism

The word "polymorphic" comes from Greek and means "having multiple forms". In programming languages, polymorphism generally has to do with types:

- A *polymorphic function* or operator is a function or operator that can be applied to arguments of multiple different types, or return results of multiple different types.
- A *polymorphic type* is an abstract type that can be instantiated to multiple concrete types.

The types in question can be static types, meaning that *names* (variables, functions, etc) in the program are associated with types before the program is executed, or dynamic types, where names are not associated with types, but where *values* created during execution are associated with types, either explicitly by including a type description in the value or implicitly by the shape and content of the value. These two concepts can be combined: Before execution, a name can be associated with a polymorphic type, and at runtime it can be associated with values that have types that are allowed by the polymorphic type. What this means depends on what kind of polymorphism is used:

- In *ad hoc polymorphism*, a function or operator name is associated with a finite set of allowed types. The types and the implementations of the function or operator at these types can be completely unrelated. For example, the operator + can in some languages add integers, add floating-point numbers or concatenate strings, which have completely different implementations. Ad hoc polymorphism is also called *overloading*.
- In *interface polymorphism*, a type is identified with the set of operations that can be applied to values of the type. Any value that supports these operations can be associated with the type. Interface polymorphism is also called *duck typing* because "If it quacks like a duck and walks like a duck, it *is* a duck". The operations in the interface are usually identified by name but can otherwise have completely unrelated implementations.
- In *subtype polymorphism*, types are arranged in a hierarchy where some types are subtypes of other types. A name declared to have a certain type can be associated to values of any type that is a subtype of the declared type. This is the main form of polymorphism used in object-oriented languages, but even languages that are

not object-oriented may have a subtype-hierarchy of number types that allow, for example, an integer to be passed to a function that expects a floating-point number.

- In *parametric polymorphism*, a name can take *type parameters* that instantiate the type of the name to a specific type. At each place where the name is used, different type parameters can be given to make different instantiations. Usually, a function that has a parametric polymorphic type uses the same implementation for all possible instantiations, at least at the source-code level.

It is possible to combine several of these kinds of polymorphism in a single language. For example, many object-oriented languages combine subtype polymorphism with interface polymorphism and parametric polymorphism. The interactions between different kinds of polymorphism can be quite complex and can lead to programs that are hard to understand for the programmer, so a language designer must be careful not to use more kinds of polymorphism than necessary.

We will, in this chapter, look at how polymorphism can be implemented in a programming language. We will treat each of the kinds above individually and look at a few common combinations.

7.4.1 Ad hoc Polymorphism

Ad hoc polymorphism is the oldest form of polymorphism used in programming languages. It dates back to at least FORTRAN in the late 1950s, where it was used to allow the same symbols for arithmetic operations on integers and reals (floating-point numbers). So I+1 would use integer addition because both arguments are of integer type and X+3.14 would use floating-point addition because both arguments are of the real type. If one argument is an integer and the other a real, the integer is converted into a real and floating-point addition is used. Not all languages using overloading on arithmetic make such implicit conversions. For example, writing 3+3.5 in Standard ML will result in a type error while both 3+3 (integer addition) and 3.0+3.5 (floating-point addition) are perfectly legal.

In both cases, an overloaded operator can be described by a set of pairs of a type and an implementation. We use the notation $(a, b) \rightarrow c$ as a type of an operation that accepts two arguments of type a and b and returns a result of type c. We describe the implementations informally. The + operator in Standard ML can be described by the following set of pairs:

$$\{(int, int) \rightarrow int, \text{ integer addition},$$
$$(real, real) \rightarrow real, \text{ floating-point addition})\}$$

The situation in FORTRAN is a bit more complex:

$$\{(int, int) \rightarrow int, \text{ integer addition}),$$
$$(int, real) \rightarrow real, \text{ convert 1st argument to real and use floating-point addition}),$$
$$(real, int) \rightarrow real, \text{ convert 2nd argument to real and use floating-point addition}),$$
$$(real, real) \rightarrow real, \text{ floating-point addition})\}$$

Note that the implicit conversions are part of the overloading and not a separate mechanism.

In the above examples, the types of the arguments provide sufficient information to select the correct implementation, but there may be operators where the result type is required to select the implementation. For example, an operator for converting a string to a number may have the following overloaded specification:

$$\{ string \rightarrow int, \text{ read integer}),$$
$$string \rightarrow real, \text{ read floating-point})\}$$

If such is the case, the compiler must keep track of both the expected result type and the types of the arguments, and there can be situations where there is not sufficient information to select an implementation: `read(s) + read(t)` can either read integers from s and t and add these using integer addition, read reals from both and use floating-point addition or a combination that reads one integer and one real, converts one argument to real and uses floating-point addition. If no unique implementation can be found, some languages choose a default (the first match in a list of implementations) while other languages report an error saying that the overloading cannot be resolved.

Many languages use overloading only for a fixed set of predefined operators (typically arithmetic), but other languages (like C++) allow user-defined overloaded functions. These are resolved in the same way as predefined overloaded operators with the only difference being that the list of overloaded operators and implementations can be extended during compilation.

Suggested Exercises: 7.1.

7.4.1.1 Overloading in Dynamically-Typed Languages

The above assumes that overloading is resolved at compile time, before the program is executed. But overloading is also found in dynamically-typed languages, where no types are present at compile time. In dynamically typed languages, each value carries a type description, so the implementation of an overloaded operator would at runtime look at the type descriptors of the arguments to select a specific implementation of the operation. This adds a small overhead when an overloaded operator is used.

In some languages, a type descriptor contains a list of pointers to implementations for all the overloaded operations supported by the type, so the code generated for an overloaded operator will fetch an implementation from the type descriptor of the argument. The main advantage of this strategy is that the number of types that an overloaded operation can support can be extended at runtime simply by adding new type descriptors containing implementations of the operator. The main disadvantage is that the implementation of an operator must be taken from the descriptor of one specific argument to the operator, so it is more complex to support operators whose implementations depend on the types of several arguments.

If there is a fixed set of overloaded operators, a type descriptor can be (a pointer to) an array of pointers to implementations of these operators in a specific order, so fetching an implementation of a specific operator is just fetching a pointer at a specific offset into the array. If overloaded operators can be added at runtime, this can not be done, so the descriptor must be an array of pairs of operator names and implementations, and a search through the array for a matching name must be performed at runtime. This search can be sped up by hashing the operator names at compile time and at runtime using a hash-table lookup using the precomputed hash key. Due to possible hash-table collisions, this is more costly than using an offset into a simple array.

Object-oriented languages use a similar mechanism for selecting method implementations. We will return to this in Sect. 9.3.

7.4.2   Interface Polymorphism

In interface polymorphism, an *interface* is a specification of a set of operators (including constructors and field names) that a type must support, and a type is said to *implement* an interface if operators meeting the specification exist for the type. The implementations of the operators for the different types can be unrelated, so interface polymorphism is related to ad hoc polymorphism. The main difference is that an interface combines several overloaded operations and that these can include constructors and field selectors.

An interface can be explicitly declared in the program (as is the case in languages like Java or Haskell) or implicitly by how a value is used in a program: The operations applied to a value define the interface that the value must implement. The latter is often used in dynamically-typed languages, where the term *duck typing* (see above) is used.

Explicit Interfaces

An explicit interface specifies a set of operations that a type must implement. A type is declared to implement an interface and the type checker will check that all the operations in the interface declaration exist for that type. The operations can (as in Haskell) be defined in a declaration that describes how an already-defined type implements an interface. Or (as in Java) a type declaration must specify all implemented interfaces when the type is declared, and all operations required for the interfaces must be declared as part of this type declaration.

In short, with explicit interfaces, it is verified at compile time that a type implements the declared interfaces, though the mechanism for binding types to interfaces may be different.

Implicit Interfaces

Implicit interfaces are typically used in dynamically-typed languages, where types are not explicitly declared but instead a property of values. In such languages, a value is deemed correctly typed if it supports all the operations performed on the value, hence the term "duck typing". The operations performed on a variable in a given context thus implicitly define an interface for the variable.

It is usually not verified that a value implements an interface as a whole. Instead, each application of an operation checks if the operation is defined for the value in question. This is done like described in Sect. 7.4.1.1.

Suggested Exercises: 7.7.

7.4.3 Subtype Polymorphism

Types can be ordered in a subtype relation: $s \preceq t$ means that s is a subtype of t. The subtype relation is normally a partial order. A partial order $\preceq$ has the following properties:

$$s \preceq s \qquad \qquad \preceq \text{ is reflexive}$$
$$s \preceq t \wedge t \preceq s \Rightarrow s = t \quad \preceq \text{ is anti-symmetric}$$
$$s \preceq t \wedge t \preceq u \Rightarrow s \preceq u \quad \preceq \text{ is transitive}$$

Intuitively, anywhere a *value* of type t can be used, it is possible also to use a *value* of type s, if $s \preceq t$. The emphasis on value here is because the situation is more complex for variables and functions, as we shall see below.

If a type is viewed as a set of values, a type denoting a smaller set is a subtype of a type denoting a larger set: $s \preceq t \Leftrightarrow Values(s) \subseteq Values(t)$, where $Values(t)$ is the set of values denoted by the type t. Another way to view subtyping is as capabilities: If $s \preceq t$, then values of type s have at least as many capabilities as values of type t: Whatever you can do to a value of type t, you can also do to a value of type s. This is the usual view of subtyping in object-oriented languages.

Subtyping is often used for numeric types, so `integer` is a subtype of `real` which is a subtype of `complex`, so you can use integers whenever reals are expected and so on. While, conceptually, the set of integers is a subset of the set of reals which, again, is a subset of the set of complex numbers, integers are not represented in the same way as integer-valued reals, and complex numbers with 0.0 as the imaginary part are not represented in the same way as the equivalent reals. So numerical subtyping is usually combined with implicit type-conversion operators similar to those used with ad hoc polymorphism (see Sect. 7.4.1).

A similar hierarchy can exist between bounded integer types. For example, in Pascal the subrange type `1..9` is a subtype of `0..10` and all subranges of integers are subtypes of the type `integer` (which is equivalent to the subrange `minint..maxint`). Here, the values-as-sets intuition works well, as integers in a subrange usually *are* represented the same way as integers from the `integer` type, so no conversion is needed. C has a similar hierarchy: `short` $\preceq$ `int` $\preceq$ `long`. Since these may be implemented by different numbers of bytes, conversion may require widening with sign extension.

In class-based object-oriented languages, a class D that extends (inherits from) C is a subclass of C. Like `integer` is a supertype of all subrange types in Pascal, most object-oriented languages have a type that is supertype to all classes. In Java, this is called `Object`. We call such a common supertype the *top element* of the subtype relation. Note that neither Pascal nor Java have a type that is a supertype of *all* types: integer is only a supertype of subrange types and has no subtype relation to, say, Boolean and in Java Object is not a supertype of primitive types (such as int) nor of array types. Essentially, only numeric types in Pascal and object types in Java are included in subtype hierarchies.

Record types (also called structs) can, like classes, form a subtype hierarchy: A record type with more fields is a subtype of a record type with fewer fields if the fields in the subtype record type have the same names and types as fields in the supertype record type. This is similar to subclasses adding fields and methods to the classes they inherit from. A record type with no fields is supertype to all record types. A dual situation occurs for sum types (also called variant types, unions or enumerated types): A sum type with more alternatives is a supertype of a sum type with fewer alternatives (as long as the alternatives in the supertype have the same names and types as the alternatives in the subtype). A sum type with no alternatives (and, hence, no possible values) is a subtype of all sum types. Using C-style notation (though C does not use subtyping for structs and unions), a record type declared as

```
struct s1 {int x; double y;};
```

is a subtype of a record type declared as

```
struct s2 {int x;};
```

where a sum type declared as

```
union u1 {int x; double y};
```

is a supertype of a sum type declared as

```
union u2 {int x;};
```

While C does not use subtypes for structs and unions, type conversion from s1 to s2 and from u2 to u1 are safe, but conversions the other way around are not. While conversion of a sum type to a sum type with more alternatives is always safe in C, it is not always safe to convert a record type into a record type with fewer fields: The fields of two such structs are in C not guaranteed to have the same offsets, except that the first field is always stored at the address of the whole struct. Using the example above, a pointer to s1 can safely be cast to a pointer to s2, but if a record type s3 has a single field double y, a pointer to s1 cannot safely be converted to a pointer to s3.

7.4.3.1 Functions and Arrays

As said above, the intuition is that if $s \preceq t$, you can give a value of type s wherever a value of type t is expected. Conversely, when you have a variable or parameter *declared to* have type t, its actual value may well be of a subtype of t such as s. Let us expand a bit on this.

Let us first focus on functions. Let us say that we have a function f whose type is $a \rightarrow b$, i.e., it takes an argument of type a and returns a result of type b. The subtype relation should then guarantee that if $c \preceq a$ then f can take a value of type c as argument and still return a value of type b: Since we can use a value of type c whenever a value of type a is required, f should have no problems with getting a value of type c.

This intuition matches the behaviour of Pascal and Java: If a function in Pascal is declared to take an argument of type 0..9 it can safely take an argument of type 3..6. No runtime check is needed, as any value in the subrange 3..6 is also in the subrange 0..9. Similarly, a Java method that takes an argument of type A will happily accept an argument of type C if C is a subclass of A, i.e., if $C \preceq A$. No runtime subtype check is needed here either, though dynamic method invocation may be required because A and C might have different implementations of methods.

Pascal allows a function that is declared to take an argument of type 0..9 to take an actual argument of a larger subrange type such as 0..100. This, however, requires a runtime check that the actual value of the argument is in 0..9. Similarly, Java can *downcast* values known to be of type A to C if $C \preceq A$. This also requires a runtime check to verify that the actual value is of a type C or a subtype of C. Downcasts can be useful because a parameter declared to have type A can have any value that has a type that is a subtype of A, including C and subtypes of C.

Both these cases can be seen as restricted instances of dynamic typing, as information about the type of a value is gathered at runtime by inspecting the value. A purely static type system would not allow values that are not statically known to belong to a subtype of the declared type and would, hence, not need any runtime type checks.

In early versions of Java, collection classes (such as Set and List) were declared to have elements of type Object. This made their methods accept elements with types that are subtypes of Object, say Shape. But whenever elements are returned from a collection, these will be declared to have type Object, regardless of their actual types. So downcasts are required whenever you extract, say, a shape from such a collection. What we really need for type-safe generic collection classes is *parametric polymorphism*, which we will look in Sect. 7.4.4.

It gets more interesting if functions can be values, i.e., if we have parameters or variables of type $s \rightarrow t$. If a variable f is declared to have the function type $s \rightarrow t$, what values can f have? The intuition is that any actual value g of f should be safe with respect to its type: g should have all the capabilities that the type of f indicates. What we know is that the functional value g will get arguments of type s (or lower) and that the return value will be used in a context where a value of type t (or lower) is expected. So it is safe if g has a value of type $u \rightarrow w$, as long as $s \preceq u$ and $w \preceq t$: A function that accepts arguments of type u will happily accept arguments of type

s, since $s \preceq u$, and if it returns a result of type w, this is fine because w is acceptable whenever a value of type t is acceptable, i.e., if $w \preceq t$.

So a functional type $u \rightarrow w$ is a subtype of $s \rightarrow t$ if $s \preceq u$ and $w \preceq t$. Note that the subtype relation on the argument types is in the opposite direction to the subtype relation on the functional types. We say that the subtype relation is *contravariant* on the argument types of function types, as opposed to *covariant* in the result types.

Given that $s \preceq t$, we can look at array types $s[]$ and $t[]$. If we assume $s[] \preceq t[]$, we should be able to use an array of type $s[]$ whenever we need an array of type $t[]$. This is fine as long as we read from the arrays: We may get an object of type s when we expect an object of type t, but that is fine: We can use objects of type s whenever we need objects of type t. But what if we store to the array? We have an array of type $s[]$ in a variable declared to be of type $t[]$, so we expect to be able to store values of type t into this array. But when we, later, extract this value from the array of type $s[]$, we get an object of type t, and this is not what we want: We may use a field or method that is available for objects of type s but not for objects of type t! So our assumption that $s[] \preceq t[]$ whenever $s \preceq t$ must be wrong. We can, similarly, see that $t[] \preceq s[]$ is also wrong. In conclusion, $s[] \preceq t[]$ only if $s = t$. This is called *invariance*. An array of type $t[]$ is, intuitively, similar to a function of type $t \rightarrow t$: We can pass it elements of type t (when we store elements in the array) and get elements of type t back (when we read elements from the array), just with sometime between these events. So if $s \rightarrow s$ is a subtype of $t \rightarrow t$ only if $s = t$, we should not be surprised by the fact that $s[]$ is a subtype of $t[]$ only if $s = t$.

In spite of this, both Java and C# use the rule that $s[] \preceq t[]$ whenever $s \preceq t$. This is unsound, as we noted above, but this is handled with runtime tests: Downcasts (that can fail) are implicitly added when storing elements to or reading elements from arrays. Only one of these is required, and Java and C# do this differently: Java adds the tests when reading from arrays, and C# when storing into arrays.

If arrays are immutable, i.e., that you after initialisation can only read from them, then $s[] \preceq t[]$ whenever $s \preceq t$. But, excepting a few functional languages, languages with subtypes rarely have immutable arrays.

References to mutable variables are equivalent to references to arrays of size 1, so two such types are only in a subtype relation if they are the same.

7.4.3.2 Conditional Expressions

If a language that uses subtypes has conditional expressions (such as $c\,?\,e_1 : e_2$ in Java), the result can come from either branch, so it must have a type that can accept both, i.e., a supertype of the types of the branches. If the branches do not have a common supertype, no safe static type can be given to the conditional expression.

If the subtype hierarchy has a top type (such as `Object` in Java), i.e., a type that is supertype to all types in the hierarchy, we can always find a common supertype to two arbitrary types in the hierarchy. If there are several different common supertypes to the types of the branches, we must choose one of these to represent the type of the result. Let us say that we have the following type hierarchy:

If the branches of a conditional have types C and D, both T and A are common supertypes. But A gives more precise information about the possible values than T: Where T allows values of types T, A, B, C and D, A allows only values of type A, C and D. So it is preferable to use A as the type for the result. In general, we want the *smallest* common supertype. There might, however, not always be a unique smallest supertype. Consider the following type hierarchy:

Now C and D have three common supertypes: T, A and B. While T is least informative, A and B are equally informative, so there is no clear choice between the two. Any choice is safe, since the actual possible values have type C or D, so we could choose arbitrarily among the smallest common supertypes. But this choice can affect whether the compiler will report type errors. Consider the assignment A x = p ? c : d where c has type C and d has type D. If we choose A as the common supertype for c and d (and, hence, for the result of the conditional expression), the assignment is type-correct. But if we choose B (or T) as the common supertype, the assignment is not type-correct, as x is (according to the type checker) given a value of type B (or T) which is not a subtype of A.

A reasonable choice is to make the type checker report an error if there is no unique smallest common supertype to the branches of a conditional. This strict rule can give type errors for programs that *could* be given valid types, but if different compilers make different arbitrary choices, one compiler might report an error while another does not, which is clearly unacceptable.

Java uses single inheritance of classes, so any two classes will have a unique common superclass. But Java allows multiple inheritance of interfaces, so the problem above does occur. See Sect. 7.4.6.2 for details.

Suggested Exercises: 7.6, 7.8.

7.4.4 Parametric Polymorphism

As the name indicates, *parametric polymorphism* adds type parameters to declarations. By substituting different types for the type parameters, the declaration can define values (or other features) for each combination of types.

To illustrate this, let us look as something as simple as the identity function: A function that returns its argument unchanged. In C, we can write the identity function for integers like this:

```
int identity(int x)
{
   return x;
}
```

This, however, only works on integers, so if we want the identity function for double-precision reals, we must write it as

```
double identity(double x)
{
   return x;
}
```

Additionally, we can't have both of these in the program at the same time, as two different functions cannot have the same name.

C++ added *templates* to solve this problem: By adding a type parameter, we can define an identity function that works on all types:

```
template <typename T>
T identity(T x)
{
   return x;
}
```

The keyword `template` indicates that the following declaration has template parameters, which in the case above is a typename passed in the template parameter `T`. C++ allows other kinds of template parameters than typenames, but we will focus on types here.

When we call the identity function defined above, we must specify a specific type argument: `identity < int > (3)` will return the integer value 3 and the call `identity < double > (3.1415)` will return the double-precision number 3.1415.

Intuitively, the *template instantiation* `identity < int >` will create an *instance* of the template by substituting `int` for `T`. The resulting instance is identical to the integer identity function shown in the beginning of this section. C++ allows functions with identical names as long as their types are different, so there is no problem in creating two different instances of the template. In languages that do not allow this, the instances can be renamed to different names.

C++ does not type-check a template declaration but, instead, type-checks each instance: When the instance `identity < int >` is created, it is type-checked like a normal (non-template) C++ function. So a C++ template is very much like a macro. The main difference is that instantiating a template (to ensure static scopes) causes an instance declaration to be added at the place of the template declaration rather than where the template is instantiated. Templates can be (and were originally) implemented as a preprocess to a compiler for a language not containing templates: The preprocess adds declarations for each template instance, naming each instance uniquely and then removes the (no longer needed) template declarations.

C++ template parameters can be numbers, which makes the template system a small functional language of its own, allowing arbitrary computation at compile time. While this is a powerful feature, it is also one of the things prevents C++ from type-checking a template before it is instantiated. Another feature that prevents this is ad hoc overloaded functions: A template might use an overloaded function or operator (like <), which can restrict the possible legal instantiations of a template. For example, the template

```
template <typename T>
T max(T x, T y)
{
   if (x<y) return y; else return x;
}
```

can only be instantiated to types where < is defined. For the same reason, different code needs to be generated for each instance, as different implementations of the overloaded operators are used.

7.4.4.1 Uniform Parametric Polymorphism

If a language has no ad hoc overloading, allows no run-time type inspection, and template parameters can only be types, it is possible to type-check a template before any instantiation. The idea is that we can prove that the template is type-safe for *all* instances by creating *one* instance and checking this.

To do this, we create a new unique type for each type parameter. These types must be incompatible with each other and with all other types, and the only operations allowed on values of these types are operations that are allowed for values of *any* type in the language. These new types are abstract: We only make new type names, but no declarations or implementations of these.

We then instantiate the template to these abstract types and check the resulting instance: If there is no type error for this instance, this will also true for any other possible instance.

The reason is that the template has no a priori knowledge about the types used in the instance (as they are created just for this purpose), so it cannot do anything with these that it could not as well do with any other types. So it can store values of these types in variables, retrieve such values from variables, pass the types as template arguments to other templates and values of these types as normal arguments to other functions, and so on, but the template can not do anything that would require knowledge about the structure of the values of the abstract type.

Note that the converse is not true: A template that generates type errors when instantiated with abstract types may well have *some* instances that are type safe—the max template above can, for example, safely be instantiated to int. All we can say is that it is not type safe for *all* instances. For example, the max template above can be safely instantiated to `int` and `double` but not to, for example, union types, structs and function types, as these do not support the $<$ operation.

If a language only allows type parameters that can be instantiated without restriction, as described above, we say that the language has *uniform* parametric polymorphism.

With uniform parametric polymorphism all instances of a template will be equivalent (as their operation cannot depend on specifics of their type parameters), so they can in principle share a single implementation. Sharing an implementation, however, requires that values have a uniform representation: No matter what type a value has, its "shape" must be the same, so passing a value as a parameter or assigning a value to a variable moves the same number of bits regardless of the type of the value. And if there are operations (such as equality) that are allowed on all types, the implementations of these operations must be identical for all types. The usual way to ensure uniform shape is to let all values fit into one machine word. If a value is, in fact, larger than one machine word, it is placed in memory and the machine word instead holds a pointer to the location of the value. So instead of passing the actual value around, a pointer to the value is passed around instead. This is called *boxed representation*, as the pointers are considered to point to "black boxes" with unknown content.

Many compilers for functional languages such as Standard ML and Haskell use boxed representation, as this allows a parametrically polymorphic function to be compiled once, independently of its instantiations, so a module containing a polymorphic function can be compiled before and shared between modules that use it. The boxed representation does, however, add a small overhead for following pointers to boxed values and allocating memory for boxed values, so some optimising compilers generate specialised instances for each different shape of value, similar to what C++ compilers do. So all types that use, say, three machine words can share one instance implementation, but this is different from the instance implementation for types that use only one machine word. The compiler MLton for Standard ML uses this approach.

7.4.5 Polymorphic Type Inference

Many languages do not require functions and variables to have declared types. Some of these, like Python and Scheme, use dynamic types, but other languages, like Standard ML, F# and Haskell, use static (but possibly polymorphic) types. Since types of variables and functions are not required to be given in the program text, the compiler must infer these types at compile time.

For example, the Standard-ML function

```
fun length [] = 0
  | length (x :: xs) = 1 + length xs
```

is inferred to have the type $'a$ `list` $->$ `int`, where $'a$ is an abstract type that can be instantiated to any type, so $'a$ `list` is a list with elements of any single type. Hence, `length` is uniformly parametrically polymorphic.

Strictly speaking, $'a$ list $->$ int is not a type, but a *type schema*, as there is an implicit type parameter. More formally, we can write the type schema for length as

$$\forall \alpha : \text{list}{<}\alpha{>} \rightarrow \text{int}$$

where α corresponds to $'a$ and list$<\alpha>$ corresponds to $'a$ list. Note that Standard ML uses postfix notation when applying a type constructor such as list to type parameters where the formal notation is closer to the C++ notation where parameters to type constructors are given in angle brackets after the type constructor name.

Type parameters are shown between $\forall$ and : after which follows the type. We show instantiation by giving type arguments in angle brackets (like in C++). So the type schema not only indicates that the type of length is polymorphic (since it has a type parameter), it also indicates that it uses an instance of the polymorphic list datatype. We can instantiate the type schema to a specific type by supplying a type argument:

$$(\forall \alpha : \text{list}{<}\alpha{>} \rightarrow \text{int}){<}\text{string}{>} = \text{list}{<}\text{string}{>} \rightarrow \text{int}$$

Since the polymorphism is uniform, we can do this for any type without needing to check for correctness with respect to the declaration of length. Note that, in ML notation, the type list<string> is written as string list.

So how do we infer this type schema from the declaration of length? We will start by an informal sketch of the idea.

length uses the polymorphic datatype list. In Standard ML, datatype declarations have explicit type parameters, so a list can be declared as[2]

```
datatype 'a list = [] | :: of 'a * ('a list)
```

This tells us that list is a polymorphic type taking a single type parameter $'a$ and that [] is a value of type $'a$ list for any type $'a$, in other words that it has the type schema $\forall \alpha : \text{list}{<}\alpha{>}$. It also tells us that :: is a constructor that takes an $'a$ and an $'a$ list and produces an $'a$ list, so in ML notation we have :: : $'a$ * $'a$ list $->$ $'a$ list, and in formal notation the schema :: : $\forall \alpha :$ $\alpha \times \text{list}{<}\alpha{>} \rightarrow \text{list}{<}\alpha{>}$, where $\times$ and $\rightarrow$ are the formal equivalents of * and ->. In expressions and patterns, :: is used as an infix operator.

When inferring a type schema for length, we annotate all uses of constructors in the declaration with instances of the type schema for the type that declares these constructors. In each instance, we apply the type schema to new, previously unused,

---

[2] The code is, strictly speaking, not correct SML, as [ ] and : : are predefined symbols that cannot be redefined.

type variables. Type variables are written as capital letters such as A and B. We also annotate uses of previously declared constants, functions, operators, and variables with their types. In the example, these are the constants 0 and 1 (both of type int) and the operator + which has type int*int -> int. Note that infix operators and constructors implicitly take pairs of arguments.

After this, we get:

```
fun length ([] : list<A>) = (0 : int)
  | length (x (:: : B*list<B> -> list<B>) xs)
      = (1 : int) (+ : int*int -> int) (length xs)
```

where A and B are new, unbound type variables. Note that unbound type variables are not the same as type parameters: We have instantiated the type parameter α with two different type variables A and B, that each represent *one* type that is as yet unknown, and may even be generalised to a new type parameter.

We now propagate types to all subexpressions. Since :: is applied to x and xs, we can infer that x has type B and xs has type list<B>, and we can infer that the result of applying :: to x and xs has type list<B>. We use this to annotate the other occurrence of xs with the type list<B>. We can do the same for the arguments and result of +. The first argument of + must have type int, and since the first argument is the constant 1, which does have type int, this is o.k. The second argument must also have type int, so we conclude that the call to length must return a value of type int. Since the result type of + is int, we get that the expression 1 + length(xs) has type int.

This gives us the following annotations:

```
fun length ([] : list<A>) = 0 : int
  | length (((x : B) (:: : B*list<B> -> list<B>) (xs : list<B>))
          : list<B>)
      = ((1 : int) (+ : int*int -> int)
          ((length (xs : list<B>)) : int)) : int
```

The first rule for length, hence, has the type list<A> -> int and the second rule has the type list<B> -> int. The recursive application of length has a parameter of type list<B> and we expect a result of type int. This gives this instance of length the type list<B> -> int.

All three instances (the two rules and the recursive call) must have the same type, so A and B must be the same type. We replace A by B, and all three occurrences of length now have the same type list<B> -> int. To get a type schema, we then *generalise* the type variable B to a type parameter α and get

$$\forall\alpha(\texttt{list}<\alpha> \to \texttt{int})$$

as expected.

This informal method uses the following steps:

1. Annotate occurrences of previously declared constants, operators, functions, and constructors with their types. If a type is polymorphic, use an *instance* of the polymorphic type by applying the type schema to new type variables.
2. Propagate types to subexpressions from operators to their argument and result expressions and so on. If one instance of a variable is annotated with a type, all other occurrences of that variable in its scope are immediately annotated with the same type. If this causes two occurrences of a variable to be annotated with incompatible types, an error is reported.
3. We should now have found types for all occurrences (both defining instances and uses) of the function for which we are trying to infer the type. These must have the same type, so we make them equal using *unification*, which we will describe in detail below. If the occurrences have incompatible (not unifiable) types, and error is reported.
4. If the resulting type for the function contains type variables, we *generalise* the type to a type schema by replacing the type variables by type parameters and quantifying these with ∀.

We will provide more detail of the type inference process in the next section.

7.4.5.1 The Hindley-Milner Algorithm

The informal description above is not really suited for implementation. Implementations of polymorphic type inference often use the *Hindley-Milner algorithm*, which we will describe below. It uses the following elements:

1. *Type environments* that binds names of variables, functions, operators, and constructors to types or type schemata. Type environments are local to each point in the program and are extended when new declarations are added.
2. A *global* set of *bindings* of type variables to types. This is updated by side effects that add new bindings.
3. A *unification* function that takes two types as arguments and either updates the global bindings of type variables so the two types are made equal (considering a bound type variable equal to the type to which it is bound) or *fails*, in which case the program has a type error.
4. A function that *instantiates* a type schema to a type by replacing type parameters with previously unused type variables.
5. A function that *generalises* a type to a type schema by replacing unbound type variables with type parameters.

A *type* is constructed from type variables (like A and B) and type constructors (like *, ->, int and list). Type constructors are applied to zero or more types to build compound types. We have written some type constructors (such as * and ->) as infix operators between their arguments and others (such as list and int) as names with parameters (if any) in angle brackets, but there is no conceptual difference between infix and prefix type constructors.

A *type schema* is a list (quantified with ∀) of type parameters (like α or β) followed by a colon and a type description that is constructed from type variables, type constructors and type parameters.

There are type-check functions for expressions, declarations, patterns and so on that work in the same way as in a normal monomorphic type checker, with the following exceptions:

1. When a name is looked up in a type environment and the result is a type schema, the schema is *instantiated* by replacing type parameters with new, previously unused, type variables.
2. Whenever a normal type checker would check if two types are equal, the Hindley-Milner algorithm tries to *unify* these instead. A successful unification (which can bind type variables to types) means the types are treated as equal, but if the unification fails, the types cannot be made equal, and a type error is reported.
3. When a declaration of a function is checked and a type is found, that type is *generalised* to a type schema, and the declared name is bound to this type schema in the extended type environment.

We will look in more detail at these below.

Instantiation

A type schema has the form $\forall \alpha_1, \ldots, \alpha_n(\tau)$, where the α_i are type parameters and τ is a type description. Instantiating this schema starts with creating n new, previously unused type variables $A_1, \ldots, A_n$ and substituting in τ all occurrences of α_i with A_i for $i = 1, \ldots, n$, so the result is a type t (that does not contain type parameters).

Unification

Unification takes two types s and t and either fails or succeeds and as a side effect updates the global set of bindings of type variables to types. It uses the following prioritised rules:

1. If $s = t$, succeed with no further bindings.
2. If s is a bound type variable A, find the type u to which A is bound and unify u and t.
3. If t is a bound type variable A, find the type u to which A is bound and unify t and u.
4. If s is an unbound type variable A and t does not contain A, bind A to t and succeed.
5. If t is an unbound type variable A and s does not contain A, bind A to s and succeed.

6. If s is of the form $c(s_1, \ldots, s_n)$ and t is of the form $c(t_1, \ldots, t_n)$, where c is a type constructor, unify s_i and t_i for $i = 1, \ldots, n$. If all of these succeed, succeed, otherwise, fail.
7. Otherwise, fail.

We need to clarify what we mean by "t does not contain A". We use the following rules:

   i. If $t = A$, t contains A.
  ii. If t is an unbound type variable different from A, t does not contain A.
 iii. If t is a type variable B bound to a type u, t contains A if u contains A.
 iv. If t is of the form $c(t_1, \ldots, t_n)$, t contains A if one of the t_i contains A.

The reason for this *occurs check* is to avoid creation of circular types: For example, unifying A with $(A*A)$ would otherwise create a circular type. Circular types may or may not have finite values (the example above would not), and the unification algorithm as described above could be nonterminating if trying to unify two circular types. It is possible to extend unification to handle circular types, but it is usually not done for type inference. Instead, the type system relies on explicitly recursive type declarations such as the one for `list` shown earlier.

We show the result of unification as a *substitution*, i.e., a list of bindings $[x_1 = t_1, \ldots, x_n = t_n]$, where x_i is a type variable and t_i is a type that may contain unbound type variables. Bound type variables are replaced by the type to which they are bound, so t_i cannot contain bound type variables. This makes the substitution *idempotent*: Applying a substitution twice to a type gives the same result as applying it once.

Let us use the above rules to unify $A*A$ and $(B\text{->}int)*(int\text{->}B)$:

1. We note that both types have the same outermost type constructor $*$, so rule 6 applies, so we need to unify arguments. So we need to unify A and $B\text{->}int$, and then unify A and $int\text{->}B$.
2. Since A is an unbound type variable, rule 4 applies. We verify that $B\text{->}int$ does not contain A, and then bind A to $B\text{->}int$ and succeed this unification.
3. We now need to unify A with $int\text{->}B$. A is now bound, so we use rule 2 and unify $B\text{->}int$ and $int\text{->}B$.
4. Again, we can use rule 6 (the type constructor is ->). So we must unify B and int and then int and B.
5. Unifying uses B and int rule 4 (since B is unbound) and binds B to int.
6. Unifying int and B. uses rule 3 (since B is now a bound type variable), so we need to unify int with int. This uses rule 6, and since there are no parameters to int, we succeed.

The resulting substitution is $[A = int\text{->}int, \ B = int]$. By applying the substitution, we find that the resulting unified type is $(int\text{->}int)*(int\text{->}int)$.

Another example is unification of $A*B$ and $B*(A\text{->}\texttt{int})$.

1. We use rule 6 and must unify A with B and B with $A\text{->}\texttt{int}$.
2. Unifying A with B uses rule 4 and binds A to B.
3. Unifying B with $A\text{->}\texttt{int}$ also uses rule 4, but we must check that $A\text{->}\texttt{int}$ does not contain B.
4. By using rule iv, rule iii, and rule i, we find that $A\text{->}\texttt{int}$ does indeed contain B (because A is bound to B). Hence, the unification fails.

Generalisation

When a function is declared, we find the type of the function by locally extending the type environment with bindings of the parameters of the function to new, previously unused type variables and then type check the body of the function using the extended environment. If this succeeds, we create a type for the function by combining the types of the arguments with the type of the body (using the -> type constructor) and then generalise this type to a type schema, which is what the function name is bound to in the type environment.

Generalisation of a type t uses the following rules:

We find all type variables $A_1, \ldots, A_n$ in t that are unbound in the global set of bindings *and* which do not occur anywhere in the type environment (before adding the new binding). We substitute these with type parameters $\alpha_1, \ldots, \alpha_n$ in t to create a type description τ. The type schema is $\forall \alpha_1, \ldots, \alpha_n(\tau)$.

The reason we only generalise type variables that do not occur in the unextended environment is that, if a type variable A that occurs in the type environment is locally generalised to α and A is later bound to a type t, we really should have bound α to t, as α represents A. But after generalisation, we have lost the connection between A and α. So to avoid this problem, we just do not generalise A if it occurs in the environment.

Summary of Hindley-Milner Type Inference

When encountering a function definition, do the following:

For each rule of the function:

1. Build an environment for local variables by processing the pattern on the left-hand side of the rule. The environment initially contains bindings for constants, operators, functions, and global variables and is extended by the following rules:

   - A variable pattern adds to the environment a binding of the variable to a new type variable and returns this as the type of the variable pattern.
   - A constructor pattern finds the types and type environments of its arguments. An instance of the type of the constructor is created, and the types of the argument patterns are unified with the types of the declared parameters of the

constructor. If this succeeds, the type environments are combined (we assume linear patterns, i.e., no repeated variables, so no unification is needed) and the combined environment is returned along with the declared result type of the constructor.

2. The environment built from the pattern is used to find the type of the right-hand side expression of the function rule using the following rules:

   - The type or type schema of a constant or variable is found in the environment. A type schema is instantiated by replacing type parameters by new type variables.
   - The type of an application of a function, operator, or constructor g is found by first finding the types of the arguments, then finding in the environment the type or type schema for g (and instantiating if a type schema). The arguments for the arguments of f found in the environment are unified with the types of the argument expressions, and if this is successful, the result type of f found in the environment is returned

3. The rule is given the type $s \rightarrow t$, where s is the type found for the pattern and t is the type found for the expression.

If there are multiple rules for the function, the types of the rules are unified. Finally, the resulting type is generalised by replacing any type variables that do not occur in the environment in which the function declaration is declared with type parameters and then quantifying these to form a type schema.

The following paragraphs add more details and special cases to the above procedure.

Recursive Declarations

If a function f is recursive, we need to know the type of f to find the type of the body of f. This might seem impossible without explicit declarations, but unification comes to the rescue: When checking the type of f, we bind f in the local type environment to a new, previously unused type variable F. When we, afterwards, construct the type for f (but before generalisation), we unify F with this type. This ensures that recursive calls to f are used at a type that is consistent with its declaration.

If several function definitions are mutually recursive (i.e., they call each other), we find the types of all of them before unifying and generalising. This means that we, before type inference, must group mutually recursive function definitions. In Standard ML, this is done explicitly in the program text (by combining mutually recursive declarations with the keyword and). In Haskell, the compiler constructs a call graph: A graph where the nodes are function names and edges represent calls. Strongly connected components in this graph are grouped into explicitly mutually recursive declarations (like in ML).

Note that, since unification is done before generalisation, all recursive calls in an instance of f call the same instance. This means that, for example, the following declaration cannot be given a polymorphic type schema by the Hindley-Milner algorithm:

```
fun f (a,0) = a
  | f (a,n) = #1 (f((a,a),n-1))
```

where #1 is an operator that takes the first component of a pair. But f *has* a valid type schema:

$$\forall\alpha((\alpha*\text{int})\text{->}\alpha)$$

This schema, however, requires that the recursive call uses a different instance of this schema than the caller, which the Hindley-Milner algorithm does not allow.

It can be seen as a weakness of the Hindley-Milner algorithm that it fails to find a type schema for such declarations, but has been proven that allowing recursive calls to use different instances than the calling instance (which is called *polymorphic recursion*, or *Milner-Mycroft typing*) makes type inference undecidable: Deciding if a valid type schema exists is as hard as solving the halting problem (see Chap. 12).

In practice, there is rarely need for such polymorphically recursive functions, so it is not a major problem that the Hindley-Milner can not infer types for them. Some languages (like Haskell), however, allow polymorphically recursive functions if their types are explicitly declared, as *checking* a polymorphically recursive function against an explicit type schema *is* decidable, even if *inferring* such a type schema is not. So the Haskell equivalent of the function above can be compiled if (and only if) a type schema like the above is explicitly given.

One thing to note is that absence of polymorphic recursion ensures that a polymorphic function is in any given program used at a finite number of instances that can be found at compile time. This means that it (unlike in C++) is safe to create all these instances at compile time—there is no risk of nontermination. The number of instances can, in theory, be extremely large, but in practice only small functions are used at more than a handful of different instances.

Polymorphic Value Declarations

So far, we have only discussed polymorphic function declarations, but it makes perfect sense to make declarations of other kinds of values polymorphic. Consider, for example, the declaration

```
val x = []
```

When we type-check the expression, we instantiate the type schema for [] to list<A>. It makes perfect sense to generalise this so x is bound to the type schema $\forall\alpha(\text{list}<\alpha>)$. This means that we can safely use it in an expression like (3::x, "a"::x), where x is instantiated to two different types (int and string). But consider the declaration

```
val y = ref []
```

where ref is an operator that creates a mutable box initialised to contain is argument (in this case $[]$). Using similar reasoning as above, ref $[]$ has the type $ref<list<A>>$, so y would have the type schema $\forall\alpha(ref<list<\alpha>>)$. This allows using y in the expression $(y := 3::!y;$ $"a"::!y)$: The three occurrences of y are instantiated to the types $ref<list<B>>$, $ref<list<C>>$ and $ref<list<D>>$. B and C are both unified with int and D is unified with $string$. But the result of the expression is the ill-typed list $["a", 3]$, so something is clearly wrong.

The problem is that the three occurrences of y are not independent: Assigning a value to one instance of y allows that value to be read through another instance. To avoid this, all instances must have the same type. This can be achieved by *not* generalising the type of y to a type schema but instead bind y to the (ungeneralised) type $ref<list<A>>$. This means that the three occurrences of y in the expression all have this type, so A is first unified successfully with int, but later unsuccessfully unified with $string$, making the expression ill-typed.

It is clear that the culprit is the assignable reference, as it is essentially possible to modify the type of its contents as a side effect. But which other types should or should not be generalised is less clear.

The original standard for Standard ML had two kinds of type variables: *Applicative* type variables that can be generalised and *imperative* type variables that cannot. In this system, the type of y has only imperative type variables (because of the reference type), so it is not generalised. This mechanism (though safe) was, however, considered too complex, so the 1997 standard replaced it with a different mechanism: There is only one kind of type variable, but a value declaration is generalised only if the right-hand-side expression is *non-expansive*. This restriction is called *value polymorphism*. Non-expansive expressions are, briefly speaking, expressions that do not contain any applications of the ref constructor nor applications of any other functions and operators, except where these are inside function abstractions (expressions of the form fn $m => e$) or inside local function definitions. Applications of constructors (except ref) are still allowed outside function abstractions.

Value polymorphism is more restrictive than using imperative type variables, as some programs that are typable using imperative type variables are not typable with value polymorphism. It is, however, usually fairly easy to rewrite programs to get around the restriction.

7.4.5.2 Structural Equivalence

In order for type inference to work, the type of a value must depend only on how it is built and used, so two values built the same way and used the same way must have the same type. This is called *structural equivalence* of types, as types are identified by structure. In contrast, *name equivalence* means that types are identified by their name, so two values may be built and used in exactly the same way but still have different types.

Standard ML, Haskell, and other languages that use Hindley-Milner-style type inference use structural equivalence, but object-oriented languages such as Java and

C# tend to use name equivalence: Two classes can have identical fields and methods, but if they are named differently, you cannot substitute a value from one with a value from the other (unless one inherits from the other). This limits the possibility of type inference in object-oriented languages: Usually types are inferred only for local variables that are instantiated to expressions of known type.

7.4.5.3 Constrained Type Variables

We said above that, after introducing the value-polymorphism restriction, Standard ML has only one kind of type variable. Strictly speaking, this is not true: Standard ML still has two kinds of type variables: *Unrestricted* type variables and *equality* type variables. The reason is that Standard ML has an overloaded equality operator (=) that works on most, but not all types (the exceptions being `real`, `exn`, function types and compound types containing these). If the equality operator is applied to a type represented by an unbound unrestricted type variable, that type variable is bound to an equality type variable. Equality type variables can only be instantiated to types that allow equality, and when generalised, they are generalised to equality-type parameters (indicated by using two quotes before the name, e.g., `"key`) that are substituted with equality type variables when instantiated.

Equality type variables are type variables that are constrained so they can only be instantiated to types that fulfil certain criteria. Such constraints on type variables and type parameters can be used for other purposes than polymorphic equality, though Standard ML does not. For example, it is possible to constrain type variables with subtype constraints or with requirements that certain overloaded operators (such as < and >) are implemented for the types they can be bound to. Java (see Sect. 7.4.6.2) allows explicit subtype and interface constraints on type parameters and the type inference in Haskell (see Sect. 7.4.6.3) can constrain type variables to types that implement specified interfaces (called *type classes* in Haskell).

7.4.6 Polymorphism in Various Languages

Though we have mentioned various languages in the sections above, we have given only fragmentary information about how polymorphism is used in these languages. We will remedy this by giving more detailed (though not complete) descriptions of polymorphism in a few specific languages.

7.4.6.1 Standard ML

Section 7.4.5.1 covers the polymorphism used in the core language of Standard ML, apart from ad hoc polymorphism used for arithmetic operators.

Standard ML, additionally, has a module language that introduces more kinds of polymorphism.

Briefly speaking, Standard ML modules consists of *signatures*, *structures*, and *functors*.

A signature is basically an interface (see Sect. 7.4.2): It specifies abstract declarations that obey specified type constraints. A structure is a collection of declarations that *implement* the specifications in the signature. A signature can import other signatures and impose constraints that selected types from these must be identical (using the `sharing` keyword). A functor is a function from structures to structures: It takes as arguments structures (that are usually declared to conform to specific signatures) and returns a structure (that may be similarly constrained). This is a form of explicit parametric polymorphism with constraints, though it is polymorphism over modules rather than over values.

For example, a signature may specify the interface of a symbol table: Abstract types for the symbol table, its keys and its values and type specifications of the operations for inserting key/value pairs in a symbol table and for looking up keys in the symbol table:

```
signature symbolTable =
sig
   type (''key, 'value) table
   val empty : (''key, 'value) table
   val insert : (''key, 'value) table -> (''key * 'value)
                      -> (''key, 'value) table
   val lookup : (''key, 'value) table -> ''key -> 'value option
end
```

A structure can provide an implementation of symbol tables using lists of pairs:

```
structure simpleTable :> symbolTable =
struct
   type (''k, 'v) table = (''k * 'v) list
   val empty = []
   fun insert table pair = pair :: table
   fun lookup [] key = NONE
     | lookup ((k1,v)::pairs) k2 =
         if k1=k2 then SOME v else lookup pairs k2
end
```

Another structure `hashTable` can provide an implementation of symbol tables using hash tables, and so on.

A compiler can then be made as a functor that is parameterised over the implementation of the symbol table:

```
functor compiler (table : symbolTable) =
struct
   ...
end
```

This functor can then be applied to a specific symbol-table implementation:

```
structure comp = compiler(simpleTable)
```

or

```
structure comp = compiler(hashTable)
```

Several implementations of Standard ML have added functors that can take functors as arguments and return functors as results, but this is not part of the 1997 standard.

7.4.6.2 Java

Java implements both ad hoc polymorphism, interface polymorphism, subtype polymorphism, and parametric polymorphism (generics), which was added in Java 5.0. While each of these alone is fairly easy to understand and implement, there are some subtle interactions between the different kinds of polymorphism that can add restrictions and complications.

In general, a type in Java is of the form

$$c \mathbin{\&} i_1 \mathbin{\&} \ldots \mathbin{\&} i_n$$

where c is a class name and the i_j are interfaces. This means that a value of this type must belong to a subclass of c and implement the interfaces $i_1 \mathbin{\&} \ldots \mathbin{\&} i_n$. Note that the class c is not required to implement the interfaces $i_1 \mathbin{\&} \ldots \mathbin{\&} i_n$: These are extra constraints on the subtypes of c that are allowed. You can, for example, let c be `Object`, so all classes that implement the interfaces $i_1 \mathbin{\&} \ldots \mathbin{\&} i_n$ are allowed.

Interfaces form a subtype relation where one interface can extend any number of existing interfaces (unlike a class that can extend only one existing class). This is called "multiple inheritance".

If all you know at compile time about a variable x is a type $c \mathbin{\&} i$, where c does not implement i, then an application $x.m()$, where m is a method implemented in i but not in c, the usual mechanism for applying a class method cannot be used (as m is not bound in the method table of c). Hence, Java (and JVM) has a fairly complex mechanism for invoking interface methods that is used in these cases.

We saw in Sect. 7.4.3 that the type of a conditional expression ($c\,?\,e_1\!:\!e_2$ in Java) is the least common supertype of the types of the branches. But while any two classes in Java have a least common superclass, the same is not true for interfaces. Though `Object` works as a common supertype for all types, even when these have interface constraints, this is not always a minimal supertype, and there may be cases where there is no unique minimal subtype. The type rule for conditional expressions in Java is, as a result, rather complicated.

Java generics (parametric polymorphism) is also complicated by subtyping. Even if `T1` is a subtype of `T2`, the two instances `C<T1>` and `C<T2>` of a generic class `C` are not in any subtype relation (unless `T1=T2`). This is because `C` can use its type argument in both covariant and contravariant roles, and it is not visible from the declaration of `C` in which roles its type argument is used. Java does, however, allow *wildcard* type arguments that can be given separate subtype and supertype constraints, which allows sub-type comparable instances to be created.

7.4.6.3 Haskell

Haskell implements parametric polymorphism and interface polymorphism.

In Haskell, interfaces are called "type classes", but should not be confused with classes from Java and other object-oriented languages, as a Haskell type class is just a collection of specifications of operations, and a type implements a type class by specifying implementations of these operations. This is done through an `instance` declaration that specifies that a type is an instance (using Haskell terminology) of a type class by specifying how the operations in the type class declaration are implemented by that type. An instance declaration can be polymorphic itself: It can specify type parameters that must be instances of certain type classes. For example, the type class `Ord` (values with an order relation) requires that any instance already implements an equality relation by specifying the constraint `(Eq a) =>`.

```
class  (Eq a) => Ord a  where
   (<), (<=), (>=), (>)  :: a -> a -> Bool
   max, min              :: a -> a -> a
```

This makes `Ord` a *subclass* of `Eq`. Like Java interfaces, multiple type-class (interface) constraints can be applied to a type class declaration.

A major difference between interfaces in Java and type classes in Haskell is how types are declared to be instances of an interface or type class: In Java, interface constraints are given when a class is declared, so it is not possible to connect an already-declared class to a new interface without rewriting the class declaration. In contrast, instance declarations in Haskell are separated from both type-class declarations and type declarations, so you can add instances to a type after it has been declared without having to rewrite the type declaration (or the type-class declaration).

We can declare that pairs of elements that implement `Ord` also implement `Ord` (using lexicographic ordering) by the following instance declaration:

```
instance (Ord a, Ord b) => Ord (a,b) where
   (x,y) < (p,q) = x<p || x==p && y<q
   (x,y) <= (p,q) = x<p || x==p && y<=q
   (x,y) >= (p,q) = x>p || x==p && y>=q
   (x,y) > (p,q) = x>p || x==p && y>q
   max x y = if x<y then y else x
   min x y = if x<y then x else y
```

which defines a lexicographic order relation on pairs using the order relations on the components of the pair.

This separation of type declaration and instance declaration also allows multiparameter type classes: Type classes relate several types by operations between them. For example, you can define a bijection type class by the definition

```
class Bijection a b where
   forward :: a -> b
   backward :: b -> a
```

A type class declaration can also define default implementations of some operations in terms of other operations. For example, we can extend the declaration of Ord above to

```
class  (Eq a) => Ord a   where
  (<), (<=), (>=), (>)   :: a -> a -> Bool
  max, min               :: a -> a -> a
  x > y = y < x
  x <= y = x<y || x==y
  x >= y = y<x || x==y
  max x y = if x<y then y else x
  min x y = if y<x then x else y
```

This means that an instance of Ord need only specify an implementation of <, as the rest can be derived from this and equality (which is defined through the (Eq a) constraint). For example, we can use the default declaration to make a simpler instance declaration for ordered pairs:

```
instance (Ord a, Ord b) => Ord (a,b) where
  (x,y) < (p,q) = x<p || x==p && y<q
```

Type variables in polymorphic function declarations can be constrained to require that instances implement specific type classes. For example, a sorting function can be defined by

```
qsort [] = []
qsort [x] = [x]
qsort (x:xs)
   = qsort [y|y<-xs, y<x] ++ [x] ++ qsort [y|y<-xs, y>=x]
```

which, since qsort uses < and >= operations that are defined in the Ord class, gives qsort the type (Ord a) => [a] -> [a]. This type is inferred from the definition of qsort using a variant of Hindley-Milner type inference.

While type classes form a subclass hierarchy, types are not ordered by any subtype relation. The subclass hierarchy can, however, be used to simplify type-class constraints. For example, the constrained type (Eq t, Ord t) => t can be simplified to (Ord t) => t, since Eq t is implied by Ord t.

The Glasgow Haskell Compiler extends Haskell with more polymorphism including *kind polymorphism*, that allows more generic definitions.

7.5 Further Reading

Types and polymorphism are studied in detail in [6]. Comparisons of language features for generic (polymorphic) programming are made in [1]. Standard ML is defined in [5], Java is described in [7], and Haskell is described in [2,4]. A discussion of different variants of Haskell-type classes can be found in [3].

7.6 Exercises

Exercise 7.1 Write the overloaded specification of the + operator in the language C using the notation from Sect. 7.4.1. Consult the conversion rules used in C before writing the specification.

Exercise 7.2 Some languages implicitly convert values of one type to values of another type to make application of an operator or function possible. For example, C converts integers to floating point if they are passed as arguments to functions that require floating-point parameters. JavaScript is much more aggressive about implicit type conversions. Describe what the results of the following operations are in JavaScript:

$$
\begin{aligned}
&1 + "2" \\
&1 * "2" \\
&"1" * "2" \\
&1 + \{\} \\
&\{\} + 2 \\
&\{1\} \\
&1+\{2\} \\
&\{1\}+2
\end{aligned}
$$

Why do you think implicit type conversion in JavaScript works like this? Consider why some cases are not symmetric.

Discuss why these rules may (or may not) be appropriate for the application area for which JavaScript is designed.

Exercise 7.3 The STUDENT example in Sect. 7.3.6 uses four digits to represent the year, but it used to be quite common for COBOL programs to use only two digits, where the first two were implied to be 19. A student record could, for example, be

```
01 STUDENT
   05 NAME PIC A(20)
   05 DATE-OF-ENTRY
      09 YEAR PIC 99
      09 MONTH PIC 99
      09 DAY PIC 99
   05 ECTS-POINTS PIC 9(3)V9
```

This was the source of the *year 2000 problem*, where years after 1999 would have smaller values than years before 2000. For example, 2022 (represented as 22) would be seen as smaller than 1960 (represented as 60). Changing old programs to use four digits instead of two had the problem that databases would use only two digits, and changing all data in all old databases was impractical. Suggest how you could handle the year 2000 problem in a school database using the STUDENT record above without changing the format in the database, but only changing how that data is interpreted.

Consider such operations as comparing 2 years to see which occurs first, subtracting two years to find the number of years between these, and adding a number of years to a year. State your assumptions.

Exercise 7.4 FORTRAN uses 1-indexed arrays, C uses 0-indexed arrays, and Pascal allows the index range to be specified. Discuss advantages and disadvantages of these design choices.

Exercise 7.5 Most languages with dynamic scoping (see Sect. 5.1.3.1) tend to also use dynamic types: Type checking, if any, is done at runtime. But it is possible to combine dynamic scoping and static typing. An example is found in some versions of BASIC: Integer variables are suffixed by %, string variables are suffixed by $, and variables that have no such suffix are floating point. FORTRAN has a similar rule: Variables beginning with letters I, J, K, L, and M are integers, while variables beginning with any other letter are floating point. Both of these, however, limit the number of different types: There are only so many letters in the alphabet, and there are only so many non-alphanumeric characters that can be used as suffixes to variables. Also, these name conventions do not reveal whether a variable is an array or a scalar.

Consider a language that has syntax identical to C but uses dynamic scoping, so if a function f calls a function g, g has access to variables declared in f in addition to global variables and variables declared in g. Note that this is the case even if g is called through a function pointer, so it isn't possible by inspection of f to see which function(s) it calls.

We want to do static type checking of this language, so no type checking is needed at runtime. We do not want to change the syntax of the language. We may impose restrictions on the relation between variable names and their types, but we will not want to restrict the number of different types (such as structs and arrays) it is possible to declare.

Suggest a method for performing static type checking given these conditions.

Exercise 7.6 Consider *fixed-point numbers*: Decimal fractions with a fixed number of digits before and after the decimal point. In a hypothetical language, we specify fixed-point number types as $m.n$, where m is the number of digits before the decimal point and n is the number of digits after the decimal point. m and n should both be non-negative integers. The numbers specified by such a type can be both positive and negative, so the type 2.1 contains numbers from -99.9 to 99.9 in steps of 0.1, and the type 0.2 specifies numbers from -0.99 to 0.99 in steps of 0.01. The type 0.0 contains only the value 0.

We want to define a subtype relation $\preceq$ on fixed-point types. We want $m.n \preceq p.q$ if a value of type $m.n$ can always be converted to a value of type $p.q$ without overflow and without loss of precision.

a. Describe necessary and sufficient conditions on the numbers m, n, p, and q that will ensure that $m.n \preceq p.q$.

b. Is there a type $a.b$ such that $a.b \preceq p.q$ for any p and q? If so, what is it?

c. Is there a type $a.b$ such that $m.n \preceq a.b$ for any m and n? If so, what is it?

d. Consider types $m.n$ and $p.q$, where $m.n \npreceq p.q$, a variable x of type $m.n$, and a variable y of type $p.q$. An assignment $y := x$ is not type safe, as x may have a value that cannot be converted to the type of y. Consider, now, a downcast operation $(p.q)x$ that converts the value of x to a value of type $p.q$, such that the assignment $y := (p.q)x$ is type safe. This is (like all downcasts) a *partial* operation: If the value can not be converted without overflow or loss of precision, a runtime error message is given. Describe what tests the downcast operation must make on the value of x to verify that the conversion can be made without overflow or loss of precision.

e. If x has type $m.n$ and y has type $p.q$, what is the most precise type you can give for the result of the expression $x + y$? Explain why.

f. If x has type $m.n$ and y has type $p.q$, what is the most precise type you can give for the result of the expression $x * y$? Explain why.

g. Consider an assignment $x := x + y$, where x has type $m.n$ and y has type $p.q$. For what values of m, n, p, and q will this assignment be type safe? How can the assignment statement be modified so it is always type safe, but still performs the same addition?

Exercise 7.7 In Java, types are bound to interfaces they implement in the declaration of the type (i.e., in a class declaration). In Haskell, a type can be declared to implement an interface (a type class) after the type itself is declared. Discuss advantages and disadvantages of these two approaches.

Exercise 7.8 In Java and C#, arrays with elements of different types are in a subtype relationship: If $A \preceq B$, then $A[\,] \preceq B[\,]$. This contradicts Sect. 7.4.3.1, where it is argued that arrays of (like references to) different types should be incomparable in the subtype relation regardless of how the element types are related. This implies that array types in Java are not statically type safe but require dynamic (runtime) checks to ensure type safety.

a. Why do you think the designers of Java and C# chose arrays to be in a subtype relationship when the elements are, even though this requires runtime type checks?

b. Describe where downcasts can be inserted to ensure runtime type safety when using arrays in Java or C#.

Exercise 7.9 Using the method sketched in Sect. 7.4.5.1, unify the following pairs of types. Note that letters A, B, ... represent type variables that are initially unbound, and a, b, c, ... represent type constructors. If the unification succeeds, show the bindings of type variables obtained through unification. If the unification fails, explain why.

a. $a(A, B)$ and $a(B, A)$.
b. $a(A, b(c))$ and $a(B, A)$.
c. $a(A, b(B))$ and $a(B, A)$.
d. $a(b(c), b(B))$ and $a(B, A)$.

Exercise 7.10 Using the informal method for type inference described in Sect. 7.4.5, do type inference for the function definition

```
fun rev ([],      ys) = ys
  | rev (x :: xs, ys) = rev (xs, x :: ys)
```

using the same list type as in the `length` example and using $s \times t$ as the type for pairs with components of types s and t. For example, the expression or pattern $(1,2)$ has type `int × int`.

Show the results of each of the four steps of the informal method.

Exercise 7.11 In Sect. 7.3.11.1, the idea of units of measure is described, and rules for addition, multiplication, and division are sketched.

Suggest a rule for when it is allowed to take the square root of a value with a unit-of-measure type, and what relation the argument and result units have to each other.

Exercise 7.12 Distance can be measured both in meters and in feet, and temperatures can be measured in both Celsius, Fahrenheit, and Kelvin. It makes sense to want to, say, add distances in feet to distances in meters, or add a temperature difference measured in Celsius to an absolute or relative temperature measured in Fahrenheit.

a. Design a syntax for declaring a unit to be related to another, e.g., declaring Fahrenheit to be related to Kelvin or feet to be related to meters. Note that the declaration should contain enough information to allow conversion between the related units.
b. If you add, say, a temperature in Fahrenheit to a temperature in Celsius, the result could be measured in either Fahrenheit or Celsius or even in Kelvin. What rules would you use to determine the unit of the result of an addition?

References

1. Garcia R, Jarvi J, Lumsdaine A, Siek J, Willcock J (2006) An extended comparative study of language support for generic programming. J Funct Program 17(02):145. http://www.journals.cambridge.org/abstract_S0956796806006198
2. Jones SLP (2003) Haskell 98 language and libraries: the revised report. Cambridge University Press, Cambridge. http://haskell.org/onlinereport/
3. Jones SP, Jones M, Meijer E (1997) Type classes: an exploration of the design space. In: Haskell workshop

4. Marlow S (2010) Haskell 2010 language report. http://www.haskell.org/onlinereport/haskell2010/
5. Milner R, Tofte M, Harper R, MacQueen D (1997) The definition of Standard ML. MIT Press, Cambridge
6. Pierce BC (2002) Types and programming languages. MIT Press, Cambridge
7. Sestoft P (2005) Java precisely, 2nd edn. The MIT Press, Cambridge

Modularisation

8

> *Complexity that works is built up out of modules that work perfectly, layered one over the other.*
>
> Kevin Kelly
>
> *Our ultimate goal is extensible programming (EP). By this, we mean the construction of hierarchies of modules, each module adding new functionality to the system.*
>
> Niklaus Wirth

In early programming languages, programs were *monolithic*: A program consisted of one file or one deck of punched cards. Reuse of code was done by copying parts of a program into another program. While this can work reasonably well for small programs, the link between the original and the copy is lost, so errors fixed in one of these are not also fixed in the other.

Modularisation is a mechanism for fixing this problem: A module is developed independently of the program that uses it, and errors need only be fixed in the original module, and the corrections can be propagated to the programs that use the module by recompiling these.

Modules can, additionally, have some abstraction features that allows a program to consists of parts that are not only physically independent modules, but also, in part, logically independent.

8.1 Simple Modules

In its simplest form, a module is just a piece of program text that can be textually included in a program—not by explicitly copying the text into the program, but by referring to the module by name (or file path), which makes the compiler or interpreter

© The Author(s), under exclusive license to Springer Nature Switzerland AG 2022
T. Ægidius Mogensen, *Programming Language Design and Implementation*,
Texts in Computer Science, https://doi.org/10.1007/978-3-031-11806-7_8

fetch the text from the module. To allow sharing, a module is typically stored in a file directory/folder that is shared among all programs that use the module. This works poorly on a system with no permanent storage, so all programs have to be read from cards or tape immediately prior to running them, which is why module systems only arose when permanently-attached disks with file systems became common.

While such simple text inclusion allows sharing of code that can be maintained independently of the programs that import this code, the code will be recompiled whenever a program that imports the code is compiled. If a program uses modules that are larger than the program itself, this overhead can be significant. For this reason, module systems often allow *separate compilation* of modules: A module is compiled independently of the programs that import the module, and the compiled code is combined with the code compiled for the program itself.

This combination (called *linking*) is not trivial: A variable or procedure in a module might be stored in different locations when included in different programs, so compiling a module not only produces code, but also information about where (relative to the start of the file) variables, labels and procedures are *stored*, and information about where these entities are *used* within the module (again relative to the start of the file). This allows the module variables and code to be placed at arbitrary addresses in memory, and all variable references, jumps and procedure calls modified to refer to the correct addresses in memory. So a module is compiled to a *linkable file*. A simple linkable file consists of three parts: A *code segment* where the compiled code is stored, but with unspecified target addresses of variable accesses, jumps and procedure calls, a *data segment* where global variables are stored, and a *relocation table* that contains the information necessary to place the code and data segments anywhere in memory, and to allow these to be accessed by the program (or other modules) that imports the module. More advanced linkable file formats allow multiple code and data segments, each with their own relocation tables.

If a language uses static types, a program that imports a module must be verified to use the variables, procedures, and other entities defined in the module in a way that does not conflict with the types of these. Without separate compilation, this is not a problem: The module is type-checked at the same time as the program that imports it. But with separate compilation, this is not so easy. A typical solution is to use a file (often called a *header file* or a *signature*) containing the necessary type information, which can be used when type-checking programs that import the module. In some languages, the header file is generated by the compiler when it compiles a module, and in other languages, it is written as a separate file by the programmer. In C, for example, the header file (using a .h file extension) is typically hand-written, though there are tools that can generate a header file from a module file (using a .c file extension). A linkable file for C has a .o file extension.

8.1.1   Shared Modules

While modules are conceptually shared between different programs, the code of a module is typically statically linked into the code for each program that uses the module. But it is also possible to have several programs that share the same module code at run time, avoiding having to store multiple copies of the module in memory.

Such shared modules (also called *dynamically linked libraries* or *relocatable modules*) are usually implemented by generating two linkable files: a shared executable file that can be located anywhere in memory, either by internally using only relative addressing or by using a relocation table, and a *stub*, that contains code that first checks if a copy of the module already exists in memory, and, if not, loads it into memory. After making sure the module is in memory, the stub finds the addresses of the exported entities and stores them in a local table. Each entity is then addressed indirectly through this table.

A shared module, once loaded into memory, usually keeps a count of the number of running programs that use the module, so it can be freed from memory when no programs use it any more. This is an instance of *reference counts*, see Sect. 4.7. Since the count is updated only when a program starts or finishes, the overhead is quite small.

A limitation of shared modules is that multiple users of the module should not be able to interfere with each other. This means that a shared module cannot use global or static variables to store information between different procedure calls, as the next procedure call might be from a different program. Also, the procedures must be *re-entrant*, meaning that one program can start executing a procedure before another program finishes doing so. This can be solved by allowing only stack-allocated variables in shared modules, so these are allocated on the stack of the calling programme, or by letting global and static variables be stored in a table in the stub included the calling program, and passing a reference to this table to all calls to procedures in the module, which must then access these variables indirectly through this table.

8.2 Modules with Abstraction

If header files are separate from the module files themselves, they do not need to specify types for *all* the entities declared in the module: Some entities declared in the module can be kept private to the module by not declaring them in the header file. This allows the maintainer(s) of the module to modify or replace the private entities without having to worry about breaking programs that use the module: They can't access these entities if they are not declared in the header file.

If a header file/signature is handwritten, the programmer can decide exactly which entities are made public. If the header file/signature is generated, the module must declare which entities are private and which are exported. One approach is to make entities public by default and require the programmer to specify those that are private. Alternatively, entities can by default be private, so exported entities are explicitly marked as such.

Abstraction mechanisms can not only determine which entities are exported or not but can also hide some information about the entities. For example, a module can export the *name* of a type, but not information about its *structure*. If creation and manipulation of values of this type are done through the use of other exported entities, the users of the module do not need to know the internals of the type. This makes the type an *abstract* type, and it allows the maintainer(s) of the module to change the internals of such abstract types completely, as long as they conform to the information revealed in the header file/signature.

If a signature does not reveal all information about the module, it can even allow multiple different modules to share the same signature. When a program imports a module, it needs only to specify the signature, and the actual identity of the module can be supplied later, when modules and program are linked together. In this context, a signature has the same relation to a module that a type has to a value: It specifies some constraints and operations that the module must implement in the same way that a type (implicitly or explicitly) specifies constraints and operations on values of the given type. See Sect. 7.4.6.1 for an example of several modules sharing a signature.

8.3 Name Spaces

When modules are written independently, it can easily happen that different modules declare functions, types, or variables using the same names.

To allow two (or more) such modules to be used by the same program, many languages allow modules to have independent *name spaces*: Each module has its own scope but allows names defined in this scope to be accessible from outside the module by prefixing the names with the module name. For example, if modules A and B both define entities named f, these can be accessed as A . f and B . f, respectively. Some languages use : : or other separators instead of a dot.

To remove the need for prefixes when accessing names in another name space, a name space can be *opened*, which merges the name space into the current scope. This can cause names already defined in the current scope to be shadowed by names defined in the opened name space, so this must be done with care, and it is generally recommended not to do this unless names defined in a name space are used *very* often in the program that imports the name space. Some module systems allow a program that uses a module to specify which entities it imports from the module, which reduces the risk of polluting the local name space when the module is opened.

8.3.1 Nested Modules

Some languages allow modules to be defined inside other modules. This allows modules to be organised in a hierarchy, so related modules are sub-modules of other modules. This hierarchy typically implies a similarly nested scope, so modules at inner levels implicitly have access to modules at outer levels.

So if module A contains two nested modules B and C (at the same level of scoping), an entity named x in module B can from inside module A be accessed by prefixing names by B, i.e., B.x, while access from C or from outside A requires a full path prefix (A.B.x).

Suggested Exercise: 8.1.

8.4   Modules and Classes

Modules and classes have a lot in common: They both define variables (fields) and procedures (methods) in a local scope, and classes are often able to declare fields and methods private, so these are not accessible from the outside. Even the dot-notation for accessing names defined in a name space is similar to the notation for accessing fields and methods in a class or object. In particular, static classes (classes where all fields and methods are static) are almost the same as modules, the main difference being that a static class usually cannot define new types, but only fields and methods. Inheritance in static classes is similar to importing and opening previously defined modules in a new module.

Dynamic classes are somewhat different, though: Here, you can define an object as a value that is an instance of a class, and inheritance works differently from module import. Mixins, which is a mechanism used in some object-oriented languages to import fields and methods from one class to another, is much closer to module import.

8.5   Modules as Parameters/Values

When signatures are separated from the modules themselves (so several modules can share the same signature), a signature can (as noted above) be viewed as a type for one or more modules. We noted above that this allows the module to be specified later than the signature, for example at linking. In some sense, the program is parameterised over all modules that match the given signature.

Some languages make this parameterisation explicit: A module can explicitly specify a module parameter constrained by a signature, and a user of the module can specify which module is passed as parameter to the parameterised module.

In Standard ML, a module without parameters is called a *structure*, while a module that takes other modules as parameters is called a *functor* because it can be viewed as a function from modules to modules. See Sect. 7.4.6.1 for more details. According to the standard, a functor cannot take other functors as parameters, only structures, but there are variants of ML that allow functors as parameters to functors. There are also variants of ML that allow modules to be passed around at run time, so a program can choose between different implementations of a signature depending on its input. This blurs the concept of a module somewhat and makes modules more similar to objects, where a signature for a module is similar to an interface for an object. See more details in Sect. 7.4.6.1.

8.6 Further Reading

More about linking can be found in [2]. A short comparison of module systems can be found in [1].

A paper about the design of the ML module system can be found in [3]. This uses a slightly different syntax than what was eventually standardised [4]. An extension (called MixML [5]) allows both mixin-like imports and modules as run-time values.

8.7 Exercises

Exercise 8.1 Find a language that allows nested modules and shows an example of a declaration of a nested module.

Exercise 8.2 Section 7.4.6.1 shows a signature for a symbol table and a structure that implements the signature using lists of pairs. Write another structure `treeTable` implements the signature using search trees.

References

1. Calliss FW (1991) A comparison of module constructs in programming languages. SIGPLAN Not 26(1):38–46. https://doi.org/10.1145/122203.122206
2. Levine JR (1999) Linkers and loaders, 1st edn. Morgan Kaufmann Publishers Inc., San Francisco, CA, USA
3. MacQueen D (1984) Modules for standard ML. In: Proceedings of the 1984 ACM symposium on LISP and functional programming, LFP'84. ACM, New York, NY, USA, pp 198–207. https://doi.org/10.1145/800055.802036
4. Milner R, Tofte M, Harper R, MacQueen D (1997) The definition of standard ML. MIT Press, Cambridge, MA, USA
5. Rossberg A, Dreyer D (2013) Mixin' up the ML module system. ACM Trans Program Lang Syst 35(1), 2:1–2:84 . https://doi.org/10.1145/2450136.2450137

Language Paradigms

9

> *I find languages that support just one programming paradigm constraining.*
>
> Bjarne Stroustrup
>
> *'Disruption' is, at its core, a really powerful idea. Everyone hijacks the idea to do whatever they want now. It's the same way people hijacked the word 'paradigm' to justify lame things they're trying to sell to mankind.*
>
> Clayton M. Christensen

9.1 What Is a Language Paradigm?

The word "paradigm" comes from Greek $\pi\alpha\rho\acute{\alpha}\delta\epsilon\iota\gamma\mu\alpha$, meaning "pattern", "example", "instance", or "object lesson". In modern language, the word is generally used to denote a group of things or concepts that share significant properties such as a defining theme or pattern of thought.

A language paradigm is, hence a selection of properties that a language can have or not have.

When concerning programming languages, paradigms usually concern properties of data flow, execution order, structuring, or combinations of these. We will look at these aspects below.

9.1.1 Data Flow

Data flow concerns how data is communicated from one part of a program to other parts, or from one execution of a piece of code to a later execution of the same piece of code. The main paradigms for data flow are

T. Ægidius Mogensen, *Programming Language Design and Implementation*, Texts in Computer Science, https://doi.org/10.1007/978-3-031-11806-7_9

Imperative.   Data is communicated by modifying the contents of locations (such as
   variables or heap addresses) that are shared between different parts of the program.
Functional/applicative.   Data is communicated by giving it as arguments to function
   calls and by returning it as results from function calls.
Logical.   Data is communicated through *logical variables*: shared locations that are
   initially uninitialised, but may be initialised by any of the program parts that share
   the locations, but not modified after initialisation, so they are write-once, read-
   many variables. Some languages allow logical variable to be rebound through
   backtracking.
Message passing.   Data is transferred as messages from one process to another.

Many languages use a combination of the above, so we classify a language by the
main method used for data flow in that language.

   Examples of almost purely imperative languages are FORTRAN 57, COBOL 60,
and many variants of BASIC: Even though these languages may have subroutines
or procedures, you can not give these parameters nor let these return results. All
values are communicated through global variables. Later variants of these languages
do allow parameters and results to function calls, but the main data flow mechanism
is still imperative.

   LISP was the first language to use mainly functional data flow, but LISP also has
mutable variables and locations, so it is not a pure functional language. Haskell and
Backus' FP languages are examples of pure functional languages.

   Logical variables are almost exclusively used in logic languages, the first of which
was Prolog. Logic languages also use parameter passing, and sometimes also function
result values. Prolog also has a limited form of mutable variable, but not all logic
languages do.

9.1.2 Execution Order

Execution order concerns the order in which different parts of the program are executed or evaluated, or how one piece of the program may be executed multiple times.
The main execution-order paradigms are

Sequential.   The syntax of the program indicates a well-defined (though possibly
   conditional) order in which execution/evaluation happens, and implementation
   of a language can only deviate from this order if the change is not observable.
   Conceptually, only one part of a program is executed at any one time.
Parallel.   Multiple operations are done at the same time, either by executing different parts of the program at the same time (thread parallelism) or by executing one
   piece of the program on multiple, different data at the same time (data parallelism).
Concurrent.   Execution of different parts (called *processes* or *threads*) of the program are *interleaved*. This can be by explicit passing of control to other parts of
   the program (coroutines) or by having outside events (such as timers, sensors, or
   availability of data) change which part of a program is executed. Concurrency

is different from parallelism because parallelism requires multiple calculations to happen at physically the same time (using multiple processors or processing elements), which concurrency does not. Conversely, parallelism does not imply passing of control between different parts of a program.

Declarative.   Execution order is mostly unspecified, so a program specifies *what* should be done, but not in which order this is done. This does not imply that computation can be done in *any* order, as there may be dependencies through data that impose a partial order on computations. Usually, the specific execution order used during execution is not observable in terms of *what* a program outputs, but it can have an effect on *when* (or even *if*) the program outputs something. This is in contrast to concurrency, where different execution orders can lead to different results.

As with data flow, many languages use a combination of several execution-order paradigms. Most early programming languages (FORTRAN 57, COBOL, LISP, ALGOL 60, and so on) are strictly sequential, but later variants of Fortran include explicit parallelism, and many ALGOL-like or LISP-like languages have concurrent features.

Functional languages and logic languages are often (mostly) declarative, but impure effects such as exceptions and input/output may impose sequential order. Declarative execution order often allows parallelism, as computations that are not data-dependent can be executed at the same time. While APL is sequential in the order in which statements are executed, operations on vectors do not specify an order in which vector elements are processed, so parallelism is possible without changing the observable behaviour, so APL is partly declarative. Pure functional languages like Haskell use almost entirely declarative evaluation order, but often require that only evaluations that *definitely* contribute to required output are done. Also, Haskell offers a mechanism (monads) for explicitly sequentialising computations by adding hidden data dependencies.

9.1.3   Structuring

Structuring is about how pieces of a program are joined to form large programs. The main paradigms for structuring are

Block structured   languages allow explicitly delimited blocks of declarations and code to be combined by nesting and sequence: A block can contain other blocks, and a block can follow another block, but two blocks can only overlap if one is properly nested within the other. A block can include both declarations and state-ments/expressions.

Procedural   languages allow procedures or functions to be declared so these can be called from other parts of a program (or even from within the procedure or function itself).

Modular   languages allow collections of declarations to be collected into named
  modules that can be used by multiple programs without repeating the declarations. A module can often hide details, so these details can be modified without
  impacting how the module is used, and a module can often be checked or compiled
  independently of the programs in which it is used. A module may be required to
  implement a specification (sometimes called a *signature*) that specifies a set of
  names that must be declared in the module and required properties of these, such
  as their types.
Object-oriented   languages structure programs using *objects*, where the word "object" is used in a specific way that differs from the day-to-day meaning of the
  word. An object is (in this context) a collection of variables (called *fields*) and
  procedures (called *methods*) that can access the fields in the same object. An object is a value, so it can be stored in variables or fields and passed as argument to
  or result from procedures or methods.
  Object-oriented languages can be *class-based* or *prototype-based*. Class-based
  languages require objects to be instances of statically declared *classes*, that are
  to objects what types are to values: An object is an instance of a class just like a
  value is an instance of a type. Classes can be related by a subtype relation (called
  inheritance or *sub-classing*). Prototype-based languages are dynamically typed,
  so instead of requiring an object to be an instance of a type, an object is constructed
  as a copy of another object (the prototype), possibly extended with more fields
  and methods. As long as an object is accesses only using field and method names
  that it defines, no runtime error occurs. This is called "duck typing".

Languages often allow several different structuring paradigms. ALGOL 60, for example, is both block-structured and procedural.

Modules in the simple form of text inclusion or separate compilation have existed
since around 1960, often as local extensions of languages that did not specify such
in their definitions. The Mesa language from 1970 introduced a module system
including specifications and implementations, but module systems did not become
widespread until Modula-2 and Modula-3 in the late 1970s. Most modern languages
have module systems.

The first object-oriented language was Simula from 1967. Simula is a class-based
language with inheritance and subclasses and is the major inspiration for later class-
based languages such as C++, Java, and C#. Prototype-based programming was introduced in SELF in 1986, and is used in many scripting languages such as JavaScript
and Lua.

9.1.4 Nomenclature

Most languages use one or more paradigms from each of the three aspects, but are
mostly designated by the paradigm(s) that the designers or users find most important. For example, most object-oriented languages are also imperative, and many
functional languages are also declarative. The word "multi-paradigm" is sometimes

used for languages that significantly support both functional, imperative, and object-oriented programming styles.

Suggested Exercise: 9.1.

9.2   A Closer Look at Some Paradigms

We have covered functional languages reasonably well in Chap. 5, and we have looked a bit at object-oriented languages in Chap. 7, but we have only briefly mentioned logic languages. In the sections below, we will look more closely at object-oriented and logic languages.

9.3   Object-Oriented Languages

We will assume basic familiarity with object-oriented languages like Java or C#. We focus mainly on the implementation aspects of class-based languages and briefly discuss the implementation of prototype-based languages.

9.3.1   Classes and Objects

A class is a set of declarations of fields and methods. From a class definition, a compiler will create information for the class: Offsets for fields and method pointers, types of fields and objects, and properties of these, such as whether they are private or public, static or dynamic, and so on.

Static fields and methods have addresses that can be computed at compile time when a class is declared, so there is no need to store these in the object or the class descriptor. We will ignore static fields and methods from now on, and assume all fields and methods are dynamic. We will also ignore private and final declarations, as the restrictions imposed by these are typically handled by type checking.

An object is created at runtime as an instance of a class. This means that it will have local copies of the fields declared in the class, and that when a method of the object is applied, the method can read and modify these local copies.

When an object is created, the compile-time information is used to create a record for the object. The record contains the local copies of the fields declared in the class. The record also contains a *class pointer* that points to a record (called a *class descriptor* or *virtual table*) that is shared by all objects that are instances of the class. This descriptor holds pointers to all methods of the class, and may also contain one or more superclass pointers.

9.3.2 Single Inheritance

A class can *inherit* or *extend* another class, called its *superclass*, which means that all fields and methods in the superclass are available in the class that inherits or extends it (called a *subclass* of the superclass). This is transitive, so a superclass of a superclass is a superclass, and ditto for subclasses.

A class can *override* method declarations from a superclass by redefining these methods. The type of a redefined method must match the type in the original declaration.

When an object is created (by calling the static constructor method of the class, usually called "new"), a record is allocated. This record has local copies of both the fields declared in its own class and those declared in its superclasses. These fields are ordered so fields in a superclass precede fields in its subclass. This means that the offset to a field in the record can be computed at compile time. The first field in the object record (at offset zero) is the pointer to its class descriptor. Note that a variable containing an object normally just contains a pointer to the object.

The class descriptor holds pointers to methods, also ordered so methods declared in a superclass precede those declared in a subclass, even if a method is overridden in the subclass. The difference is that an overridden method points to the implementation declared in the subclass, while a method declared in a superclass and not overridden points to the implementation declared in the superclass. As with fields, the offsets to methods in the descriptor can be computed at compile time.

The class descriptor also holds a pointer to the descriptor of the superclass (if any). This is used for subclass tests (downcasts); we will shortly see how. The superclass pointer is the first field in the class descriptor (at offset zero). The constructor method is static, so it is not in the descriptor. There can, however, be implicitly declared methods such as a `forward` method for copying garbage collection. Pointers to implementations of these (if any) are placed directly below the superclass pointer but before pointers to implementations of the class methods.

Figure 9.1 shows declaration of three classes and creation of four objects. Class A inherits `Object`, which is the top element in the class hierarchy and is a superclass of all classes. It declares a field n and a method f. Additionally, a constructor method is implicitly declared. Class B inherits A, so it has the fields and objects of A and declares a new field m and a new method g. Class C inherits B, so it has the fields and objects of A and B. It declares no new fields, but overrides the definition of method f. Note that the type of the new f is the same as the original. Below the class declarations are some variable declarations and assignments. The expression new A calls the implicitly defined constructor method for class A. This allocates a record containing a class descriptor pointer and the field n. The following statement sets n to 5. Other objects of type A, B, and C are allocated and their fields initialised. The assignment a2 = c; is allowed because a variable of type A can hold an object of type C (which is a subtype of A). The call a2.f(3) calls the method f that is declared in C because the value of a2 is an object of type C. The method is found in the class descriptor of the object, not the variable. This is called *dynamic method calls*. Hence, the print statement will print 14. Only the constructor methods are

Fig. 9.1 Declaration of
classes and objects

```
class A inherits Object {
    int n;
    int f(int a) { return n + a; }
}

class B inherits A {
    int m;
    void g() { m *= n; }
}

class C inherits B {
    int f(int a) { return n - a; }
}

A a1 = new A;
a1.n = 5;
A a2 = new A;
a2.n = 7;
B b = new B;
b.n = 9;
b.m = 13;
C c = new C;
c.n = 17;
c.m = 19;
a2 = c;
print a2.f(3);
```

static. The method f needs to access the fields of the object, so the object itself is passed as an implicit parameter to f, so the call is compiled as a2.f(a2, 3) and the method is compiled as if it was declared as

```
int f(C this, int a) { return this.n - a; }
```

This implicit parameter is similar to the static link used for accessing non-local variables in Sect. 5.2.3. Object-oriented languages typically allow methods to explicitly access this parameter (often called this or self).

Figure 9.2 shows the records and class descriptors for the objects and classes declared in Fig. 9.1. Names like f_A denote a pointer to the code for the method f as declared in the class A. The far right box is the previous value of a2 (before the last two lines of Fig. 9.1), as indicated by the light-grey arrow from a2. This reference no longer exists at the end of Fig. 9.1), so the (now unreachable) box will be removed by the next garbage collection.

When a method is applied, the statically computed offset is used to find the method pointer in the class descriptor, and then this method is called through its pointer. Every method has an implicit parameter that holds a pointer to the object from which the method is invoked. When a method accesses a field, it is accessed by the statically computed offset through this object pointer. The call a2.f(3) from Fig. 9.1 is compiled to code that does the following:

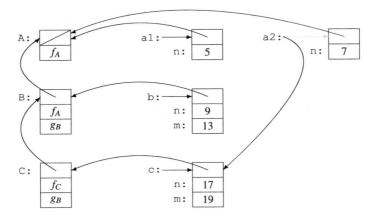

Fig. 9.2 Memory state at the end of Fig. 9.1

1: Evaluate the expression 3 to the value 3.
2: Find the descriptor pointer to C at offset 0 from a2.
3: f has a global, static offset 1 that is the same in all subclasses of A. Find the implementation f_C of f at the offset 1 in C.
4: Call f_C with the parameters (a2, 3).
5: When f_C evaluates n − a, it accesses n through the pointer to a2 that it was given as the first, implicit parameter this to f_C. So, the expression n − a generates code corresponding to this.n − a.

Subtyping means that if B is a subclass of A, an object bb of type B can be used whenever an object aa of type A is expected. Since bb has all the fields expected of aa at the same offsets in the record, and all the methods of A (possibly overridden) in its class descriptor at the same offsets, this works as expected. If, furthermore, C is a subtype of B, a variable x declared to be of type A can hold an object cc of type C, so calling x.f(11) can call the f method implemented in class C instead of the f method implemented in class A. This is the essence of dynamic (virtual) method calls.

Recursive method calls need not be virtual: If a method calls itself, its address is known at compile time. It is a bit more complicated when a method calls another method in the same class. The other method can have been overridden, so there are two choices: Call using a virtual/dynamic call (in which case the overriding method is called), or call the method directly (in which case the original method is called). There is no obvious answer to which is better, so it is a design choice that should be documented.

Since a variable x of type A can hold objects of type A, B, or C, it can be useful to test which type it actually has. If it is verified that its value has type B, fields and methods declared in B (and not in A) can be used. This is a form of dynamic typing. To verify that the value of x has type B, we look at the class descriptor that x points to. If this is the class descriptor for B, we know x to be of this type. However, since all subtypes of B are also considered to be of type B, a different class descriptor does not imply that the value is not of type B—the class descriptor could be from a subtype of B such as C. So to test if a value is of type B, we need a loop:

1: Find the class descriptor pointer *d* of the value.
2: If *d* points to the class descriptor of B, return true.
3: If *d* is a null pointer, return false.
4: Set *d* to the contents of the superclass pointer in *d* and go to step 2.

A downcast is done the same way: A downcast to type B is an identity function guarded by a type test.

Suggested Exercise: 9.2.

9.3.3 Multiple Inheritance

With multiple inheritance, a class can inherit from two or more superclasses. For example, a class C can inherit from two unrelated classes A and class B. This has several consequences:

1. If both A and B have a field named x of different types, which of these are used in C?
2. If both A and B implement a method called f, which implementation is used in C?
3. If A stores a field x at offset *k* and B stores a field y at offset *k*, which offsets should be used for x and y in C?
4. The same as above for offsets to method pointers in the class description.

Issues 1 and 2 can be solved by precedence: If A is mentioned before B in the list of classes that C inherits, the fields and methods of A are used when there is a conflict. This can, however, lead to type errors: If B has a method f not found in A, f is accessible from C. If both A and B have a field x, the field x from A is accessible from C. If f uses x, it must use the x from A, which may have a different type than the x from B that it expects. A similar problem occurs if a method in C calls a method that exists in both A and B, but with different types. If we disallow overlap between A and B, the *diamond problem* occurs: If A and B both inherit from a common superclass S, they will, by necessity, overlap. A solution can be to allow overlap if the overlapping fields and methods are inherited from S, but disallow if they are defined or overridden in A or B.

Issues 3 and 4 are more tricky. A simple solution is to require every field and method in the program to have a unique, global offset. This means that when a new class is declared, all its fields and methods have offsets that follow the offsets used by all classes declared before this, even if it does not inherit any of these. This is a huge waste of space, as an object will have many empty slots in its record. This can be reduced by using indirections: Class descriptors use unique global offsets for all fields and methods, and for each field, the descriptor holds a (non-unique) offset into the object record. To access a field, the unique offset of the field name is used in the class descriptor to find the non-unique offset in the object record. Class descriptors have many empty slots, but since these are allocated only once per class, this is tolerable. An alternative is to use hashing: A field or method name is hashed into a small offset, and all fields and methods with this offset are stored in a linked list at this offset in object records and class descriptors. There is still waste, but (with a suitably small hash table size) much less. Access is, however, much slower even though translating names to hash codes can be done at compile time.

Both of the above methods allow dynamic class loading: If you use unique global offsets, a freshly loaded class will just use offsets higher than those already used. When using hashing, a new hash table is created for the new class. But if the whole hierarchy is known in advance, the method using global unique offsets can be optimised using graph colouring: Two classes are said to *interfere*, if they both inherit from the same superclass or one is a subclass of the other. If two different classes do not interfere, they can use the same offsets for their fields and methods, but if they do interfere, offsets of new (non-inherited) fields of these classes must be different. By using graph colouring (as in register allocation), a minimal set of non-interfering offsets can be found. But when a new class is added, the graph colouring must be redone and the code recompiled with new offsets, so the method does not work well with dynamic class loading.

Type checks are also more complicated when there is multiple inheritance: There is no single superclass pointer, so several chains of superclass pointers must be searched to determine if an object is of a type that is a subclass of a specified class.

So while multiple inheritance can be useful, the complication of implementing it correctly and efficiently is a barrier that makes many language designers choose single inheritance. With static classes or interfaces, many of the issues can be resolved at compile time, so some languages allow multiple inheritance of these while allowing only single inheritance for non-static classes. For example, interfaces in Java can use multiple inheritance.

9.3.4 Prototype-Based Languages

Prototype-based object-oriented languages have objects but not classes. Instead of (mostly) static type checking, prototype-based languages rely on *duck typing*: Type errors are only reported (at runtime) if an object is accessed using a method or field it does not possess.

Prototype-based languages, like class-based languages, use records containing fields and descriptors containing method pointers, but methods are identified not by offsets into the descriptor, but by name, so the descriptor has a mapping from names to method pointers. This mapping can be implemented as a list or sorted tree of name/value pairs, or as a hash table. The descriptor also contains a mapping of field names to offsets in the object record.

New objects are usually constructed by *cloning* another object, called the *prototype* and then later updating the fields. When cloning an object, new fields or methods can be added. If these have the same names as existing fields or methods, these are overridden.

If no new fields or methods are added, the descriptor is shared with the prototype, but if new fields or methods are added, a new descriptor is made.

There is no superclass pointer, as there are no superclasses, downcasts, or type tests. Multiple inheritance is not normally supported, as you clone a single prototype object. It is, however, possible to extend an object with all fields and methods of another object, so a similar effect can be achieved.

Suggested Exercise: 9.3.

9.4 Logic Languages

We have only briefly mentioned logic languages, and since these are less well known than functional and imperative languages and radically different from these, we give a short introduction to these.

In a logic language, you express a program as a set of logical predicates, and running a program is done by asking if a logical query containing variables can be made true relative to the program by instantiating the variables.

For example, if the program is a set of predicates that determines if a triangle with integer edge lengths is a right-angled (Pythagorean) triangle, you can use the program to test if a specific triangle is Pythagorean or, by specifying only two edges of the triangle, to see if a third edge length exists that would make the triangle Pythagorean (and what that edge length would be). You can even use the program to list *all* Pythagorean triangles by demand. Logic languages are used mainly for database programming and artificial intelligence.

Logic languages originated with the language Prolog (short for "programming with logic") in the 1970s. Since then, many other logic languages have been developed, some of which combine logic and functional languages and some of which extend the logical predicates of the original Prolog with arithmetic constraints. We will, in this chapter, focus on Prolog, as this provides a basic understanding of the issues in implementing logic languages.

9.4.1 Pure Prolog

Pure Prolog is a subset of Prolog that is restricted to use only logically sound features, whereas full Prolog has extensions that break logical soundness and, hence, must be used with care. We will return to full Prolog in Sect. 9.4.4.

Pure Prolog works on logical statements about values that are built from function symbols and variables. A function symbol is either an integer constant or a sequence of letters and digits that starts with a lowercase letter. A variable is a sequence of letters and digits that starts with an uppercase letter. Usually, more characters are allowed, but we will stick to this simple characterisation. Function symbols that are not numbers may have parameters, which are separated by commas and enclosed in parentheses. Variables do not have parameters.

Examples of values are

A	a variable
nil	a function symbol without parameters
cons(13,nil)	a function symbol with two parameters that are both function symbols.
cons(X,Y)	a function symbol with two parameters that are both variables.

We call a value *ground* if it does not contain variables. In the examples above, the second and third values are ground.

A *goal* is a predicate symbol that can have parameters that are values. A predicate symbol has the same form as a function symbol—they are only distinguished by context. Examples of goals are

true	a predicate symbol without parameters
false	a predicate symbol without parameters
pythagorean(3,4,5)	a predicate symbol with three parameters that are all function symbols
pythagorean(A,B,C)	a predicate symbol with three parameters that are all variables.

A *clause* is a logical statement that is declared to be true. This can either be a *fact*, which is a goal followed by a period, or an *implication*, which is a goal followed by the symbol :- (which is read as "if" and corresponds to the logical implication symbol ⇐) and a list of goals separated by commas (which can be read as "and") and terminated by a period. Examples of clauses are

```
true.
pythagorean(3,4,5).
pythagorean(A,B,C) :-
    square(A,X), square(B,Y), square(C,Z), sum(X,Y,Z).
```

The three first clauses above are facts, and the last (which is split over two lines) is an implication that states that A, B, and C form a Pythagorean triple when the sum of the squares of A and B equals the square of C—assuming suitable definitions of the predicate names square and sum. Clauses have only one goal on the left-hand side of the :- symbol and there is no explicit negation, so the clauses are in the class of so-called *Horn clauses*.

A *predicate definition* is a list of clauses where the facts and left-hand sides of implications have the same predicate symbol and number of arguments. So, the two clauses for pythagorean above form a predicate definition.

A program consists of a list of predicate definitions. It is assumed that *only* goals that are consequences of these predicates are true and that *all* consequences of the predicates are true. This is called *the closed-world assumption*.

A simple example of a Prolog program is shown in Fig. 9.3. It starts by listing a set of facts about the parentage of a number of persons. Note that the names of these persons are written with lowercase initials, as they would otherwise be variables and not symbols. Next come two clauses that define a predicate called `parent` that states that a parent is either a mother or a father, followed by clauses defining predicates `grandparent`, `ancestor`, `siblings`, and `cousins`. Note that the right-hand side of the clause for `grandparent` uses a variable Z that does not occur on the left-hand side. Such variables are implicitly existentially quantified, so the clause states that Y is a grandparent of X if there exists a person Z such that Z is a parent of X and Y is a parent of Z. Similar existentially quantified variables are used in the last three clauses.

Running this program is done by formulating a query containing a goal and asking the Prolog system if this is true. For example, the query

```
?- parent(isabella, mary).
```

will return `true`, as this is a logical consequence of the clauses in the program. We can also ask `?- grandparent(isabella, Y).` which will return Y =

```
mother(christian, mary).
mother(isabella, mary).
mother(mary, henrietta).
mother(frederik, margrethe).
mother(joachim, margrethe).
mother(felix, alexandra).

father(christian, frederik).
father(isabella, frederik).
father(mary, john).
father(frederik, henri).
father(joachim, henri).
father(felix, joachim).

parent(X, Y) :- mother(X, Y).
parent(X, Y) :- father(X, Y).

grandparent(X, Y) :- parent(X, Z), parent(Z, Y).

ancestor(X, Y) :- parent(X, Y).
ancestor(X, Y) :- parent(X, Z), ancestor(Z, Y).

siblings(X, Y) :- parent(X, Z), parent(Y, Z).

cousins(X, Y) :- grandparent(X, Z), grandparent(Y, Z).
```

Fig. 9.3 A Prolog program about family relations

```
list(nil).
list(cons(A,As))  :- list(As).

append(nil,Bs,Bs)  :- list(Bs).
append(cons(A,As),Bs,cons(A,Cs))  :- append(As,Bs,Cs).
```

Fig. 9.4 A Prolog program using lists

henrietta. We can ask for more solutions by typing a semicolon, which will give us Y = john. Further semicolons will give us Y = margrethe and Y = henri. Asking ?- siblings(X, frederik). will give us X = frederik, X = joachim, X = frederik, and X = joachim. We get X = frederik as a result because the rules do not say that you are not a sibling of yourself. Pure Prolog does not allow negative statements, so we can not express this restriction. We get the same results several times because there are several ways to find these results. For example, siblings(joachim, frederik) is true both because they share a mother and because they share a father. So the query ?- cousins(X, Y). will list each result four times because there are four ways in which two people can be cousins. It will also make a person a cousin of him/herself, and it will list, for example, both X = christian, Y = isabella and X = isabella, Y = christian because it is a symmetric relation.

Another example program is shown in Fig. 9.4. The program defines two predicates: list and append, each defined by two clauses. Intuitively, the first clause states that nil is a list and the second predicate states that a value of the form cons(A,As) is a list if As is a list. The second predicate defines what it means to append lists. The first clause for the append predicate states that the empty list (nil) appended to Bs is equal to Bs if Bs is a list. The second clause states that a value of the form cons(A,As) appended to a value Bs is a value of the form cons(A,Cs) if As appended to Bs is equal to Cs.

In general, a query is the symbol ?- followed by a list of goals separated by commas and terminated with a period. Examples of queries are

```
?- pythagorean(3,4,5).    a ground query.
?- list(A), append(A,A,A).  a non-ground query consist-
                          ing of two goals linked by a
                          shared variable.
```

Running a program is done by specifying a query. The execution will then find an instantiation of the variables in the query that makes the query a consequence of the clauses in the program. If no such instantiation exists, the program execution responds with "no", indicating that no solution exists. If a solution is found, it is possible to ask for more solutions.

A solution is given in the form of a *substitution*, which is like the substitutions used in the Hindley-Milner algorithm (Sect. 7.4.5.1) with the following differences:

- We bind logic variables to values instead of type variables to types.
- We use function symbols instead of type constructors.
- When looking for new solutions, we will *unbind* some variables, so they can later be bound to new values.

The values may contain unbound variables. The intended meaning is that any values that these variables may have to give valid solutions to the query. To find solutions, we will use unification as in the Hindley-Milner algorithm with the differences mentioned above.

Figure 9.5 shows an example of running a query with respect to the program in Fig. 9.4. The first line is the query (terminated with a period). The two following lines report that one possible solution is

```
[As = nil, Bs = cons(1, cons(2, cons(3, nil)))]
```

After pressing semicolon, the Prolog system reports another solution

```
[As = cons(1, nil), Bs = cons(2, cons(3, nil))]
```

Note that the bindings to As and Bs have been unbound and rebound to new values. By pressing semicolon again, we get two more solutions before the Prolog system returns `false`, indicating that no more solutions exist. Some Prolog systems write `no` instead of `false`.

9.4.2 List Notation

For readability, Prolog uses a list notation similar to the notation used in functional languages like ML and Haskell. For example, a list of the first four integers can be written as [1, 2, 3, 4]. The empty list is written as [], and a list starting with head

```
?- append(As,Bs,cons(1,cons(2,cons(3,nil)))).
As = nil,
Bs = cons(1, cons(2, cons(3, nil))) ;
As = cons(1, nil),
Bs = cons(2, cons(3, nil)) ;
As = cons(1, cons(2, nil)),
Bs = cons(3, nil) ;
As = cons(1, cons(2, cons(3, nil))),
Bs = nil ;
false.
```

Fig. 9.5 Running a query

```
list([]).
list([_|As]) :- list(As).

append([],Bs,Bs) :- list(Bs).
append([A|As],Bs,[A|Cs]) :- append(As,Bs,Cs).
```

Fig. 9.6 A Prolog program using list notation

A and tail As is written as `[A | As]`. So, the list `[1, 2, 3, 4]` can, equivalently,
be written as `[1 | [2, 3, 4]]` or `[1, 2, | [3, 4]]`. Furthermore, an underscore
can be used as an unnamed variable (a wildcard). Using this notation, the program
in Fig. 9.4 can be written as in Fig. 9.6.

Suggested Exercise: 9.4.

9.4.3 Resolution

Running a query as shown in Fig. 9.5 is done by logical resolution. We will omit
the mathematical theory behind resolution and present an operational view of how
resolution is implemented in Prolog.

Given a query $?- p_1(x_1), p_2(x_2), \ldots, p_n(x_n) .$, where p_i are predicate symbols
and x_i are lists of terms that may contain variables, we look for a clause in the
program that uses the predicate symbol p_1. Let us say that this clause has the form

$$p_1(y_0) :- q_1(y_1), q_2(y_2), \ldots, q_m(y_m) .$$

where q_i are predicate symbols and y_i are lists of terms. We start by *renaming* this
clause so it does not have variables in common with the query. The reason is that
variables in the clause are local to the clause, so to avoid name clashes when we
combine the query and the clause, we make sure that there are no common names.
This gives us a clause

$$p_1(y_0') :- q_1(y_1'), q_2(y_2'), \ldots, q_m(y_m') .$$

We then try to unify the goal $p_1(x_1)$ with the goal $p_1(y_0')$. If the unification succeeds
with a substitution Θ, we replace the original query with

$$?- \Theta \left(q_1(y_1'), q_2(y_2'), \ldots, q_m(y_m'), p_2(x_2), \ldots, p_n(x_n) \right) .$$

That is, we replace the goal $p_1(x_1)$ in the query with the (renamed) right-hand side
of the matching clause and then replace variables with values as indicated in the
substitution Θ. We then continue by applying resolution to the new query, until the
query is empty. More bindings are added to the substitution during this process.
The solution is given by applying the resulting substitutions to the variables of the
original query.

If the unification of $p_1(x_1)$ and $p_1(y_0')$ fails, we can try other clauses with the same function symbol p_1 on the left-hand side: All bindings that were made when attempting unification of $p_1(x_1)$ and $p_1(y_0')$ are undone, so the variables can be rebound to new values.

If there are no untried clauses, the current path of investigation does not lead to a solution, so we go back and try a different clause for an earlier resolution step (again undoing all bindings made in the mean time). If this also fails, we go back to an even earlier resolution step, and so on, until we either find a solution or there are no further resolution steps to go back to, in which case, we report that there are no solutions (by printing `false`). This is called *backtracking*.

When a solution is presented to the user, the user can press semicolon to force backtracking, so the Prolog system looks for further solutions.

We can use Fig. 9.5 as an example. We start with the query

```
?- append(As,Bs,cons(1,cons(2,cons(3,nil)))).
```

The first clause in the predicate for append in Figure 9.4 is renamed to

```
append(nil,Bs01,Bs01) :- list(Bs01).
```

This is unified with the first (and only) goal in the query, yielding the substitution

```
[ As = nil,
  Bs01 = cons(1,cons(2,cons(3,nil))),
  Bs = cons(1,cons(2,cons(3,nil))) ]
```

The resulting query is

```
?- list(cons(1,cons(2,cons(3,nil)))).
```

This does not match the first clause of the `list` predicate, so we try the second clause. We first rename the clause to

```
list(cons(A02,As03)) :- list(As03).
```

and then unify, yielding the new substitution

```
[ A02 = 1,
  As03 = cons(2,cons(3,nil)) ]
```

and the resulting query

```
?- list(cons(2,cons(3,nil))).
```

After a few more steps, we get the query

```
?- list(nil)
```

which matches the first clause of the predicate for `list`. The resulting query is the empty query, so we have found a solution.

We apply the resulting substitution to the variables from the original query, giving the result

$$[\,\texttt{As} = \texttt{nil},$$
$$\texttt{Bs} = \texttt{cons(1,cons(2,cons(3,nil)))}\,]$$

which, apart from notation, is the first solution shown in Fig. 9.5.

If the user presses semicolon to ask for more solutions, we backtrack. The queries involving the list predicate do not have any untried matching clauses, so we go all the way up to the clause for append, where we try the second clause instead of the first (while undoing all bindings made when trying the first clause). The second clause renames to

append(cons(A04,As05),Bs06,cons(A04,Cs07))

:- append(As05,Bs06,Cs07).

which successfully unifies with the query, resulting in the substitution

$$[\,\texttt{As} = \texttt{cons(1,As05)},$$
$$\texttt{Bs} = \texttt{Bs06},$$
$$\texttt{A04} = \texttt{1},$$
$$\texttt{Cs07} = \texttt{cons(2,cons(3,nil))}\,]$$

When applying this substitution to the right-hand side of the clause (which replaces the old goal in the query), we get the new query

?- append(As05,Bs06,cons(2,cons(3,nil))).

This matches the first clause of append, yielding the substitution

$$[\,\texttt{As05} = \texttt{nil},$$
$$\texttt{Bs06} = \texttt{cons(2,cons(3,nil))}\,]$$

and the resulting query

?- list(cons(2,cons(3,nil)))

which succeeds. The result is obtained by applying the resulting substitution to the variables in the original query, yielding

$$[\,\texttt{As} = \texttt{cons(1,nil)},$$
$$\texttt{Bs} = \texttt{cons(2,cons(3,nil))}\,]$$

The two remaining solutions can be found by backtracking in a similar way.

Given a query, we can draw a *resolution tree*. The root node is the initial query and the children of a node are found by resolving the leftmost sub-query of the query with all the different matching clauses in the program ordered by their occurrences in the program. The edges of the resolution tree are labeled with the new bindings added by the resolution steps restricted to the variables in their parent nodes. Leaves of the tree are either queries that match no clause (so no solution can be found), or empty queries (marking that a solution is found). We will draw the latter as □.

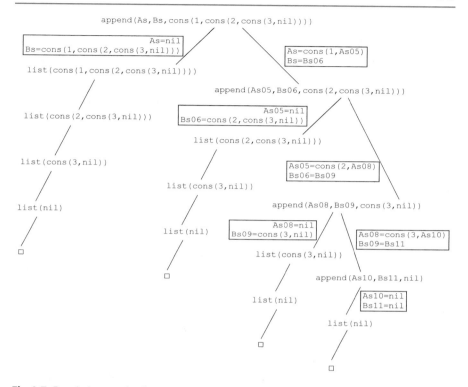

Fig. 9.7 Resolution tree for the query ?- append(As, Bs, cons(1, cons(2, cons(3, nil)))))

As an example, the query ?- append(As, Bs, cons(1, cons(2, cons(3, nil)))).
and the program shown in Fig. 9.4 (as used in the example above) gives the resolution
tree shown in Fig. 9.7. The substitution on the left branch gives one solution, and
by composing the substitutions on the other paths, we get other solutions. For
example, following the rightmost path gives As=cons(1, cons(2, cons(3, nil)))
and Bs=nil. Since the resolution tree is complete, these are all the solutions.

A resolution tree can be infinite, so there can be an infinity of solutions. There can
also be infinite paths that do not lead to any solutions. Hence, a depth-first search of
the resolution tree might go down an infinite path and miss solutions in paths to the
right of this in the tree.

So depth-first search of the resolution tree is not logically complete. But if breadth-
first search is used, resolution is *sound* and *complete* for Horn clauses: Any solution
found by resolution will be valid (soundness), and any valid solution can be found by
resolution (completeness). Even when there are only finitely many valid solutions,
breadth-first search may, however, not terminate, as there can be infinite branches
that never lead to solutions. So after finding all valid solutions, a breadth-first search
procedure may keep searching forever for more solutions without finding any. But

depth-first search may not even find all valid solutions (or even one) before it goes down an infinite, unproductive path.

Nearly all Prolog systems use depth-first search as this is in most cases much faster and less memory-hungry than breath-first search. To reduce the chances of going down infinite paths in the resolution tree, most Prolog systems add control operators that can cut off branches of the search tree. We will look at these in the next section.

Suggested Exercises: 9.5 and 9.6.

9.4.4 Full Prolog

Implementations of Prolog usually relax the requirements of soundness and completeness, as sound and complete implementations are costly. The first victim is completeness: A breadth-first search is expensive, so depth-first search is chosen.

The second victim is soundness: The occurs-check in unification is expensive when a variable is bound to a large value, so this check is often omitted (or made optional). This omission allows circular substitutions like [X = f(X)]. Such substitutions represent pseudo-solutions that are not valid in a model of finite trees.

It should be noted, that for pure Prolog, all finite (non-circular) solutions found by such an implementation are valid, so this does not impact soundness of the reported finite solutions—and the infinite solutions can easily be detected. The main consequence is rather a further reduction in completeness: The circular structures produced by unification without occurs-check can lead to nontermination that prevents further valid solutions from being found.

Depth-first search can search infinite, unsuccessful branches of the resolution tree and never get to later, potentially successful branches. In order to avoid some of these unsuccessful searches, *full Prolog* adds *control operators* that can limit backtracking. While the control operators may be used to prevent search in infinite branches and, hence, allow more solutions to be found, use of these can also prevent search in branches that may contain valid solutions, so completeness as a whole is neither better nor worse than in pure Prolog.

The most common control operators are *cut* (written as !), *negation as failure* (written as \+), and delays, which we will look at below. Additionally, full Prolog also provides arithmetic on numbers.

9.4.4.1 Cut

Cut is an operator that prevents backtracking: If a cut is encountered on the right-hand side of a clause, goals to the left of the cut on the same right-hand side are not backtracked, nor are the other clauses of the same predicate. Consider the Prolog program in Fig. 9.8. Without the cut, a query ?- p(X). would return the results X=3 and X=4, but because backtracking to find more solutions for q(A) gets to the non-terminating third clause, it would loop forever and not return X=7, even though

Fig. 9.8 Example of
program using cut

```
p(A)  :-  q(A),  !,  r(A).
p(7).

q(3).
q(4).
q(5)  :-  q(5).

r(3).
```

it is a valid consequence of the logical rules. In fact, the query `?- p(7).` would succeed.

With the cut placed as shown, the cut is encountered as soon as the goal `q(A)` succeeds with the binding `A=3`. This means that, when `r(3)` yields an answer and backtracking is done, `q(A)` is not retried and nor is the second clause of `p`. So while no further solutions are returned, execution will terminate rather than end in an infinite loop. Note that the query `?- p(7).` will still succeed because the cut has scope only within the rule in which it occurs.

Since cut only limits backtracking (cuts away branches in the resolution tree), it will not compromise soundness. But it can give some surprising results: In pure Prolog, if a query `?- f(A).` succeeds with a substitution `A=w` for some value w, then the query `?- f(w).` will also succeed. With cut, this is no longer true. Consider the program shown in Fig. 9.9. Note that the predicate `fail` will always fail, as there is no clause that can make it succeed. The query `?- f(A).` will succeed with the substitution `A=4`, because `g(A)` fails due to the cut in the first rule for `g`. But the query `?- f(4).` will fail, as `g(4)` succeeds. This means that variables in answer substitutions are no longer truly universally quantified. Generally, cuts must be used with care.

9.4.4.2 Negation as Failure

In pure Prolog, there is no negation. This limits the expressive power compared to full first-order logic, where a clause can have any number of positive and negative goals. To regain some of this power, full Prolog includes a limited form of negation called *negation as failure*. Negation of failure works like normal negation except when it comes to unbound variables: With true negation, the formula $\exists X : \neg p(X)$ is equivalent to $\neg(\forall X : p(X))$. But with negation as failure (written as `\+`), $\exists X : \+ p(X)$ is read as $\neg(\exists X : p(X))$. This means that $\+(\+ p(X)) \neq p(X)$, as the double negation using `\+` unbinds all variables that resolving $p(X)$ binds.

Fig. 9.9 Program with
non-monotone behaviour

```
f(X)  :-  g(X),  !,  fail.
f(4).

g(3)  :-  !,  fail.
g(X).
```

Negation as failure is implemented like cut: a goal of the form \+ p is rewritten into the goal p' where p' is implemented with the clauses

```
p' :- p, !, fail.
p'.
```

So if p succeeds, p' fails, and if p fails, p' succeeds. But in neither case will any variables be bound.

\+ is unsound if viewed as an implementation of "real" logical negation, *except* when it is used on goals without unbound variables. For this reason, some Prolog implementations can delay resolution of negated goals until all variables in the goals are bound. This can, however, keep some goals delayed until after all non-negated goals have been resolved. To preserve soundness with respect to logic, the delayed goals must be treated as false, so if any delayed goals remain, the query fails. While this strategy can keep the logic sound, it is far from complete. Some built-in operators in Prolog implicitly use negation as failure. For example, X\=Y (X is not equal to Y) is actually short for \+ X=Y, which will always fail if one or both of the variables are unbound (since they can be unified).

9.4.4.3 Delays

Unbound variables can both cause nontermination because they can be instantiated to an infinite number of values, and they are an issue for cut and negation as failure, as noted above. So many Prolog systems allow delaying a goal until a specified variable is bound. The goal freeze(X, p) delays search for solutions to p until X is bound to a non-variable value. This can help guide a search to avoid going down infinite paths, but it can leave goals forever delayed. To remedy this, the goal frozen(X,Q) unifies Q with the conjunction of all goals that currently wait for X to be bound, allowing these to be inspected and possibly executed (using the call predicate). A more general delay is found in some systems (such as SWI Prolog): when(c, p) which delays p until the condition c is true, where c can test if variables are bound to non-variables, are ground, or if two variables can safely be determined to be equal or different (i.e., they are sufficiently bound that any further bindings will not change the result).

Delays allow coroutines to be implemented: A goal can be delayed until a variable is bound to a message, whereupon it is resumed and can later delay itself or activate other delayed goals by instantiating variables to messages.

9.4.4.4 Arithmetic

In pure Prolog, numbers are just symbols: There are no built-in operations to operate on them (apart from comparing them for equality). While it is possible to encode numbers as, say, lists of digits or bits and program arithmetic operations explicitly as predicates, this is not very efficient. So full Prolog has built-in operations for arithmetic operations and numeric comparison. For example, the goal A<B is true if A and B are bound to numbers x and y, respectively, and $x < y$. Similarly, if

x is not less than y, the goal will fail. If either x or y is bound to a non-number value, a runtime error is reported. But what if A or B (or both) are not bound at all? Logically, the unbound variables should be bound to values that make the goal true and backtracking should ensure that all such values are eventually tried. But there is an infinite number of solutions, so instead most Prolog systems report a runtime error if one or both of the operands are unbound variables. Note that reporting an error is different from failing the goal, as the program can backtrack when a goal fails, but not when an error is reported.

Arithmetic expressions are implemented by the is pseudo-predicate. Goals using this pseudo-predicate have the form X is e, where e is an arithmetic expression involving variables and constants and the usual arithmetic operators. As with comparison, arithmetic expressions will cause runtime errors not only if any variables in the expression are not bound but also if they are bound to non-numbers. If all variables are bound to numbers, the expression is evaluated and the result is unified with X, which may be a variable or a number constant. Both integer and floating-point arithmetic is usually available.

9.4.5 Other Logic Languages

While Prolog as described above (and minor variants thereof) is the original and most widespread logic language, there are a number of logic languages that share the essential logic features of pure Prolog, but are extended in various ways.

9.4.5.1 Constraint Logic Languages

While Prolog generates runtime errors for arithmetic constraints and expressions that contain unbound variables, *constraint logic languages* attempt to solve these constraints mathematically, and present solutions that combine substitutions with constraints that must be obeyed by the unbound variables. Attempts are made to reduce these constraints and detect when they are unsatisfiable. Satisfiability of general arithmetic constraints is undecidable, so most constraint logic languages solve only linear constraints and postpone any other constraint until all variables in the constraint are bound to values (so it can just evaluate the constraint and check it), or until the constraint is sufficiently instantiated to be linear.

There are constraint logic languages for constraints over integers, reals, and finite domains.

9.4.5.2 Functional-Logical Languages

There are several different approaches that lay claim to this title.

One approach (called *Lambda Prolog*) is to extend the value domain with lambda expressions that can contain free (unbound) variables. Lambda expressions can be unified like other terms, but unification also embodies beta equivalence (reduction of expressions), so two lambda expressions that are not syntactically equal but beta equivalent will successfully unify. Unification, hence, becomes undecidable (as beta equivalence is undecidable). Furthermore, even when decidable, a most general unifier of two lambda terms may not exist. Hence, Lambda Prolog uses a simplification procedure that may stop before completing unification. If unification is incomplete, a set of residual constraints are postponed until variables in these are instantiated or output as part of a solution. This is similar to how non-linear constraints are delayed in constraint logic languages.

Another approach for combining functional and logic languages is to allow unification of the results of applying functions to values with arguments. For example, the goal f(X)=g(X), where f and g are functions (and not just uninterpreted function symbols, as in pure Prolog), finds values of X such that the equality is obeyed. An example of this is the language Curry.

A third class of languages that may be called functional-logical is languages that borrow features from functional languages such as polymorphic types and higher-order functions, but not in a way that requires unification over domains more complex than in pure Prolog. Mercury and Visual Prolog are examples of such languages.

9.5 Further Reading

The language SELF and prototype-based object-oriented programming are described in [8].

Traditional full Prolog is described in [7]. More in-depth description of implementation techniques for Prolog can be found in [1,3].

Constraint logic programming is described in [4].

Lambda Prolog is described in [5].

Mercury and its implementation is described in [6], and Visual Prolog is described in [2].

9.6 Exercises

Exercise 9.1 For each of the following programming languages, what is the primary paradigms for data flow, execution order, and structuring?

a. Pascal
b. Python
c. APL

Exercise 9.2 Add the lines

```
b = new C;
b.m = 7;
b.n = a2.n;
```

to the end of Fig. 9.1.

a. Show the memory state at the end of the modified Fig. 9.1 by modifying Fig. 9.2.

Exercise 9.3 Consider this Java program:

```
class A {
  void f () {System.out.println("A");}
  void g () {this.f ();}
}

class B extends A {
  void f () {System.out.println("B");}
}


public class Foo {
  public static void  main (String [] args) {
    B b = new B();
    b.g ();
  }
}
```

a. What does this program output, and why?
b. If we change the second line to

```
private void f () {System.out.println("A");}
```

what is then the output, and why?

Exercise 9.4 Find for each of the following pairs of Prolog values a most general unifier. If no unifier exists, explain, briefly, why the unification fails.

a. f(A,B,A) and f(X,X,3).
b. h(a,b) and h(A,A).
c. h(a,b) and h(A,B,C).
d. h(k(A),B) and h(B,k(C)).
e. h(k(A),B) and h(B,A).

Exercise 9.5 Draw in the style of Fig. 9.7 a resolution tree for the query

```
?- append(As,cons(B,Bs),cons(1,cons(2,nil))).
```

with respect to the program shown in Fig. 9.4.

Exercise 9.6 Install SWI-Prolog on your computer. On Linux, you can install it using the package system (on Ubuntu, search for SWI-Prolog in the Software Center). For Windows and MacOS, you can find SWI-Prolog at http://www.swi-prolog.org/download/stable. You can also find documentation there.

Quick guide: To run a program, start Prolog with the command `swipl` or `prolog`, which starts the Prolog REPL.

At the `?-` prompt write `compile('program.pl')`. to load your program. Run it by writing a query (remember to end with a period). You can ask for more solutions by writing a semicolon. If you don't want any more solutions, press **Enter**. If you ask for (more) solutions, and there are none, SWI-Prolog will write `false` and return to the prompt.

Write the program in Fig. 9.3 to a file and load it into SWI Prolog.

a. Run the query `?- ancestor(isabella, X).` and show all results.
b. Rewrite the second clause of `ancestor` to
    `ancestor(X, Y) :- ancestor(X, Z), parent(Z, Y).`
    reload the program and rerun the query above. Explain the different behaviour.

Exercise 9.7 Install SWI-Prolog on your computer (see Exercise 1.8).

SWI-Prolog uses the list notation shown in Sect. 9.4.2. As an example, a predicate for testing whether an element X is an element of a list Ys can be written as

```
elementOf(X,Ys) :- append(_,[X|_],Ys).
```

The `append` predicate is predefined when you start SWI-Prolog, so you don't need to type it in.

(a) Load a program consisting of the above predicate into SWI-Prolog and run the query
     `?- elementOf(2,[1,2,3,4,3,2,1]).` Explain the result.
(b) Write a Prolog predicate `subSet` such that `subSet(X,Y)` is true if X is a subset of Y, i.e., if all elements of X occur in Y. You can use `append` and `elementOf`, but not any library functions.
(c) Make a predicate `square4` that given an 4×4 matrix M represented by list of lists verifies that all the following properties hold for M:

     1. Every row in M contains all the numbers from 1 to 4.
     2. Every column in M contains all the numbers from 1 to 4.
     3. Both the diagonals of M contain all the numbers from 1 to 4.

Hint: The easiest way to extract columns and diagonals is to define `square4` as

```
square4(M) :-
  M = [[A11,A12,A13,A14],
       [A21,A22,A23,A24],
       [A31,A32,A33,A34],
       [A41,A42,A43,A44]],
  additional goals.
```

where the additional goals can use, e.g., `[A11,A22,A33,A44]` to represent one of the diagonals. It is possible to write this predicate using only the predicates mentioned earlier (`append`, `elementOf`, and `subSet`), but you can add extra helper predicates if you prefer. Do not use any library functions.

(d) Use the above to find all solutions to the query

```
?- square4([[1,2,3,4],A,B,C]).
```

References

1. Aït-Kaci H (1991) Warren's abstract machine: a tutorial reconstruction. MIT Press, Cambridge, MA, USA. http://wambook.sourceforge.net/
2. de Boer TW (2009) A beginners' guide to visual Prolog version 7.2. Prolog Development Center. http://wiki.visual-prolog.com/index.php?title=A_Beginners_Guide_to_Visual_Prolog
3. Kursawe P (1987) How to invent a Prolog machine. New Gener Comput 5:97–114. https://doi.org/10.1007/BF03037460
4. Marriott K, Stuckey PJ (1998) Programming with constraints: an introduction. MIT Press, Cambridge, Mass
5. Miller D, Nadathur G (2012) Programming with higher-order logic. Cambridge University Press. http://books.google.dk/books?id=vbX3pwAACAAJ
6. Somogyi Z, Henderson F, Conway T (1994) The implementation of Mercury, an efficient purely declarative logic programming language. In: ILPS workshop: implementation techniques for logic programming languages
7. Sterling L, Shapiro E (1994) The art of Prolog: advanced programming techniques, 2nd edn. MIT Press, Cambridge, MA, USA
8. Ungar D, Smith RB (1991) SELF: the power of simplicity. LISP Symb Comput 4(3):187–205. https://doi.org/10.1007/BF01806105

Domain-Specific Programming Languages

10

> *Everything we design is a response to the specific climate and culture of a particular place.*
>
> Norman Foster
>
> *Domain work is messy and demands a lot of complicated new knowledge that doesn't seem to add to a computer scientist's capabilities.*
>
> Eric Evans

New programming languages are usually designed because the designer is not satisfied with existing languages. This dissatisfaction can have many different causes: The designer may find the notation used in previous languages verbose, clumsy or opaque, the designer may find that certain data structures are not well supported, that certain kinds of computation are not easily expressible, or that it is difficult to reason about programs.

Often, these points of critique are found when working with a specific problem domain, and the designer finds it easier to design a new language specifically for the problem domain than it is to keep fighting with an existing language to express domain-specific concepts. Additionally, the designer may find it difficult to communicate with domain experts when they use notations and concepts that are far removed from the notations and concepts used in programming languages. Thirdly, the designer may want domain experts to be able to write small programs on their own without having to learn all of the complexities associated with a traditional programming language.

Languages designed for specific problem domains or for use by specific groups of non-programmers are called *domain-specific languages*, or DSLs for short. In this chapter, we will look at some characteristics of DSLs and how these can be designed and implemented.

T. Ægidius Mogensen, *Programming Language Design and Implementation*,
Texts in Computer Science, https://doi.org/10.1007/978-3-031-11806-7_10

10.1   GPLs Versus DSLs

General-purpose languages (GPLs) are programming languages intended for a broad range of problem domains, and typically for use by trained programmers. Languages like C, Java, Haskell, and Python are in this category.

Domain-specific languages (DSLs) are programming languages intended for either a narrow range of problem domains or for use by a certain type of non-programmers (and sometimes both). Languages like HTML, LaTeX, SQL, Excel, and R are in this category.

The dichotomy between GPLs and DSLs is not strict, it is a matter of degree. Many GPLs were originally designed with specific problem domains in mind, but have expanded to be used in many other domains as well. For example, C was designed for writing operating systems and systems programs but is now used for almost all types of programming. Similarly, Java was originally intended for writing *applets*, small programs running in a browser, but is now also used for almost everything. Similarly, many even highly specialised DSLs can be used for general-purpose programming if the programmer is sufficiently persistent, and many DSLs evolve over time to include features for general-purpose programming.

So what really distinguishes GPLs and DSLs? It can be a matter of intent only: The language was designed either for general-purpose programming or for a specific problem domain. But it can also be more concrete: A domain-specific language can use notation from the problem domain and have concepts from this domain built-in rather than having to be modelled using more general concepts. Also, where a GPL is typically Turing complete (capable of expressing all computable functions), DSLs can be more limited. For example, SQL in its original form (as in the SQL86 or SQL92 standards) does not allow general computation, but later extensions such as CTE and stored procedures make SQL Turing complete. HTML (discounting the use of embedded scripting languages such as JavaScript), also, is not Turing complete.

Regardless, it is a matter of degree: A language can be more or less domain-specific, with languages like Algol and Java on one end of the spectrum and languages like HTML and SQL on the other end. At this end of the spectrum, the border between programming languages and programs, in general, begins to blur. There is no theoretical distinction between programs and data, so if a program P takes an input C that controls the behaviour of P on its other inputs, is C then a program and P an interpreter for the language in which C is written? Similarly, any program that produces data that is used as input to another program can be considered a compiler.

Take, for example, a search engine like Google. A query for Google is not just a set of keywords, but you can also use special notation to restrict the domain names of the sites being searched, how old the material it finds can be, and so on. So you can argue that Google is or contains an interpreter for a simple query language. Similarly, a program that takes command-line parameters can also be seen as an interpreter for a language that specifies these parameters.

We will not try to make hard distinctions but note that specialisation can increase programmer productivity: If a language that is highly specific to a domain is used, it can take a lot less time to write a program to solve a problem—as long as the problem is within the domain in question. Solving problems outside this domain can be difficult or even impossible. An analogy is tools: A Swiss army knife can be used for a lot of different tasks, including opening wine bottles and (un)screwing screws. But it is easier and faster to open a wine bottle using a tool specifically designed for that purpose, and to (un)screw a screw, a "real" screwdriver is usually better. On the other hand, a corkscrew is next to useless for (un)screwing screws, and a screwdriver is next to useless for opening wine bottles.

Then there is the question of who is going to use the language for writing programs. A trained programmer is used to working with general purpose languages, but being able to use a GPL effectively and correctly requires significant training. A more specialised tool or language can be easier to learn, especially if it uses concept and notation with which the user is already familiar.

10.2   When Should You (Not) Design a New DSL?

A DSL has some advantages over GPLs, some of which we have already discussed:

- A DSL can potentially increase productivity within the domain.
- A DSL can use notation and concepts known to domain experts, which can help domain experts to understand programs and allow them to write simple programs. Also, programs in a DSL may need less documentation because it uses notation that would otherwise have been used for documentation purposes.
- A DSL can be written to either guarantee certain properties or make it possible to analyse programs to determine these.
- An implementation of a DSL can employ domain-specific optimisations not usually found in implementations of GPLs.
- A program written in a DSL can have multiple different well-defined semantics, for example, an execution semantics (when inputs are known) and a simulation or analysis semantics (when they are not).
- Training non-programmers to use a DSL may be easier than training them to use a GPL.
- If some element of the problem domain changes, it may be sufficient to handle this in the implementation of the DSL rather than having to rewrite all programs. For example, if dates need to use four-digit years instead of two-digit years, a language that has dates as a built-in concept can make this change just a matter of changing how dates are represented in the language, where using a GPL may require inspection and modification of a large code base.

On the other hand, there may be good reasons to use a GPL instead:

- The problem domain may not be specific enough or may not have features that lend themselves to domain-specific notation or optimisation.

- Designing, implementing, and maintaining a DSL is a significant investment.
- Interfacing with other software may be difficult.
- If the intended users already know a GPL, training them to use a DSL is an extra investment.

In the other extreme, you might want to write a program with command-line parameters or a GUI instead of designing and implementing a full-blown DSL. This may be simpler to use and implement than a DSL, but there are pitfalls:

- A GUI might require a sequence of menu choices and numeric/string inputs that are mostly the same in every use of the program. Using a textual notation that can be stored and edited may be easier than repeatedly entering almost the same choices. This is why many programs with GUIs support scripting: Specifying a sequence of GUI interactions in a file, so they can be "played back" later.
- While command-line parameters can be stored and edited, they are usually just a sequence of options and values without structure, so they can be hard to read.

If a typical GUI interaction or command line includes more than a dozen choices or values, it might be better to use a DSL instead.

10.3   How do You Design a DSL?

Let us say that you have decided to design a DSL. How do you then proceed to do so?

The first step is to identify the problem domain for which the language is intended. The domain should be narrow enough that assumptions about the domain can be exploited in the design, but not so narrow that it is rarely applicable. A good start is to see how problems in the domain are currently handled: If it is common to modify an existing program to solve a related problem, it might be a good idea to extract the common part and the different parts of these programs and make a language that assumes the common part, so only the different parts need to be expressed. And if tasks are frequently solved manually, it may be an idea to see if these tasks are amenable to semi-automation using a language. An outcome of the identification step may well be that a DSL is *not* the best solution.

Once you have identified the domain, the next step is to collect domain knowledge. This can be by establishing use cases, interviewing domain experts, reading domain literature, and so on. This knowledge is then used for *domain analysis* and *theory building* to establish suitable notation, data structures, properties, and so on, that can be employed in the language design. This should be done in collaboration with users and domain experts, so their experience and expertise can be exploited to avoid misunderstandings and omissions of important properties and use cases.

The third step is the concrete language design. This should primarily build on the domain analysis and theory building from the previous step and not prematurely jump to using concepts and notation from GPLs: What is natural for the language designer and implementer may not be so for the users or domain experts. For example, a priori deciding on object-oriented modelling and notation may be a mistake, even when this is natural for a programmer to do, since it is unlikely that non-programmers will find these abstractions natural. Similarly, over-engineering should be avoided: It can be tempting to add features (such as recursion or polymorphism) that make the language more powerful for general-purpose programming, but if these features are rarely or never going to be useful in the problem domain, they will just add confusion.

Nevertheless, the design process should not ignore programming language theory or experience: These are needed to ensure that the language is unambiguous and implementable with sufficient efficiency. Also, knowledge of which properties and language features are amenable to automatic analysis and verification may be useful. Knowledge of a wide range of language paradigms and features is useful for picking well-understood design elements that fit the domain: If you only have a hammer, every problem looks like a nail, and if you only know one kind of programming language, this is what your designs will look like.

10.4 How do You Implement a DSL?

Implementing a DSL is not really very different from implementing a GPL, except that the DSL is typically a smaller language. Additionally, you can often exploit existing language implementations to make your work easier.

The four most common approaches to DSL implementation are:

Embedded language:	The language is built as a library or framework within an existing language.
Language extension:	Domain-specific features are added to an existing language.
Language restriction:	An existing language is restricted to have only the features relevant to the problem domain.
Stand-alone language:	Implemented using a traditional interpreter or compiler with its own parser, type system, etc.

We will look at these below, using a subset of the SQL SELECT statement as an example. The syntax of this is shown in Fig. 10.1. **RelOp** is either = or <, and **Constant** is a numerical constant or string. An example of a SELECT statement is

`SELECT name FROM students WHERE enrollmentYear < 2012`

which should find the names of all students from the student database who were enrolled prior to 2012.

$$\mathit{SelectStatement} \rightarrow \texttt{SELECT}\ \mathit{Columns}\ \texttt{FROM}\ \textbf{TableName}\ \mathit{WhereClause}$$

Columns	→ **ColumnName**
Columns	→ *Columns* , *Columns*
WhereClause	→ WHERE *Condition*
WhereClause	→
Condition	→ *Value* **RelOp** *Value*
Condition	→ *Condition* AND *Condition*
Value	→ **ColumnName**
Value	→ **Constant**

Fig. 10.1 Simplified SELECT-statement syntax

10.4.1   Implementation as Embedded Language

Most GPLs have abstraction and modularisation features that allow a package of types and functions to be built while hiding implementation details from the user, restricting use to be through a well-defined interface. Domain-specific concepts can be modelled in a module or set of related modules (sometimes called a *framework*), so a user can use the full features of the language to combine the concepts that are exposed in the interface.

While this approach blurs the distinction between implementing a language and writing a module, you can not call any set of types and functions an embedded DSL: A DSL should have a syntax and semantics that is (mostly) independent of how it is implemented: The language in which the DSL is embedded (the host language) just implements the syntax (perhaps as abstract syntax) and semantics (perhaps exploiting that parts of the semantics can be expressed directly in the host language).

Looking at the SQL subset in Fig. 10.1, we must represent this syntax using only features from the host language. One possibility is to use a string containing the concrete syntax, e.g.,

`"SELECT name FROM students WHERE enrollmentYear < 2012"`.

The embedded language then has to implement a function executeQuery that takes this string as an argument and returns a list or array of student names. This method of implementing the syntax has a number of problems:

- The syntax is not checked at compile time, as the compiler will accept any string as an argument to executeQuery.
- executeQuery has to implement a parser that at runtime parses the string before or while executing the query.
- If the query string is built at runtime, for example using a user-supplied string to represent a number in a comparison, this string has to be "sanitised" to prevent parts of this string from being interpreted as query syntax. Otherwise, this can lead to a class of security problems called *SQL injection*.

```
datatype Value = Column of string
               | StringConst of string
               | Number of int

datatype Condition = == of Value * Value
                   | << of Value * Value
                   | AND of Condition * Condition

datatype WhereClause = WHERE of Condition
                     | ALL

datatype SelectStatement =
    SELECT_FROM of string list * string * WhereClause
```

Fig. 10.2 SQL syntax representation in ML

Nevertheless, this is a common method of embedding SQL in languages like Java. An alternative implementation of the syntax is by defining a data structure that represents the syntax as abstract syntax. In ML, this can be represented by the datatypes as shown in Fig. 10.2.

The query example would then be represented as the data structure

```
SELECT_FROM (["name"], "students",
    WHERE (<< (Column "enrollmentYear", Number 2012)))
```

In ML, it is possible to declare that ==, <<, and AND are infix operators. Doing this allows writing the above as

```
SELECT_FROM (["name"], "students",
    WHERE (Column "enrollmentYear" << Number 2012))
```

Other functional languages such as Haskell and F# implement similar data types, but with somewhat different syntax.

We still need to implement a function `executeQuery` that takes the representation of the query as an argument and returns a list of student names, but

- `executeQuery` does not need to parse the query from a string, it can use pattern matching instead,
- The syntax of the query is checked at compile time, since a syntax error would give a syntax error or type error in the host language,
- Even if input strings are used as values, these will never be interpreted as SQL syntax, so SQL injection is avoided.

In languages that do not have similar data types, e.g., most object-oriented languages, an approach called *method chaining* is often used. Here, a database would be an object that implements a constructor `Database` that takes the name of a database and returns an instance of a class `Rows` that represents the list of rows in the database. `Rows` implements methods `SELECT`, `WHERE_EQ`, and `WHERE_LT`. The `SELECT` method takes a list of column names (e.g., represented as a string with comma-separated names) and returns the rows reduced to the columns given in the `SELECT` method argument. The `WHERE_EQ` method takes two arguments which are instances of an abstract `Value` class that has sub-classes for column names, strings, and numbers. `WHERE_EQ` returns another instance of `Rows`, so you can add more conditions before calling the `SELECT` method. The example query can be implemented by the expression.

```
Database("students").
  WHERE_LT(Column("enrollmentYear"),Number(2012)).
    SELECT("name")
```

where `Column` and `Number` are constructors for subclasses of the abstract `Value` class. Note that `SELECT` is called after the `WHERE` clause, since it operates on the rows after they have been filtered by the `WHERE` clause.

Method chaining has pretty much the same advantages as using a datatype to represent the syntax:

- The program does not need to parse the query,
- The syntax of the query is checked at compile time, since a syntax error would give a syntax error or type error in the host language,
- Even if input strings are used as values, these will never be interpreted as SQL syntax, so SQL injection is avoided.

It does, however, have a few limitations that were not present in the datatype approach:

- The syntax looks less like the concrete syntax, as methods like `SELECT` and `WHERE_EQ` have to be called in the order they are to be executed, even if this is not the order in which they are given in the concrete syntax.
- Method chaining allows only a linear chain of method calls, so a condition with `AND` is represented as two consecutive `WHERE` clauses rather than a single `WHERE` clause with two sub-conditions.
- Building a query at runtime is more complicated.

There are other approaches to embedding DSLs in a host language, but they are usually variants of the above: Syntax is represented either as a value (with different degrees of checking) or as a combination of objects or functions where types are used to restrict how these are combined, which allows some degree of compile-time checking of DSL syntax.

The advantages of implementing a DSL as an embedded language are:

- It is usually easier to implement a DSL as an embedded language than it is to make or modify an interpreter or compiler.
- A programmer using the DSL can embed a DSL program inside a program that uses all the features of the host language, such as graphing libraries and user interaction.
- It is easy to interface programs written in the DSL with other programs, as long as they can be interfaced with the host language.

The disadvantages are:

- You are limited to use the syntax of the implementation language, which may be far from the traditional domain notation.
- Error messages are often expressed in terms of the underlying implementation language and not in terms of concepts from the domain. This can make the language unsuitable for non-programmers, even if they only use the domain-specific features.
- It may be impossible to statically verify domain-specific properties (if these can not be modelled in the type system of the host language), so these may have to be checked at runtime.

Some host languages may be better suited than others for embedding DSLs:

- A powerful macro system can allow notation closer to the problem domain.
- An expressive type system can statically verify syntax and possibly even simple domain-specific properties.
- Good abstraction mechanisms can hide implementation details from the user of the language.

10.4.2 Implementation by Preprocessor

As with embedded languages, the DSL is built on top of an existing language, but a new syntax is added which a preprocessor to the original compiler or interpreter expands into structures in the original syntax. This allows almost arbitrary domain-specific notation.

A preprocessor is in essence a simple compiler, but it need not parse the full syntax of the language: It can copy most of the input unmodified to the output, only making modifications when it sees a keyword or symbol that marks the language extension. For example, a preprocessor can look for the keywords SELECT, FROM, WHERE, and AND and do something with the program text that immediately follows these keywords while keeping the rest of the program text untouched. Typically, the DSL syntax is expanded into something that looks like an embedded DSL, but more complex static checks can be made, and static errors can be expressed in terms of the concrete syntax rather than the expanded host-language syntax. The idea is that most of the user code will be written in the (almost) unmodified host language, but that bits of DSL code can be inserted into the code and then be expanded/translated into the host language by the preprocessor, which keeps all non-DSL parts of the code unchanged.

As with embedded languages, you can easily interface with other programs written in the host language (as you can mix DSL code with code in the host language), and you freely exploit all the features of this language, but you can also restrict which features in the original language is available, for example, outlawing features that make it difficult to maintain desired domain-specific properties. The latter requires writing a full parser rather than a simple keyword search as described above.

Regardless, runtime errors are reported in terms of what the preprocessor emits, so not only do the error messages not use domain concepts, the reported position of the error is a place in the processed program and not a place in the original program. Additionally, DSL syntax can not be built at runtime.

10.4.3 Implementation as Compiler/Interpreter Modification

The DSL is built on top of an existing language by modifying a compiler or interpreter for the existing language, typically by adding new productions to the grammar and code in the parser, type-checker and interpreter or compiler to handle these extra productions. In the SQL example, the productions in Fig. 10.1 are added to the grammar of the host language. This may cause ambiguities which must be handled in the way ambiguities are usually handled (by specifying precedences or adding keywords or symbols that disambiguate the syntax).

The advantages and disadvantages are more or less the same as when using a preprocessor, but modifying a compiler or interpreter for the host language allows also runtime errors to use domain-specific concepts and precise positions, and domain-specific optimisations can be added to the compiler.

Modifying a compiler or interpreter can be more work than writing a preprocessor, and you may be tied to a specific version of the compiler or interpreter, as porting the modifications to new versions can be a major effort.

10.4.4 Implementation as Stand-alone Language

This requires building a complete implementation such as an interpreter or a compiler. This gives complete freedom in notation, it can make error messages very precise, and it can implement exactly the features that are relevant for the domain, no more and no less.

In the SQL example, parser, type-checker, and either interpreter or compiler for the grammar in Fig. 10.1 must be made more or less from scratch.

The advantages of a stand-alone language are:

- Full domain-specific notation, including diagrams and complex formula notation, can be used.
- Domain-specific properties can be guaranteed or verified statically.
- Errors can be expressed in terms of domain-specific concepts.
- More advanced domain-specific optimisations can be used.
- It is possible to implement multiple different semantics for the same language.

The main disadvantages are:

- Requires implementation and maintenance of a full compiler or interpreter.
- DSL syntax can not be built at runtime.
- Interfacing with other programs may be difficult. It usually involves communication using files or pipes rather than just method or function calls.

Even when implementing a DSL as a stand-alone language, you might want to modify the syntax. For example, some stand-alone DSLs use XML-based syntax, as this eases parsing—you can specify the grammar using DTDs or XML Schema, parse programs by using a standard XML parsing library, and even interpret or compile them with help of XML APIs such as XSLT and DOM.

10.5 Examples of DSLs

We will now look at a few DSLs and, in particular, what makes them different from GPLs, both in terms of design and implementation.

10.5.1 Scratch

Scratch [6] is one of many languages designed for teaching children to program. As such, the problem domain is not so much the kind of problems you solve with the language, but the kind of programmer that will use it. It is mainly used for making small interactive animations (and has built-in support for this), but that is secondary to its main purpose, which is teaching.

To make the language accessible to beginners, programs are built by joining graphical blocks, as shown in Fig. 10.3, which shows two concurrent processes—one that changes between two different pictures of a bat (wings up, wings down), and one that moves the bat across the screen.

In spite of being targeted at beginners, Scratch support advanced concepts such as recursion and concurrency.

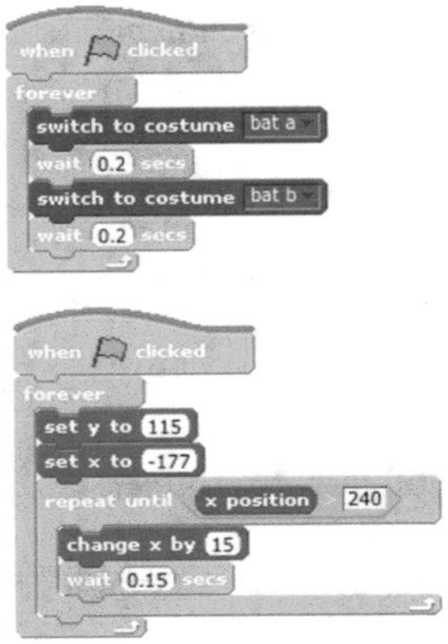

Image source and license: `https://commons.wikimedia.org/wiki/File:Code_for_a_flying_`
`bat_in_Scratch-_2013-04-07_19-26.png`

Fig. 10.3 A small Scratch program

10.5.2   TEX and LATEX

TEX [4] is a type-setting system. It can be seen as a markup language (similar to HTML) in the sense that most text represents itself, but embedded codes can modify the appearance of the text. But, unlike HTML, TEX contains a Turing-complete language for writing *macros* that allow users to program both advanced layout, cross-references, and arbitrary computations. TEX is block structured (using curly braces) and uses dynamic binding. Parameter passing is by text, so if a macro uses its argument several times, any formatting or calculation done in the argument is done each time. Dynamic scoping allows the macro to influence this formatting and calculation by redefining variables, macros, and properties used by the argument text.

What LATEX [5] has added on top of TEX is mainly features for structuring documents into chapters, sections, figures, theorems, and such. LATEX is modular, and many packages exist that extend LATEX for almost any kind of type-setting, including sheet music and electronic diagrams. While TEX and LATEX are mainly used for writing scientific papers, textbooks, and presentations, LATEX has been used also for writing game books, poetry, dictionaries, and even an interpreter for the BASIC language.

10.5.3   Graphviz

Graphviz (https://graphviz.org/) is a domain-specific language for visualising trees and graphs: You describe a graph using textual notations, and Graphviz will convert this to an image. For example, the input

```
digraph G {
   main -> parse -> execute
   main -> {init, cleanup}
   execute -> {make_string, printf, compare}
   init -> make_string
   main -> printf
}
```

produces the image

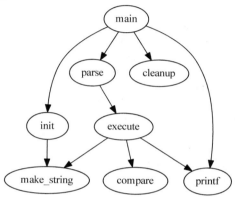

Note that Graphviz handles the layout automatically. Adding the line

```
compare -> main
```

to the list above yields a quite different layout:

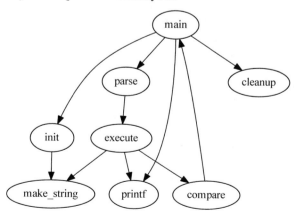

There are six different layout algorithms to choose from. There are options for differ-ent node shapes, directed and undirected graphs, edge labels, clustering, and much more. There is a large number of different output formats including PDF, bitmaps, and vector markup languages.

10.5.4 OpenSCAD

OpenSCAD (http://openscad.org/) is a functional language for creating 3D models for use with, e.g., 3D printers. Its main way of building models is through constructive solid geometry, where you can create union, intersection, and difference of solids such as spheres, cylinders, and cubes. It also uses linear extrusion of 2D objects (such as polygons or text) into 3D. For example, you can create a triangular prism by extruding a triangle.

OpenSCAD can export to STL format, which is accepted by many renderers (such as Blender) and can be "sliced" for 3D printing.

As an example, an OpenSCAD program and the resulting model are shown in Fig. 10.4. OpenSCAD uses the term "module" for a function that creates a 3D object. The module `digit` creates a text image of a digit given as a parameter, extrudes it to a 3D figure, and translates it away from the centre. The module `example` has no parameters. It adds four rotated digits to a sphere and makes three cylindrical holes in the sphere by subtracting three rotated cylinders. Finally, the call `example()` creates the model specified by the module.

OpenSCAD is a stand-alone DSL, including a build-in editor for programs. But a variant of OpenSCAD called OpenJSCAD (https://openjscad.com/) is an embedded DSL in JavaScript. This means that, for example, `rotate` and `translate` in OpenJSCAD are methods instead of functions.

10.5.5 Troll

Troll [9] is a language used for calculating probabilities of dice rolls in games. It takes its roots in the dice notation used by Dungeons & Dragons, where, for example, `3d10` means rolling and adding three ten-sided dice, but extends this notation to cover mechanisms used in other languages, such as counting how many dice are over a certain threshold, re-rolling dice until a condition is met, counting sets, and many other combinations found in board games and role-playing games.

Troll is implemented as a stand-alone language, and has two related but different semantics: You can either run a Troll program to get one or more random rolls of the specified dice, or you can run it to calculate a probability distribution of the possible outcomes. Both semantics are implemented by interpretation but use different value domains: When generating random results, a value is a multiset of numbers, and when calculating probabilities, values are finite, discrete probability distributions.

As an example, the following Troll definition counts the number of different results you get when you roll five ten-sided dice:

```
count different 5d10
```

```
$fs = 0.05;  // Don't generate smaller facets than 0.1 mm
$fa = 2;     // Don't generate larger angles than 5 degrees

// Make 3D upright digit 12 units from centre
module digit(d) {
     translate([0,-12,0])
     rotate([90,0,0])
     linear_extrude(height=4, convexity=4)
       text(d,
            size=10,
            font="Bitstream Vera Sans",
            halign="center",
            valign="center");
}

// Add four digits to sphere and make three cylindrical holes
module example() {
    difference() {
      union() {
        for (i = [1:4])
            rotate([0,0,45+90*i]) digit(str(i));
        sphere(d=20);
      }
    rotate([90,0,0]) cylinder(d=12, h=20, center=true);
    rotate([0,90,0]) cylinder(d=12, h=20, center=true);
    rotate([0,0,90]) cylinder(d=12, h=20, center=true);
  }
}

// create model
example();
```

Fig. 10.4 OpenSCAD program and resulting model

If you ask Troll to generate, say, six random samples of this, you might get the answers 4, 4, 3, 3, 5, and 4. If you ask Troll to generate a probability distribution, it will output the distribution

```
Value    % =              % >=
    1:    0.01            100.0
    2:    1.35            99.99
    3:    18.0            98.64
    4:    50.4            80.64
    5:    30.24           30.24

Average = 4.0951
Spread = 0.72681221096
Mean deviation = 0.54728352
```

From this, we can see that rolling exactly four different values has a probability of 50.4%, and that getting at least four different values has a probability of 80.64%. Additionally, we see that the average number of different values is 4.0951 and we also get the spread and mean deviation of the results. The web server for Troll (https://topps.diku.dk/~torbenm/troll.msp) will, additionally, show a bar chart of the probabilities.

Troll includes text formatting. For example, the definition

```
"Str |>Dex|>Con|>Int|>Wis|>Chr" || 6'sum largest 3 4d6
```

generates random D&D attribute sets such as

```
Str 11
Dex  8
Con 13
Int 14
Wis 16
Chr  9
```

Explanation: The quoted string generates a text box of six left-aligned lines containing the attribute abbreviations. The |> symbol is a left-aligned newline. The expression sum largest 3 4d6 adds the largest 3 of 4 six-sided dice, and the 6' prefix generates six of these and converts them to six lines of right-aligned text. The || operator concatenates the two text boxes side by side.

Troll also allows recursive function definitions, so it is Turing complete. As an example, the following function returns the multiset of digits of a number:

```
function digits(x)=
  if x>9 then
    {x mod 10, call digits(x / 10)}
  else x
```

The curly braces here denote building a multiset. Nested multisets are automatically flattened and sorted, so {3, {2, 3}} is equivalent to {2, 3, 3}.

When calculating probabilities, the recursion is bounded to a finite user-specified depth, as unbounded recursion can create infinite probability distributions.

10.5.6 CRL

There are several languages called CRL, but we here address a *cashflow reengineering language* [8].

In this context, a *cashflow* is a financial paper specifying a sequence of payments over a period of time, such as a loan that is paid back in instalments and where interest accrues. *Cashflow reengineering* is a process where a bank issues new cashflows by redirecting the payments of other cashflows. For example, a new cashflow can be made by adding the interest payments from several other cashflows, but not the payments on the principal, which are redirected to yet another new cashflow.

CRL was designed as a language that allows bankers to specify how new cashflows are created from existing cashflows. A design goal was to make the language usable by non-programmers, so it is extremely simple. Also, the banker has to account for all of the incoming payments and ensure that no incoming payment is used twice. For this reason, CRL uses a simple linear type system that ensures that all values are used *exactly* once. This is an example where a DSL can statically verify a domain-specific property that, at best, can be verified at runtime if a GPL is used. An example definition in CRL is

```
declarations
  fraction = 0.7

input
  cashflow a, b

structure
  c = a + b
  (d,e) = Divide(c, fraction)

output
  cashflow d,e
```

The declarations section defines constants that are used in the rest of the program. The input section declares names of incoming cashflows. The structure section redirects cashflows: First, cashflows a and b are added into a variable c. Then, this is split into to cashflows d and e using the fraction defined in the declarations section. Finally, the resulting cashflows are output in the output section. Note that each variable is defined once and used once, which is ensured by the linear type system. The type system can handle somewhat more complex cases: In an if-then-else statement, a cashflow can be used arbitrarily often in the condition (as checking the balance of a loan does not affect it), but the two branches must consume and produce the same set of cashflow variables.

Like Troll, CRL has two semantics: One that issues payments when they are due, and one that uses Monte Carlo simulation to calculate expected earnings based on probabilistic assumptions about interest rates and defaults on payments.

10.5.7 Futhark

Futhark [3] (named after the Norse runic alphabet) is a language for doing parallel computations on graphics processors. Its aim is to provide a higher abstraction level than, for example, CUDA or OpenCL, which are embedded languages for programming graphics processors. Futhark, in fact, compiles to OpenCL.

Futhark is a pure functional language that supports recursion and loops, but mainly uses whole-array operations such as map, filter, reduce, and scan. It uses *uniqueness types* (a form of linear types) to ensure that code written in imperative style can be done without visible side effects and that recursive functions can avoid copying whole arrays.

An example is the following program for matrix multiplication:

```
fun main(x: [n][m]i32, y: [m][p]i32): [n][p]i32 =
  map (\xr -> map (\yc ->
                  reduce (+) 0 (zipWith (*) xr yc))
              (transpose y))
    x
```

Compare with the inner-product function in Backus' FP language shown in Sect. 6.4.

Note that array parameters have size variables and that the declarations constrain the number of columns of x to be the same as the number of rows of y and that the result has the same number of rows as x and the same number of columns as y.

Futhark is not intended for stand-alone programs, but for writing compute-intensive cores that are called from programs written in a GPL (such as C or Python).

10.6 Further Reading

A full book [2] has been written about DSLs. An annotated bibliography about domain-specific languages can be found in [1]. Another article [7] focuses on methodology, and has many references to specific DSLs.

10.7 Exercises

Exercise 10.1

a. Discuss to what extent JSON and XML can be considered DSLs.
b. Discuss to what extent a notation for regular expressions is a DSL.

Exercise 10.2 The DSL that has arguably been most successful in being used by non-programmers is Excel, the spreadsheet program in Microsoft's Office package.

Discuss which properties of Excel make it suitable for non-programmers, and which properties that might hinder this.

Exercise 10.3 An online implementation of Troll can be found at https://topps.diku.dk/~torbenm/troll.msp. The page has links to both a quick reference guide and a manual with a complete description of the language.

a. Use Troll to solve Project Euler Problem 205 (https://projecteuler.net/problem=205).
b. Solve Project Euler Problem 205 using a general-purpose language. Compare the two solutions in terms of speed, size, effort to program, and readability by people who are familiar with neither language.
c. Use Troll to solve the following problem:
   You roll 6 six-sided dice and collect sets of equal values, add up the values in each set, and then take the largest such sum.
   For example, if you roll 5 2 2 5 2 3, you have a set of one 3 (with the sum 3), a set of three 2s (with the sum 6), and two 5s (with the sum 10), so the result of this roll is 10.
   What is the average result?

Exercise 10.4 Modify the OpenSCAD program in Fig. 10.4 so the hollowed-out sphere is surrounded by the digits 1–5 instead of 1–4.

References

1. van Deursen A, Klint P, Visser J (2000) Domain-specific languages: an annotated bibliography. SIGPLAN Not 35(6):26–36. https://doi.org/10.1145/352029.352035, http://doi.acm.org/10.1145/352029.352035
2. Fowler M (2010) Domain specific languages, 1st edn. Addison-Wesley Professional
3. HIPERFIT Research Centre (2017) The Futhark language. (Retrieved March 2017). http://futhark-lang.org/
4. Knuth DE (1986) The teXbook. Addison-Wesley Professional
5. Lamport L (1986) Latex: a document preparation system. Addison-Wesley Longman Publishing Co., Inc, Boston, MA, USA

6. Maloney J, Resnick M, Rusk N, Silverman B, Eastmond E (2010) The Scratch programming language and environment. Trans Comput Educ 10(4):1–16. https://doi.org/10.1145/1868358.1868363. http://doi.acm.org/10.1145/1868358.1868363

7. Mernik M, Heering J, Sloane AM (2005) When and how to develop domain-specific languages. ACM Comput Surv 37(4):316–344. https://doi.org/10.1145/1118890.1118892. http://doi.acm.org/10.1145/1118890.1118892

8. Mogensen TÆ (2003) Linear types for cashflow reengineering. In: Broy M, Zamulin AV (eds) Perspectives of system informatics: 5th International Andrei Ershov memorial conference, PSI 2003, Akademgorodok, Novosibirsk, Russia, July 9–12, 2003. Revised Papers. Springer, Berlin Heidelberg, pp 13–21. https://doi.org/10.1007/978-3-540-39866-0_2

9. Mogensen TÆ (2009) Troll, a language for specifying dice-rolls. In: Shin SY, Ossowski S (eds) Proceedings of the 24th symposium on applied computing, pp. 1910–1915. https://doi.org/10.1145/1529282.1529708

Specifying the Semantics of a Programming Language

11

> *Semantics, or the study of meaning, remained undeveloped, while phonetics made rapid progress and even came to occupy the central place in the scientific study of language.*
>
> Roman Jakobson
>
> *It is easier to change the specification to fit the program than vice versa.*
>
> Alan Perlis

As we noted in Chap. 3, syntax concerns the textual or graphical *form* of programs, but not what these programs *mean*. The meaning of programs is the concern of *semantics*.

Semantics of programming languages can be defined loosely or precisely and informally or formally. It is not necessarily the case that informal specifications are imprecise or formal specifications are precise, so these are orthogonal aspects of specification. In this chapter, we will briefly describe various ways that language semantics can be specified.

A distinction is often made between *static* and *dynamic* semantics. Static semantics concern types or other aspects of non-syntactic correctness of programs that can be checked or inferred before the program is executed, while dynamic semantics concern what happens during execution. We have informally discussed types in Chap. 7, but not how these are specified, so we will look into this in this chapter.

Suggested Exercise: 11.1.

11.1 Informal Specification

Informal specification, as the name indicates, does not use formal notation or reasoning as the main medium for specification of language semantics. Instead, a natural language such as English is used, supplemented with examples.

Informal semantics specification was used in early language definitions, such as the FORTRAN, COBOL, and ALGOL 60 reports, but even today, most programming languages are informally specified. For example, the Java Language Specification [2] is more than 700 pages of English text, including code examples. In comparison, the ALGOL 60 report [1] is 17–40 pages (depending on the page format) and the Pascal User Manual and Report [5] (which defines the language and includes examples) is around 170 pages.

The advantage of informal specification is that the writer and reader of a specification do not need to know any formalism apart from the English language (or whatever natural language is used). The disadvantage is that natural languages such as English are verbose, ambiguous, and not amenable to formal or automatic processing. For example, it is not possible to formally verify an implementation of a language against its specification if the specification is written in English. For this reason, informal specification usually employ many examples with descriptions of expected behaviour, such that these can be used for testing an implementation.

Sets of example/test programs that cover all aspects of a language specification are called *validation suites* and can be very large. For example, typical compiler validation suites for the ISO C standard include more than 50,000 lines of code. An issue with such validation suites is that they are themselves prone to errors, so they may give false positives or false negatives when testing a compiler. If a validation suite is free from errors, it can at best detect errors in a language implementation, but it can never prove that the implementation is correct—only that errors are unlikely to be found by casual users of the implementation. A validation suite tends to grow over time, as cases are found where implementation errors escape detection by the previous validation suite.

Another problem with validation suites is that specifications (in particular informal specifications) often allow multiple different behaviours to be correct. This is called *under-specification*. For example, the size of integers and the behaviour of rounding in arithmetic can be unspecified. In C, the result of $(-3)/2$ can be either -1 or -2 depending on whether division rounds towards 0 or towards $-\infty$, both of which are allowed by the specification, as long as any single implementation is consistent. A test for this should allow either result and also check sufficient cases to render consistency probable.

11.2 Specification by Reference Implementation

A common strategy for language specification is to provide an implementation of the language and elevate the behaviour of this implementation to standard.

An advantage of this form of specification is that it is precise—to the extent that the language in which the reference implementation is written is precise. To avoid such imprecisions, reference implementations can be written using only simple features and not attempting any form of optimisation, so it reflects the desired behaviour even if it does not reflect the desired efficiency. But the common case is that a reference implementation is written to be a useful implementation, which makes it more error prone and harder to understand.

It is possible to formally verify that an implementation conforms to a reference implementation, but that requires formal specification of both implementation languages or, at minimum, that the implementation languages are identical and that the chosen language specifies sufficient equivalence rules to allow proofs that two different programs are equivalent. If a reference implementation applies optimisations and exploits all useful features of the implementation language, this can make formal verification all but impossible. The fact that equivalence of programs written in Turing-complete languages is undecidable does not make it any easier. An additional complication is that a correct compiler does not need to produce the same code as a reference compiler, it just needs to produce that is equivalent to this, which elevates the equivalence property to a meta-level.

A reference implementation can be useful when building a verification suite: Any test program can be executed on the reference implementation to find the desired behaviour. It is even possible to generate programs randomly and use these to test for identical behaviour on the reference implementation and the tested implementation. Random test programs will usually not be sufficient, though, as they rarely cover corner cases.

A problem with a reference implementation is that it can over-specify behaviour: If the language is intended to allow some freedom in, say, the order of evaluation, a reference implementation can restrict this freedom, as any deviation from the behaviour of the reference implementation will be considered erroneous.

11.3   Formal Specification

A formal specification is similar to a reference implementation, except that the language is specified/implemented using a mathematical or logical formalism instead of another programming language. The advantage of using a formalism is that formalisms are usually simpler than "real" programming languages and structured in ways that make proving properties of semantics easier than if the semantics are specified by an interpreter or compiler written in a "real" programming language.

Furthermore, formal specifications can be more *abstract*, i.e., by not specifying the size of integers, the layout and management of data in memory, the exact sequence of operations, and so on, that a reference implementation has to make concrete.

The most common forms of formal language specification are *denotational* and *operational*. Denotational semantics are similar to compilers: A program is translated into another language, in this case, a language of domains (set-like mathematical objects) and functions over these, so a program is specified by a function from input to output (or events to events). Operational semantics are similar to interpreters: A language is specified by a set of logical rules such that execution of a program on specific input leading to specific output forms a logical proof. The proof can have the form of a sequence of state transitions from an initial state to a final state—this is called *small-step semantics*—or it can be tree-structured to allow some freedom in the order in which execution happens and even that sub-computations can be done at the same time—this is called *big-step semantics*.

In both cases, the semantic specification is *syntax directed*: Each grammar rule in a syntax for the language is represented by one or more semantic rules. A program is represented by its abstract syntax tree, and for each node in the syntax tree, a rule is applied. In operational semantics, this rule can use state-dependent conditions to decide which rules (if any) are applied to the sub-trees, but in denotational semantics, the same rule is applied to all instances of a grammar rule, so all state-dependent behaviour is handled by the mathematical function into which a program is translated.

Operational semantics is the most common form of formal semantics for programming languages, and the notation used for operational semantics is also commonly used to specify type systems. For this reason, we will focus on operational semantics in this chapter. For denotational semantics, we refer to the Further Reading section at the end of this chapter.

We begin by introducing the notation for environments and semantic rules that are commonly used for both type systems and operational semantics. We will then look at the type system specification, operational semantics and static semantics, where the latter concerns well-formedness criteria for programs.

11.3.1 Notation for Logic Rules

An operational semantics or type system is specified by a set of logic rules, where a given set of premises (also called "antecedents") imply a conclusion. The premises, if any, are written above a horizontal line, and the conclusion is written below the line. As an example, the *modus ponens* rule from logic can be written as

$$\frac{A \Rightarrow B \quad A}{B} \text{ (ModusPonens)}$$

saying that if A implies B and A is true, then we can conclude that B is true. The parenthesised text to the right of the rule names the rule, but has no logical meaning.

Similarly, the transitive rule for logical implication can be written as

$$\frac{A \Rightarrow B \quad B \Rightarrow C}{A \Rightarrow C} \text{ (Transitive)}$$

stating that if A implies B and B implies C, then A implies C.

We will for type systems and runtime semantics use a specific instance of this notation, which we will describe below. Different texts about semantics and type systems use different instances of the general notation, but they are usually similar to what we will use.

11.3.2 Environments

Nearly all programming languages use names that can be bound to types, values, functions, program points (labels), and so on. A semantic specification will need to operate on *environments*: mappings from names to information about these names. In semantic rules, we use a notation where an environment is written as a list of bindings, each of the form *name* $\mapsto$ *info*, where *info* can be a value, a type, or any other form of information we may need. For example, an environment that maps x to the value 3 and y to the value 4 is written as $[x \mapsto 3, \ y \mapsto 4]$.

We use Greek letters such as ρ, σ or τ to denote environments, often with a subscript if several environments are used in a rule. We can use environments as functions, so $\rho\, x$ is the value that x is bound to in the environment ρ. It is considered an error if x is not bound in ρ, but we can test if it is by a condition $x \in Dom(\rho)$, where Dom is a function that finds the *domain* of a mapping.

We can also update an environment: $\rho[y \mapsto 4]$ is a new environment that is created by adding the binding $[y \mapsto 4]$ to ρ. If there is already a binding for y in ρ, this is overridden. Note that ρ itself is not modified as a side effect—a new expanded or modified environment is created. Semantic rules do not have side effects, all behaviour is described as explicit functions or relations between values and environments.

11.3.3 Judgements

Semantics and type systems use logical judgements such as "the expression 2+3 has type `int`" or "the expression 2+3 evaluates to 5", but we use formal notation instead of free-form text. A typical judgement has the form

$$context \vdash syntax : values$$

where the context is usually one or more environments as shown in Sect. 11.3.2 above, but it can be some other form of context. If there are several environments, they are separated by commas. The $\vdash$ symbol (called "turnstile") can be subscripted with a letter or symbol that identifies the kind of judgement. For example, $\vdash_E$ can indicate that the judgement concerns expression (indicated by the nonterminal E). In many cases, such subscripts are not needed as the form of the judgement (e.g., the number of environments in the context, the kind of syntax used, or the shape of values) identifies its kind. The syntax part of a judgement describes the kind of program syntax that the rule covers. Semantic rules assume that parsing has been done and an abstract syntax tree has been built, but we use notation similar to concrete syntax but with (possibly subscripted) nonterminals denoting subtrees in the abstract syntax tree. For example, `while` E `do` S describes any while loop with condition E (which is an expression) and body S (which is a statement). Similarly, $E_1 + E_2$ describes an expression built from two subexpressions E_1 and E_2 and the infix operator +. The colon symbol can be replaced by other symbols such as $\downarrow$ when talking about expressions evaluating values. Values can be types, numbers, truth values, program states, and even relations between such. For example, a judgement of the form

$$\rho \vdash S : \sigma_1 \rightsquigarrow \sigma_2$$

can state that, in an environment ρ, a statement S transforms a state σ_1 into a new state σ_2. We use a Greek letter for states, as a state is a mapping from names to values.

Just like Greek letters are metavariables denoting environments and stores and nonterminals are used as metavariables denoting syntax, we can also use metavariables denoting values and types. We use lowercase letters in Italic font for such metavariables. Note that we use both syntactic operator symbols (such as +) and semantic operator symbols (such as +). Syntactic operator symbols are just text, but semantic operator symbols have their usual mathematical meaning. Note that the turnstile and arrow symbols have no a priori meaning—they are just notation. Their meaning is defined by semantic rules.

11.3.4   Semantic Rules

A semantic rule has the form

$$\frac{judgement \quad \cdots \quad judgement}{judgement}\text{(name)}$$

The judgements above the line are antecedents (preconditions) that must all be true for the judgement below the line (the conclusion) to be true. In addition to judgements as described in Sect. 11.3.3 above, we also allow logical statements such as $m = n + 1$, $\rho(x) = n$, $x \in v$ and so on. When not explicitly otherwise stated, such statements have their usual meaning. The antecedents are separated by space (usually several letters wide), and the order has no implicit significance. It is, however, customary to have antecedents that produce values occur before antecedents that use these values. The name of a rule is used in explanatory text to refer to the rule. When doing so, the name is always parenthesised.

Semantic rules are *syntax directed*. This means that the syntax descriptions used in rules must represent syntactically correct subtrees of the original program syntax tree. The usual case is that the syntax in a conclusion is the right-hand side of a production (possibly with subscripted nonterminals) and that the syntax part of antecedents are (subscripted) nonterminals found in the conclusion, but subtrees can be stored in environments or program states and extracted from these and used in antecedents. This is useful for representing closures and defining the semantics of recursion and loops. But we never allow an antecedent to use syntax that is not a syntactically correct subtree of the original, full program syntax tree: We can not build new syntax during type checking or execution.

A semantic rule is similar to a clause in a Prolog program, see Sect. 9.4, and most semantic rules can, indeed, fairly easily be expressed in Prolog. The horizontal line in a semantic rule is in Prolog represented with the :- symbol, with antecedents on the right and the conclusion on the left. A judgement is represented as a goal: A predicate symbol with context, abstract syntax, and values as arguments. Names of rules are not directly represented in Prolog, but can be added as comments.

11.4 Type Systems

A type system specifies when a program is statically type-correct, so they use environments that map names to types and rules that given premises about the types of subexpressions, substatements, or declarations conclude something about the type of an expression, statement, or program.

We will illustrate formal specification of type systems by a tiny functional language that has integers, pairs, and function types. Types and expressions in this language are specified by the grammar in Fig. 11.1.

The operators `fst` and `snd` take, respectively, the first or the second component of a pair. The two last productions of nonterminal E specify function application and anonymous function definitions. The grammar is highly ambiguous, but we assume ambiguities are resolved during parsing, and parentheses used in the concrete syntax for disambiguation can be removed during parsing. The abstract syntax is conceptually a tree structure.

The type system must ensure that addition is only performed on integers, that `fst` and `snd` are only applied to pairs, that only functions are applied to arguments, and that the type of an argument corresponds to the declared type in the function that is applied.

Recall that we use (possibly subscripted) nonterminals as metavariables, so N will in the rules below denote the text of any number constant, X will denote any variable name, and T will denote any type that can be built from the nonterminal T. We use a function $valOf$ to map number constants into semantic numbers. For example, $valOf(42) = 42$.

Judgements for the type system are of the form $\tau \vdash E : T$, where τ denotes a type environment that maps variable names to types, E denotes an expression, and T denotes a type. The intended meaning of this judgement is that, given a type environment τ, the expression E has type T. Note that, even though T is a nonterminal, it doesn't occur in the syntax part of the judgement, so we are allowed

$$T \rightarrow \texttt{int}$$
$$T \rightarrow (T \mathbin{\texttt{*}} T)$$
$$T \rightarrow (T \mathbin{\texttt{->}} T)$$

$$E \rightarrow N$$
$$E \rightarrow X$$
$$E \rightarrow E + E$$
$$E \rightarrow (E, E)$$
$$E \rightarrow \texttt{fst}\, E$$
$$E \rightarrow \texttt{snd}\, E$$
$$E \rightarrow E\, E$$
$$E \rightarrow \texttt{fun}\, X : T \mathbin{\texttt{->}} E$$

$$N \rightarrow \textbf{num}$$
$$X \rightarrow \textbf{id}$$

Fig. 11.1 Syntax of tiny functional language

$$\frac{}{\tau \vdash N : \texttt{int}}\,(\text{Const}) \qquad \frac{}{\tau \vdash X : \tau(X)}\,(\text{Var})$$

$$\frac{\tau \vdash E_1 : \texttt{int} \quad \tau \vdash E_2 : \texttt{int}}{\tau \vdash E_1 + E_2 : \texttt{int}}\,(\text{Plus}) \qquad \frac{\tau \vdash E_1 : T_1 \quad \tau \vdash E_2 : T_2}{\tau \vdash (E_1, E_2) : (T_1 \ast T_2)}\,(\text{Pair})$$

$$\frac{\tau \vdash E : (T_1 \ast T_2)}{\tau \vdash \texttt{fst}\, E : T_1}\,(\text{Fst}) \qquad \frac{\tau \vdash E : (T_1 \ast T_2)}{\tau \vdash \texttt{snd}\, E : T_2}\,(\text{Snd})$$

$$\frac{\tau \vdash E_1 : (T_1 \text{->} T_2) \quad \tau \vdash E_2 : T_1}{\tau \vdash E_1\, E_2 : T_2}\,(\text{Apply})$$

$$\frac{\tau[X \mapsto T_1] \vdash E : T_2}{\tau \vdash \texttt{fun}\, X : T_1 \text{->} E : (T_1 \text{->} T_2)}\,(\text{FunDef})$$

Fig. 11.2 Type rules for tiny functional language

to build types that are not found in the program text. T is, in this context, a value—just one that has a tree structure specified by a grammar. In the rules below, expressions used in antecedents of a rule are always subexpressions of the expression used in the conclusion of the rule. This is the typical case for type systems.

We specify the type system for the functional language using the rules in Fig. 11.2.

The rule (Const) says that a number constant is of type $\texttt{int}$. The rule (Var) states that a variable has the type to which it is bound in the type environment. Recall that we can use environments as functions. There are no antecedents to these rules, except the implicit premise that x must be bound to a type in τ.

The rule (Plus) states that both arguments and the result of addition must be integers. If more arithmetic operators are added to the language, similar rules need to be added to the semantics.

The next three rules concern building and accessing pairs: If you build a pair (rule (Pair)), it has a pair type, and if you use $\texttt{fst}$ or $\texttt{snd}$ (rules (Fst) and (Snd)), the argument must have a pair type, and the result will have the type of the first or second component of the pair type, respectively.

The rule (Apply) says that the expression E_1 must have a function type, that the expression E_2 must have a type that matches the argument part of this function type, and that the resulting application has a type that matches the second part of the function type. The rule (FunDef) extends the type environment with the declared type of the argument variable and finds the type of the function body using the extended environment. The declared argument type and the type of the body are used to build a function type. Note that (FunDef) uses both a syntactic colon ($\texttt{:}$) and a semantic colon (:).

We can use the type system to prove, for example, that, if x is bound to the type $\texttt{int}$ in the environment, then the expression $\texttt{fst}\,(7,\ 5)\ +\ x$ has type $\texttt{int}$. The proof (shown in Fig. 11.3) is a tree that combines the rules, with the conclusion at the root (lowest) and rules without antecedents at the leaves (highest).

The top two rules in Fig. 11.3 say that 7 and 5 are integers. The conclusions of these rules are used as premises in the rule that concludes that $(7,\ 5)$ is a pair of two integers. This conclusion is then used as a premise to a rule that concludes that

$$\dfrac{\dfrac{}{[\mathsf{x}\mapsto\mathsf{int}]\vdash 7:\mathsf{int}}\text{(Const)}\quad \dfrac{}{[\mathsf{x}\mapsto\mathsf{int}]\vdash 5:\mathsf{int}}\text{(Const)}}{\dfrac{[\mathsf{x}\mapsto\mathsf{int}]\vdash (7,5):(\mathsf{int}*\mathsf{int})}{\dfrac{[\mathsf{x}\mapsto\mathsf{int}]\vdash \mathtt{fst}\ (7,5):\mathsf{int}}{[\mathsf{x}\mapsto\mathsf{int}]\vdash \mathtt{fst}\ (7,5)+\mathsf{x}:\mathsf{int}}\text{(Fst)}\quad \dfrac{}{[\mathsf{x}\mapsto\mathsf{int}]\vdash \mathsf{x}:\mathsf{int}}\text{(Var)}}\text{(Plus)}}\text{(Pair)}$$

Fig. 11.3 Proof tree for type correctness

`fst (7, 5)` is an integer. This conclusion is together with the conclusion of a rule that concludes that `x` is an integer to conclude that `fst (7, 5) + x` is an integer.

Since such proof trees can get pretty big, they are rarely written or printed out in full. Instead, programs (type checkers) are made that internally construct such proofs but only print or store the final conclusion.

Suggested Exercises: 11.2 and 11.3.

11.5   Operational Semantics

An operational semantics for a programming language L is, in essence, an interpreter for the language L written as a set of semantic rules, and execution of a program with a certain initial state corresponds to using these rules to build a proof that the program finishes with a certain final state or value.

We show two examples of operational semantics: One for the small functional language used in Sect. 11.4, and one for a small imperative language.

11.5.1   Operational Semantics for a Functional Language

We use the same grammar as in Sect. 11.4, but instead of operating on types, we operate on values. We need values to represent numbers, pairs, and functional values. A functional value is a *closure*, i.e., a tuple of a variable name, an expression and an environment. The following grammar describes the set of values:

$$v \rightarrow I\!N$$
$$v \rightarrow (v, v)$$
$$v \rightarrow (X, E, \rho)$$

where ρ is an environment that binds variables to values. We use judgements of the form $\rho \vdash E \downarrow v$ to say that, in the environment ρ, the expression E evaluates to the value v. $I\!N$ represents the set of natural numbers, as distinct from N, which the set of number constants. We use a function $valOf : N \rightarrow I\!N$ to map number constants to values, and we use mathematical addition $+$ (as distinct from the syntactic addition operator +) to add numbers. A triple (X, E, ρ) represents a closure consisting of a

$$\frac{}{\rho \vdash N \downarrow valOf(N)}\,(\text{Const}) \qquad \frac{}{\rho \vdash X \downarrow \rho(X)}\,(\text{Var})$$

$$\frac{\rho \vdash E_1 \downarrow m \quad \rho \vdash E_2 \downarrow n}{\rho \vdash E_1 + E_2 \downarrow (m+n)}\,(\text{Plus}) \qquad \frac{\rho \vdash E_1 \downarrow v_1 \quad \rho \vdash E_2 \downarrow v_2}{\rho \vdash (E_1, E_2) \downarrow (v_1, v_2)}\,(\text{Pair})$$

$$\frac{\rho \vdash E \downarrow (v_1, v_2)}{\rho \vdash \texttt{fst}\, E \downarrow v_1}\,(\text{Fst}) \qquad \frac{\rho \vdash E \downarrow (v_1, v_2)}{\rho \vdash \texttt{snd}\, E \downarrow v_2}\,(\text{Snd})$$

$$\frac{\rho_1 \vdash E_1 \downarrow (X, E_3, \rho_2) \quad \rho_1 \vdash E_2 \downarrow v \quad \rho_2[X \mapsto v] \vdash E_3 \downarrow w}{\rho_1 \vdash E_1\, E_2 \downarrow w}\,(\text{Apply})$$

$$\frac{}{\rho \vdash \texttt{fun}\, X : T \rightarrow E \downarrow (X, E, \rho)}\,(\text{FunDef})$$

Fig. 11.4 Rules for evaluating expressions

parameter name X, a function body E and an environment ρ representing the scope in which the function is defined. See Sect. 5.3 for more detail about closures.

The semantic rules for evaluating expressions are shown in Fig. 11.4.

Note that we use the symbol $\downarrow$ where the type rules use :. We use the same names for rules as we did in the type system. The context makes it clear whether we refer to a type rule or an evaluation rule.

The rule (Const) states that a number constant evaluates its value. The rule (Var) states that a variable evaluates whatever it is bound to in the environment. The rule (Plus) states that to evaluate an addition expression, you first evaluate the two subexpressions to m and n and then add these (using mathematical addition).

The next three rules concern pairs. To evaluate a pair expression (rule (Pair)), you first evaluate the subexpressions and build a pair from their values. When applying `fst` to an expression (rule (Fst)), you first evaluate the expression to a pair, and then return the first component. Applying `snd` (rule (Snd)) works analogously.

When applying one expression to another (rule (Apply)), you first evaluate the first expression (E_1) to a closure (X, E_3, ρ_2) and the second expression (E_2) to any value v. The expression (E_3) in the closure is then evaluated in the environment (ρ_2) from the closure, extended by binding the variable X from the closure to v. The resulting value is the value of the application. The rule (FunDef) for anonymous functions just builds a closure from the argument variable, the body, and the current environment. Note that this implements static scoping. Unlike in the type rules, we have a rule here (rule (Apply)) where the syntax part of an antecedent is not a subexpression of the syntax part of the conclusion: E_3 is not found in the conclusion. But E_3 is a subexpression of the entire program, for (assuming evaluation starts with an empty environment) it must be part of a closure evaluated by rule (FunDef), which creates closures from expressions that are found in the program text.

Suggested Exercise: 11.4.

11.5.2   Relating Type Systems and Operational Semantics

If a program is type correct according to the rules in Sect. 11.4, all semantic rules in the operational semantics will always succeed. For example, when `fst` is applied to an expression, we know from the type system that this expression *will* evaluate a pair, and when we add two expressions, we know that these evaluate to numbers. It is possible to formally prove this property from the rules for the type system and the operational semantics, but we refer interested students to the Further Reading section for details about this.

Robin Milner coined the phrase "Well-typed programs don't go wrong" to cover the relation between type correctness and runtime behaviour. Some runtime errors, for example, division by zero or stack overflow, can not be prevented by correct types, but a large class of errors can.

11.5.3   Operational Semantics for an Imperative Language

Operational semantics are not only useful for describing the semantics of functional languages. We specify the syntax of a tiny imperative language shown in Fig. 11.5.

The semantics are (informally) like in Pascal and C: `skip` is the empty statement that does nothing. $X := N$ gives the variable X the value of N, $X{+}{+}$ increments X, $X{-}{-}$ decrements X, `if` checks if the variable is different from 0, and if so executes the `then` branch, and otherwise the `else` branch. The `while` statement executes the body statement until the variable becomes 0 (which may be at entry to the loop, after a finite number of iterations, or never).

We use environments to represent stores that bind variables to values. A statement takes a store and returns a modified store, which we represent with judgements of the form $\vdash S : \sigma \rightsquigarrow \sigma'$, where σ and σ' represent stores and S is a statement. Stores map variables to values. This judgement states that S transforms the store σ into a new store σ'.

The operational semantics for statements is shown in Fig. 11.6 and is specified by one or more semantic rules for each statement type.

The (Skip) rule states that `skip` leaves the store unchanged. This rule has no premise—the conclusion is always true.

Fig. 11.5 Syntax of tiny imperative language

$$S \rightarrow \texttt{skip}$$
$$S \rightarrow S\texttt{;}\, S$$
$$S \rightarrow X\texttt{:=}N$$
$$S \rightarrow X\texttt{++}$$
$$S \rightarrow X\texttt{--}$$
$$S \rightarrow \texttt{if}\,X\,\texttt{then}\,S\,\texttt{else}\,S$$
$$S \rightarrow \texttt{while}\,X\,\texttt{do}\,S$$

$$N \rightarrow \textbf{num}$$
$$X \rightarrow \textbf{id}$$

$$\frac{}{\vdash \texttt{skip}:\sigma \rightsquigarrow \sigma}\,(\text{Skip}) \qquad \frac{\vdash S_1:\sigma \rightsquigarrow \sigma_1 \quad \vdash S_2:\sigma_1 \rightsquigarrow \sigma_2}{\vdash S_1;S_2:\sigma \rightsquigarrow \sigma_2}\,(\text{Semi})$$

$$\frac{}{\vdash X:=N:\sigma \rightsquigarrow \sigma[X \mapsto valOf(N)]}\,(\text{Assign})$$

$$\frac{}{\vdash X\texttt{++}:\sigma \rightsquigarrow \sigma[X \mapsto (\sigma(X)+1)]}\,(\text{Incr}) \qquad \frac{}{\vdash X\texttt{--}:\sigma \rightsquigarrow \sigma[X \mapsto (\sigma(X)-1)]}\,(\text{Decr})$$

$$\frac{\sigma(X) \neq 0 \quad \vdash S_1:\sigma \rightsquigarrow \sigma'}{\vdash \texttt{if } x \texttt{ then } s_1 \texttt{ else } s_2:\sigma \rightsquigarrow \sigma'}\,(\text{If1})$$

$$\frac{\sigma(X) = 0 \quad \vdash S_2:\sigma \rightsquigarrow \sigma'}{\vdash \texttt{if } x \texttt{ then } s_1 \texttt{ else } s_2:\sigma \rightsquigarrow \sigma'}\,(\text{If2})$$

$$\frac{\sigma(X) \neq 0 \quad \vdash S:\sigma \rightsquigarrow \sigma' \quad \vdash \texttt{while } X \texttt{ do } S:\sigma' \rightsquigarrow \sigma''}{\vdash \texttt{while } X \texttt{ do } S:\sigma \rightsquigarrow \sigma''}\,(\text{While1})$$

$$\frac{\sigma(X) = 0}{\vdash \texttt{while } X \texttt{ do } S:\sigma \rightsquigarrow \sigma}\,(\text{While2})$$

Fig. 11.6 Rules for statement execution

The (Semi) rule states that, if S_1 transforms the store σ to a new store σ_1 and S_2 transforms σ_1 to σ_2, then $S_1;S_2$ transforms σ to σ_2. The order in which the two antecedents are specified does not really matter, but it is usual to specify them left-to-right according to value dependencies.

The next three rules (Assign), (Incr), and (Decr) specify how variable updates change the store. These, also, have no premises.

Rules (If1) and (If2) define the behaviour of the if-then-else statement. Rule (If1) is for the case where X is non-zero, and (If2) is for when X is zero, so we have $\sigma(X) \neq 0$ as antecedent in (If1) and $\sigma(X) = 0$ as antecedent in t(If2). We use multiple rules for the same statement to represent multiple possible outcomes. For a deterministic language, we want exactly one of the rules to match any given situation. Since X is either zero or non-zero, this is the case here.

Rules (While1) and (While2) define the semantics of the while loop. Again, we have one rule (While1) for $\sigma(X) \neq 0$ and another (While2) for when $\sigma(X) = 0$. (While1) says that, when $\sigma(X) \neq 0$, the body S of the loop is executed to find a new store σ', and then the whole loop is re-entered using this new store. (While2) simply states that if $\sigma(X) = 0$, the loop finishes without updating the store. Note that the syntax parts of the antecedents are parts of the program syntax tree.

We complete the semantics with a rule for executing programs:

$$\frac{\vdash P : [x \mapsto n] \rightsquigarrow \sigma}{\vdash_P P : n \rightsquigarrow \sigma(y)}$$

This rule states that with input n, a program P runs (as a statement) in an initial store binding the variable x to n, which leads to a final store σ. The value of the variable y in σ is the output from the program. We subscript $\vdash$ with P in the conclusion to distinguish judgements for programs (that map values to values) from judgements for statements (that map stores to stores).

Example Execution

We consider the program:

```
y := 0; while x do x--; y++
```

Executing this program with input 1 gives the proof shown in Fig. 11.7 (with rule names omitted and rotated to fit the page). It should be evident that such proofs can become very large, so they are seldom written out.

11.5.3.1   A Word of Warning

If we extend the syntax of the imperative language in Fig. 11.5 with the production

$$S \rightarrow \texttt{repeat num } S$$

with the intended meaning that $\texttt{repeat } n \ S$ repeats S exactly n times, it can be tempting to define this semantics by rules such as these:

$$\frac{}{\vdash \texttt{repeat } 0 \ S : \sigma \rightsquigarrow \sigma} \qquad \frac{n > 0 \quad \vdash S : \sigma_1 \rightsquigarrow \sigma_2 \quad \vdash \texttt{repeat } (N-1) \ S : \sigma_2 \rightsquigarrow \sigma_3}{\vdash \texttt{repeat } N \ S : \sigma_1 \rightsquigarrow \sigma_3}$$

but these rules break the restriction that the syntax part of a judgement must be a subtree of the original program, as the second rule builds syntax that is not found in the original program. A correct way of handling this is to introduce a different form of judgement for handling the iteration: $n \vdash_r S : \sigma_1 \rightsquigarrow \sigma_2$ states that executing S n times transforms σ_1 to σ_2. Note that n is not in the syntax part of the judgement. We have, for clarity, subscripted the turnstile with r to distinguish the judgement more clearly from the normal statement execution judgement. We can now use the rules

$$\frac{valOf(n) \vdash_r S : \sigma_1 \rightsquigarrow \sigma_2}{\vdash \texttt{repeat } N \ S : \sigma_1 \rightsquigarrow \sigma_2}$$

$$\frac{}{0 \vdash_r S : \sigma \rightsquigarrow \sigma} \qquad \frac{n > 0 \quad \vdash S : \sigma_1 \rightsquigarrow \sigma_2 \quad (n-1) \vdash_r S : \sigma_2 \rightsquigarrow \sigma_3}{n \vdash_r S : \sigma_1 \rightsquigarrow \sigma_3}$$

Note that the numbers that are modified are not found in the syntax part of the judgements in the rules. It may seem harmless to create new syntax in semantic rules, as long as the rules specify the meaning of the new syntax, but it makes it harder to prove properties about program behaviour. So we will not allow it.

Suggested Exercise: 11.6.

$$\dfrac{\sigma_1(x)\neq 0 \qquad \dfrac{\vdash x--:\sigma_1\leadsto\sigma_2 \quad \vdash y++:\sigma_2\leadsto\sigma_3}{\vdash x--;\ y++:\sigma_1\leadsto\sigma_3} \quad \dfrac{\sigma_3(x)=0}{\vdash \texttt{while x do x--; y++}:\sigma_3\leadsto\sigma_3}}{\vdash\texttt{while x do x--; y++}:\sigma_1\leadsto\sigma_3}$$

$$\dfrac{\vdash \texttt{y := 0}:\sigma_0\leadsto\sigma_1 \qquad \vdash\texttt{while x do x--; y++}:\sigma_1\leadsto\sigma_3}{\vdash\texttt{y := 0; while x do x--; y++}:[x\mapsto 1]\leadsto\sigma_3}$$

$$\vdash_P \texttt{y := 0; while x do x--; y++}:1\leadsto 1$$

where

$$\sigma_0 = [x\mapsto 1]$$
$$\sigma_1 = [x\mapsto 1, y\mapsto 0]$$
$$\sigma_2 = [x\mapsto 0, y\mapsto 0]$$
$$\sigma_3 = [x\mapsto 0, y\mapsto 1]$$

Fig. 11.7 Proof tree for executing `y := 0; while x do x--; y++`

$$\frac{}{c \vdash \texttt{skip} : \rhd []}\,(\text{LSkip}) \qquad \frac{(S_2 :: c) \vdash S_1 \rhd \lambda_1 \quad c \vdash S_2 \rhd \lambda_2}{c \vdash S_1 \,;\, S_2 \rhd (\lambda_1 \cup \lambda_2)}\,(\text{LSemi})$$

$$\frac{}{c \vdash X := N \rhd []}\,(\text{LAssign}) \qquad \frac{}{c \vdash X\texttt{++} \rhd []}\,(\text{LIncr}) \qquad \frac{}{c \vdash X\texttt{--} \rhd []}\,(\text{LDecr})$$

$$\frac{c \vdash S_1 \rhd \lambda_1 \quad c \vdash s_2 \rhd \lambda_2}{c \vdash \texttt{if } x \texttt{ then } s_1 \texttt{ else } s_2 \rhd (\lambda_1 \cup \lambda_2)}\,(\text{LIf})$$

$$\frac{}{c \vdash L : \rhd [L \mapsto c]}\,(\text{LLabel}) \qquad \frac{}{c \vdash \texttt{goto } L \rhd []}\,(\text{LGoto})$$

Fig. 11.8 Rules for building label environment

11.5.4 Unstructured Control

We replace the while-loop from the imperative language with labels and jumps:

$$S \to L :$$
$$S \to \texttt{goto } L$$

where L is a label name. For each label name L, there is exactly one occurrence of $L :$ in the program, but there can be any number (including 0) of occurrences of $\texttt{goto } L$.

Like with variable names, we need an environment for label names. But to what should a label L be bound? It should represent the position of the occurrence of $L :$ in the program, but we don't really have a notion of addresses for statements. We can not just map a label to a statement in the program, since the label points not only to the following statement but to all the statements that follow the label. So, instead, we map L to a list of statements. We denote such lists by c (possibly with subscript). We choose the letter c because a sequence of statements represents a continuation of the current statement. We use [] for the empty continuation and $(S :: c)$ to represent a continuation created by adding S in front of the continuation c.

We define an environment λ that binds labels to such statement lists by using logical rules over the syntax of the program: The judgement $\vdash S : c \rhd \lambda$ states that statement S with continuation c creates the label environment λ.

We define this by the rules in Fig. 11.8.

Note how c is extended in the rule for semicolon. We use $\cup$ to combine two environments with disjoint domains.

In the rule for programs, we use the above to build a λ for the whole program in an empty continuation, and then use this λ and an empty continuation when executing the body of the program (using modified statement execution rules):

$$\frac{[] \vdash P \rhd \lambda \quad \lambda, [] \vdash P : [\texttt{x} \mapsto n] \leadsto \sigma}{\vdash_P P : n \leadsto \sigma(\texttt{y})}$$

We must now modify the execution rules for statements to use λ and a continuation, and we must replace the rules for the while loop with rules for labels and jumps. We add a new judgement for executing a continuation: $\lambda, c \vdash_C \sigma \leadsto \sigma_1$ states that, given a label environment λ, executing the continuation c transforms state σ to σ_1. We show rules for this judgement and the modified judgement for statements in Fig. 11.9.

$$\frac{}{\lambda, [\,] \vdash_C \sigma \rightsquigarrow \sigma} \text{(EmptyContinuation)} \qquad \frac{\lambda, c \vdash S : \sigma \rightsquigarrow \sigma_1}{\lambda, (S :: c) \vdash_C \sigma \rightsquigarrow \sigma_1} \text{(NonemptyContinuation)}$$

$$\frac{\lambda, c \vdash_C \sigma \rightsquigarrow \sigma_1}{\lambda, c \vdash \texttt{skip} : \sigma \rightsquigarrow \sigma_1} \text{(Skip)} \qquad \frac{\lambda, (S_2 :: c) \vdash S_1 : \sigma \rightsquigarrow \sigma_1}{\lambda, c \vdash S_1 ; S_2 : \sigma \rightsquigarrow \sigma_1} \text{(Semi)}$$

$$\frac{\lambda, c \vdash_C \sigma[X \mapsto valOf(N)] \rightsquigarrow \sigma_1}{\lambda, c \vdash X := N : \sigma \rightsquigarrow \sigma_1} \text{(Assign)}$$

$$\frac{\lambda, c \vdash \sigma[X \mapsto (\sigma(X)+1)] \rightsquigarrow \sigma_1}{\lambda, c \vdash X++ : \sigma \rightsquigarrow \sigma_1} \text{(Incr)}$$

$$\frac{\lambda, c \vdash_C \sigma[X \mapsto (\sigma(X)-1)] \rightsquigarrow \sigma_1}{\lambda, c \vdash X-- : \sigma \rightsquigarrow \sigma_1} \text{(Decr)}$$

$$\frac{\sigma(X) \neq 0 \quad \lambda, c \vdash S_1 : \sigma \rightsquigarrow \sigma'}{\lambda, c \vdash \texttt{if } x \texttt{ then } s_1 \texttt{ else } s_2 : \sigma \rightsquigarrow \sigma'} \text{(If1)}$$

$$\frac{\sigma(X) = 0 \quad \lambda, c \vdash S_2 : \sigma \rightsquigarrow \sigma'}{\lambda, c \vdash \texttt{if } x \texttt{ then } s_1 \texttt{ else } s_2 : \sigma \rightsquigarrow \sigma'} \text{(If2)}$$

$$\frac{\lambda, c \vdash_C \sigma \rightsquigarrow \sigma_1}{\lambda, c \vdash L: : \sigma \rightsquigarrow \sigma_1} \text{(Label)} \qquad \frac{\lambda, \lambda(L) \vdash_C \sigma \rightsquigarrow \sigma_1}{\lambda, c \vdash \texttt{goto} L : \sigma \rightsquigarrow \sigma_1} \text{(Goto)}$$

Fig. 11.9 Semantics for unstructured control

Continuations are handled by the rules (EmptyContinuation) and (NonEmptyContinuation): An empty continuation does not change the state, while a continuation of the form $(S :: c)$ is executed by executing S in context of the continuation c. This way, the statements in a continuation are executed in sequence—unless this sequence is interrupted by a jump.

Rule (Skip) says that execution continues to the continuation directly. Rule (Semi) executes the first statement S_1 in a continuation constructed by adding the second statement S_2 to the front of the current continuation c. This way, S_1 can skip S_2 entirely by jumping. Rules (Assign), (Incr), and (Decr) modify the state and then continue with the continuation. Rules (If1) and (If2) are unchanged from Fig. 11.6, except that λ and c are added. Rule (Label) is similar to rule (Skip) and says that execution continues directly to the continuation, and rule (Goto) states that execution continues at the continuation to which the label is bound.

The complexity of handling `goto` above shows that structured control is easier to formalise than unstructured control—basically because structured control, like semantics, is syntax-directed. That said, operational semantics *can* handle unstructured control, including exceptions and continuations, which are handled in a way similar to jumps.

11.5.5 Nontermination and Nondeterminism

A program execution is a finite proof using the rules from the operational semantics. A finite proof can only describe a terminating execution, so nontermination is, unlike in denotational semantics, not explicitly modelled, but only implicitly by not allowing infinite proofs. Similarly, runtime errors are modelled by not having proofs, usually because the premise of a rule can not be made true.

But what if there is more than one proof for a given program with given input, yielding different results?

The rules we gave for the small imperative language do not allow multiple proofs, as whenever there are multiple rules for the same statement, these have disjoint premises (such as $\sigma x = 0$ and $\sigma x \neq 0$), but it is possible to define semantics where there are overlapping rules. This introduces nondeterminism: An execution can follow multiple different paths (yielding multiple different proofs). If this is the case, a proof just shows one possible execution, and you need to find all possible proofs to find all possible executions. Also, a proof is a terminating, error-free execution, so if a nondeterministic choice in a program chooses between a nonterminating execution and a terminating execution, there is only a proof for the terminating case, so this case is indistinguishable from the case where the program always terminates. This is called *angelic nondeterminism*: Paths that lead to errors or nontermination are ignored, and only error-free terminating paths are considered. This is similar to the nondeterminism found in nondeterministic finite automata (NFAs): An NFA recognises a string if a path to an accepting state exists, even if other paths lead to non-accepting states or to states that do not define transitions on the current symbol. While this form of nondeterminism is easy to model using operational semantics with overlapping rules, other forms require more explicit modelling.

11.6 Static Semantics

The forms of semantics we have discussed so far are mostly about runtime behaviour of programs: Assuming a well-formed program, what does it compute given a specific input? Semantics for runtime behaviour is called *dynamic semantics*, but almost as important is specifying what programs are well-formed. This is called *static semantics*.

Static semantics encompass syntax, static types, and similar properties that can be (and normally are) checked prior to running a program. Syntax is usually specified using formal grammars, such as context-free grammars, and type correctness is often specified informally by statements such as "the types of the arguments given to a function call much match the types specified in the function declaration", but type systems can also be specified formally, as we saw in Sect. 11.4.

The imperative language that we presented in Sect. 11.5.3 does not have an interesting type system because all values are integers, and variables are not declared. Variables *do* need to be initialised before they are used, but that is not a decidable property, so this is checked at runtime, where the operational semantics will fail to

$$\frac{P \lhd \lambda \quad \lambda \vdash P}{P \sqrt{}}\text{(ProgramOK)}$$

$$\frac{}{\vdash \texttt{skip} \lhd \emptyset}\text{(SkipLabels)} \qquad \frac{\vdash S_1 \lhd \lambda_1 \quad \vdash S_2 \lhd \lambda_2 \quad \lambda_1 \cap \lambda_2 = \emptyset}{\vdash S_1 ; S_2 \lhd (\lambda_1 \cup \lambda_2)}\text{(SemiLabels)}$$

$$\frac{}{\vdash X := n \lhd \emptyset}\text{(AssignLabels)} \qquad \frac{}{\vdash X{+}{+} \lhd \emptyset}\text{(IncLabels)} \qquad \frac{}{\vdash X{-}{-} \lhd \emptyset}\text{(DecLabels)}$$

$$\frac{\vdash S_1 \lhd \lambda_1 \quad \vdash S_2 \lhd \lambda_2 \quad \lambda_1 \cap \lambda_2 = \emptyset}{\vdash \texttt{if } X \texttt{ then } S_1 \texttt{ else } S_2 \lhd (\lambda_1 \cup \lambda_2)}\text{(IfLabels)}$$

$$\frac{}{\vdash L: \lhd \{L\}}\text{(LabelLabels)} \qquad \frac{}{\vdash \texttt{goto } L \lhd \emptyset}\text{(GotoLabels)}$$

$$\frac{}{\lambda \vdash \texttt{skip}}\text{(SkipOK)} \qquad \frac{\lambda \vdash S_1 \quad \lambda \vdash S_2}{\lambda \vdash S_1 ; S_2}\text{(SemiOK)}$$

$$\frac{}{\lambda \vdash X := n}\text{(AssignOK)} \qquad \frac{}{\lambda \vdash X{+}{+}}\text{(IncOK)} \qquad \frac{}{\lambda \vdash X{-}{-}}\text{(DecOK)}$$

$$\frac{\lambda \vdash S_1 \quad \lambda \vdash S_2}{\lambda \vdash \texttt{if } X \texttt{ then } S_1 \texttt{ else } S_2}\text{(IfOK)}$$

$$\frac{}{\lambda \vdash L:}\text{(LabelOK)} \qquad \frac{L \in \lambda}{\lambda \vdash \texttt{goto } L}\text{(GotoOK)}$$

Fig. 11.10 Rules for correctness of label usage

produce a proof because an uninitialised variable is not bound in the environment. But the variant with labels and jumps that we presented in Sect. 11.5.4 is a bit more interesting, since it does have some static requirements that are not specified in the grammar: No label can be declared twice in the program, and all labels to which jumps exist in the program must be declared. We can specify this by the semantics rules. We use two sets of rules: One to collect the set of labels that are defined in the program while checking that no label is defined twice, and then a set of rules to check that all jumps are to defined labels, as seen in Fig. 11.10.

Rule (ProgramOK) states that a program p is well formed (signified by a check mark) if p defines the set of labels λ and p calls only labels in this set.

Rules (SkipLabels) to (GotoLabels) collect the set λ of labels, and rule (SemiLabels) verifies that there are no duplicates by checking that unions are disjoint. We use standard set notation.

Rules (SkipOk) to (GotoOk) check that jumps are to labels found in the set λ. Only rule (GotoOk) is non-trivial—the rest just apply the rules to subexpressions (if any).

These rules do not verify that variable names and label names are well-formed, this is assumed to be already verified during lexical analysis. Since there are rules for every production in the grammar and only for these, you might think that syntactic correctness is verified by the rules. This is, however, not the case, as the rules do not consider ambiguities in the grammar that would be resolved during syntax analysis. In the example above, associativity of semicolon and precedence of semicolon relative to if-then-else is not specified. It is fairly common for semantic rules (both static and dynamic) to omit parentheses, indentation and similar grouping mechanisms that are used only for syntactic disambiguation: It is assumed that these are used during syntax analysis and removed by the parser, which will produce a syntax tree where ambiguities are resolved.

11.7 Languages That Have Formal Semantics

Few mainstream programming languages have complete, formal semantics, and when they do, the formal semantics are usually not part of the official definition of the languages, but something written *a posteriori* to reflect the informal specification that the official language definition provides. An exception is Standard ML, which in the standard document defines the language through operational semantics in a style similar to the one used in this chapter. This includes both static and dynamic semantics.

Older standards for Pascal and C have *almost* complete formal semantics, but these are not part of the standard documents, and have not been maintained to follow later developments of these languages.

Many mainstream languages, including Java and Haskell, have formal semantic descriptions of significant subsets. These subsets are large enough that the formal semantics can be used to reason about nontrivial programs and to guide implementations of the languages.

Many small research languages have complete formal semantics, where the formal semantics are used both to make the meaning of programs precise, but also to prove properties of these languages, such as reversibility, freedom from certain kinds of errors, and so on. For example, we stated in Sect. 11.5.1 that the type rules in Sect. 11.4 ensure that execution will never apply fst to something that is not a pair, and similarly to the other operations. This can, in fact, be proven formally from the type rules and the execution rules.

11.8 Further Reading

An introduction to formal semantics covering both denotational and operational semantics can be found in [7]. A less formal introduction to operational semantics can be found in [4]. Harper [3] explains a broad range of language concepts using formal, operational semantics. The Definition of Standard ML [6] has complete formal semantics of the language.

11.9   Exercises

Exercise 11.1 Which of the following properties are semantic and which are syntactic (i.e., not semantic)?

a. The program never tries to divide a number by 0.
b. The program never tries to access a variable that has not been initialised.
c. The program does not contain recursive function definitions.
d. Some parts of the program are never executed.
e. The program never reaches a state where integer variables a, b, c and n have the following properties: $0 < a \leq b, n > 2$, and $a^n + b^n = c^n$.

Exercise 11.2 Use the type rules from Sect. 11.4 to prove that, in an environment that maps y to int, the expression fun x : int -> x + y has type (int -> int).

Exercise 11.3 Extend the type rules from Sect. 11.4 with a rule for an if-then-else expression:

$$E \rightarrow \text{if } E \text{ then } E \text{ else } E$$

The condition must be an integer expression, and the two branches must have the same type, which is also the type of the if-then-else expression.

Exercise 11.4 Extend the operational semantics from Sect. 11.5.1 with rules for an if-then-else expression:

$$E \rightarrow \text{if } E \text{ then } E \text{ else } E$$

If the condition evaluates to a non-zero value, the then-branch is chosen, otherwise the else-branch is chosen.

Exercise 11.5 We extend the simple functional language from Sect. 11.4 with pattern matching and let-expressions. We, first, add the following rules to the syntax:

$$E \rightarrow \text{let } P = E \text{ in } E$$

$$P \rightarrow X$$
$$P \rightarrow N$$
$$P \rightarrow (P, P)$$

An expression of the form let $P = E_1$ in E_2 evaluates E_1 to a value v, matches the pattern P to v, and if the pattern does match, binds variables in P to the corresponding parts of v, so these variables can be used locally inside E_2. If the pattern does not match, this is a runtime error.

The type of the pattern P must be compatible with the type of the value v. The rules for when a pattern is compatible with a type can be informally specified as

- A variable is compatible with any type.
- A number constant is compatible with the type `int`.
- A pattern (P_1, P_2) is compatible with a type $(T_1 * T_2)$ if P_1 is compatible with T_1 and P_2 is compatible with T_2.

Patterns and let-expressions work the same way as the similar constructs in Standard ML and F#.

Note: You can assume (without checking) that, in a pattern (P_1, P_2), P_1 and P_2 contain disjoint sets of variables. In other words, you can be sure that there are no repeated variables in patterns.

a. Extend the type system shown in Sect. 11.4 with rules for `let` expressions and patterns. Note that the rules for patterns should check that a pattern is compatible with a given type, and produce an environment that binds the variables in the patterns to their types. This environment should be composed with the environment of the let-expression and used for evaluating the body of the let-expression. You can use the notation $\tau_2 \circ \tau_1$ for composing τ_1 and τ_2 (in such a way that bindings in τ_2 shadow those in τ_1 that bind the same names, if any). The notation for a pattern p being compatible with a type t and producing an environment τ is $t \vdash p \hookrightarrow \tau$.

b. Using the notation from Sect. 11.5.1, write semantic rules for evaluation of `let` expressions and matching of patterns to values (producing environments). A pattern not matching a value is not explicitly reported as an error—there just are no rules that can be applied. The notation for a pattern P matching a value v and producing an environment ρ is $v \vdash P \twoheadrightarrow \rho$. You can use $\circ$ to compose value environments in the same way that it is used to compose type environments. You can use $=$ to compare values to constants.

c. If we modify pattern matching so repeated variables are allowed in patterns, with the semantics that all occurrences of the same variable in a pattern must be of the same type and (at run time) match the same value, what changes are required in the type rules and semantic rules made above? Show the modified rules. It is only the rules for pairs that need to be modified, so you need only show these.

Note: Be careful to use notation consistent with the notation used in Sects. 11.4 and 11.5.1 (with the extensions described above).

Exercise 11.6 We extend the language from Sect. 11.5.3 with a repeat-until loop:

$$S \to \texttt{repeat } S \texttt{ until } X$$

Informally, the semantics is that the body statement is repeated until the variable becomes non-zero, but at least once. So the variable is tested after each iteration, where the while-loop tests the variable before each iteration, and the loop is exited when the variable is non-zero, where a while-loop exits when the variable is zero. Extend the operational semantics from Sect. 11.5.3 to include the repeat loop.

Exercise 11.7 Section 11.4 shows the syntax of a simple functional language. This can, with a few modifications, be expressed as terms in SWI Prolog. For example, SWI Prolog allows *, ->, +, ,, and : as infix function symbols, so the only differences are that variable names must be wrapped in a function symbol, there must be parentheses around the arguments to `fst`, `snd` and `fun`, and function applications must use an explicit infix operator (we use ^). We use the following modified syntax:

$$T \rightarrow \mathtt{int}$$
$$T \rightarrow (T * T)$$
$$T \rightarrow (T \mathtt{->} T)$$

$$E \rightarrow N$$
$$E \rightarrow \mathtt{var}(X)$$
$$E \rightarrow (E + E)$$
$$E \rightarrow (E , E)$$
$$E \rightarrow \mathtt{fst}(E)$$
$$E \rightarrow \mathtt{snd}(E)$$
$$E \rightarrow (E \mathtt{\ ^\ } E)$$
$$E \rightarrow \mathtt{fun}(X : T \mathtt{->} E)$$

Note that numbers are not wrapped by function symbols, as the Prolog predicate $number(V)$ can be used to check if a value V is a number. Note, also, that the parentheses are required where shown in the grammar.

We represent type environments as lists of pairs of the form $(X : T)$, for example `[(x:int), (y:(int->int))]`. We add new bindings to the front of the list, and use the following predicate to look up in environments

```
lookup(X,[(X:T)|_],T).
lookup(X,[(Y:_)|E],T) :- X\=Y, lookup(X,E,T).
```

A type judgement of the form $\tau \vdash E : T$ is represented in Prolog as (τ `\-` $E : T$), where we define `\-` as an infix operator. So the type rules

$$\overline{\tau \vdash N : \mathtt{int}} \qquad \overline{\tau \vdash X : \tau(X)}$$

can in Prolog be written as

```
(Tau \- N : int)   :- number(N).
(Tau \- var(X) : T) :- lookup(X,Tau,T).
```

To define the required infix operators and the rules above, start your Prolog program with the lines

```
?- op(1100,xfx,\-).

lookup(X,[(X:T)|_],T).
lookup(X,[(Y:_)|E],T) :- X\=Y, lookup(X,E,T).

(_ \- N : int) :- number(N).
(Tau \- var(X) : T) :- lookup(X,Tau,T).
```

Note that we have used wildcards to avoid the "singleton variable" warning. Your task is now to

a. Rewrite the remaining type rules in Sect. 11.4 to SWI Prolog using the representations described above.
b. Run the query `?- [(x:int)]  (fst((7,5))+var(x)) : T.` and show the answers you get.
c. Run the query `?- [] \- fun(x:T1 -> (var(x),3)) : T.` and explain what the result means.
d. Run the query `?- [] \- fun(x:T1 -> var(x)^var(x)) : T.` and explain what the result means. Is the result valid with respect to the grammar for types shown above?

References

1. Backus JW, Bauer FL, Green J, Katz C, McCarthy J, Naur P, Perlis AJ, Rutishauser H, Samelson K, Vauquois B, Wegstein JH, van Wijngaarden A, Woodger M (1963) Revised report on the algorithmic language Algol 60. Commun ACM 6(1):1–17
2. Gosling J, Joy B, Steele GL, Bracha G, Buckley A (2014) The Java language specification, Java SE 8 Edition, 1st edn. Addison-Wesley Professional
3. Harper R (2012) Practical foundations for programming languages. Cambridge University Press, New York, NY, USA
4. Hüttel H (2010) Transitions and trees: an introduction to structural operational semantics. Cambridge University Press . https://www.cambridge.org/catalogue/catalogue.asp?isbn=9780521147095
5. Jensen K, Wirth N (1975) Pascal user manual and report, 2nd edn. Springer-Verlag
6. Milner R, Tofte M, Harper R, MacQueen D (1997) The definition of standard ML. MIT Press, Cambridge, MA, USA
7. Winskel G (1993) The formal semantics of programming languages: an introduction. MIT Press, Cambridge, MA, USA

Exploring the Limits

12

The enemy of art is the absence of limitations.
Orson Welles

Once we accept our limits, we go beyond them.
Albert Einstein

In this chapter, we will explore limits as they relate to programming language design in several different ways:

- How limits of computation can affect language design?
- What sort of limits it may be reasonable to impose on programs in a language?
- Some designs push the limits in various ways.

So while these have the word "limit" in common, they are actually quite different concepts.

12.1 Limits of Computation

We have several times in the book mentioned the notion of Turing completeness: A language is said to be Turing complete if it can compute all the functions that a Turing machine can. The Church-Turing thesis states that no realisable programming language can compute functions that are not computable by a Turing machine, so all languages that are Turing complete have the same computational power. Most mainstream programming languages are (if they have unbounded storage) Turing complete, but some domain-specific languages are not. But why not make a language Turing complete if you can?

© The Author(s), under exclusive license to Springer Nature Switzerland AG 2022
T. Ægidius Mogensen, *Programming Language Design and Implementation*,
Texts in Computer Science, https://doi.org/10.1007/978-3-031-11806-7_12

This brings us to Rice's Theorem, which informally can be stated as

Theorem 12.1 *In a Turing complete language, all non-trivial semantic properties of programs are undecidable.*

To understand this theorem, we need to clarify what the words in the theorem mean:

- A *semantic property* is a property that pertains to the observable runtime *behaviour* of programs, and not on their *form*. For example, "Will this program ever terminate?" is a semantic property, while "Does this program contain more than seven function definitions?" is not. Properties that are not semantic are called *syntactic*, even if they do not pertain to the syntax of the language.
- A property is *trivial* if either all programs have this property or none do. For example, in a language without null pointers, the property "Can this program raise a null-pointer exception that is not caught?" is trivial, which it is not in a language that allows null pointers and exceptions.
- A property is *undecidable* if there is no algorithm that for *all* values can determine if the property holds or not for that value. This does not prevent the existence of an algorithm that for *some values* can determine if the property holds or not.

A consequence of Rice's Theorem is that, if we want to design a language in such a way that we for *all* programs p in a language can decide if a semantic property holds for p, we have the following choices:

- We can make the property trivial: We can design the language in such a way that all (or no) programs have this property. An example is the absence of null-pointer exceptions, which we can make trivial by excluding null pointers.
- We can restrict the language so it is not Turing complete. This does not automatically make all semantic properties decidable, but any semantic property can be made decidable with sufficient restrictions.

One interesting semantic property is termination (also called "the halting problem"): Is the program guaranteed to terminate on any finite input? A consequence of Rice's theorem is that termination is not decidable for a Turing-complete programming language. However, there are many interesting programming languages that guarantee termination for all programs on all inputs. For example, in a structured imperative programming language without recursive function or procedure calls, and where the only loop construct is a for-loop where the number of iterations is known when the loop is entered (a type-2 loop), all programs will always terminate. This can be shown easily:

1. Since there is no recursion, all function and procedure calls can be fully unfolded in finite time.
2. A program containing no loops is trivially terminating for all inputs.

3. If the body of a loop is terminating for all initial states (values of variables), then the loop will terminate for all initial states. By induction, this is true also for finite nestings of loops.

Such a language is by no means useless: It can do linear algebra, sorting, prime factorisation, graph colouring, and lots more. In fact, most practical problems can be solved using such a language: If the time bound for solving a problem can be computed using for loops only, the problem itself can also be computed using for loops only:

1. Compute the bound in variable T.
2. Use T as the number of iterations for a for-loop.

Termination does not need to be a trivial property in order to be decidable: Any language where memory is bounded by a computable function of the size of the input has decidable termination. For any given input, there are only finitely many different memory states, so a non-terminating computation must eventually repeat a state. So, a simulation that remembers all previous states will in finite time either terminate because the simulated computation terminates or stop and report nontermination when it detects a repeated state.

Another semantic property is equivalence of programs: Do two programs always exhibit the same observable behaviour if they are given the same inputs? For any single input, this is decidable if the language has memory bounded by input size as above, but when we talk about *all* inputs, this is not always the case. Some languages, such as regular expressions, have decidable equivalence, but other languages, such as context-free grammars, do not, even though determining whether a string is recognised by a grammar is decidable.

So, if you want to guarantee a certain property of all programs, you can make that property decidable and reject programs that do not have the property. An alternative is to allow Turing completeness but specify an incomplete decision procedure: One that will reject all programs that do not have the property, but which may also reject some programs that do have the property. This ensures that all programs that are not rejected will have the desired property. If the language is defined to be the subset of programs that are not rejected by the decision procedure, the property is trivial on this subset.

An example is type safety: You can define a program to be type safe if it only performs operations on values for which the operations are defined. Runtime checks can ensure this and report an error if a violation is detected. But if we want to know *before* running the program that it will for no input ever report a violation, this is in fact undecidable for a Turing-complete language, as it is a semantic property of the program. A static type system (for example, type inference) can guarantee that programs that are not rejected by the type system do, indeed, never cause runtime type errors. But if the type system is decidable (and the language Turing complete), it will have to reject some programs that would, in fact, *never* cause runtime type errors.

If we say that only statically type-correct programs are valid programs, we have in essence restricted the language in such a way that the semantic property "Never causes runtime type errors" is a trivial property: All programs in the language exhibit this property.

In summary, if we want to be able to determine if a semantic property holds for a program before running it, we can either

1. Restrict the language, so the property is trivial. The language can still be Turing complete, or
2. Restrict the language, so the property is non-trivial, but decidable. The language can not be Turing complete.

For general-purpose languages, option 1 seems to be the best choice, as many problems require Turing completeness. For domain-specific languages, the choice is not so obvious: If the problem domain does not require Turing completeness, it may be best to choose option 2. For example, while a type system can make runtime type safety a trivial semantic property even in a Turing-complete language, it can not make equivalence of programs decidable, as that will never be a trivial property unless all programs are equivalent. Guaranteeing termination can be done either way: By making it a trivial property (by ensuring that all programs terminate), or by making it a nontrivial, but decidable property. In neither case can the language be Turing complete.

Suggested exercises: 12.1

12.2 Limits on Program Features

Here, we talk about numeric limits on the uses of a certain feature in a program, for example:

- How deeply can scopes be nested?
- How many arguments can a function at most have?
- How many characters are allowed in a variable name?
- What is the largest integer value?
- How many elements can there at most be in a tuple or record?
- How many dimensions can a multidimensional array have?

We will argue that the only *reasonable* design choices for such limits are 0, 1, or no limit (i.e., unbounded), with 2 *occasionally* also being a reasonable choice. Here, 0 means that the feature is not included in the language.

Let us look at the examples above:

How deeply can scopes be nested?   Some early programming languages like FOR-
    TRAN, COBOL, and APL had flat scopes: All variables are global, and procedure
    declarations can not be nested. This makes the limit 1.

Other early languages, such as ALGOL 60 and LISP, on the other hand, allow arbitrarily deeply nested scopes, and function declarations can freely be declared within other function declarations. Hence, no limit.

In the C programming language, function declarations can not be nested, but blocks can be arbitrarily deeply nested, so the limit is 1 for function declarations and none for variable scopes.

In no mainstream languages are scopes limited to 2, 3, or some such arbitrary constant greater than 1, and it is hard to see where such a limit would make sense. It can, however, make sense to make the limit be 0: If no procedures are allowed (as was the case in the first FORTRAN version), or if no named variables are used.

How many arguments can a function at most have?   In COBOL and a few other languages, procedures have no arguments. This can be a reasonable (if somewhat limiting) choice in a language that primarily uses side effects to handle data flow. ALGOL 60 and most ALGOL-inspired languages allow any number of parameters to functions (though some implementations may impose an upper bound). This also seems reasonable.

Functions in Standard ML and Haskell strictly speaking have exactly one argument each, but since that argument can be a tuple, it is not a significant limitation. Also, by letting a function return another function, *currying* can be used to get an effect similar to multiple arguments even without using tuples.

So restricting functions to at most one or exactly one argument can make perfect sense, but limiting the number of arguments to 2, 3, or 17 does not make a lot of sense.

How many characters are allowed in a variable name?   In mathematics, variables are usually one letter, but variables can have numeric subscripts and use letters from non-Latin alphabets (such as Greek letters). This has worked well for mathematics for centuries, so it does not seem an unreasonable choice. Few languages allow subscripted variable names, Plankalkül being an exception. And in Plankalkül variables are, indeed, one letter with a numeric subscript. There are also variants of BASIC where variable names are limited to one letter and a sequence of digits— not as a subscript, but following the letter.

But names consisting of single subscripted letters are not very informative, so most programming languages allow more. FORTRAN originally allowed six characters in variable names, and COBOL (following Grace Hopper's idea that names should be descriptive) allowed 30. Some languages (such as ALGOL 60 and Pascal) do not specify an upper limit, but allow implementations to impose limits. For example, Pascal just requires at least eight significant characters, allowing characters after this to be ignored.

It may seem unlikely that any programmer will use a variable name with more than 30 characters, but not all programs are written by humans: Some programs are generated by other programs, and some programs are made as transformations of other programs. Such generators or transformers often add extra characters to names from their input, so any fixed limit is likely to eventually be a problem. The main reason for imposing a limit on names is to ease language implementation:

A symbol table can be implemented as an array of fixed-length strings. But most modern programming languages can handle variable-length strings with no significant overhead, so there is no good reason to limit variable names to anything less than the maximum length of a string, which is often bounded only by the available memory.

In the opposite extreme, a language can not have named variables at all. John Backus' FP language is an example of this approach.

So, again, the reasonable choices seem to be 0 (no named variables), 1 (though with subscripts), and unbounded.

What is the largest integer value?   This is more contentious. Most programming languages allow integers up to the size of an integer register, which is machine specific. C, for example, does not specify the size of the int type, except that it should be large enough that a pointer can be converted to an integer and back again without losing information. Java specifies integers to be 32 bits, because that is what the Java Virtual Machine uses.

COBOL represents integers as strings of digits, where each variable has a specified number of digits, but there is no language-imposed upper bound on the number of digits.

Pascal allows both bounded integer types such as $-10..10$ and a type named integer, the size of which is implementation dependent. It defines a constant maxint that defines the largest integer in the integer type, but the language definition does not specify what the range of numbers should be—not even a minimum range.

Some languages, such as Haskell, Scheme, and Python allow integers to be unbounded (except by available memory). In such languages, large integers are represented by linked lists of smaller integers, and arithmetic operations are implemented as loops that operate on these lists. To make operations on small integers relatively efficient, an integer can be represented as either an odd machine word, where the $n-1$ most significant bits represent the number (as described in Sect. 4.7), or as a pointer (which is an even machine word) to a linked list of numbers.

Generally, a bounded integer range can easily be a problem, as problem sizes are likely to increase between the time a program is written and the time it is retired. So, unbounded integers do seem like the best solution. Unbounded integers do, however, carry an overhead: They are more costly to work with, both in terms of time and space, than machine integers (though the overhead is only significant for large numbers). A solution can be to have both explicit subranges and unbounded integers, basically Pascal types where the integer type is unbounded. If a programmer knows that the range of values is bounded, he/she can specify this as an explicit subrange, but if not, the unbounded integer type can be used.

So, for this particular feature, reasonable choices are not exactly 0, 1, 2, or unbounded, but rather that *if* number types are bounded, the type should specify the bounds, and there should preferably be no upper limit on these bounds. Alternatively or additionally, an unbounded integer type can be included.

How many elements can there at most be in a tuple or record?   A language may not have tuples at all, in which case the bound can be seen as either 0 (there are no tuples) or 1 (a value is equivalent to a tuple with one element). But if the language does support tuples, what are then reasonable bounds for their size?

Unsurprisingly, unbounded seems like a good answer: There is no *a priori* reason tuples should be bounded to, say, 7 or 42 elements, and machine-generated programs are likely to break any fixed bound an implementation may impose. But there is another reasonable answer: 2. Tuples with two elements are pairs, which is the most common tuple size, and any tuple can be built using nested pairs. Indeed, LISP has pairs as the only tuple type and uses this to build lists of arbitrary size. Nested pairs are a bit more verbose than tuples with multiple elements, though.

So when it comes to tuples, it seems that the reasonable limits are no tuples at all, pairs, or arbitrary tuples.

It is rather more cumbersome to build multi-field records from records with two fields each, so for records with named fields, the reasonable limits are 0 (no records) or unlimited.

How many dimensions can a multidimensional array have?   A language may not have arrays at all (early versions of LISP and ML did not), and some languages (such as Standard ML) have only one-dimensional arrays. If elements of arrays can be other arrays, multidimensional arrays can relatively easily be represented as arrays of arrays, so this is not a serious limitation. Though arrays of arrays may be slightly less efficient than native two-dimensional arrays, they have the advantage that the rows of two-dimensional arrays need not have the same size, so you can make, for example, triangular arrays. In C, the notation for accessing an element of a two-dimensional array is the same as the notation for accessing an element in an array of arrays, so it is mainly when allocating arrays that arrays of arrays are slightly more verbose than true multidimensional arrays—you may need an explicit loop when you allocate arrays of arrays.

Early versions of FORTRAN supported arrays of dimensions up to 3, but elements could only be numbers, so arrays of arrays were not possible. The limit of three dimensions was probably motivated in the application area (numeric computation), where vectors and matrices are common, three-dimensional arrays are occasionally used, but higher dimensions very rarely. While arrays of arrays are not possible, it is possible for a programmer to use a one-dimensional array to emulate a higher-dimensional array by calculating positions explicitly. For example, in a $3 \times 3 \times 3$ array implemented as a one-dimensional array of 27 elements, the position of element (i, j, k) is $9i + 3j + k - 12$ (since indices range from 1 to 3 in all dimensions).

Two-dimensional arrays are relatively common, whereas arrays of higher dimensions are not, so it may be somewhat reasonable to support one-dimensional and two-dimensional arrays directly, but require higher dimensions to be implemented as arrays of arrays. If arrays of arrays are not allowed, it does not seem reasonable to limit the number of dimensions.

The main lesson of this section is that a language designer should carefully consider if a feature should be bounded or not, and if a bound is chosen, this should nearly always be 1, though occasionally 2 can be reasonable also. A feature may, of course, not be included at all in a language, in which case the bound is 0.

Suggested exercises: 12.3

12.3   Languages at the Limit

We will now look at a few cases of programming languages that in some way push the boundaries of traditional computation, including reversible programming languages and quantum programming languages.

12.3.1   Reversible Programming Languages

Most programming languages are designed to be implemented on traditional computers, built from traditional logic elements such as AND, OR, and NOT gates. Even memory is built from such gates.

Gates like AND and OR lose information: It is not possible to determine what the inputs were if you only know the outputs. The NOT gate does not lose information, and is, indeed, its own inverse, but it is not sufficient by itself for general logic—you need at least one multi-input gate such as NAND for general logic.

Information loss is an integral part of most programming languages and models: In a Turing machine, a tape cell can be overwritten in such a way that the original content can not be retrieved, and in lambda calculus, a function can discard its argument by not using it. An example is the function $\lambda a.\lambda b.a$, which when applied to two values discards the second. Even a deterministic finite automaton can have two transitions into the same state on the same symbol, which makes it impossible to (deterministically) go back to a previous state.

So is this a problem? Not really, unless we look at thermodynamics. Using the laws of thermodynamics, it can be shown that erasing a bit of information dissipates a small amount of heat, and *no matter which technology is used*, there is a fixed lower limit (called *the Landauer limit*) to how small that amount of heat can be. This limit is quite small: $(KT \ln(2)$ joules, where K is Boltzmann's constant and T is the temperature in Kelvin. At room temperature, this is about 2.75×10^{-21} joules—several orders of magnitude smaller than the energy used when switching a gate in CMOS technology. But if the requirement for ever-increasing compute power for the same energy consumption increases, this small amount of heat may become significant in a few decades.

But, since the problem is information loss, a way out may be to build computers from gates that do not lose information, i.e., gates that implement bijective functions from their inputs to their outputs. The NOT gate is an example, but as noted it is not sufficient for general computation. There are, however, gates that are universal for bijective functions: Any bijective function from N bits to N bits can be built by composing such gates. An example is the Toffoli gate, which takes three input bits, passes the first two through unchanged, and flips the third bit if both of the first two bits represent the true logic value. Using 0 for false and 1 for true, a Toffoli gate can be represented by the following table:

input			output		
0	0	0	0	0	0
0	0	1	0	0	1
0	1	0	0	1	0
0	1	1	0	1	1
1	0	0	1	0	0
1	0	1	1	0	1
1	1	0	1	1	1
1	1	1	1	1	0

Using such gates, we can (at least in theory) build a computer that can compute all bijective computable functions with no theoretical minimum energy use. There *will* be some energy use (nothing is free), but it can, in theory, be much smaller than the Landauer limit. Single reversible gates that can operate using less power than the Landauer limit have been constructed, but no complex circuitry has yet been constructed from these gates.

The restriction that such a computer can only compute bijective functions is a limitation, but not a severe one: Any non-bijective function can be extended to a bijective function by adding extra outputs, whose size is in the worst case the same as the size of the inputs (and can, indeed, be the inputs themselves).

Traditional programming languages can be implemented in such reversible computers, basically by storing information that would otherwise be discarded: Every time a value is written to a variable, a copy of the previous contents is stored on a stack. The amount of extra space needed to do so is, however, very large—in the worst case, proportional to the number of computation steps. So, it makes sense to program reversible machines using reversible programming languages, where no variable is ever modified in an irreversible way.

12.3.1.1 Designing a Reversible Programming Language

A programming language is reversible if every operation it performs is reversible. We will, using a simple imperative language as example, see what this implies. We start from a traditional (irreversible) language and then modify this to be reversible. The syntax of the irreversible language is shown in Fig. 12.1.

Values are integers, **var** represents variables, Exp represents expressions, and **p** represents procedure names. A procedure is simply a named statement, and a program consists of a statement and a list of procedure definitions. Executing a program is done by executing the statement that is not inside a procedure definition. Procedures

Fig. 12.1 A simple
irreversible language

$$Program \rightarrow Stat\ Proc^*$$

$$Proc \quad \rightarrow \texttt{procedure}\ \mathbf{p}\ Stat\ \texttt{end}$$

$$Stat \quad \rightarrow \mathbf{var} := Exp$$
$$Stat \quad \rightarrow \texttt{read}\ \mathbf{var}$$
$$Stat \quad \rightarrow \texttt{write}\ \mathbf{var}$$
$$Stat \quad \rightarrow Stat\ ;\ Stat$$
$$Stat \quad \rightarrow \texttt{if}\ Exp\ \texttt{then}\ Stat\ \texttt{else}\ Stat$$
$$Stat \quad \rightarrow \texttt{repeat}\ Stat\ \texttt{until}\ Exp$$
$$Stat \quad \rightarrow \texttt{call}\ \mathbf{p}$$

have global scope and can call each other recursively. Variables are also global and have undefined values until initialised (with a `read` statement or assignment).

We leave expressions unspecified, except noting that expressions include constants, variables, arithmetic, and comparison operators such as addition, subtraction, and equality. When used as a condition, a variable is considered true if it contains a non-zero value.

The language is not reversible for several reasons:

- A `read` statement or assignment overwrites the previous value of the variable in such a way that it can not (in general) be retrieved.
- After executing a conditional statement, we have no information about which branch was executed.
- After executing a loop, we do not know how many iterations were taken.

We will now see how we can modify the language to avoid these problems.

We first look at the assignment statement $\mathbf{var} := Exp$. This is obviously not reversible, as we discard the previous contents of the variable. We can, however, make reversible variants of this by using *reversible updates*:

$$Stat \rightarrow \mathbf{var}\ \mathrel{+}= Exp$$
$$Stat \rightarrow \mathbf{var}\ \mathrel{-}= Exp$$

Adding a value to a variable can be reversed by subtracting the same value, and vice versa, so these two updates are inverses of each other—assuming the variable is not used in the expression Exp. For example, the statement $x\ \mathrel{-}=\ x$ is not reversible, as the resulting value of x is 0 no matter what value it had before. So, we impose the syntactic restriction that a variable can not be used on the right-hand side of an update of that variable. We also add a statement that swaps the contents of two variables:

$$Stat \rightarrow \mathbf{var} <\text{-}> \mathbf{var}$$

This is not strictly necessary, as we can swap the contents of two variables by a sequence of reversible updates, but it is convenient to have.

We also overwrite variables in `read` statements. We could do as for reversible updates and make a `read` either add the read value to the variable or subtract

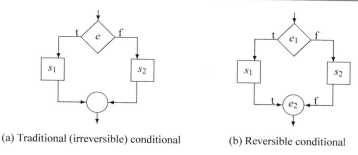

(a) Traditional (irreversible) conditional   (b) Reversible conditional

Fig. 12.2 Traditional and reversible conditionals

the read value to the variable. This would make the inverse of a `read` statement another read statement (just with a different update operator). But it is more useful to make the inverse of a `read` statement a `write` statement: When running a program backwards, the input will be the output of a forwards run and vice versa, so if input to a program is read with `read` statements, and output printed with `write` statements, it makes sense to make these inverses of each other. But, in the current form, a `read` statement is not the inverse of a `write` statement: A `read` statement will forget about the previous value of the variable, while a write statement does not modify the contents of the variable. To solve this, we say that a statement of the form `write x` will clear x to 0 after writing its content. To make `read x` the inverse of this, we must require x to be 0 before it is read. If this is not the case, a runtime error will be issued.

When programs can fail due to runtime errors, the concept of reversibility becomes a bit more muddled. All we can say is that, if a program given an input sequence $x_1, \ldots, x_m$ runs to completion without runtime errors, giving the output sequence $y_1, \ldots, y_n$, then running the program backwards with the input sequence $y_n, \ldots, y_1$ will succeed, giving the output sequence $x_m, \ldots, x_1$. Note that the input and output sequences are reversed when running backwards, as what is output first when running forwards will be read last when running backwards.

We next look at the sequencing statement $s_1 ; s_2$. If both statements are reversible, this is reversible: If $\bar{s}_1$ is the inverse of s_1 and $\bar{s}_2$ is the inverse of s_2, then the inverse of $s_1 ; s_2$ is $\bar{s}_2 ; \bar{s}_1$. So, a reversible language can use the traditional sequencing statement without modification.

The conditional `if e then` s_1 `else` s_2 is another matter. For example, the statement `if x then x -= 1 else x += 0` gives x the value 0 both if x initially has the value 1 and when it initially has the value 0. The reason for this irreversibility becomes clear if we show the conditional as a flowchart, as shown in Fig. 12.2a.

The problem is clear: The join point has two incoming arrows but no information to determine which was used.

We can, however, fix this by adding an exit condition as shown in Fig. 12.2b. A condition in a circle is a *join condition*: If you enter via the arrow marked t, the condition must evaluate to true, and if you enter via the arrow marked f, the condition

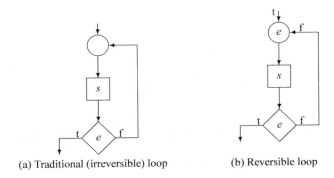

(a) Traditional (irreversible) loop   (b) Reversible loop

Fig. 12.3 Traditional and reversible loops

must evaluate to false. If this does not hold, a runtime error is issued. If the statements s_1 and s_2 are not allowed to modify any variables used in the condition e_1, the value of the condition will be the same at exit as at entry, so we could reuse e_1 as join condition, and we would be sure that the join will always succeed. The restriction against modifying variables in the condition makes programming difficult, though, so instead, we modify the conditional to be of the form if e_1 then s_1 else s_2 fi e_2, where e_2 can be different from e_1, and there is no restriction on the statements (other than that they must be reversible). The cost is that the join can fail.

To invert the flowchart in Fig. 12.2b, we reverse the arrows, replace diamond boxes (branches) with circles (joins), replace circles (joins) with diamond boxes (branches), and reverse the statements s_1 and s_2. Note that the inverse of a conditional is conditional of the same form.

We also illustrate the problem with loops using its flowchart, as shown in Fig. 12.3a.

Again, the problem is clear: The join point has no information to determine from where it is entered. We note that the condition e will be false when we return from the bottom of the loop to the top of the loop, so it makes sense to use e also in the join point and require it to be true when the loop is first entered, as illustrated in Fig. 12.3b. This means that the syntax of the loop is unchanged, but we add a test at the entry of a loop: If e is false when we enter the loop, a runtime error is reported. There is no need to check e again when we return to the top of the loop since we already know it to be false, but it is not harmful to do so. It is possible to modify the semantics of the loop, so the condition at the join point will never fail. We discuss this in an exercise.

The last thing to consider is procedure calls. There is really nothing that needs to be done: If the procedure body is reversible, a call to the procedure is also reversible. But we can exploit the reversibility by allowing a call to a procedure to choose whether it should be executed forwards or backwards. If call p executes p forwards, we can use the statement uncall p to run it backwards.

In summary, the reversible language has the syntax shown in Fig. 12.4, with the following restrictions:

Fig. 12.4 A simple reversible language

$$Program \to Stat\ Proc^*$$

$Proc$	$\to$ procedure **p** $Stat$ end

$Stat$	$\to$ **var** += Exp
$Stat$	$\to$ **var** -= Exp
$Stat$	$\to$ **var** <-> **var**
$Stat$	$\to$ read **var**
$Stat$	$\to$ write **var**
$Stat$	$\to$ $Stat$; $Stat$
$Stat$	$\to$ if Exp then $Stat$ else $Stat$ fi Exp
$Stat$	$\to$ repeat $Stat$ until Exp
$Stat$	$\to$ call **p**
$Stat$	$\to$ uncall **p**

- In a variable update, the updated variable can not occur o the right-hand side of the update operator. This can be checked at compile time.
- A variable in a read statement must be zero before reading. This must be checked at runtime.
- The condition at the end of the conditional (after the fi keyword) must be true if the first branch was chosen and false if the second branch is chosen. This must be checked at runtime.
- When a loop is entered from the outside, the loop condition must be true. This must be checked at runtime.
- All variables are initialised to 0 when execution starts, and they must be returned to zero when the execution ends. The latter must be checked at runtime.

Each statement is reversible, as shown in Fig. 12.5, where $R(s)$ denotes the inverse of the statement s. Inverting a complete program can be done by inverting the main statement and leaving the procedures unchanged (because any calls to these procedures will be replaced by uncalls) or, alternatively, reversing all statements in the program except calls and uncalls.

If integers are unbounded, this language is complete for bijective reversible functions. It is somewhat more difficult to program in this language than it is to program in a similar irreversible language, but it gets easier with a bit of training. Below, we show a few examples of programs and their reversible counterparts.

$$R(x\ {+}{=}\ e) = x\ {-}{=}\ e$$
$$R(x\ {-}{=}\ e) = x\ {+}{=}\ e$$
$$R(x\ {<}{-}{>}\ y) = x\ {<}{-}{>}\ y$$
$$R(\text{read}\ x) = \text{write}\ x$$
$$R(s_1\ ;\ s_2) = R(s_2)\ ;\ R(s_1)$$
$$R(\text{if}\ e_1\ \text{then}\ s_1\ \text{else}\ s_2\ \text{fi}\ e_2) = \text{if}\ e_2\ \text{then}\ R(s_1)\ \text{else}\ R(s_2)\ \text{fi}\ e_1$$
$$R(\text{repeat}\ s\ \text{until}\ e) = \text{repeat}\ R(s)\ \text{until}\ e$$
$$R(\text{call}\ p) = \text{uncall}\ p$$
$$R(\text{uncall}\ p) = \text{call}\ p$$

Fig. 12.5 Reversing statements

```
                                    read n;
        read n;                     f += 1;
        f := 1;                     repeat
        repeat                        t += f*n;
          f := f*n;                   f -= t/n;
          n := n-1                    f <-> t;
        until n=0;                    n -= 1
        write f                     until n=0 || f=1;
                                    write f
```

Fig. 12.6 Traditional and reversible factorial programs

```
                                    read m;
        read m;                     read n;
        read n;                     repeat
        repeat                        write g;
          t := m mod n;               g += m mod n;
          m := n;                     m <-> n;
          n := t                      g <-> n
        until n=0;                  until n=0 || g=0;
        write m                     write g;
                                    write m
```

Fig. 12.7 Traditional and reversible gcd programs

The first example is a program for computing the factorial of a function. Since $0! = 1! = 1$, we restrict this to inputs greater than 0, so the computed function is bijective. This is shown to the left in Fig. 12.6, while the reversible counterpart is shown to the right. In order to make the loop condition true at entry to the loop, we add an extra condition f=1. This will not make the loop exit prematurely, because (unless the input is 1), f will be greater than 0 after any number of iterations. Since we do not have *= operator, we must use a temporary variable t and do the equivalent of f *= n in three steps.

A more complicated example is the greatest common divisor function (gcd). Gcd is not, a priori, a bijective function. For example, $gcd(x, y) = 1$ whenever x and y are mutually prime. So, to make it bijective, we must add extra outputs, called *garbage outputs*. We use an extra variable g that is written out at the beginning of every iteration, clearing it in the process. It starts by being 0, so we add this to the loop condition as entry condition. In later iterations, g will be a copy of the previous value if m, so the program will output first 0, then the sequence of values of m, and finally the greatest common divisor of the inputs. When running backwards, this sequence must be given in reverse, ending with the 0. It is possible to reduce the garbage to copies of the input rather than one number per iteration, but that gets complicated if there are no structured data or local procedure variables. The programs are shown in Fig. 12.7.

Suggested exercises: 12.4, 12.5.

12.3.2 Quantum Programming Languages

We will not try to explain quantum programming in depth, but note that it differs from traditional programming in using quantum bits (qubits) instead of traditional bits. Qubits can be:

- In a *superposition* of 0 and 1, written as $a|0\rangle + b|1\rangle$, where a and b are complex numbers and $|a|^2 + |b|^2 = 1$. This represents a mix of 0 and 1 with a parts 0 and b parts 1.
- *Entangled*, so operations on one of the entangled qubit affects all the qubits with which it is entangled. Entanglement is created whenever one qubit affects the value of another qubit.

A quantum state is a vector of (possibly entangled) qubits. For example, a vector of two qubits can be described as

$$a|00\rangle + b|01\rangle + c|10\rangle + d|11\rangle$$

where $|a|^2 + |b|^2 + |c|^2 + |d|^2 = 1$.

An operation on a vector of qubits must be both *reversible* and *unitary*, which means that it can be represented as a *unitary* matrix.

A matrix of complex numbers is unitary if it is square and its conjugate transpose is its own inverse. The conjugate transpose is obtained by transposing the matrix and then replacing every number by its complex conjugate, where the complex conjugate of the complex number $a + ib$ is $a - ib$.

We can modify the reversible language above for quantum computation by adding operations to create bits that are superpositions of 0 and 1. Example: The Hadamard transform:

$$H_1 = \frac{1}{\sqrt{2}} \begin{pmatrix} 1 & 1 \\ 1 & -1 \end{pmatrix}$$

which maps $|0\rangle$ to $\frac{1}{\sqrt{2}}|0\rangle + \frac{1}{\sqrt{2}}|1\rangle$ and $|1\rangle$ to $\frac{1}{\sqrt{2}}|0\rangle - \frac{1}{\sqrt{2}}|1\rangle$. Note that the Hadamard transform is its own inverse.

To emulate controlled negation operations such as the Toffoli gate (which is a three-input gate that inverts its third input if the two first inputs are 1), an update **var** $\hat{} = Exp$, which does a bitwise exclusive or of variable and the value of an expression, can be added.

Note that a common misconception is that a quantum computer, by operating on a superposition of all possible bit vectors, in essence can perform operations in parallel on all the superimposed bit vectors. While this is to some extent true, it ignores an important point: When you read the output of a quantum computer, the superimposed state collapse to just one of its component states, which is a classical state. It is random *which* of the classical states the superimposed state collapses to, so you can only read out the result of the computation for one random of the exponentially many superimposed classical input states. What gives quantum computation its power is that it is *sometimes* possible to get constructive interference of useful quantum states and destructive interference of useless quantum states, thus making it is more likely (but still not certain) that the collapsed output state contains useful information. If the likelihood is high enough, the total time used for repeating calculations until a useful result is obtained can be smaller than for classical computation. But finding algorithms that do this is not trivial.

12.4 Further Reading

A more precise formulation of Rice's theorem and more about computability can be found in [2].

An imperative reversible programming language similar to the one described in Sect. 12.3.1 is described in [3]. A simple reversible functional language is described in [4].

A survey of quantum programming languages can be found in [1].

12.5 Exercises

Exercise 12.1 Consider which of the following properties of programs are trivial, decidable, or undecidable. If they are not decidable, can they be made decidable by modifying or restricting the language? How?

a. A C program will never follow a null pointer.
b. A Standard ML program will never follow a null pointer.
c. A downcast in a Java or C# program will always succeed.
d. In Python, a program will not make an integer calculation that overflows. Division by zero is not considered overflow.

Exercise 12.2 Consider a simple imperative language with the following features:

- There are eight global variables A, ..., H, each capable of holding a 16-bit two-complement number.
- Assignment statements can set a variable to a constant value, add one variable to another, or subtract one variable from another.
- There is an if-then-else statement that can choose between two statements depending on whether a variable is 0 or non-zero.
- A statement can be a (possibly recursive) call to a procedure that has no arguments and return value (but can do side effects on the global variables).
- A program consists of a finite number of procedures, the first of which is called to run the program.
- The body of a function is a sequence of statements.

Is termination (the Halting Problem) trivial, decidable, or undecidable for this language? Argue your answer

Exercise 12.3 Consider the following language features and discuss which limits are reasonable for these features (c.f. Sect. 12.2):

a. The number of classes from which a class can inherit.
b. The number of alternatives in a conditional statement or expression.
c. The number of alternatives in a sum type or enumerated type.
d. The number of results from a function call.
e. The number of different types in a program.
f. The number of different precedence levels of user-defined operators.

Note that there can be more than one reasonable limit for each of these.

Exercise 12.4 Use the reversible language presented at the end of Sect. 12.3.1 to make a program that, given a number $n > 0$, computes $fib(n)$, where fib is the Fibonacci function. It should output at most one other (garbage) output.

Exercise 12.5 The reversible loop described in Sect. 12.3.1 and Fig. 12.3b gives an error message if the condition e is false when the loop is first entered.

An alternative is to skip the loop entirely if e is false when the loop is first entered, jumping directly to what comes after the loop.

a. Draw a flowchart in the style of Figs. 12.2 and 12.3 for this modified behaviour.
b. Is this flowchart reversible? Argue your answer.
c. If the flowchart you drew is not reversible, can it be modified to be reversible while retaining the alternative behaviour described above?

Exercise 12.6 In the reversible language presented in Sect. 12.3.1, all variables are global.

We wish to add statically scoped local variables by introducing a block statement of the form

$$\{\text{int } \textbf{var}=0; \ Stat\}$$

which creates a local scope in which a new variable is available. This is a simplified form of block statements as found in C, Java, etc.

a. What restrictions or runtime tests are required for this to be reversible? You can take inspiration from the restrictions and runtime tests used in Sect. 12.3.1.1.
b. What is the inverse of the block statement? You should not introduce new statement forms—it can be reversed without introducing new language elements. Use notation as in Fig. 12.5

c. The reversible gcd program in Fig. 12.7 prints a garbage value in every iteration. This can be avoided by using recursion and local variables, so the program prints only the inputs (in their original forms) as garbage in addition to the result. Show how this can be done. Be careful to use only reversible features with the restrictions that these impose.

Exercise 12.7 In the reversible language presented in Sect. 12.3.1, all variables are global, and procedures have no parameters. We now modify the language so there are only local variables. Local variables are declared using the block statement from exercise 12.6. To allow procedures to interact, we want procedure calls to have parameters, so we change the syntax of procedure declarations and calls to

$$Proc \rightarrow \texttt{procedure } \mathbf{p} \, (\, Vars \,) \; Stat$$

$$Vars \rightarrow \mathbf{var}$$
$$Vars \rightarrow \mathbf{var}, \, Vars$$

$$Stat \;\; \rightarrow \texttt{call } \mathbf{p} \, (\, Args \,)$$

$$Args \rightarrow Arg$$
$$Args \rightarrow Arg, \, Args$$

where we, for now, leave the form of Arg unspecified. As in most other programming languages, no parameter name can occur twice in a procedure declaration header.

Discuss each of the parameter-passing methods listed below:

- What is the form of Arg? For example, are arguments restricted to variables or can they be arbitrary expressions? Note that the restrictions might not be the same as in traditional, non-reversible languages.
- What restrictions on arguments in procedure calls and use of parameters in procedure bodies are required to make procedure calls reversible, where reversing a call is done by changing `call` to `uncall` and vice versa? Explain why these restrictions are needed.
- With these restrictions, how well suited is the parameter-passing method for programming in the reversible language?

The parameter-passing methods to discuss are

1. Call-by-value
2. Call-by-reference
3. Call-by-value-result

References

1. Gay SJ (2006) Quantum programming languages: survey and bibliography. Math Struct Comp Sci 16(4):581–600. https://doi.org/10.1017/S0960129506005378

2. Jones ND (1997) Computability and complexity: from a programming perspective. MIT Press, Cambridge, MA, USA. http://www.diku.dk/~neil/Comp2book.html

3. Yokoyama T, Axelsen HB, Glück R (2008) Principles of a reversible programming language. In: Proceedings of the 5th conference on computing frontiers, CF'08, ACM, New York, NY, USA. pp 43–54. https://doi.org/10.1145/1366230.1366239. http://doi.acm.org/10.1145/1366230.1366239

4. Yokoyama T, Axelsen HB, Glück R (2012) Towards a reversible functional language. In: Vos A, Wille R (eds) Reversible computation. Lecture Notes in Computer Science, vol 7165. Springer Berlin, Heidelberg. pp 14–29. https://doi.org/10.1007/978-3-642-29517-1_2

Index

© The Editor(s) (if applicable) and The Author(s), under exclusive license to Springer   321
Nature Switzerland AG 2022
T. Ægidius Mogensen, *Programming Language Design and Implementation*,
Texts in Computer Science, https://doi.org/10.1007/978-3-031-11806-7

Printed in the United States
by Baker & Taylor Publisher Services